HISTORIC TEXTS AND INTERPRETERS IN BIBLICAL SCHOLARSHIP

General Editor:
Professor J. W. Rogerson (Sheffield)

Consultant Editors:
Professor C. K. Barrett (Durham)
Professor R. Smend (Göttingen)

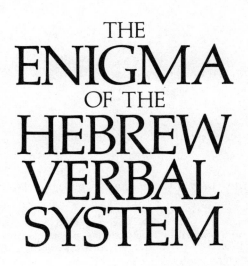

THE
ENIGMA
OF THE
HEBREW
VERBAL
SYSTEM

SOLUTIONS FROM EWALD
TO THE PRESENT DAY

Leslie McFall

The Almond Press · 1982

HISTORIC TEXTS AND INTERPRETERS
IN BIBLICAL SCHOLARSHIP, 2

British Library Cataloguing in Publication Data:

McFall, Leslie
    The enigma of the Hebrew verbal system:
    solutions from Ewald to the present day. -
    (Historic texts and interpreters in Biblical
    scholarship, ISSN 0263-1199; 2)
    1. Hebrew language - Verb
    I. Title   II. Series
    492.4'7   PJ4645

    ISBN 0-907459-20-X
    ISBN 0-907459-21-8 Pbk

Published by
The Almond Press
P.O. Box 208
Sheffield S10 5DW
England

Printed in Great Britain
by Redwood Burn Limited
Trowbridge, Wiltshire
1982

TABLE OF CONTENTS

APPENDICES

PUBLISHER'S NOTE

The original title of this work was: A Critical Examination of the Principal Theories of the Hebrew Verbal System between 1827 and 1954 with Particular Reference to the Waw Consecutive Problem. While splendidly accurate it was clearly too unwieldy to use as the published title. The latter has been reached - as often - by a process of suggestion and counter-suggestion between author, general editor and publisher. Dr. McFall remains diffident about the sub-title, not wishing to convey any impression that he might be offering here an account of the many and specialized lines of current research on the Hebrew verbal system. His work is essentially an historical survey - hence its appearance in our new series - and its main treatment is indeed of theories advanced between 1827 and 1954. On the other hand, he is of the view that no fundamentally new solution has appeared since 1954 that has received significant support. Hence his study serves both to "preface" current research and, broadly speaking, to bring the reader, in terms of principal contributions, up to the present consensus. In doing so it clarifies the origins and nature of theories which have survived, influentially, over very many decades and continue prevalent amongst biblical scholars today. It is with these dimensions in mind that I believe "from Ewald to the present day" reflects both the historical scope of the work and its fundamental spirit - which is forward-looking, into the present day and beyond.

David M. Gunn
The Almond Press

PREFACE

This book is a reproduction of the author's dissertation submitted to the University of Cambridge for the Degree of Doctor of Philosophy in 1981. The only material change has been the addition of an index of Scripture texts. Throughout the work references to scholarly works have been made in an abbreviated form. This has both reduced the bulk of the notes and suppressed to a non-confusing minimum the use of op.cit., ibid., and loc.cit. Sources are indicated in round brackets by the date of publication followed by the page references, e.g.: (Driver, 1982:103). Where an author has published two or more works in the same year a lower case letter (a, b, c) follows the year of publication, thus: (Poebel, 1939a:227). The notes are together on pp. 217-33 and the method of numbering them is explained on p. 217. Throughout this work the symbols qtl and yqtl stand for the Suffix- and Prefix-forms respectively, hence the omission of the dot under the t.

I would like to thank Prof. J. W. Rogerson, the series editor, and Dr. D. M. Gunn of The Almond Press, for including the book in Historic Texts and Interpreters in Biblical Scholarship.

This book could not have been written without the goodwill and assistance of many friends. I wish particularly to thank Rev. Prof. J. A. Emerton, my supervisor for the entire period of research, for his helpful blend of criticism and guidance. I am indebted to Dr. John L. Dawson and the staff of the Cambridge Linguistic Computing Centre for the help afforded me in coding the Hebrew text. My thanks are due also to Rev. J. Sturdy, Dr. C. Hemer and Mr. D. Dykes. The daily work of research would have been immeasurably less convenient without the resources, facilities and financial support of Tyndale House Library, for which I would like to thank the Council and the Warden, Rev. D. Kidner. For my early instruction in the Hebrew language I owe an inestimable debt of gratitude to the Principal and Staff of the South Wales Bible College, Glamorgan, and to Mr. D. F. Payne and Dr. G. Wenham of Queen's University, Belfast. For the time granted to me to type this work in its present form I wish to thank the Council of the Belfast Bible College. Lastly, I would like to thank my mother and my wife for their steady encouragement and sacrificial support.

Leslie McFall
Belfast Bible College

INTRODUCTION

The germ of this dissertation began in 1965 when the author undertook a course on Biblical Hebrew at the South Wales Bible College. The standard explanation given for the waw consecutive/conversive and the use of the so-called tenses in Hebrew appeared illogical to him then as it does now.

Interest in the phenomenon of the waw consecutive/conversive was further aroused during a course of exegesis on the Hebrew Text when it became apparent that translators and exegetes appeared to have considerable latitude in some passages on the choice of English tense to be used in translating the Hebrew verb-forms (cf. p. 36 below). In contrast to this situation the translation and exegesis of the Greek NT was free from such diversity of tense translation, and in fact the tense of a Greek verb was sometimes important (cf. 'the blood of Jesus Christ his Son cleanseth [καθαρίζει, 'keeps on cleansing'] us from all sin' 1 John 1:7).

The central difficulty in the Hebrew verbal system has been, and still is, the correct understanding of the two principal verb forms, the Prefix- and Suffix-forms (i.e. yqtl and qtl), and their respective waw consecutive constructions (i.e. wayyqtl and wqtl).

If a correct understanding of the Hebrew language is the only basis for sound exegesis, and if the heart of a language is its verbal system, then it must be conceded that in the case of Hebrew we have not yet acquired a correct understanding of that language, and consequently we lack a sound basis for exegesis of the OT Scriptures. It is a cause for concern that Hebraists in the 20th century find the HVS an enigma on occasions. A correct understanding of the HVS would not only make the OT a thrilling body of Eastern wisdom and learning to read and appreciate, but it might well provide us with the much needed key to the verbal systems of other ancient Semitic languages.

The earliest known attempt to explain the difficulties in the HVS was the Waw Conversive theory which was put forward by Jewish grammarians in the 10th century A.D. This was adopted by Christian Hebraists from the earliest days of the Reformation and still has its supporters to-day. However, with the publication in 1827 of Samuel Lee's Hebrew grammar, in which he opposed the Waw Conversive solution, the way was opened up to find a more acceptable understanding of the consecutive constructions and the principal verb forms.

The present work is a selection of the principal theories published between 1827 and 1954 dealing with the central difficulty. The work of each of the following authors has been examined and evaluated: S. Lee (1827), H. Ewald (1834), I. Nordheimer (1841), S. R. Driver (1874), W. Turner (1876), J. A. Knudtzon (1889), H. Bauer (1910), G. R. Driver (1936), and T. W. Thacker (1954). The six different approaches represented in the above theories have been examined with a view to further research into the problems of the HVS by future scholars. The author has no solution of his own to put forward, but knowing the impenetrable nature of the problem the acclaimation of a host of scholars justly awaits the scholar, or more probably, the group of scholars who can provide them with a solution to the HVS. So far it has eluded the grasp of eminent men of learning and will continue to do so until considerably more homework and pure research is carried out more cautiously and more painstakingly in the future.

A particular thorn in the side of the author throughout the period of research has been the phenomenon known as tone shift, involving the 1st and 2nd pers. masc. sing. of the w̲q̲t̲l̲ form. To a greater or lesser extent all the theories use it in some manner to support their solution. This phenomenon had to be investigated, albeit cursorily; the results appear in Appendix 2.

Although we have found fault with every solution to the HVS examined in this work, and in some cases found it necessary to criticise the work of individuals, it has been done solely in the interests of clearing away the myths and presuppositions that have prevented research in the past and to avoid making the same mistakes.

The writer is conscious that he criticises the work of men who were more learned in the Hebrew and cognate languages, and to whom he owes his own stock of knowledge of the sacred language. Nevertheless, as Bernard of Chartres (12th century) so aptly put it:

> We are like dwarfs seated on the shoulders of giants; we see things more clearly than the ancients and more distant, but this is due neither to the sharpness of our own sight nor the greatness of our own stature but because we are raised and borne aloft on that great mass.

1.1 A BRIEF SURVEY
ON THE UNDERSTANDING OF THE HVS BEFORE 1827

Hebrew grammar in one sense probably never had a beginning, since embryonic grammatical observations are to be found scattered throughout the Talmud and the Midrashim.[1] The Massorah was the real cradle of Hebrew Grammar. The Massoretes, like the grammarians, differentiated between the several forms of the words found in the biblical text. They collected similar words into groups, registered the peculiarities of the text and formulated the rules governing the spelling and reading of the same. But their work shows no traces of grammatical categories, nor of any examination of the forms of the language as such. Their chief concern was to preserve the written form of the text and its correct pronunciation. In order to safeguard the delicate shades of pronunciation they introduced the Tiberian punctuation system. The Massorah, then, paved the way for grammar. The extremely accurate system of pointing enabled the grammarians to determine the laws of Hebrew phonetics and etymology.

Long before Hebrew had become a subject of grammatical study there appeared what may be regarded as the earliest products within Judaism of reflection on the elements of the language, namely, the classification of the consonants and the vowels. The former can be found as part of the peculiar cosmogony of the Sefer Yezirah, and the latter in the Massoretic vocalization—the most important legacy that the Massoretes bequeathed to the grammarians.

The connecting link between the Massoretes and the grammarians was undoubtedly Aaron ben Moses ben Asher (commonly called Ben Asher). He worked in Tiberias in the first half of the tenth century. He was descended from a family of Massoretes which can be traced back through six generations. It was his last revision of the Massorah that formed the basis for our present Massoretic text. However, in his work, Dikduke ha-Te'amim, his theory on grammatical forms already shows the influence of Arabic which was not completely ousted as the vernacular of Palestine until about AD 800.

Every science has its precursory stage and pioneers, and so it was in the case of Hebrew grammar as an independent subject for investigation. Jehuda ibn Koreish is the first one known to us. He lived in Morocco some time between 850 and 900 and was an elderly contemporary of Saadia Gaon. In an extant letter to the Jewish community at Fez—his grammatical works were lost—he makes a plea for the study of Hebrew. In this long letter he makes

a strong plea for comparative Semitic studies, recommending the use of
Arabic, Aramaic, and the Mishnah, to elucidate the Bible. He views the study
of the Hebrew language as the best bulwark against the arbitrary deductions
of the Karaites. With his great successor, however, the study of Hebrew
grammar begins in real earnest.

1.1.1   Grammarians from Saadia Gaon (882-942)
to Judah Hayyuj (940-1010)

1.1.1.1   Saadia ben Joseph, or, more commonly, Saadia Gaon.

He was born in Dilaz, Fayum, in Upper Egypt. When he was twenty
(some say thirty) he produced his first major work, the <u>Argon</u>, a Hebrew
dictionary. Three years later he moved to Palestine and was there until he
was called to be head or Gaon of the Sura academy.

Saadia nowhere states why he took up grammatical studies; but we may
infer from his works the kind of pressures that made this a necessity.
Firstly, Karaism had made serious inroads into Babylonian Jewry, so that
the academies were beginning to lose their importance. Secondly, he was
disturbed by the style of the Piyyut poets and the confusion of grammatical
categories. And thirdly, he lived in an Arabic environment and was conver-
sant with Arabic learning, including their grammatical treatises.

His dependence on Arabic grammars is quite evident; see Skoss, 1955:
11-16, 57-60. Following the Arab grammarians he classifies the language in
the three usual divisions: nouns, verbs, and particles.[1] He wrote most of
his work in Arabic and this appears to have influenced his understanding
of the HVS. We find him, for example, forming a Hebrew equivalent for the
Past Continuous (or the Past Habitual) Arabic tense: kāna yaf'al, viz.
hawāh yabō'. A remarkable Arabism in his otherwise BH style, is the use of
the Prefix-form after the auxiliary verb instead of the participle: אשר
היה הייתה בה תצלוץ 'by which you were wont to terrorize every
man' (C. Rabin, 1943a:135). His Hebrew is closer to BH than to MH, so
much so that Rabin (<u>op. cit.</u>) finds it easier to point out where it differs
from BH than to try to describe his style. From our point of view Saadia's
verbal system is closer to MH than to BH. He uses the Prefix- and Suffix-
forms in place of the consecutive constructions.

It is interesting that Japheth ha-Levi (better known as Jephet ben 'Ali
or Abū al-Basrī), who was a contemporary of Saadia and who entered into lengthy

disputes with him has this to say about the consecutive forms in Genesis
28: 20-21 (Japheth was a Karaite grammarian in Jerusalem):[1]

> If one objects to us that וְהָיָה has also a ! [Japheth is opposing
> Saadia's(?) and another commentator's interpretation that והיה
> belongs to the protasis of vv. 20-21a, which would make it a
> hypothetical future perfect.] we will reply that the וֹ in והיה
> is not the same as the וֹ in והאבן! nor the same as in וְכָל אֲשֶׁר;
> because the וֹ in וְהָיָה serves [to put this word] in place of
> יְהֶיה , and this is waw 'atīdī [וו עתיד i.e. 'waw of future'].
> It is the same as in וְהַחֲרַמְתִּי [Num. 21:2], which [waw] is in
> place of אַחֲרִים ; in והיה ל- [Jud. 11:31] which is in place of
> אהיה ; and in וּנְתַתִּיו ל- [1 Sam. 1:1,11], which is in place of
> אֶתְּנֶנּוּ .

From this it is quite clear that at the beginning of the 10th century the
'waw of future' was known among the Karaites and possibly among orthodox
exegetes such as Saadia in Palestine.

Saadia was aware of only two verbal themes, namely, Qal and Hiphil, which
he tabulates using the root שמע. It was left to David Kimhi, some 300
years later, to produce the first grammar containing the seven verbal conjugations familiar to Hebraists today. Saadia enumerates only seven vowels.
This shows that the Massoretic vowel system was forgotten in some academies.
Some time later, under the influence of Latin grammar, Kimhi set out five
long and five short vowels. Earlier, under Arabic influence, Ibn Janah put
forward a system very close to Arabic.

The triliteral root system was unknown to Saadia, and was not fully
discovered until Hayyuj's time (ca. 1000). The Arab grammarians, on the
other hand, knew about it in the 9th century at the latest, from whom Hayyuj
learnt about it.[2]

Saadia uses the MH tense system though it is not certain how he regarded
the consecutive constructions. He makes both the participle and the infinitive
with pronominal suffixes serve for the Present tense (Skoss, 1955:10-13).

Unfortunately, the direct influence of his Kutub al-Lugah on later
grammarians was rather short-lived. Ibn Janah gives quotations from this
grammar found in Saadia's commentaries and adds that he never saw it nor
did it get to Spain. Similarly, Abraham ibn Ezra evidently knew of it only
from Dunash's remarks. Profiat Duran (ca. 1403) tells us that Saadia wrote
three grammatical works which 'did not reach us'. However, his commentaries
and other works were read, especially in Spain, with the result that there
was a remarkable shift from Talmudic to grammatical studies. The study of
Hebrew grammar became the 'in thing' during the next century. Grammatical
accuracy was the criterion by which all literary compositions were judged.

Grammar was taken up by statesmen, such as Samuel ha-Nagid, by poets and philosophers, and not just the 'theologians' and professional grammarians.

1.1.1.2   Menaḥem ben Saruḳ (ca. 910–ca. 970)
He was a very gentle person who devoted himself almost exclusively to classical Hebrew in his grammatical works. His Maḥberet was the first complete Hebrew dictionary of the Bible; it was, so far as we know, the first grammatical work to be written in Hebrew. Up until his time everything was written in Arabic, though the next generation reverted to writing in Arabic. The result was that only the works of Menaḥem and Dunash were available to the non-Arabic speaking Jews of Europe. We find Rashi relying on Menaḥem's Maḥberet and Jacob ben Meïr Tam defending it against Dunash's criticisms, apparently unaware of the latest discoveries, especially Ḥayyuj's, that were appearing in Arabic on Hebrew grammar.

Dunash was a pupil of Saadia, and Menaḥem read Saadia's commentaries (but not his grammar apparently); consequently, Jewish scholarship in Spain owed not only its pronunciation (Sephardic) but its beginnings to Babylonian Jewry.

As regards the grammatical importance of Menaḥem's dictionary, it should be noted that he had no systematic knowledge of the forms of the language. He is groping his way towards the triliteral root system. His work is based entirely on the premise that where a consonant is not found in all its inflexions it does not belong to the stem (ש ר ש). Thus in the case of נ ס ה the stem would be only ס, since this letter alone remains after the affixes have been removed. In other words, no portion of the stem can ever disappear in the course of inflexion. The consequences of such a principle were disastrous. The four classes of verbs פ"י , ע"ן , ל"ה , and ע"ע immediately disappeared.[1]

Under the entry 'Waw' Menaḥem clearly thought that the waw possessed a converting influence on the verb to which it was prefixed. He says:[2]

> To every word [i.e. verb, here] which refers to something past, an event [lit. 'a thing'] that is past and completed, if one prefixes to such a word the letter waw, the meaning of this word is changed into another.

Here Menaḥem agrees with Japheth ha-Levi's understanding of the consecutive forms.

No sooner had Menaḥem's Maḥberet appeared than it was fiercely criticised by Dunash ben Labrat (ca. 920–ca. 980), whose family came from Bagdad, although he himself was born in Fez. The language of his criticisms

was extremely coarse even given the fact that scholars in that age vied with
each other in the use of opprobrious epithets and slanderous insinuations.
Abraham ibn Ezra (1092-1167) praises Dunash stating that 'he was the only
one before Ḥayyuj who awakened somewhat from that slumber of ignorance which,
like a deep sleep, still held others in its bonds' (see W. Bacher, 1882:87).
However, Dunash did not go beyond the statement that the first, second, or
third root-letter is weak and may be eliminated. It was through the study of
Arabic which enabled him, like Ḥayyuj at a later period, to arrive at this
knowledge. He was a diligent comparative lexicographer (Jastrow, 1887:122).

1.1.1.3   Judah ben David Ḥayyuj

He was born in Fez around 940, but lived permanently at Cordova,
where he died around 1010. According to Kimḥi (Miklol, preface) 'he found
Hebrew grammar perverted in his day.' He was the first to establish the
triconsonantal system of Hebrew stems, following the Arabic model. He, too,
was the first to discover the true relation of the quiescent letters (י"ה'א),
and their changes. He also arranged the verbs into their present conjugations, though he considered Puʻal and Hophal as one conjugation. He adopted
the root פעל in the standard paradigm straight from the Arabic grammars.
It was an unfortunate choice because while the verb is a strong one in Arabic
it is a weak verb in Hebrew. Had Ḥayyuj been a more independent worker than
he was, he would almost certainly have made a better choice. He did not see
the difficulties in using this root, but his successors did. Abraham ibn
Ezra exchanged it for שמל , while Kimḥi adopted פקד , and this was later
changed for קטל by J. A. Danz (1654-1727) in his grammar of 1696, because
the root occurred in the other known Semitic languages of his day. It was
Ḥayyuj who first introduced the designation of the letters of the root as
the Pe, the Ayin, and the Lamedh, from the Arabic root فعل .

It was not without good reason that both Ibn Ezra and Kimḥi regarded
him as 'the chief of grammarians'. His two works, Kitab al-Afʻal Dhawat
Ḥuruf al-Lin (The Book of Verbs Containing Weak Letters) and Kitab al-Afʻal
Dhawat al-Mathalain (The Book of Verbs Containing Double Letters) gave him
a pre-eminent place among grammarians of the Middle Ages. The significance
of his discovery, which enabled others to view the Hebrew Language as an
intricate structure, cannot be overestimated.

Abu al-Walid Merwan ibn Janah—more commonly, Ibn Janah—was a contemporary of Ḥayyuj, some say his pupil (his dates are ca. 990-1050), completed
the work begun by Ḥayyuj. His writings were also in Arabic. Moses ibn

Gikatilla (11th cent.) and later Abraham ibn Ezra translated most of the works of Ḥayyuj and Ibn Janah into Hebrew for the benefit of European Jewish scholarship. It is strange that while we reach the high water-mark of Hebrew lexicography in the 11th century, we find Ibn Janah complaining in the preface to his grammar, that a knowledge of the Hebrew language was only looked upon in his time as a secondary thing. Even more remarkable is the fact that Ibn Janah himself did not fully understand the vowel and accent systems, which had been thoroughly mastered by the Massoretes in the 7th cent.

1.1.2   Grammarians from Judah Hayyuj to the Kimhi Family (1235)

We pass over a number of grammarians chiefly because we do not know very much about their work, men such as Samuel ha-Nagid (993-1055), the great Spanish statesman who wrote a grammar with twenty-two sections, none of which is extant. It would require a study in itself to reconstruct Rashi's understanding of the consecutive forms. Moses ibn Gikatilla (11th cent.), Moses ibn Ezra (1070-ca. 1140), Judah ha-Levi (1085/6-ca. 1140), Solomon ben Judah ibn Gabriol (1021-1058), and Abu Ibrahim Ishak (11th-12th cent.), contributed to the knowledge of Hebrew grammar, many of them interested in the comparative approach. The period under review was not one of great new advances in the study of grammar, rather it was a period of consolidation in which all the recent gains were purified and perfected for those times. The grammarian who did more than any other to foster the study in Europe was Abraham ibn Ezra.

1.1.2.1   Abraham ben Meïr ibn Ezra (1092/3-1167)

Better known as Ibn (Aben) Ezra, he is remembered for his wanderings around Europe between 1140 and 1167 imparting to the Jewish communities the fruits of Spanish scholarship. These communities had been cut off from Spanish Jewry, and hence the benefits of Arab science, medicine, and linguistic studies. Now all this became theirs through the teaching of Ibn Ezra. In Rome (ca. 1140) he produced his grammar in good Hebrew, based for the most part on his Arabic sources. According to Rabin (1943b:91) his Hebrew is more Mishnaic than Rashi's Hebrew; hence Ibn Ezra thought in terms of a true tense system. While in Rome he translated Hayyuj's works and so brought this valuable contribution to the notice of European grammarians.

Ibn Ezra was a well educated person and had read extensively. According to
Issac Broydé (The Jew. Encycl., 1904, vol. 7, p. 73) Ibn Ezra was very
familiar with Japheth ha-Levi's commentaries and it is possible that he
assimilated Japheth's 'waw of future' explanation through them (see 1.1.1
above). Ibn Ezra's grammar was very soon eclipsed by those of the Kimhi
family. David Kimhi quotes Ibn Ezra's view of the consecutive forms, with
approval it would seem. After Ibn Ezra the great majority of grammars are
written in Hebrew.

1.1.2.2   The Kimhi family

Joseph ben Issac Kimhi (ca. 1105–ca. 1170), the father of David
Kimhi (1160–1235), fled to Provençe during the Almohade persecutions in
southern Spain. He probably met Ibn Ezra in 1160. He followed Ibn Ezra in
some particulars, e.g. in the use of the root שׁמר in his paradigms. Ibn
Ezra, on the other hand, quotes Kimhi's commentaries. Both men were well
equipped to popularize Judaeo-Arabic learning among the Jews of Europe.
Both were kept busy translating Arabic works. As far as his contribution
to original research is concerned he was not outstanding. He introduced
the long and short vowels under the influence of Latin.

His son Moses, about whom little is known, wrote a short grammar.
Elias Levita (1469–1549) later wrote annotations to it and it became the
most widely used 'elementary Hebrew grammar' among the Protestant and
Catholic scholars of Europe after it had been translated into Latin by
Sebastian Münster in 1531.

David, the youngest of the family, became the most illustrious
representative of his name. His contribution, on the whole, was not original.
His Mikhlol was the Gesenius grammar of his age, being the most comprehensive exposition of Hebrew grammar ever written. It was never surpassed
until some 600 years later. In 1952 William Chomsky translated it with
critical notes. Unfortunately, he has replaced Kimhi's grammatical terminology with what he assumes are their modern equivalents (see p. xxix).
In such a delicate area as the HVS this has proved disastrous. On page 74
note 82 he informs the reader that he has rendered Kimhi's terms, עָבַר
(past), עָתִיד (future), and בֵּינוֹנִי or עוֹמֵד (present), by their modern
equivalents, Perfect, Imperfect, and Participle, respectively. He then
reminds the reader to give these terms the meaning, past, future, and
present, since the mediaeval grammarians thought in terms of Indo-Germanic

tenses. Would it not have been wiser to use Past, Future, and Present, and then for the convenience of the modern reader to point out their modern equivalents in a footnote? As it is, the reader must remind himself each time he comes across the term 'consecutive' that it does not mean 'consecutive', but something else. To make matters worse, we read in the Introduction (pp. xxvi-vii), 'Among the significant grammatical concepts and terms originated by the Kimḥis and generally accepted by modern grammarians, are those of the Dagesh lene and the Waw consecutive'. This is misleading. The cross-referenced footnotes lead eventually to p. 78 note 100, where we read the following:

> Kimḥi seems to be the first to have sensed the peculiar character of the Waw consecutive, since he designates it by a special term הַשֵּׁרוּת 'ו and devotes a paragraph to a discussion of its uses and vocalization (Lyk ed. 48b, etc.). His predecessors made no clear distinction between the Waw Consecutive and the Waw Copulative, although they observed their respective functions...'

We have noted already (1.1.1) that Kimḥi's predecessors did make a distinction between the terms and functions of the <u>waw</u> conversive and the <u>waw</u> copulative. The following quotation from Kimḥi's <u>Sepher Mikhlol</u> (Venice, 1546:12b[in St. John's Coll., Cambridge]) shows that there is no essential difference between his understanding of the phenomenon and that of Japheth ha-Levi and Menaḥem ben Saruḳ:[1]

> And you must know that it is the custom of the tenses in the Holy Language to be employed: a past in the place of a future, that is [the forms with the prefixed] letters אית״ן , and this is for the most part in prophecies, because the matter is as clear as though it had already passed, seeing that it has already been decreed. Likewise, a future in the place of a past, [such] as [occurs with] אז. Also, a future or a past in the place of a participle, as if to say one was doing such and such [a thing] continually; there is no need to illustrate them as they are so numerous, and you can recognize every one of them by the context.
> And with the particle אז 'then', a future usually comes in the place of a past, as אָז יָשִׁיר מֹשֶׁה [Exod. 15:1 'then sang Moses'] . . .And the sage Rabbi Abraham Aben Ezra wrote that this is the custom in the language of Ishmael [D. Kimḥi did not know Arabic], and he moreover wrote that so it is allowable to use them [i.e. the past and future tenses] in speaking of a present tense in the same manner as [we read] פָּנָיו יְכַסֶּה [Isa. 6:2 'he was covering his face'], וַיָּנֻעוּ אַמּוֹת הַסִּפִּים [Isa. 6:4 'and the foundations of the thresholds were shaking'];for seeing that there is no form in the language for the intermediate tense [i.e. the present tense] , they refer to it by means of a past or future tense. . .

In his <u>Mikhlol</u> he gives examples where the 'future' refers to a past time antecedent to the time referred to by another verb preceding it. He says:[2]

And there is a ׀ which points to a time that is past before [the past action of] the verb that is before it [in the text] , 'Behold, Thou wast angry, and we sinned' וַנֶּחֱטָא קָצַפְתָּ , meaning, For we had previously sinned, therefore Thou wast angry with us. [Also] 'A man will die when he has been ill', meaning, 'when he had previously been ill, for before he dies he will be taken ill and be sick.'

Other examples he cites are, Lev. 9:22; Jud. 4:21, Exod. 16:20, and 14:21.

Now, whatever the term שָׁרוּת may mean lexically, and Ben Yehuda's dictionary (1909, vol. III, pp. 7462-3) shows that the word has a very general meaning, e.g. service, use, etc. As used by Kimchi the word is intended to cover the phenomenon where one tense is substituted by another that has a waw prefixed to it (עָבָר בִּמְקוֹם עָתִיד). It is misleading, therefore, to single out Kimḥi from among the 11th-12th century grammarians and credit him with the discovery of the Waw Consecutive idea.

With David Kimḥi we come to the end of what we may call the period of consolidation that set in after the initial period of discovery (Saadia to Ibn Janah). The next period is characterized by the translation and dissemination of works written in Arabic.

1.1.3   Grammarians from Kimhi to Elias Levita (1468-1549)

Most historians of Jewish literature are agreed that the period 1250-1500 saw a gradual decay in grammatical research among the Jews. There did not appear to be anything left to do after the Mikhlol appeared. On the other hand Talmudic studies grew and absorbed the attention of Jewish scholarship. The knowledge of the cognate languages, especially Arabic and Syriac/Aramaic, was lost. Because of strict adherence to the authority of the older grammarians independent grammatical inquiry was, on the whole, paralysed and checked.

Besides Elias Levita at the beginning of the 16th century, we know of a number of influential grammarians in this period (e.g. Profiat Duran, ca. 1360-1412, Moses ben Shemtob, ca. 1486, and others), but we shall pass over these to the Tibbon family and their contribution to the study of grammar.

1.1.3.1   The Tibbon family

This family of translators lived in southern France after Judah ben Saul ibn Tibbon (1120-1190) fled from Spain in 1148. His son, Samuel ben Judah (ca. 1150-ca. 1230), his grandson, Moses (ca. 1240-1283), his great grandsons, Judah ben Moses, Samuel ibn Tibbon, and Jacob ben Machir (1236-1304) were all prolific translators. Indeed, a veritable industry grew up around competent translators in this period. By 1300 almost every major Arabic work had been translated.

The syntax of this translation Hebrew was distinctly Arabic.[1] They slavishly followed every turn of the Arabic original leading them to imitate the etymological similarities of the Arabic words. One of these devices was to introduce Hebrew words that were similar in sound to their Arabic counter-parts, even though their meanings were not exactly alike nor etymologically connected. For example, Arabic taṣrīf 'grammatical inflexion' becomes ṣērūf in Dunash's translation; though nᵉṭīyah would have been more appropriate as a loan-translation. The waw consecutive is called waw 'oṭepet, from the Arabic 'aṭafa, which means 'to incline, bend', whereas in Hebrew the word means 'to turn aside' (cf. BDB p. 742). Could there be a reference to the conversive waw here? The waw that 'turns aside' the natural tense of the verb-form for another.

1.1.3.2   Elijah Levita (1468-1549)

Better known as Elias Levita, he taught Hebrew to, among others, Cardinal Aegidius of Viterbo in exchange for Greek lessons. He published his first grammar for the Cardinal in 1518. This work and the grammar of Abraham de Balmes (ca. 1450-1523) were the first to introduce the term waw hippuk to denote the waw conversive, and the term waw hibbur to denote the waw copulative. De Balmes was the first to treat the syntax (harkaḇah) as a special part of grammar.

We give here Levita's view of the consecutive constructions.[2]

1.   Know that to convert a past action into a future [action] a waw with sheva must be prefixed to it, as can be seen before שׁמֹר : וְשָׁמַר יהוה which is the same as וִישְׁמֹר , likewise וְשָׁמְרוּ בְנֵי ישראל is the same as וִישְׁמְרוּ ; and always it is pointed with sheva, except in the case of the מבשׁלים [i.e. before the 2nd pers. pl., the labials בומ״ף , and the gutturals אהח״עצ] since these convert the sheva of the waw either into a shurik, pathah, or hiriq.

2.   And if one asks me how I know whether this is waw hibbur or waw hippuk, [the rule is] when a past action with waw is preceded by a past this is waw hibbur, for example: מִי פָעַל וְעָשָׂה ['Who has wrought and done it?'], and וַיִּקְרָא זֶה אֶל זֶה וְאָמַר ['And one cried unto another and said']. In these two examples the waw is copulative: in the first, on account of [the verb] being pre-ceded by a past action, in the second, on account of its being

preceded by וָאֶרְאֶה אֶת יְהוָה ['I saw also the Lord...' Isa. 6:1].

3.   And know that the custom in the writings is to speak a language [peculiar to it, thus] a past action in place of a future
one, and a future action in place of a past one. This is [found]
for the most part in the prophetic writings, but very seldom in
the historical books.

4.   In the first and second person singular of the past action,
the waw hibbur may also be distinguished from the waw hippuk, by
the place of the accent; and the accent, generally, will
determine the case. An accent on the penultima shows that the
waw is copulative, for example, וְאָכַלְתִּי חַטָּאת הַיּוֹם ['and if I
had eaten the sin offering to-day...' Lev. 10:19].

After Levita the study of Hebrew grammar declined among the Jews. Whether
this was a reaction to the intense interest that the Humanists and Christians
were taking in the language, or whether they felt the work of discovery and
clarification had gone as far as it could, it is not possible to say. The
research into Hebrew grammar passed into Christian hands from this period,
and remained there for the next few centuries.

1.1.4   Hebraists from Johann Reuchlin (1455-1522)
           to N. W. Schroeder (1721-98)

Prior to Reuchlin there were few Christian Hebraists (See Pick, 1884:
474). Notwithstanding the great reverence shown by the early Christian Fathers
for the OT, the only persons who distinguished themselves in their knowledge
of Hebrew were Origen and Jerome.[1]

In the Middle Ages some knowledge of Hebrew was preserved in the Church
by converted Jews and learned monks; but there was no continuous tradition
such as characterized Judaism. The Church did not always make it easy to learn
Hebrew since it regarded anyone who took an interest in things Jewish as a
Jew. Not unnaturally, Orthodox Jews refused to teach non-Jews Hebrew. Added
to this was the difficulty of obtaining Hebrew manuscripts and the scarcity
of books in general. Yet in spite of all the difficulties, men—Humanist and
Christian—were determined to learn the Hebrew language.

Conrad Pellicanus (d. 1556) wrote the first Hebrew grammar for Christian
scholarship in 1504. In 1506 Reuchlin produced his grammar which was
immediately adopted as the best of its kind. It was based almost entirely
on Kimḥi's grammar. It reflects, therefore, the Kimḥian view of the HVS. He
says (p. 145):[2]

The letter of the alphabet waw is also a copulative conjunction
signifying 'and' as in Gen. 1:1, 'In the beginning God created the

heaven and the earth.' Sometimes indeed it is not a conjunction,
because it does not join something to something, as in Gen. 22:4,
for while we read, 'On the third day, however, he saw the place
far off with raised eyes,' the Hebrew really says, 'On the third
day and Abraham raised his eyes.' But this <u>waw</u> only converts the
future into the past and vice versa, as can be seen even at the
beginnings of books...

Sebastian Münster (1489–1552) and Paul Fagius (1504–1549) were both
pupils of Levita. Fagius was called to Cambridge as King's Reader in Hebrew,
while Münster laboured in Basle. Münster translated Levita's works into Latin,
and published a revised edition of Reuchlin's grammar (1537), thus opening
up the Hebrew language to any who cared to learn it. His understanding of
the HVS was no different from that of his master. He says:

> When <u>waw</u> is prefixed to verbs, it has two meanings, namely,
> <u>waw</u> הַפּוּךְ , which is conversive, and <u>waw</u> הַבּוּר , which is
> conjunctive. It is termed <u>waw</u> הַפּוּךְ when it is not a copula
> but with the pathah changes future into past, and with the shewa
> changes past into future.... (1544:40)

John Udall translated Pierre Martinez's Hebrew grammar into English in
1593 (first published in Latin at Paris in 1567). It was the first Hebrew
grammar in English. On the HVS it reads (pp. 195–6):

> It [the <u>waw</u> conjunctive] doth also sometimes change the preter-
> perfect tense into the second tense [<u>i.e</u>. the future], but then
> the accent of the first and second person singular masculine is
> for the most part changed, as Deut. 30[:19] וּבָחַרְתָּ. . . The
> like is sometimes done in the third person feminine, as Exod.
> 26, 23 [<u>sic</u>. 26:33] וְהִבְדִּילָה. . . But ‫ו‬ changeth the second
> future tense into the preterperfect tense, as Job 6, 1 וַיַּעַן
> . . . The same doth the Adverb אָז , as Josh. 10, 12 . . . some-
> times the same change is made without ‫ו‬ , as Job 4, 16 . . .

He also notes (p. 42) that 'The preter tense and the second future are used
often indefinitely, as Psalm 1, 1.'

In John Davis' translation of Johann Buxtorf's 1653 grammar, translated
in 1656, we read (pp. 22ff.):

> ‫ו‬ Vau when sheva is prefixed to the preterperfect tense, often-
> times turneth the preter tense into the future: and with a pathah
> daghesh following it turns the future tense into the preter-
> perfect tense. . . . A tense is either finite or infinite. The
> finite is either the preter tense, or the future tense: for the
> Hebrews have no proper present tense.

In Buxtorf's 1651 grammar we read (p. 94):

> A preterite for the future and a future for the preterite, now
> simply, as in the prophets, now on account of the prefixed <u>waw</u>
> . . . . For in a continuous sentence, the following tense is most
> often attracted to the preceeding.

In the 18th century Albert Schultens (1686–1750) wrote his epoch-
making Institutiones (1737), in which he put the study of grammar on a
new basis, and introduced comparative Semitic philology. In his treatment
of the tenses he says there are strictly only two, Praeteritum and Futurum
(p. 257). T. K. Cheyne is mistaken when he says (1893:69): 'Like Ewald he
[i.e. Eichhorn], was not merely a Hebraist but a Semitic philologist, and
propagated that sound doctrine of the so-called Tenses, which is due to that
patriarch of learning, Albert Schultens.' Schultens was a long way from
Ewald's theory of the HVS as can be seen in his edited version of the Arabic
Grammar of Erpenius, in which he retains the old names Praeteritum and Futurum,
answering to the terms used by the Arabs, El-Mādi and El-Mustaqbalu, and by
Jewish grammarians, 'Abar and 'Atīd.

However, during the 18th century scholars became increasingly discontented
with the conversive theory. The first recorded protest against the theory
appears to have been made by Johann Simonis, who declared: 'God Himself can
not change a past into a future' (1753:217).[1]

Robert Lowth gives vent to his frustration in the XV Lecture of his
Lectures on the Sacred Poetry of the Hebrews (1829:125; but written in 1753)
as follows:

> In another point, it must be confessed, they [the prophetic writers]
> differ essentially from other writers [i.e. in other languages],
> namely, when they intimate past events in the form of the future
> tense: and I must add, that this is a matter of considerable
> difficulty. If we resort to the translators and commentators...
> they do not so much as notice it, accommodating as much as possible
> the form of the tenses to the subject and the context, and explain-
> ing it rather according to their own opinions....If again we
> apply to the grammarians, we shall still find ourselves no less
> at a loss...they neither explain the reason of it, nor yet are
> candid enough to make a fair confession of their own ignorance.
> They...have always at hand a sort of inexplicable and mysterious
> enallage or change of the tenses, with which, rather than say
> nothing, they attempt to evade a closer inquiry; as if the change
> were made by accident, and from no principle or motive: than
> which nothing can be conceived more absurd or impertinent.

New ideas sprang up to account for the daghesh accompanying the waw
(see Schulz, 1900:11ff.) as scores of grammarians sought to explain every
facet of the language to their pupils.[2]

Only when we come to N. W. Schröder (1721–1798) do we meet with a new
departure from the Jewish view of the HVS, which had dominated every grammar since Levita's time. In his Institutiones (1785:261; first ed. 1766)
he says:

Apart from these various usages, the Future form has another usage which is clearly unique and peculiar to the Hebrews, in that it receives the force of our past, and designates a matter as really past, not, however, by itself and absolutely, but in relation to a past action which has preceded it. For when a number of events are to be narrated that follow one another in some kind of continuous series, the Hebrew writers consider the first action as past, the others, however, which follow it, on account of what has gone before are considered as future, since something is described which in relation to another past action is itself later and future, so it may be called the Relative Future.

Schröder appears to have been the first to introduce the distinction between Absolute and Relative future; but he does not abandon the old notion that the verb forms, as such, express the tense of the action.[1]

1.1.5   Hebraists from N. W. Schroeder to Samuel Lee (1783-1852)

On the assumption that the two forms indicated true tenses, i.e. past (qtl) and future (yqtl), numerous theories were put forward to explain the use of the future form in narrating past events. One such theory was that of G. C. Storr (Observationes....1779:161):

So if אמר֜י ו has the meaning, 'will he speak?', in the Hebrew idiom, it denies that he will speak. Moreover, to the phrase 'he will not speak' can be added this force, 'he will not speak any more because he has spoken: he has made an end of speaking.

Storr's reasoning appears to be that the expression 'will he speak?' implies a negative answer; the reason being that he has already spoken. The Hebrew expression 'will he speak' is the same as 'he spoke'. Storr made this suggestion on the assumption that the daghesh in ו אמ֜רי concealed the He interrogative.

J. G. von Herder (1744-1803) in his Vom Geist... (1782-3, transl. J. Marsh, 1833:37) suggests that Hebrew had only one tense, or rather that the two tenses are essentially aorists, that is, undefined tenses. He expresses the opinion that all poetry and history exhibit actions and events as...

vividly present to the senses. . . . The Hebrews. . . like children aim to say the whole at once, and to express by a single sound, the person, number, tense, action and still more. How vastly must this contribute to the sudden and simultaneous exhibition of an entire picture!

F. Burgess (JSL, 3/1853:425) notes that in Gesenius' time (1786-1842) the grammars of Dauz (sic. Danz [ius], 1654-1727) and Vater (1771-1826) were

most in repute in German universities. He thinks Danz treated the subject
very arbitrarily (see W. Bacher, 1904:75 for the numerous eds. of this grammar), while J. S. Vater followed no definite plan, and was often led astray
by false views (see Bacher, op. cit., for eds.).

J. Bate in his grammar (1751:16) considers Hebrew to have only two tenses,
a Present (which included the past) and a Future. He gives no examples to
illustrate this statement. A little later W. H. Barker (1773:18), along with
the majority of Hebraists of his day, states that the two tenses are 'the
perfect and the future'; but adds (p. 31): 'ו....Denotes succession, if
prefixed to a verb future, the action must be understood to be future to the
time of which the writer is speaking, not in which he is speaking...'.
G. Fitzgerald appears to agree with Barker, but he limits its application
to simple Prefix-forms used for the past (1813:89). He accepts the conversive
explanation for the consecutive constructions. A. Bayly put forward the idea
that the Past or עבר is 'expressive of an action done in a time present,
past, or at the same time with or before another action:. . .עתיד is
expressive of an action done in a future time, and after another action, or
event' (1773:27).

Typical of the 18th century bewilderment over the tenses in Hebrew is
C. Bayly's statement: 'The Tenses are often used promiscuously especially
in the poetic and prophetic books' (1782:22). The participle was unanimously
called the Present tense since Levita's time. However, even this did not go
unchallenged; W. H. Barker states: 'The present they [the Hebrews] know
nothing of, nor indeed is there, in reality any such thing: for all time is
transient; every portion of it, until it arrives, is future, the instant it
hath arrived, it is no more' (1773:18).

Though W. Gesenius (1786–1842) made great advances in the thirteen
editions of his grammar, from 1813 to 1842, he never departed from the
conversive theory, as can be seen in B. Davies' translation of the 15th
edition (1852:79ff.). However, when the task of revising Gesenius' grammar
fell to his pupil, E. Rödiger, he immediately adopted Ewald's grammatical
terms, Perfect and Imperfect. This can be seen from T. J. Conant's translation of the 17th edition (1857:93ff.).[1]

Independently of Schröder, Phillip Gell suggested that every genre or
category of literature was comprised of major and minor systems. A major
system, for example, may be an historical narrative. It will commence with

a governing verb that sets the narrative in its true historic period. This will be followed by subordinate verb forms which retain their own individual tense. The temporal power of the governing, or initial, verb is inducted, or passed on, to the subordinate verbs by means of the <u>waw</u> conjunctive; hence his term 'the <u>waw</u> inductive' (1818:45). The major system, he held, may be broken up by minor systems, such as digressions, speeches, and so on, each of which will have an initial, or governing, verb of its own, but the major system is resumed again using the subordinate verb form. The advantage of this view, he says, is that it banishes 'the barbarism of ‧ conversive' (p. 45).

1.1.6   Conclusion

In this brief survey we have traced the rise of Hebrew grammar among the Jews, and in particular their statements regarding the tenses. Two conclusions may be drawn from the survey.

(1) The pronouncements of medieval Jewish grammarians do not inspire us with confidence in the light of our present knowledge of the Hebrew language and comparative Semitic philology. Some time after the Tiberian system of vocalization was perfected by the Massoretes the principles behind their work were forgotten. <u>It took centuries to recover them</u>.

(2) In the explanation of the tenses no appeal is made to a body of tradition, such as the Massoretes, that would inspire one to accept the conversive theory as a serious contender for a solution to the HVS.

The basis of the conversive solution appears to rest on an inductive study of the Hebrew verb forms, on the one hand, and the translation of these forms, on the other hand. If so, and Japheth ha-Levi (10th cent.) and Elias Levita (16th cent.) are examples of it, then there can be no stable solution, since <u>there will be as many solutions as there are different languages in the world to translate the Hebrew</u>. It was probably assumed in Europe at that time that every language in the world had a tense system; therefore it was natural for them to look for the Indo-European tense system in BH.

1.2.   THE THREE MAIN THEORIES CURRENT IN 1827

In this section we shall summarize the three main solutions put forward before 1827. They each have in common the assumption that the Hebrew verbal system is a tense system.

The waw conversive theory originated with the Jewish grammarians, and this explanation was bequeathed to the Christian universities of Europe in the early part of the 16th century. This solution dominated the grammars, writings, and commentaries of Christian Hebraists until the grammars of Lee and Ewald broke new ground in 1827.

In this section no attempt is made to provide a comprehensive, nor exhaustive, list of grammars which support the conversive theory. The few dozen mentioned are intended to show just how ubiquitous was this particular explanation in the schools and universities of Europe.

1.2.1   The Jewish Conversive Theory

This theory was deceptively simple. It was noted that when the qtl form occurred alone without any prefixed waw it was normally translated by the Past tense. When the yqtl form occurred alone it was normally translated by the Future tense. When either of these forms occurred with a prefixed waw it was normally translated by the opposite tense, i.e. weqtl was a future, and wayyqtl was a past.[1] This led the early grammarians to conclude that the prefixed waw was the cause of the conversion, hence there grew up the Waw Conversive theory. Hebrew had the same three tenses as any other language:

$$(קָצַר) \quad \text{qtl} = \text{Past}$$
$$(קוֹצֵר) \quad \text{qōtēl} = \text{Present}$$
$$(קָצִיר) \quad \text{yqtl} = \text{Future}$$

As time went by, however, it soon became apparent that there were a significant number of exceptions; these were:

(1) cases where the waw was prefixed to the verb but the translation did not require the tense to be changed, and

(2) cases where the waw was not prefixed to the verb but a change of tense was required in the translation.

In order to obtain the complete statistics on the extent of the exceptions it was decided to take an English translation of the Hebrew OT, in this case the RSV, and tabulate how each Hebrew verb form had been translated.[2]

The results can be seen in Appendix 1. Of particular interest is Table 3,
where out of a total of 14,972 wayyiqtol forms, no less than 14,202 have
been translated by the past tense. No wonder Kimḥi remarked: 'There is no
need to illustrate them as they are so numerous, and you can recognise
every one of them by the context.' Once it was assumed that the waw (ַו)
was prefixed to the future yiqtol form, then the conversive power of the
waw would be necessarily conceded, and the statistical argument would prove
decisive, as it apparently did until the 19th century.

1.2.1.1   Criticisms of the Conversive theory.

First of all we shall point out the difficulties inherent in this
view, before outlining its basic weaknesses.

(1) If one were to assess the HVS on the basis of the statistics of Table 3,
then a strong case can be made out for the theory. However, if one takes
into account the other four Tables a more complex picture emerges. But before
passing on to these other Tables it is interesting that there are 30 examples
in Table 3 where the wayyiqtol form had to be given a future translation. The
problem arises; How can the same verb, with the same prefixed waw, be translated in one context as a past, and in another as a future? For example:

(a) וַיִּקְרָא
   Past — 'God called the light Day,' (Gen. 1:5)
   Future — 'And his name will be called...' (Isa. 9:6[Heb. 5])[1]

(b) וַיָּשֶׂם
   Past — 'And there he put the man...' (Gen. 2:8)
   Future — 'He will make her wilderness as Eden,' (Isa. 51:3)

(c) וַיָּשֶׁב
   Past — 'Then he brought back all the goods,' (Gen. 14:16)
   Future — 'He will bring back on them...' (Ps. 94:23)

(d) וַיִּרְאוּ
   Past — 'and the men were very much afraid.' (Gen. 20:8)
   Future — 'Then all men will fear,' (Ps. 64:9 [H.10])

(e) וַיִּשְׁמַע
   Past — 'When Abraham heard that his kinsmen...' (Gen. 14:14)
   Future — 'and he will hear my voice.' (Ps. 55:17[H.18])

(f) וַתְּהִי
   Past — 'And they had brick for stone...' (Gen. 11:3)
   Present — 'Truth is lacking,' (Isa. 59:15)
   Future — 'the government will be upon his shoulder,' (Isa. 9:6)[2]

(2) Table 4 shows that there are 774 examples of yiqtol translated by the
past tense and another 423 as Past Modal (i.e. past conditional/subjunctive).
Here we have cases where no waw is prefixed to the verbs yet they have been
converted in translation. How can the same verb, without any prefixed waw, be
translated in one place as a past and in another as a future? For example:

(a) אַעֲלֶה
   Past — 'I brought you up from Egypt,' (Jud. 2:1)
   Future — 'I will bring you up out of...Egypt,' (Ex. 3:17)

(b) יִקָּרֵא _{Past} 'a prophet was formerly called a seer.' (1 Sm. 9:9)
Past / Future

(b) יִקָּרֵא— Past 'a prophet was formerly called a seer.' (1 Sm. 9:9)
— Future 'No longer shall your name be called Abram.' (Gen. 17:5)

(c) תִּזְרַע— Past 'Egypt...where you sowed your seed.' (Deut. 11:10)
— Future 'For six years you shall sow your seed.' (Ex. 23:10)

(3) If we look at Table 2 we see <u>qtl</u> verbs translated by the future and the
past. Again, how can the <u>same verb</u>, without any prefixed <u>waw</u>, be converted
in one place but unconverted in another? For example:[1]

(a) נָתַתִּי— Past 'I have given you every plant...' (Gen. 1:29)
— Future 'I will give you a son...' (Gen. 17:16)

(b) הָיְתָה— Past 'And the earth was without form...' (Gen. 1:2)
— Future 'my husband is old, shall I have pleasure?' (Gn. 18:12)

(c) לָקַחְתִּי— Past 'Whose ox have I taken?' (1 Sam. 12:3)
— Future 'I will take it by force.' (1 Sam. 2:16)

(d) בָּזְזוּ— Past 'all the spoil...Israel took for their booty,' (Jos. 11:14)
— Future 'the lame will take the prey.' (Isa. 33:23)

(4) Table 1 shows that <u>w^eqtl</u> forms can be translated by the future and the
past even though they <u>both</u> have the prefixed <u>waw</u>. For example:

(a) וַהֲקִמֹתִי— Past 'I set watchmen over you,' (Jer. 6:17)
— Future 'I will establish my covenant...' (Gen. 6:18, 17:7,19)

(b) וְנָתַתִּי— Past 'I applied my mind to seek...' (Ecc. 1:12 [Heb. 13])
— Future 'I will give to you...' (Gen. 17:6, 26:4)

Elias Levita (see p. 11 above) taught that: 'An accent on the penultima
shows that the waw is copulative', <u>i.e.</u> <u>waw hibbur</u> and <u>waw hippuk</u> could be
distinguished by the position of the tone in the first and second person
singular masculine of <u>w^eqtl</u> verbs. Once again, while the rule holds good
for a large number of such forms, why is the tone on the <u>ultima</u> in the first
example cited above if the tone distinguishes between conversive <u>waw</u> and
copulative <u>waw</u>? (A full investigation into the tone shift is given in
Appendix 2.)

(5) Table 5 shows that <u>w^eyiqtol</u> forms can be translated by the past and
future tenses even though <u>both</u> have the same prefixed <u>waw</u>. For example:

(a) וְאָבוֹא— Past 'I have gone up the heights of the mountains,' (Is. 37:24)
— Future 'I will come upon him while he is weary,' (2 Sam. 17:2)

(b) וְאוֹרִיד— Past 'I have put down the inhabitants...' (Isa. 10:13)
— Future 'I will bring down their strength...' (Is. 63:6)

(c) וָאַרְבֶּהוּ — Past 'And I blessed him and made him many,' (Is. 51:2)
וְאַרְבֶּה — Future 'And I will multiply you exceedingly,' (Gen. 17:2)

(d) וְאֶתְּנָה— Past 'I delivered Jacob to destruction,' (Isa. 43:28)
— Present 'thou desirest not sacrifice; else would I give it,' (Ps. 51:16 [Heb. v.18])
— Future 'And I will make my covenant...' (Gen. 17:2)

The basic weaknesses of this theory are:

(1) The definition of yiqtol as the Hebrew Future tense was too restrictive.
It is that and more if we are to go by the way it has been translated into
English, Latin, French, etc. There are over 700 examples of it translated by
the Past tense; over 3,300 examples as a Present against 5,400 examples as
a Future. Indeed, every mood and tense in the English language is required
to translate this form.

(2) The definition of qātal as the Hebrew Past tense was too narrow. It is
that and more, since our statistics show that every tense and mood in the
English language is required to translate it.

(3) The fact that each of the five Hebrew forms requires every tense and
mood, with the exception of the Imperative in the case of wayyiqtol, to translate them shows that any attempt to draw one-to-one equivalents with the
Indo-European tense system is going to meet with insuperable difficulties,
as we have shown already.

(4) The hundreds of exceptions to the mysterious power of the conversive waw
do not prove the rule but flagrantly contradict and violate it. A more
cautious medieval Jewish grammarian might have stated the Rule with greater
accuracy if he had written: The waw conversive 'converts' yiqtol only when the
Past tense is required by the translation, and it does not 'convert' when the
translation does not require it'. In which case it ceases to be a grammatical
rule and becomes a rule of thumb for translators after they have made their
translations.

(5) Possibly the most damaging criticism that could be made of this theory
is that it is based on a linguistic non sequitur. Clearly it would be a non
sequitur to argue that because tenses must be used to translate modern
tenseless languages,[1] that therefore these languages must have a tense system
comparable to the language used to translate them. In other words, it is a
fallacy to argue the verbal system of another language on the basis of translation equivalents. Yet this is precisely how the theory was argued: 'and
you can recognise every one of them from the context', i.e. the translation
context (Kimḥi). On this premise Hebrew would have as many verbal systems as
there are languages to translate it, and none of its own.

We have no reason to suspect that the native, Hebrew-speaking, OT
writers were constantly having to use the 'conversive waw' rule to get their
tenses right. If they did, we would have to conclude that they were not very

consistent.

There is no known parallel to the _waw_ conversive theory in any other
language. The problem only arose when it came to _translating_ the Hebrew
into another language which had a totally different 'tense' system. The
theory only arises when we enter the complex area of translation. That would
appear to be the original context and point of origin for the theory.[1]

Notwithstanding the weaknesses of this theory Christian Hebraists, on
the whole, accepted it without question up until 1827 and beyond. There
were at least two reasons for this. Firstly, as a general rule the conversive idea seemed to solve all the problems of translating the Bible into
the European languages, especially in the 16th century. Secondly, Hebrew
was the Jews' language, and since they had handed down this explanation
from the 10th century, at the latest, it must have appeared foolhardy to
challenge it.[2] These two factors effectively paralysed any enquiry into this
linguistic phenomenon until the early 19th century.

While the theory has been abandoned by the majority of modern Hebraists
it still has a few modern supporters.[3]

1.2.2   The Relative Tense Theory

The earliest alternative explanation for the seemingly promis-
cuous use of the Hebrew verb forms appears to be that put forward by N. W.
Schroeder in his _Institutiones ad fundamenta linguae Hebraicae_, published
in 1766. On p. 340 he says:[4]

> Apart from these various usages, the Future [i.e. yqtl] has yet
> another [use]--unique and peculiar to the Hebrews, in that it
> receives the force of our Past, and designates a matter as truly
> past--not however by itself nor absolutely, but in relation to
> some preceding past event--for when different events are to be
> narrated, which follow the one from the other in some kind of
> continuous series, the Hebrews consider the first as past, the
> others, however, which follow--as future on account of the pre-
> ceding [past]. Since this describes something which, in relation
> to another past event, is itself later and future, it may be
> called the _Future relativum_.

Schroeder, of course, accepted the current designation of the yqtl form as
a Future tense, and qtl as the Hebrew Past tense. His Present tense was
the Participle (cf. p. 52). But with his conception of the relative use
of the Future and Past tenses he abolished the need to 'convert' these
tenses, and freed Hebraists from the conversive crutch to explain the HVS.

The starting-point for the relative use of the Future and Past tenses
may have begun with the observation that there were too many exceptions to
the Conversive waw theory, and that the waw prefixed to qtl did not really
'convert' it into a Future (yqtl). Rather, when a future event was considered to be so certain of happening, it was considered by the speaker as
being as-good-as-done. Now for the sake of translating this Hebrew concept,
the equivalent in another language may be, in the majority of cases, the
Future tense. Hence the Past used for a future event was, in reality, a
relative Past tense, i.e. from a point in the future an action, which was
future from an absolute present viewpoint, could be described as 'Past'.
It was immediately recognised that one could do the same with past events,
i.e. from a point of time in the past all actions between that point and
the absolute Present can be viewed as future to it.

The year after Schroeder published his explanation Samuel Johnson
published his grammar, An English and Hebrew Grammar (London, 1767), in
which he put forward the same idea:

> There are two tenses Praeter and Future...but there is something
> very peculiar in the use of the tenses in Hebrew....the Future
> tense is not only used to signify an action to be done hereafter
> ...but also any past action in consequence of a former expressed
> in the Praeter; as Gen. 1:1, In the beginning God created בָּרָא,
> and v.2 וַיֹּאמֶר and God said, and so on; there is a long series
> of past actions expressed by the future; because then future, or
> in consequence of He created. (p. 32)

W. H. Barker writes in the same vein in his A Plain Grammar of the Hebrew
Language (1773:18):

> The Hebrew acknowledges only two [tenses]; the perfect and the
> future. The first represents an action done, the other to be done.
> The present they know nothing off, nor indeed is there, in
> reality, any such thing: for all time is transient; every portion
> of it, until it arrives, is future, the instant it hath arrived,
> it is no more.

Concerning the prefixed waw he says:

> It denotes succession, if prefixed to a verb future, the action
> must be understood to be future to the time of which the writer
> is speaking; not in which he is speaking. (p. 31)

G. Fitzgerald in his grammar (Dublin, 1813), while accepting the idea that
the future is often put for the perfect sees...

> the futurity of the verb referring to the time of, not to the
> time in, which the Historian is writing; as גֶּפֶן מִמִּצְרַיִם תַּסִּיעַ
> "Thou shalt bring (or transplant) a vine out of Egypt," for, Thou
> hast brought, Ps. lxxx. 9, by which is intimated, that that which
> was once future, or to come, has been accomplished, viz. The
> transplanting the Children of Israel, like a choice vine out of

Egypt. Thus also in Deut. (iv. 41) we read אָז יַבְדִּיל מֹשֶׁה
שָׁלֹשׁ עָרִים "Then Moses <u>shall</u> <u>sever</u> three cities," for severed.
(p. 89)

But then we have an inexplicable lapse into the Conversive theory to explain
the forms with prefixed <u>waw</u> (<u>cf</u>. p. 89), with the statement of Lyons (1735:
15) that these tenses 'are often used promiscuously' (p. 88).

1.2.2.1   Criticisms of The Relative Tense Theory.

        In the Conversive theory the standpoint of the writer remained
constant, as it were, and the time-scale shuttled back ('converted future')
and forth ('converted past'). In this theory we have the reverse situation,
where the standpoint of the writer is shuttled up and down the fixed time-scale
in line with the time <u>of</u> which the writer is writing.

        While this theory had the advantage of giving a consistent function to
the two Hebrew verb forms, which was not the case in the Conversive theory,
nevertheless the explanation of how <u>yqtl</u> forms came to be used of past events
is muddled. We may illustrate the confused thinking behind the explanation as
follows.

Past	Present	Future		
QTL	///YQTL//////		RELATIVE TENSES	
	Qtl	///YQTL/////		
	Past	Present	Future	ABSOLUTE TENSES

If the top set of tenses represents the relative Past, Present, and Future
tenses, and the lower set the absolute or actual Past, Present, and Future
tenses, then it can be seen that the <u>qtl</u> events on the absolute scale become
the future or <u>yqtl</u> events on the relative scale. From the relative Present
standpoint all the <u>qtl</u> absolute Past events will be viewed as future events,
hence the use of the <u>yqtl</u> form to describe them.

        If, however, one extends the relative Future events so that they over-
lap the absolute Future events, the weakness in the theory can be seen:

Past	Present	Future			
QTL	/////// YQTL ///////////// YQTL ///////////				
	QTL	/// YQTL ///// YQTL ///////////			
	Past	Present	Future		

It is clear that the use of <u>yqtl</u> for the Relative <u>and</u> Absolute Future tenses
is because the Future refers to events which <u>lie in the future in relation</u>

to the Present standpoint of the writer, and not because they are describing
past events.

Another weakness with this theory is the idea that a future tense can
be used to relate past historical events.

This theory suffers the same faults as the Conversive theory with
respect to its narrow definition of yqtl as a Future and qtl as a Past tense.[1]

1.2.3   The Waw Inductive Theory

This theory was another attempt to circumvent the Conversive
theory. It took as its starting point the following observation: Connection,
generally in Hebrew, implies communication, i.e. the communicating of the
whole, or part, of the meaning of a preceding word, clause, or sentence,
connected with it; of which connection waw is most commonly the sign: the
waw indicates a communication of power, to produce the effect, flowing from
the former to the latter (Gell, 1818:4). An example of this would be Psalm
107:11,12:

11. ‏כִּי הִמְרוּ אִמְרֵי־אֵל וַעֲצַת עֶלְיוֹן נָאָצוּ :
12. ‏וַיַּכְנַע בֶּעָמָל לִבָּם כָּשְׁלוּ וְאֵין עֹזֵר :

'for they had rebelled against the words of God, and spurned the counsel of
the Most High. [Lit. And] Their hearts were bowed down with labour; they fell
down, with none to help.' It is argued that the causal power of v. 11 flows
into v. 12. Similarly, it is argued, the power of a negative, once expressed,
is communicated by means of connection to a succeeding word or clause, without the repetition of the negative, cf. Ps. 44:19, Job 30:20. Hence it is
concluded, a communication of the time, or temporal power, of a preceding
or governing verb, to another which follows, and connected with the former
generally by waw, is more properly that operation, which is said to be
produced by waw conversive, than any change of tense (cf. Gell, p. 6).

John Bellamy (1818:xxxvi-vii) had this to say of the conversive theory:

> I shall prove that the ‏וֹ‏ vau, has nothing to do with converting
> one tense to another: it is absurd to suppose any thing of the
> kind;...I shall now proceed to develop the system which appears
> to be regular throughout the scriptures.
>   When a verb at the beginning of a subject is written in the
> preter tense, and connected with verbs following which describe
> an action taking place after the action described by the first
> verb; such following verbs are written in the future form, because
> the actions described by them are future to the action described
> by the first verb at the beginning of the subject. And they are

translated in the <u>preter</u>, because the) <u>vau</u> connects the preter
tense of the first verb, which is connected with the same order,
meaning and application, as is signified by the first verb.
   Example. Gen. i.1, the first verb is בָּרָא <u>bara</u>, <u>he</u> <u>created</u>,
which is connected with וַיֹּאמֶר <u>vayomer</u>, <u>and</u> <u>he</u> <u>said</u>, in the 3d
verse; וַיַּרְא <u>vayare</u>, <u>and</u> <u>he</u> <u>saw</u>,...which verbs describe actions
after the action described by the first verb: therefore, being
actions future to the first <u>preter</u>, they are written in the <u>future</u>
form....they are translated in the preter tense, because the)
<u>vau</u> connects the preter tense of the first verb.

In this solution the <u>form</u> of the verb only tells the reader that the action
takes place <u>after</u> the preceding verb, but its tense is that of the preceding
verb which is conducted to it by means of the prefixed <u>waw</u>. In the case of
Direct Speech style (Prophetic speeches),where the order of verb forms is
reversed, Bellamy says (p. xxxviii):

   ...when a verb written in the future tense at the head of a subject
   precedes a verb in the <u>preter</u> <u>tense</u>, which has the) <u>vau</u>, prefixed
   with the vowel Sheva, then the future time of the first verb is
   connected by the) <u>vau</u>, and carried to the following verb in the
   same proposition, though written in the preter form; because it
   describes an action which takes place future to the verb at the
   beginning of the subject.

   In the same year that Bellamy published his Bible, Philip Gell published
his <u>Observations</u> <u>on</u> <u>the</u> <u>Idiom</u> <u>of</u> <u>the</u> <u>Hebrew</u> <u>Language</u> (1818). He renamed the
conversive <u>waw</u>, the 'waw inductive', because:

   When Verbs are connected in Hebrew (the connexion being generally
   indicated by the sign) prefixed to the latter), the Power,
   whether temporal or modal, of the first or Governing Verb is
   communicated from it, and inducted into the Verb following. And
   whatever be the power proper to the latter Verb, it still retains
   its use subordinately; but that which is inducted becomes the
   prevailing power. If a third Verb follow in connexion, and so on,
   the power communicated from each successive Verb to that next
   following, without destroying its proper subordinate power, is
   the same as was previously inducted into the former. (p. 8)

But on p. 13f. he makes a significant alteration to his Theorem, namely, that
subordinate preters (<u>i.e.</u> <u>qtl</u> verbs) do not keep/retain their subordinate
past tense:

   It is evident that when the Sacred Writers <u>intend</u> any order to be
   observed in their narrations or speeches, using the particle)
   before the verbs to maintain it, each circumstance is related in
   the order in which it occurs; and subordinate present or future
   tenses only are ever wanted for such a purpose. There is no
   occasion for a tense to express, <u>after</u> a forementioned event,
   another which occurred antecedently, or was <u>past</u> in relation to
   it: that is, there is no occasion for any temporal power in subordinate preters, corresponding with that of subordinates in other

tenses. Subordinate preters, therefore, seem never to have any
proper temporal power of their own, as subordinate presents and
futures have; and they are made a generally disposable force; by
which any narration or speech may be expressed, without implying
the order of the acts involved in it. They have only the inducted
power of the Governing verb.

1.2.3.1   Criticisms of the Waw Inductive Theory

        This theory combines the weaknesses of the two previous theories.
It has the weakness of the waw conversive's narrow definition of the yqtl
and qtl forms, and the weakness of the Relative Tense theory where the Future
tense (yqtl) is used to relate past historical events. Future actions on a
relative or absolute time-scale are, by definition, non-past events: Future
tenses can only refer to future actions.

        An internal weakness is its arbitrariness. While yqtl has a Governing
and a subordinate Future tense, qtl has only a Governing Past tense but no
subordinate Past tense 'only the inducted power of the Governing verb'.

        Gell is incorrect when he says: 'There is no occasion for a tense to
express, after a forementioned event, another which occurred antecedently,
or was past in relation to it.' We have quoted two examples from Kimhi's
Mikhlol on p. 9 which illustrate such an occasion.

        There are many examples where stories, and even complete biblical books,
begin with a wayyqtl form.[1] Since the prefixed waw is not a conversive waw,
but an inductive waw, what tense is being inducted? In the absence of a
governing verb these stories must begin with a Future tense.

        There are many examples where qtl and yqtl verbs do not have a prefixed
waw, yet they have been translated as though they had an inductive waw before
them. If it is the waw that is the cause of the induction how are we to
explain these cases?[2]

* * * * * *

        In the next section we shall look at nine different approaches to the
HVS, with a view to evaluating them for any cumulative contribution they may
provide towards a solution to the vexed problems of the tenses in Hebrew.
It has not been possible to cover all the works relating to our topic in the
period under review in this dissertation. This selection of works represents
the fruits of diligent research in the problems of the Hebrew Verbal System
between 1827 and 1954 by many able scholars.

**THEORIES ON THE HEBREW VERBAL SYSTEM
BETWEEN 1827 AND 1954**

1.3.   THE MAIN THEORIES ON THE HVS BETWEEN 1827 and 1954

The central difficulty of the HVS has been, and still is, the
correct understanding of the two principal verb forms: the Prefix- and
Suffix-forms and their consecutive waw constructions. These difficulties
have been a challenge to many scholars down through the centuries and have
attracted and taxed the minds of great men of learning. It can also be said
that the same problems have repelled equally able men because the situation
in Hebrew appears to be insoluble.

It is a fact that no fundamentally new solution to the HVS has appeared
since 1954 that has received significant support from Hebraists and Semitists.
The majority of scholars still go back to two 19th century theories, those
of H. Ewald (1835) and S. R. Driver (1874), to explain the HVS; yet neither
of these theories has been the subject of special investigation to our knowledge.

The period 1827 – 1954 covers the most active and formative period of
investigation into the HVS. In this period we can trace the precursors of
many of the modern theories and approaches. Indeed, some modern theories,
which have been put forward as 'new' discoveries, were already anticipated
in this period.[1] Perhaps one of the benefits of the present work may be that
the duplication of past theories, which have been tried, found wanting, and
hence discarded, will be prevented in the future.

Perhaps, also, the present selection of principal theories, published
between 1827 and 1954, will arouse new interest in an old problem; for what
greater goal can the OT scholar have than to understand the 'oracles of God'
as they were originally given in the Hebrew language? Yet just this is
denied us in the realm of its verbal system.

Progress in many sciences, especially the more complex subjects, is
often a cumulative affair. The work of previous researchers and pioneers is
accepted, improved, and made the basis for further research. If progress is
to be made in the universally acknowledged difficult area of the HVS then the
cumulative findings of previous researchers must be made available if future
researchers are to have a basis from which to proceed, and on which they can
build. Since no thoroughly detailed work or criticism of the following theories
has been published to date it is hoped that this work will meet that need. The
theories examined are: S. Lee (1827), H. Ewald (1834), I. Nordheimer (1841),
S. R. Driver (1874), W. Turner (1876), J. A. Knudtzon (1889), H. Bauer (1910),
G. R. Driver (1936), and T. W. Thacker (1954).

1.3.1   The Two Tense Theory of Samuel Lee

Lee (1783–1852) was Regius Professor of Hebrew at the University of Cambridge from 1831–48. He received the D.D. from the University of Halle on the recommendation of Professor Wilhelm Gesenius (1786–1842). He was quite a remarkable man in that he taught himself Latin, Greek, Hebrew, Aramaic (Targumic), Syriac, Arabic—he was Professor of Arabic at Cambridge when he 36 years old— Persian, Hindustani, and Ethiopic. For details of his life see A. M. Lee (1896).[1]

Six years before Lee produced his first Hebrew grammar he entered into the dispute over Bellamy's controversial translation of the Bible, but he gives no hint of his own understanding of the tenses at this time. Indeed, in the context of the dispute, he appears to acquiesce in the conversive theory which Bellamy ridiculed. He says at one point, 'Your note on the ꜱ vau prefixed deserves no remark' (1820:126). However, some of Bellamy's criticism of the waw conversive were later endorsed by Lee in 1827.

He also tells us that he read Philip Gell's work (1818) with care, and that while it evinced considerable acuteness and research, it did not appear to him to advance the subject beyond what Schroeder has said; and it left a large number of cases unaccounted for, while other cases had been accounted for in too metaphysical a fashion to make his solution probable (1827:xv).

Some time between 1821 and 1827 Lee began reading the works of Arab grammarians—he was made Professor of Arabic in 1819—with a view to a solution of the HVS. He tells us that it was in these works and grammars that he found his solution to the HVS. He was strongly impressed with the difference between the Oriental and Western way of thinking. This led him to reject Latin and Greek terms and categories to explain the Hebrew language. His approach is set out in the Preface to his 1827 Grammar. Unlike many scholars of his day he freely acknowledged his sources and also his indebtedness to the Arab grammarians for the application of their methods to the Hebrew language (1827:344ff.; 1840:163; 1850:198).

The following are the main points in Lee's understanding of the HVS.

1.3.1.1   The Origin of the Verb Forms

Central to Lee's view of the tenses—though not necessarily essential—is the suggestion that the qtl form is formed on a Concrete noun, and the yqtl form on an Abstract noun (1827:341). In this he says that he is following the Arab grammarians (1850:195; 1827:189ff.), who hold that the verbs are derived from the _masdars_, which Lee says are nouns; therefore verbs are derived from nouns. He did not deny that nouns could, after the formation of verb forms, be formed from verbs.

The principal argument used in favour of the verb being derived from the noun is that the former is clearly a compound form (1827:109-35, 193; 1850:194). It follows, therefore, that the elements which make up the verb form must be older than the formation of the compound form. In Lee's opinion once the suffixed pronoun is removed in the case of qtl forms we are left with a Concrete noun (1827:190), and in the case of yqtl forms, an Abstract noun. According to his approach the addition of one or other of the pronouns to any noun will always have the effect of investing it with the powers of a verb (1827:193).

The other arguments used in favour of the verb being derived from the noun are as follows. Firstly, there are some classes of verbs which do not exhibit the original three root consonants in the third person singular qtl, i.e. those verbs which have ‌‌ or ‌‌ for the middle radical; they are found complete in the noun, but defective in the verb. In some cases the noun appears in a defective form, in which case it is never found complete in the verb. Secondly, the variation in the last vowel of qt()l is more naturally accounted for in the noun than in the verb (1827:105-7, noun forms II, III, and X). He notes that a noun having the same vowel is almost universally found to exist.

Thirdly, the yqtl form is formed from the infinitive which is a verbal noun (1827:210); and the infinitive, when pronounced with some emphasis, will become imperative in significance (in this he says he is following Schroeder). According to his Lexicon the infinitive/imperative form of the verb is a simple primitive segolate noun, and nothing more (1840:vii). They are said to be generally Abstract nouns (1827:xiv).

Fourthly, both yqtl and the Participle, when used absolutely, refer to the present moment, and both are very similar in meaning. The Participle denotes continuity of action in the present (1850:205). Now since the participle is not inflected for tense, such as we observe in the Greek language (e.g. Pres. Ptc. παιδεύων ; Fut. Ptc. παιδεύσων; Aorist Ptc. παιδεύσας), but are inflected only for number and gender they are in this respect no different than nouns (1827:xiv). In relation, then, to the Greek participles, Lee denies that Hebrew has participles in that sense (1850:194). He is quite

adamant that Hebrew participles involve no tense whatsoever, and a better
general designation, in his opinion, would be verbal concrete nouns (1847:
51).

Lastly, the early Jewish grammarians held that the verb proceeded from
the noun (1827:189); likewise the 'best native grammarians of Arabia' (1850:
195).

The natural conclusion he drew from this line of reasoning was that
the noun, not the 3rd masc. sing. form of the verb, ought to be considered
as the root (1827:78-9); this, however, does not affect the arrangement of
his Lexicon (1840:vii). We now look at his conception of the HVS in closer
detail.

1.3.1.1.1   The qtl form

The starting point of Lee's analysis of this verb form was the
observation that a verb in a conjugated form either is, or must be, considered as being compounded with a pronoun, and consequently is in an unfit
state to be considered as a primitive word (1827:79). Without these pronouns, as well as every other affix, one has arrived at the 'root'; therefore every root is considered to have been a noun originally (1827:80).
Thus the three Qal forms: פָּקַד , פָּקֵד , and פָּקוֹד , correspond to the
noun forms: פֶּקֶד , פֵּקֶד , and פָּקוֹד (1827:190, 105-7). Nouns of these
forms are generally concrete, and may designate substances (אָדָם man,
בָּשָׂר flesh) or epithets (חָכָם a wise man, רָשָׁע a wicked man). In the
latter case he doubts whether the Hebrews ever considered words of this
kind as adjectives (1827:105).

Lee argues that while the participle has some affinity of form with
yqtl it is not a verb. Participles, he argues, are nothing more than attributes 'into the etymology of which nothing having the least connection with
tense has ever entered' (1827:214). He considers חָכָם wise, רָחוֹק distant,
and גָּדֵל growing, as being participles just as much as פּוֹקֵד visiting
(1827:214; 1847:51). Reasoning, then, from the fact that the Hebrew verbs
are made up of nouns and pronouns, and that the participle is a noun having
a concrete meaning, Lee arrived at the conclusion that since the participle,
at least in some forms, is practically identical with yqtl it is the origin
for the yqtl tense in Hebrew (1850:195).

Lee accounts for the past tense function of qtl as follows. The participle contains no fixed tense within itself (unlike the Greek participles).

The form קֹטֵל or קֹטֵל signifies some one 'killing' at any time, past,
present, or future, as the context may require. But where no such determining
context is given, the prior existence of an agent (or patient, in the case
of the passive) must necessarily be implied. But since the action is placed
prior to the agent as far as the form goes this may be taken to mean that
the verbal action has priority over the agent, previous possession of the
verbal sense being plainly implied; hence, he argues, this is how the קֹטֵל
form obtained its past notion (1850:196).[1]

He held that each of the Hebrew tenses has only one primary and proper
meaning, namely, qtl is Past, and always Past in some sense, and yqtl is a
Present tense either relatively or absolutely (1827:341–4; 1851:472,485).
In his debate with Ewald, Lee makes it clear that his Past (qtl) is not the
same thing as a completed action (1847:57ff.). An action may be past but not
finished, e.g. 'I have loved thee (אֲהַבְתִּיךְ) with an everlasting love'
(Jer. 31:3). The verb here will signify a time that is past, but it does
not mean, therefore, that ever since that time Yahweh has ceased to love
Israel. The very statement evinces the contrary, namely, that the love formerly shown would be continued everlastingly. If, however, one uses a verb
signifying completion, finish, ending, closing, concluding, perfecting, or
the like, then indeed the tenses may imply completed action; which, however,
would not be done merely by the form used (1847:59). Thus Lee argues that
neither of the verb forms can imply in themselves finished or unfinished
action, only the context can settle this point. In 1 Kings 15:1 the verb
מָלַךְ really has the force of 'he began to rule', whereas in v. 2 we are
told that Jeroboam 'reigned for three years in Jerusalem'. In both instances
the contexts determine whether the action is finished or unfinished, or just
begun. Lee interprets the two actions in 1 Kings 15:1-2 as Past tenses, and
that, apparently, is all that the verb forms can convey in themselves: they
cannot tell us anything about the state or stage that an action has reached.

1.3.1.1.2 The yqtl form

Here again Lee analyses the form into a noun and prefixed pronoun. The noun form he identifies as the infinitive, which is really a
segolate noun found in three forms: קֶטֶל, קְטֶל, and קְטֶל (1827:191).
Although the infinitive and the imperative are identical in form, he thinks
the infinitive is older than the imperative because the latter is inflected

for person (1827:210)). The infinitive (or verbal noun) generally has an
abstract meaning (1827:94–5), and implies action, passion, or neutrality,
depending on whether its sense is active, passive, or neuter. Neither tense
nor person is shown in any determinate manner, e.g. קְטֹל will signify
'killing' as to action; הִקָּטֵל 'being, or becoming, killed'; as to time,
present action, present passion, or present neutrality, would seem to be
meant. This being so, he feels quite justified in arguing that in attaching
the personal pronouns to the infinitive, in order to form the verb, present
action, present passion, and the like, would seem to be intended (1850:
194–5).

He objects to the suggestion that his Present (yqtl) tense indicates
unfinished action, chiefly on the grounds of the origin of the form. A noun
may, he argues, whether of the abstract/infinitive or concrete/participle,
signify action, accident, etc. This meaning, then, must necessarily be
indefinite in every point of view: finish or unfinish can have no place here;
because no word can in itself carry more than its own notion, as to action,
in it. If any other notion is to be added, this must be done by the addition
of some other word or words. If we now supply the pronominal affixes to
either of these nouns, he continues, we shall have action, etc., had in view,
restricted to some extent by these affixes. But these affixes carry nothing
with them implying either finished or unfinished action. He concedes that
the abstract noun so augmented will imply unfinished action, or no end to
such action; but rejects the idea that it must also imply continuous or
frequentative action. The form itself does not warrant that assumption. It
is left to the context to determine whether any action is continuous, repet-
itive, frequentative, etc. (1847:57–8).

Lee next draws a distinction between 'future tense' and 'future signification'. He acknowledges that the imperative has a future signification as
also the infinitive on which the Present is formed (1851:478). In Lee's
understanding of the Indo-European tense system there is no strictly grammatical future tense (1847:371). In English, 'I will do', says grammatically
nothing more than, 'I am willing to do': 'I shall do', than, 'I now ought
to do', etc. In his view, action, taking place at all, necessarily implies
time present to this action (1851:486). So as far as he is concerned every
action must take place in its own present tense time.[1] For this reason, and
because certain yiqtol forms cannot admit a future signification, he is con-
tent to read yqtl as a Present tense in every context.

He draws no distinction between the meaning or tense of the simple yqtl

and <u>wayyqtl</u>: both are Present tenses either absolutely or relatively. He lists
the following examples where the <u>yqtl</u> verbs cannot be given a future meaning:
אִוָּלֵד Job 3:3;   אֹמֵר, וַיַּגִּיד 3:11; אֶקְרָא 3:12; יָנוּחַ, וְאֶשְׁקוֹט 3:13;
אֶהְיֶה 3:16; and other examples in Ps. 97 (1851:479).

He gives an impressive list of quotations by Arab grammarians to the
effect that <u>yqtl</u> is a Present tense, see 1827:344-63; 1847:12-17, 57-92,
370-1; 1850:193-5. The <u>yqtl</u> consecutive is equivalent to the Historic Present
of Greek and Latin (1847:72). This interpretation is borne out by the LXX and
the Greek NT where the Present tense is sometimes used to relate past events,
e.g. 'And in those days cometh(παραγίνεται) John the Baptist' (Matt. 3:1)
(see 1847:74-6; 1827:350; 1850:198; 1851:479). In his grammar (1827:350) he
gives examples where the Aorist is used for present and future actions and
where the Present tense is used for the past and the future, and considers
these usages to be influenced by the Hebrew idiom.

1.3.1.2   The Relative Uses of the Tenses.

Since Hebrew has only two tenses—a Past (<u>qtl</u>) and a Present
(<u>yqtl</u>)—but no Future, these two tenses have a relative and an absolute
function which can cover the future sphere.

By 'absolute' he means: If we suppose any writer to be commencing a
narrative, he must necessarily speak of past, present, or future time, with
reference to the period at which his statement is made. To this period it
will be in his power to recur whenever it may suit his purpose to do so, e.g.
'And God called [calls, וַיִּקְרָא =Hist. Pres. tense] the light Day, and the
darkness he called[=Absol. Past, קָרָא] Night', Gen. 1:5.

By 'relative' tenses, he means: A writer may speak of the past, present,
or future events, with reference to some other period or event already introduced into the context, e.g. Isa. 9:6, 'For unto us a child is born [יֻלַּד,
relative past: 'has been born'], unto us a son is given [נִתַּן], relative
past: 'has been given']; and the government shall be [וַתְּהִי, relative
present: 'the government is'] upon his shoulder: and his name shall be called
[וַיִּקְרָא], relative present: 'his name is called'] Wonderful....'. Thus every
tense in this prophesy is used in a relative sense with respect to some
point in the future (1827:342-51).

The rules governing the use of the tenses are regulated by two general
principles. Firstly, the writer may set out from the period in which he
commences his narrative by transporting himself and his listener back to the

beginning of his story or narration, and follow the different circumstances
and events as they took (take) place; in which case the events will be dated
from the preceding event and not from the absolute standpoint of the writer/
narrator.[1] Or secondly, he may represent events which are believed will
certainly take place, as having already taken place (1827:360). In this way
Lee can account for the different 'tenses' in what appear to be their
'opposite' spheres.

He dismisses the idea that the waw has the power to change one tense
into another:

> How a particle, which has not the least reference to time, could
> change the tense proper for a certain form of the verb, few
> perhaps have been able to see: for my part I never could see the
> most distant connection between this particle and the tense of
> any verb. (1827:361)

The fact that biblical books begin with this waw does not trouble him, since
other books begin with it prefixed to nouns, e.g. 1 Kings, Ezra, and Exodus.
The writer may take the liberty of transporting himself and his reader into
former times without the usual notice, i.e. by some term expressive of past
time, or a verb in the qtl form. There may have been an ellipsis of some
adverb, or the verb הָיָה . He suggests that the prefixed waw may have an
illative function (1827:53-4, 163, 201) but this is retracted in a later
work (1847:76 f'note *).

1.3.1.3   An Assessment of Lee's Theory

Lee's solution was the first to provide a consistent meaning for
the two forms that did not break down very easily. Up until his Grammar
appeared the consecutive forms were treated as if they were distinct grammatical forms, with some form of 'conversion' needed to bring the HVS into
line with the Indo-European tense system. His theory was revolutionary in
that it severed any connection with the Western way of thinking. He was
going against three centuries of Jewish/Christian teaching on the subject,
which probably accounts for the very full documentation of his view.

He lived in an age which did not encourage scholars to acknowledge
their sources, and plagiarism was quite common, yet he gives full credit
to the Arab grammarians for the Two Tense solution. Despite this acknow-
ledgement it is not altogether certain that the majority of these grammarians did regard the yqtl form as a Present tense; indeed, Lee notes that
they call yqtl verbs which follow the leading qtl verb the Future (1827:347).

There are certain difficulties, however, if yqtl is to be regarded as
a Present tense, either in a relative or an absolute sense. Firstly, it
would imply that the action _is_ _in_ _progress_ and hence not yet completed. But
in 2 Sam. 14:5 we read: וַתֹּאמֶר אֲבָל אִשָּׁה־אַלְמָנָה אָנִי וַיָּמָת אִישִׁי׃
'And she answered, Of a truth I am a widow woman, and mine husband is dead.'
It is hardly likely that וַיָּמָת has a present tense significance here, _i.e._
'and my husband is dying'. She is obviously referring to a _past completed_
event. Secondly, yqtl is used of past events. We give just two examples:
Job 3:3 'Let the day perish wherein I was born (אִוָּלֶד)', and Isa. 51:2
'Look to Abraham your father and to Sarah who bore you (תְּחוֹלֶלְכֶם).' In
neither case is a Present tense translation suitable. Thirdly, since the
Present (yqtl) and the Past (qtl) tenses do not indicate formally whether
they are to be taken in a Relative or Absolute sense this leads to some
ambiguity as the rapid switch from Relative to Absolute time is unpredictable.
Where the Historic Present is used in Greek and Latin there is no such sudden
switches of tenses. The following passage will illustrate this point.

Isaiah 45:1-5

Past	אָמַר יְהוָה לִמְשִׁיחוֹ לְכוֹרֶשׁ	כֹּה		1a
Past	אֲשֶׁר־הֶחֱזַקְתִּי בִימִינוֹ לְרַד־לְפָנָיו גּוֹיִם			1b
Present in the Past	אֲפַתֵּחַ לִפְתֹּחַ לְפָנָיו דְּלָתַיִם			1c
	יִסָּגֵרוּ׃ לֹא וּשְׁעָרִים			1d
	אֵלֵךְ לְפָנֶיךָ אֲנִי			2a
Present in the Future	אֲיַשֵּׁר וַהֲדוּרִים			2b
	אֲשַׁבֵּר נְחוּשָׁה דַּלְתוֹת			2c
Past in the Future	אֲגַדֵּעַ׃ בַרְזֶל וּבְרִיחֵי			2d
	וְנָתַתִּי לְךָ אוֹצְרוֹת חֹשֶׁךְ וּמַטְמֻנֵי מִסְתָּרִים			3a
	תֵּדַע כִּי־אֲנִי יְהוָה הַקּוֹרֵא בְשִׁמְךָ אֱלֹהֵי יִשְׂרָאֵל׃	לְמַעַן		3b
	לְמַעַן עַבְדִּי יַעֲקֹב וְיִשְׂרָאֵל בְּחִירִי			4a
Present in the Future	לְךָ בִּשְׁמֶךָ וָאֶקְרָא			4b
	אֲכַנְּךָ			4c
	יְדַעְתָּנִי׃ וְלֹא			4d
	אֲנִי יְהוָה וְאֵין עוֹד זוּלָתִי אֵין אֱלֹהִים			5a
	אֲאַזֶּרְךָ			5b
	יְדַעְתָּנִי׃ וְלֹא			5c

Lee's interpretation of this passage is as follows:

> The second preterite, וְהֶחֱזַקְתִּי [1b] seems here to refer to time anterior to that of אָמַר, with which the declaration commences ....The next two, אֲפַתֵּחַ [1c] and יִפָּגֵרוּ [1d], though presents or futures to וְהֶחֱזַקְתִּי[1b], seem, nevertheless, to be anterior to אָמַר [1a] as to tense. In the next place, אֵלֵךְ [2a], אֲיַשֵׁר [2b], and אֲגַדֵּעַ [2d] are evidently present or future to אָמַר [1a], and consequently, in a tense future to אֲפַתֵּחַ[1c] and יִפָּגֵרוּ [1d]. In the last place, וְנָתַתִּי [3a] is manifestly future with respect to the preceding verb אֲגַדֵּעַ [2d], &c.: and תֵּדַע [3b], which is present or immediately to this, may be considered as referring to something still further removed into futurity. (1827:350)

Between 1d and 2a the writer is thought to have switched his standpoint from 'Present in the Past' to 'Present in the Future'. At 3a he has transported himself so far into the future that he can look back on future events and speak of them as past events. Unfortunately Lee does not tell us how he would translate vv. 4, 5. If we look at some translations of these verses we can see a variety of interpretations.

	AV	RSV	RV/NEB	NIV
4b	Past	Present	Past	Present
4c	Past	Present	Past	Present
4d	Past	Present	Past	Present
5b	Past	Present	Future	Future
5c	Past	Present	Past	Past

Of particular interest is 5b, for here the verb אֲאַזֶּרְךָ has been translated as a Past, Present, and Future action. It clearly cannot be all three. Lee's theory does not help us to solve the difficulty because the decision to describe this action as a 'Present in the Past' or 'Present in the Present' or 'Present in the Future' is a subjective one. In fact it makes perfectly good sense to translate vv. 1-5 by the past tense throughout, particularly if the writer is living _after_ the major conquests of Cyrus (described in these verses) but _before_ the Return and the rebuilding of Jerusalem and the Second Temple (prophesied in 44:26 and 45:13). In favour of a past tense throughout it should be noted that the two infinitives לְרַד and לְפַתֵּחַ (v.1) go with the verb הֶחֱזַקְתִּי. But between these two infinitives is the yqtl verb אֲפַתֵּחַ which would appear to describe Yahweh's past help to Cyrus. It also highlights the blindness of His servant Cyrus if Yahweh has done everything in vv. 1c - 4c for him yet he, Cyrus, ' has not perceived/recognised/known' Him. Yet despite this Yahweh says that Cyrus _will_ perform all His purposes for Israel (44:28; 45:13). Now if we accept Lee's view that 1c and 1d are 'Presents in the Past', and the syntax is in favour of that view, why are the next four yqtl verbs in v. 2 regarded as 'Presents in the Future'? Why could they not also be 'Presents in the Past'?

For the three reasons given above regarding the yqtl verb as the Hebrew Present tense this theory does not do full justice to the wide use of this form. Yqtl can be used of past, present, and future, actions; but also for completed actions in the past: 'I brought [אַעֲלֶה] you up from Egypt' Jud. 2:1, and action contemplated in the future: 'I will bring [אַעֲלֶה] you up out of the affliction of Egypt' Ex. 3:17. Obviously אַעֲלֶה is not used as a tense form if tense relates the time of an action to some other time, usually the moment of speaking, otherwise it could not be used of past and future events, unless, of course, it is in fact a 'Present' tense in some sense. Obviously it cannot be a Present tense in the sense of the English 'I build', 'I dig', 'I die', since these imply unfinished action; whereas 'I brought you up from Egypt' is a finished/completed action.

We have already noted that yqtl cannot be restricted to any tense, nor can it be restricted to any aspect, i.e. unfinished, finished, iterative, etc. Although Lee has found a common meaning for yqtl in any time sphere, he has restricted it to unfinished action. The strength of his Relative/Absolute tense explanation lies in the way he has marshalled the comparative Semitic evidence. This can be seen throughout his writings, especially in his criticisms of Ewald's theory (1847:53, 55, 69-70, 46), and his other works (1827: 347, 344-5, 353; 1850:194).[1]

1.3.1.4   Modifications of the Two Tense Solution

In 1751 Julius Bate put forward the idea that there were only two tenses, or times, in Hebrew, namely, the Present (including the Past) and the Future (1751:16). We hear nothing more about it until D. H. Weir put it forward as a rival theory to Lee's in 1849.

Weir held that the imperative and the participle were the primitive forms on which all the other verb forms were built (1849:309). From the imperative was derived the infinitive (the infin. abs. he deemed to belong to a later stage of the language) which formed the basis for the yqtl form (p. 328). From the participle was formed the qtl form (p. 312). He observes that the participle 'has most frequently the signification of the present', and asks: 'Why, then, not come to the conclusion that the פֹקֵד form also denotes present time?' (p. 312). He concluded that Hebrew had only two tenses, a Present (qtl) and a Future (yqtl). No doubt, he says, there is a past reference; but that is only implied; the state described is present. In proof

of this he appeals to the stative verbs, יָדַצְתִּי, זָכַרְתִּי, and שָׂנֵאתִי.
In this approach he reverses the functions given to the forms by Lee, since
Lee had contended that yqtl always and only had a Present tense meaning in
context. Weir simply transferred the Present tense function to qtl and agreed
with Lee's principle that the writers were in the habit of transporting themselves to the period when the events of which they spoke took place.

He rejects Ewald's term Perfect (or finished/completed action), because
this term can apply only to one class of verbs—active verbs (p. 318). He
points out:

> It is of these that Ewald speaks; for to these only the terms
> he employs seem properly to apply. In other verbs, describing
> a state of being or existence, nothing is more common than the
> use of the פָּרֵק form to denote a present state,—a state, which
> may indeed be continued from the past, but which may also be con-
> tinued into the future. In such cases this form cannot strictly
> be said to denote what is finished in opposition to what is not
> yet finished. Thus when the Psalmist says פֵּם-זָקַנְתִּי, 'now I am
> old,' it is plain the tense does not denote what is finished
> and done, for his old age was not then over, but simply a state
> or condition actually existing. (p. 318)

To get round the problem of yqtl (his Future) used to describe past
events he falls back on the Relative Tense theory (pp. 320, 327), that is,
that the writer describes as present not the time at which, but the time of
which he was speaking. He outlines the principle which unites all the functions of yqtl as follows:

> In viewing a continued series of past events, the Hebrews,
> instead of looking back towards the commencement of the series,
> take their station in thought at the commencement, and, looking
> forward from thence, view its gradual development. (p. 321)

However, he then goes on to say that yqtl has only one function—to denote
strictly future time, never present time (p. 322). Wayyqtl does not so much
indicate the succession of actions, as the simple fact that each action is
future in relation to the preceding one (p. 326).

When he comes to discuss the functions of weqtl (consec. Suffix-forms)
he maintains that it denotes present time, 'yet not in an emphatic manner'
(p. 327). He accounts for its functions as follows:

> When a future series of events is described, the futurity of
> the series is indicated by the first verb, or some term connected
> with it, and in those that follow the present tense [i.e. וְקָטַל]
> is adopted—the use of the present denoting the intimate connect-
> ion between the members of the series. Gen. iii. 22. 'And now
> lest he put forth his hand (יִשְׁלַח) and take also of the tree
> of life (וְלָקַח) and eat (וְאָכַל) and (וְחַי) live for ever.'
> (p. 328)

He points out that if _qtl_ is a Present tense this would account for
its use after the imperative better than the suggestion that it is a Past
or Perfect (p. 328). Instead of _qtl_ indicating a future action as being
past, or as-good-as-done, Weir suggests that it indicates 'that the event
is as certain as if actually present' (p. 329); because in Hebrew 'an action
done and a present action seem to be one and the same thing' (p. 318). He
considers that the very mention of an action as performed implies that the
action spoken of is regarded by the speaker as actually present (p. 318).

1.3.1.4.1   Weir's Contribution

There are a number of positive points raised by Weir which
highlight the weaknesses in the theories of Lee and Ewald. The first is his
observation that Ewald's Perfect and Lee's Past fail to account for numerous
intransitive verbs which cannot be taken to mean finished or past action
(p. 312). By assuming _qtl_ is really the Hebrew Present, i.e. 'done before
his eyes' (1850:495), and therefore existing in the present, he sidesteps
the issue whether the activity is over and done with, or still going on
(having begun in the past. Cf. Greek Perfect).

Lee's reply to Weir's dictum that 'an action done and a present action
seem to be one and the same thing' is scathing: 'Disregarding the paradoxes
which it involves, it can lay claim to nothing beyond a thorough-going tissue
of assumption' (1850:201. Cf. J. G. Murphy, 1851:220). Lee also points out
that if _qtl_ is a Present tense in Hebrew it stands apart from all the other
Semitic languages (1850:196).

The advantage of _qtl_ = Present is that it abolishes the abrupt changes
of standpoint required by Lee's theory. For example in Gen. 1:5 we have the
sentence:

$$\text{וַיִּקְרָא אֱלֹהִים לָאוֹר יוֹם} \mid\mid \text{וְלַחֹשֶׁךְ קָרָא לָיְלָה}$$

	2nd Standpoint:	1st Standpoint:
LEE:	'Past as viewed from the writer's own Present'	'Present in the Past'
WEIR:	'Present in the Past'	'Future in the Past'

According to Lee the writer is actually present to hear God speak the word
'Day' (1st Standpoint), but then the writer reverts to his own era and from

this new position (2nd Standpoint) records what God called the darkness as the writer looks back across the intervening centuries.

Weir's understanding of this verse assumes that וַיִּקְרָא is future in relation to the preceding verb, but once the speaker mentions the 'darkness' before he mentions the verb קָרָא the 'darkness' coming at the head of the sentence gives existence to it; hence it is already present and therefore the Present tense (קָרָא) follows it (p. 332). However, if וַיִּקְרָא only tells us what God will in the future call the light, this is incongruous in view of the present action of the second part of the construction.[1]

Lee strongly criticised Weir's interpretation of Gen. 1:1. Weir seems to have been embarrassed with his present tense translation of בָּרָא 'In the beginning God creates the heavens and the earth'. He argued that it is present in relation to בְּרֵאשִׁית, and that the writer has taken the liberty of transporting himself to the beginning. Lee argues that the writer has done this commencing at v. 3; but it seems that both men are assuming the principle of transportation to the time of the events to clear up the use of the verb forms.

Weir's solution raises more problems than it solves. On the origin of the verb forms he considers the imperative to be the oldest verb form 'which would naturally come first into use, especially in a primitive state of society' (p. 309). From it sprang the infinitive, which, when provided with personal pronominal affixes became the yqtl or Future form. Qtl, on the other hand, is said to be formed from the participle provided with suffixes (p. 311). His explanation of how qtl acquired its Present tense meaning is open to many objections, especially the view that—

> In the present tense [פָקַד], the object of which action, &c.,
> is affirmed, is regarded as already before the mind of the speaker
> or writer, and therefore the most prominent position is assigned
> to the action affirmed of that object. (p. 311)

The chiastic structure of Hebrew sentences is well known now, but Weir gives the position of the verb a significance it cannot have in Direct Speech style. Also, if the Present tense (qtl) is the participle with suffixes, what, then, is the difference between the 3rd masc. sing. qtl form and the masc. sing. participle?

There appears to be some confusion in Weir's understanding of yqtl's meaning. First he states that it is strictly a Future tense—not a Present tense (p. 322), but then later he says:

> The Hebrews were accustomed to regard and describe past events
> as present, because they transported themselves...to the period
> ...and thus viewed and described [them] as if they were spec-

tators of them.

> It is evidently a natural principle: quite in accordance with the habits of thought and expression prevalent in a simple state of society. To throw one's self back on former days—forgetting one's own position—and pourtray, as if from actual observation, what had taken place long before....

> In primitive times, too, the memory of historical events seems to have been preserved by means of paintings....The American tribes...employed it as a means of transmitting the knowledge of past events, while writing was altogether unknown among them ....Many specimens of Eastern historical painting still remain. It is, therefore, probable that the first historical narrative was simply a description of a series of historical paintings; these were, perhaps, under the writer's eye, and the events delineated on them would thus be very naturally described by him as if he were himself present a spectator of them all.(pp. 314-5)

But he seems to have forgotten that the yqtl form is the one used for this historical writing, and not his qtl Present tense form. It was no wonder that Lee accused Weir (also Ewald and Murphy) of plagiarism (1850:197, 484).

1.3.1.4.2   The Anterior-Posterior Theory of J. G. Murphy

Another variation of Lee's theory appeared in 1850. This was J. G. Murphy's Anterior-Central-Posterior (= Qtl - Participle - Yqtl)theory. His main contention was that the speaker/writer took up a position in the neighbourhood of the action, and described the events in relation to his position to them, e.g. in describing creation the writer goes back in imagination (1850:197) until he comes to the initial verb בָּרָא . He takes his stand next to this event, but on his own side of it, not beyond it. 'For in the first place,' argues Murphy, 'he has a tacit consciousness of his own time, and thence his imagination has carried him towards the event. When he first meets it, therefore, he finds himself on his own side of it, and to go farther [back],...is unnecessary, if not unnatural' (p. 197). He says of the phrase, וְרוּחַ אֱלֹהִים מְרַחֶפֶת 'and the Spirit of God moving':

> This constitutes the centre of the series. An event after this belongs to the counter-part of the series, and is conceived to be after the point of view, and therefore described by the posterior tense [yqtl] with the conjunction prefixed....This is a specimen of that antithesis or symmetrical contrast which is familiar to the Hebrew thinker. In some instances of it the extremes are the points of view [i.e. qtl and yqtl]; in others, as in this, the centre [i.e. the participle] is fixed upon, from which there is a retrospective view, he has done, and then a prospective, he goes on to do.' (p. 197)

In a connected series of past events, according to Murphy, the writer transports himself to a single point in time and from that <u>fixed</u> <u>standpoint</u> he contemplates events as either anterior (<u>qtl</u>), central (participle), or posterior (<u>yqtl</u>), (p. 222).

He gives the following reasons for his view that the two verb forms indicate Anterior (= an action ended) and Posterior (= an action to begin) tenses. Firstly, the structure of the forms themselves. In the former the order of the elements is: verbal stem, pronominal suffix; in the latter: pronominal prefix, verbal stem, <u>i.e.</u> the reverse of the former. In his judgment the pronominal element represents the relative position of the subject to the action, represented by the verbal stem. In the case of <u>qtl</u> since the verbal stem <u>precedes</u> the suffix, <u>i.e.</u> the subject, the action must precede or have existed before the subject: <u>mutatis</u> <u>mutandis</u> in the case of <u>yqtl</u>.[1]

Secondly, there is a strict antithesis in the use of the forms. <u>Qtl</u> initiates a series of past events; <u>yqtl</u> initiates a series of future events.

Thirdly, the presence of the participle to denote the mid-way position between these two extremes implies that <u>qtl</u> and <u>yqtl</u> must indicate the extremes on either side of the present participle (p. 201).

He quite strongly rejects the idea that <u>qtl</u> and <u>yqtl</u> indicate absolute tenses, <u>i.e.</u> the relation of the scene of action to the time of the narrator; rather, he argues, they denote the relation of the action to a contemplated time point in its own scheme, as before, at, or after that point of time (pp. 194, 201, 217).

We can illustrate the principle behind Murphy's theory using the following symbols: 0 represents an event/action, and + the position of the writer in relation to the action. The symbol ⟶ represents the perspective of the writer, whether he is looking forward (Posterior) or backward (Anterior) to the events he is describing. In prose accounts events would be seen as follows:

1st	2nd	3rd	4th	5th	6th
0 ⟵ +	+ ⟶ 0	+ ⟶ 0	+ ⟶ 0	+ ⟶ 0	+ ⟶ 0

In describing future events the perspective would be reversed, thus:

1st	2nd	3rd	4th	5th	6th
+ ⟶ 0	0 ⟵ +	0 ⟵ +	0 ⟵ +	0 ⟵ +	0 ⟵ +

Murphy contrasts the two perspectives as follows:

> The historian views events as causes, the prophet as effects.
> The former regards the actual progress and order of their occur-

rence, and, therefore, when he has marked off antecedent time by
an anterior tense, he notices the beginnings of events as coming
first....The latter regards the actual progress and order of
their specification according to the plan he has laid down of
the future scene, and, consequently, when he has defined the
commencement by an initial tense, he conceives himself at the
opposite extreme, contemplating the successive ends he proposes
to be accomplished in the entire procedure. The one is always at
some point within the whole group of events described, and as
an intelligent and attentive observer notices them as they
successively come into existence; the other is always without
the cumulative series of events designed, pondering them with
thoughtful premeditation as he maps out their successive accomplishment. (p. 199)

This modification of the Two Tense theory suffers the defects of the
Relative Tense theory (1.2.2.1), which need not be repeated here. A difficulty occurs over the position of the writer once he has embarked on a description of a series of past events using the wayyqtl form. Is each new
action/event viewed as future in relation to the immediately preceding action/
event, or future to the very first action/event of the series? Murphy prefers
to think that it is the former (p. 196-7). This implies that each wayyqtl,
though future in relation to the immediately preceding verb, is automatically
transformed into a past event as soon as the writer has passed over it, or
spoken it.

Murphy's use of the order of the compound elements making up the
morphology of qtl and yqtl in support of his view is not very convincing.
The pronominal affixes are not entirely prefixed in the case of yqtl verbs
as he suggests (p. 201), but appear at both ends of the verb stem.

* * * * *

1.3.2   The Perfect-Imperfect Theory of G. H. A. von Ewald

Heinrich Ewald (1803-1875) was the pupil of Johann Gottfried
Eichhorn (1752-1827) who produced a grammar in 1827. In the same year Ewald
(who says he was only 22 years of age, 1847:380, but see his biography
written by T. W. Davies, 1903) produced his first Hebrew Grammar. This was
also the year in which Lee put forward his fully developed theory of the
HVS. In his first grammar Ewald followed the teaching of Johann Jahn (1750-
1816) with respect to the terminology of the Hebrew tenses. Jahn called
them the First and Second Aorists having abandoned the terms Past and Future.
The general principle of his new theory was stated in the following words:

Aoristus primus sistit <u>rem perfectam</u>, <u>jam praesentem</u>, jam praeteritam, jam
<u>futuram</u>.
Aoristus secundus sisit rem <u>imperfectam</u>, jam praesentem, jam praeteritam, jam
<u>futuram</u>.[1]

In accordance with this new view, later writers on Hebrew Grammar named the
two forms <u>Perfect</u> and <u>Imperfect</u>. In his first grammar Ewald heads the rules
on the Hebrew tenses (1827:524 §277), <u>Die Zwei Modi</u>. <u>Tempora aorista</u>, and
Lee regards his rules as 'very much of a piece with those laid down by Jahn'
(1847:369). Ewald agrees that he modified his view of the HVS <u>after</u> the publication of his first grammar (1847:380). In his first Arabic Grammar (1831-3)
he introduces the terms <u>Perfect</u> and <u>Imperfect</u> for the first time (vol. II,
p. 112), not with the special senses they have in Latin and Greek grammar,
but in their etymological meaning, as signifying <u>complete</u> and <u>incomplete</u>.
So while the terminology may have been suggested by Jahn's definition, the
concepts were Ewald's, though Lee accused him of plagiarism (Lee, 1847:
366ff.)

In Ewald's reconstruction Hebrew has six grammatical forms: two plain, two
modified or progressive, and two absolute or re-simplified.[2] The last pair
were the latest forms to appear (<u>i.e.</u> w^eyqtl = Future, and w^eqtl = Past), and
these replaced the Consecutive forms as early as the later times of the OT
(especially in Ecclesiastes). The first pair belong to the earliest stage in
the formation of the verb with the second pair came into use very soon
afterwards. We shall examine each of these pairs in turn.[3]

1.3.2.1   The Simple Forms: Perfect and Imperfect

These first pair denote or represent 'the two grand and opposite
aspects under which every conceivable action may be regarded'. He postulates
the following evolutionary process to account for their origin. Man has first
acted, passed through an experience, and sees before him something that is
finished; but this very fact reminds him of that which does not yet exist.
The former, or positive side, is that of objective contemplation of action;
the latter, or negative side, is the higher, subjective side of individual
human thought and inference. Hence the speaker views everything either as
already <u>finished</u>, and thus <u>before</u> him, or as <u>unfinished</u> and non-existent,
but possibly <u>becoming</u> and <u>coming</u>. At this early stage there was nothing whatever corresponding to the three-fold distinction of time, past, present, and

future, that distinguishes later languages. In fact, he argues, no language
can start from anything threefold. Both in thought and language every distinction is at first drawn between no more than two things. Just as in the sphere
of personality there is, first of all, a distinction made merely between I and
you (sg.), and these two are only afterwards distinguished from the absolutely
remote he. In the case of all existent things we see the same process; first
of all a distinction is made between the animate and the inanimate, and then,
in the former class, between the masculine and the feminine. Likewise in the
primitive languages the distinction of three tenses is not a feature of the
original tense division. The original distinction was between Complete and
Incomplete (or Non-existent), and this, later on, gave rise to the tense distinction: Past and Future, but no Present tense.

Although the two ideas of Complete and Incomplete led to the distinction
between Past and Future, these natural distinctions of time are far removed
from the cold intellectuality of the Indo-European languages (1879:3). The
primitive languages generally afford the freest scope to the imagination, and
view everything in an exceedingly animated and emotional manner. This being
so, and in virtue of the power and freedom accorded to the imagination, the
ideas of Completeness and Incompleteness may also be used relatively. In this
way the speaker can represent an action either as Complete or Incomplete
(going on and coming) in whichever of the three simple divisions of time
(past, present, and future) he envisages the action taking place (p. 3)

1.3.2.2   The Use of the Perfect

It is used of actions which the speaker from his present regards
as actually past and therefore complete. It is used of actions which are
regarded as finished but which reach right into the present. This applies
particularly to stative verbs such as זָכַרְתִּי, יָצְאתִי, and חָפַ֫צְתִּי. It is
also used of actions that will occur only in the future to indicate what
would then appear as past, e.g., 'they shall suffer until the time when she
shall have brought forth (עַד־עֵת יֹלֵדָה)' (Mic. 5:2).

The most striking use of the Perfect occurs when through the inclin-
ation or lively fancy of the speaker future actions and events are regarded
as being already as good as finished. This usage is confined to impassioned
discourse where the poet or prophet describes the future as an experience
while in the ecstatic state (p. 6). Where it occurs in unimpassioned des-

scription it is usually in more brief and rapid utterances such as Isa. 19:7.
It occurs regularly in ordinary discourse in conditional propositions and
when it is combined with <u>waw</u> consecutive.

Irrespective of the time sphere in which the Perfect is used it <u>always</u>
denotes <u>completed</u> action whether actual or imagined.

1.3.2.3.   The Use of the Imperfect

This form is used to describe incomplete action, also what does
not yet exist, what is going on or progressing towards completion. It may
indicate what is to take place in the future relative to some preceding
action. From the basic idea of Incompleteness there arise two distinct
meanings which are very widely different from one another. Firstly, what is
stated absolutely to be incomplete refers to time and is therefore a mere
time-form or tense. Secondly, what is stated to be dependent on something
else is set forth as in a particular '<u>kind</u> of being, which hence becomes
more a <u>mood</u> than a <u>tense</u>' (p. 7).

Ewald goes on to make a subdivision within the use of the Imperfect to
denote (a) the absolute distinction of time, <u>i.e.</u> the future absolutely, what
does not yet exist, and (b) it can view what is incomplete as '<u>becoming</u>, as
just arising and continuing, but not yet gone by' (p. 7). Within this latter
use he makes a further subdivision, (i) the incomplete action can be set
forth as incipient, or (ii), as continuing in this incipiency (p. 7). In
modern languages these will be translated by the Present tense.

The Imperfect may also, with equal propriety, indicate what was <u>becoming</u>
<u>realized</u> <u>in</u> <u>the</u> <u>past</u>. This is done when the speaker, 'fancying that he is
lingering within the sphere of a definite past, looks down on what was <u>then</u>
<u>being</u> <u>realized</u>, and thus transports the hearer directly into the time when
the thing was taking place' (p. 8). In prose, this usage is normally confined
to certain cases and combinations such as, שָׁרֶם , אָז, and especially to the
constant case of <u>waw</u> consecutive.

The use of the simple Imperfect to depict a past event as if it were
present must not be thought to be the same as the Imperfect consecutive, even
though the result is the same, <u>i.e.</u> both present the past as a vivid present.
The use of the simple Imperfect in this way is exceptional, and hardly once
occurs in prose (an example of it occurs in 1 Kgs. 21:6)(p. 9). It is used
when the speaker is thinking more of the mere thing itself than of the time

of the action, as in Num. 23:7. The desire is to produce a more graphic
representation of events and is equivalent to the Historical Present tense
of Latin, Greek, and the Indo-European languages.

Another function of the form is to express the special idea of duration,
continuance, or even repetition; because that which endures is also incomplete
(p. 9). Even in the case of the present, when used to express what is usual,
or customary, the Imperfect is preferred to the Perfect for expressing these
ideas.

The Perfect is sometimes used interchangeably with the Imperfect to
express the Present according as the thing is depicted as just completed,
or still going on, as קָא בָּאֹת אֵי , Gen. 16:8, 42:7, and מֵאַיִן תָּבֹא 'whence
comest thou?'. The latter is the more frequent construction, cf., Jos. 9:8,
Jud. 17:9, 19:7, and 2 Sam. 1:3. The two forms may also be exchanged merely
for the sake of variety in poetic parallelism. The distinction between the
two is often very slight, because that which occurs in the present may easily
be viewed as already complete with the 'Perfect of volition and fancy', and
thus as existent. This is possible in a language which does not yet possess
any settled form for the Present, strictly so called (p. 8).

1.3.2.4   The Consecutive Forms

A noticeable feature in Ewald's presentation of his ideas on the
HVS is his constant use of the cases of the noun to illustrate the moods of
the verb. He likens the indicative mood to the nominative case and the voluntative (Jussive and Cohortative) to the vocative, since these represent the
subjective or impassioned feelings of the speaker (p. 14).

To illustrate the consecutive tenses he draws the following analogy.
As the preposition and its subordinated noun, so also may a conjunction and
its subordinated verb form an inseparably close combination, in which the one
member conditions the other, and the exact sense is given by both only in this
close connection. He suggests, on the basis of this analogy, that the copulative waw prefixed to the verb forms does not mean simply and, but, like the
English then, or so, indicates more emphatically the consequence of an action.
In order to distinguish this and from the conjunctive and he places a stress
mark over the former ánd, and notes: If this, or a similar conjunction, be
combined with a tense or mood, progressive, connective, and therefore relative
tenses and moods are formed (p. 18). These are:

(a) The Relatively-Progressive Imperfect.

Two points should be carefully noted concerning this form (wayyqtl). Firstly, the conjunctive way- (= ·ו) is the amalgamation of two particles, i.e. ו and * אז. Secondly, the Imperfect form to which this compound conjunction is prefixed is the voluntative or shortened Jussive form. It is not the simple Imperfect that is found occasionally describing a vivid present in the past.

The compound particle *אז ו > ·ו is 'a temporal particle referring to the past' (p. 19), and corresponds to the augment ἐ- in the Greek Imperfect tense; thus παιδεύεσθον , Present tense, but ἐπαιδεύεσθον Past Imperfect.[1] This augment, or prefixed ánd in Hebrew, 'throws an action into the sphere of the past' (p. 19).[2] It is found prefixed only to the voluntative Imperfect and 'transfers an action that is taking place back into the past' (p. 20), and attaches it there at some point already mentioned, in its necessary sequence, and in such a way that it can be perceived in its beginning there. This composite verb form can never, by its very nature, stand by itself absolutely, but must always relate to a previous action. This relatively-progressive Imperfect 'exactly answers to the Greek aorist'; it is always attached by the compound (or emphatic) ánd to a qtl verb already mentioned, or assumed (p. 20). Poets, however, may sometimes omit the emphatic ánd in order to depict the past more vividly, as if it were present. But this does not affect the meaning of the Imperfect, any more than in those instances where the Greek aorist is used without the augment (p. 22). Poets may also omit the emphatic ánd or replace it with the conjunctive and, without affecting the meaning of the Imperfect.

(b) The Relatively-Progressive Perfect.

This is the antithesis in every respect to the relatively-progressive Imperfect, and this extends to their forms. The compound augment (*אז ו) in front of the verb is dropped, and this allows the ו to become a simple conjunction once more. But to compensate for this, the tone is so strongly placed on the final syllable of the verb, that one would would think the augment had originally been suffixed to the verb. It is as if the progressive Imperfect sought to attach its initial syllable to what had gone before and which was past, and the progressive Perfect sought to attach its final syllable to what lies ahead of it, i.e. the future (p. 23).

The meaning of the rel. prog. Perf. is the same as the simple Imperfect, and the meaning of the rel. prog. Impf. is the same as the simple Perfect (1836:374 §611). The following is Ewald's own explanation for the apparently opposite use of the verb forms:

> The copula ׀ and is prefixed to each of the two tenses in such a manner that this union forms a new whole, and two new forms accordingly arise....the one cannot be without the other....That which is really peculiar in this is, that the copula connects the opposite tense to the preceding one, i.e. that which is conceived as finished or past, as already existing [i.e. qtl], is followed by that which is conceived as unfinished and being done [i.e. (way-)yqtl], and vice versā [i.e. in prophesy future yqtl's are followed by (wᵉ-)qtl's] ; the imagination therefore advances from what is done to what is doing [i.e. qtl...yqtl], and from what is doing to what is done [i.e. yqtl...qtl] . For what is actually past [qtl] , assumed as a beginning, advances to ever new progressive development; that which not yet exists [yqtl], however, when once admitted as certain, advances, at least in thought to what exists and has come to pass [qtl]. On the one hand, the imagination sets out from what is distant and past [qtl], descends into the present [i.e. 'present in the past'] and beholds the ever new consequences, the ever new progress of the past, and, as it were, accompanies the successive moments as they proceed out of the past [using the yqtl form]; on the other, it sets out from what is near, what is unfinished [yqtl], mounts up into the distant reality and calmly anticipates their consequences as sure and certain [using the qtl form].
> (J. Nicholson's transl., 1836:166)

The line diagram given by Ewald to illustrate his thinking is not very clear or helpful. We might illustrate his view as follows:

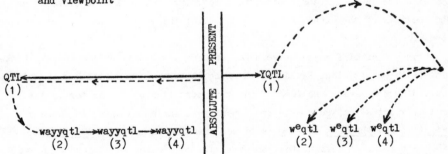

The first verbs are to be taken in an absolute sense; verbs (2), (3), and (4) are to be viewed as relatively-progressive.

1.3.2.5   The Two Absolute Tenses

Ewald has very little to say about these forms which replaced
the consecutive forms eventually. The Perfect + ן with a past meaning replaced
the Imperfect progressive form; the Imperfect + ן (copulative) with a future
meaning replaced the Perfect progressive form. The only reference to their
origin states simply that they were 'derived from no. 2' (1870:166 §233),
i.e. from the relatively-progressive forms.

The Perfect + ן with a past meaning is distinguished from the Relatively-
progressive Perfect by the position of the tone. In the former it is on the
penultima syllable, in the latter on the ultima syllable where this is per-
missible.

1.3.2.6   A Critical Analysis of Ewald's Theory

If we are to believe Ewald his work was entirely original (1847:
379-381). After his 1835 grammar was published he was handed a copy of Lee's
grammar that same year, but returned it 'as the most cursory inspection convinced me that it was a thoroughly unsatisfactory book' (1847:379-80).

Ewald introduced the terms Perfect and Imperfect in his Arabic Grammar
(1831-3), before he used them in his Hebrew Grammar. This alone shows that
he was well advanced in his new understanding of the so-called tenses, and
it would seem that he and Lee arrived independently at a solution that incorporated the idea of transporting the reader/listener backwards or forwards
to the time of the events being related, i.e. the vivid or Historical Present
tense.

The chief difference between Lee and Ewald was that while Lee was thinking in terms of tense, Ewald was thinking in terms of aspect/modes of action;
but both were taking the idea of the transportation of the writer to the
actual event(s) as their main presupposition. While Lee spoke in terms of
Relative and Absolute tenses, Ewald was speaking in terms of Relative and
Absolute modes of action. Lee, however, saw no special significance in the
prefixed waw, whereas Ewald thought that the significance of the Relative
action depended on the combination of the waw with the verb form. He called
the function of this waw the waw consecuutivum (or relativum).

Whether primitive man did divide every conceivable action into the two
grand and opposite aspects of finished and non-existing action is pure speculation. It seems highly unlikely that every language in the world has these

'two grand and opposite aspects' as the starting point for the development
of its verbal system. In any case why should the two opposite aspects be
between finished and non-existing action? It is questionable whether the
opposite aspect of 'finished' is 'non-existing'. The natural opposite of
'finished' is 'unfinished', and the opposite of 'existing' is 'non-existing'.

1.3.2.6.1   The Compound Particle *אַז וְ > וַ

Ewald tries to make a distinction between the simple Imperfect
used as a 'vivid present' in the description of past events, which he regards
as rare in prose, and the 'relatively-progressive Imperfect', which is likewise used as a 'vivid present'. He argues that the Imperfect to which וַ is
prefixed is the jussive Imperfect and not the longer or indicative Imperfect.
The rel.-prog. Imperfect (or consecutive Imperfect) does not retain the jussive meaning of this Imperfect, for, says Ewald, the use of this form transports the hearer directly into the time when the thing was taking place (p. 8).
If this is so it leaves us with the question: What is the basic difference
between the simple Imperfect and the consecutive Imperfect given that both of
them are used as 'vivid presents' when describing past actions?

Ewald noticed that the consecutive Imperfect had a heavy prefixed waw
(וַ) which he says not only throws the action back into the past but attaches
it there to a preceding action. He conjectures that this heavy waw is the
amalgamation of *אַז and וְ, and that *אַז 'is a particle of time referring to
the past' (p. 19). He goes on, quite illogically, to conjecture that this
past particle dropped out of the Perfect consecutive, and in compensation
the tone was shifted to the last syllable (in the 1st pers. sg. and 2nd masc.
sg.). But if the Perfect (qtl)form indicates complete, and therefore past
action, what was the point of prefixing a 'past particle' to it? Why would
one prefix a 'past particle' *אַז plus וְ before a Perfect that is intended to
refer to future action?

It is possible that in choosing אַז to lie behind וַ Ewald was thinking
of the particle אָז 'then', which marks both action and time sequence. If so,
how is this equivalent to the prefixed augment in the Greek tenses?

Another difficulty is the absence of this past augment in Hebrew before
the simple Imperfect when used of past events if it was so indispensable to
the relatively-progressive meaning. The hypothesis that poets and prophets

dropped the augment but retained the relatively-progressive meaning, which
he stressed was inseparable from this meaning, shows how arbitrary and subjective the theory becomes when actually applied to the language. The difficulties are only made worse in the speculation that the same poets and prophets could use the conjunctive waw in place of the relatively-progressive waw
but with a relatively-progressive meaning.

The weaknesses of Ewald's theory are, therefore: Firstly, he has failed
to establish the possibility that ־ן could be an amalgamation of a particle
such as יִךְ and the simple conjunctive waw; nor, indeed, has he established
the need for such a particle. Secondly, he does not explain why the Perfect
consecutive needs to have a past particle before it, when it refers to future
action. Thirdly, he has failed to establish any demonstrable difference,
either morphologically or semantically, between the simple Imperfect and the
relatively – progressive Imperfect when used of past events.

1.3.2.6.2   The Consecutive Imperfect and the Greek Aorist

The consecutive Imperfect is used to describe past events as
coming into being, or to use Ewald's words, 'the speaker, fancying that he
is lingering within the sphere of a definite past , looks down on what was
then being realized, and thus transports the hearer directly into the time
when the thing was taking place' (p. 8). On p. 22 he says it is used 'to
depict the past more vividly'. But on p. 20 he says, 'this imperfect (which,
apart from the and which ever adheres to it, exactly answers to the Greek
aorist)....'. The Greek aorist does not transport the hearer directly into
the time of the event, nor does it have a relatively-progressive meaning,
nor does it describe events as coming into being. It is difficult to know,
then, how it 'exactly answers to the Greek aorist'.

1.3.2.6.3   Conflicting Views on the Meaning of the Consecutive Imperfect

In his reply to Lee Ewald strongly rejects the idea that the
consecutive Imperfect is used as an Historical Present tense.(1847:384-5).
He accuses Lee of failing to notice the—

> extraordinary case in which the narration...introduces past events
> as if they were present, because it, for some particular reason,

then rather regards the mere importance of the events themselves
....Such an extraordinary use of the so-called presens historicum
is, indeed, possible in every language; but it is really aston-
ishing that Professor Lee considers the apocopated imperfect
with Vau consequutivum (as וַיֹּאמֶר 'and he spoke') to belong to
this class. Does he not know that this form is not at all an
extraordinary one [which is how Ewald views its presens historicum function], but the altogether ordinary and necessary description of the simple past time, as soon as ever the succession
of thought or of time is to be expressed? Does he not know that
וַיַּעַשׂ as far as tense is concerned, cannot signify any thing
whatever but Καὶ ἐποίησε?

But in his Syntax (1879:8) he says:

But the imperfect may also, with equal propriety, indicate what
was becoming realized in the past (praesens praeteriti); for,
in the case of a thing that is to be viewed as having simply
occurred, and gone by, prominence may be assigned, in animated
description, to the one side of its occurrence,—the moment when
it actually happens. This is done when the speaker, fancying that
he is lingering within the sphere of a definite past, looks down
on what was then being realized, and thus transports the hearer
directly into the time when the thing was taking place....In
prose, this usage, though not entirely absent, is nevertheless
confined to certain definite cases and combinations; e.g. to the
construction with טֶרֶם 'before'... אָז 'then'...especially, however, to the constant case of Vau consecutive,...

Ewald fell into the error of arguing from translations, just as the earlier
Jewish grammarians had done to justify their Waw Conversive theory, and Lee
had no difficulty in demolishing his arguments. Lee was able to bring forward
examples where wayyqtl forms had been translated by the future in the Greek
versions (1847 :74ff.).[1] Once Ewald had conceded that the wayyqtl was used
as an Historical Present, it was purely subjective to limit its application
to a few occasions.

His remark that the simple Imperfect,when used as a present in the
past,is rare,is not borne out by our statistics; it occurs over 770 times.
If this simple Imperfect can have the 'past particle' וְ prefixed to them
in over 300 cases and retain their 'present in the past' function, then the
prefixed augment וְ cannot be identical with the past augment ἐ- in the
Greek Imperfect tense.

Our diagram of Ewald's relatively-progressive forms shows that as soon
as the writer mentions the first past action, using a qtl form, the writer
travels to that point of time in imagination and then moves toward the absolute present using the wayyqtl forms. But if וְ really is the equivalent of
the Greek ἐ- then wayyqtl is a tense and not a mood; there would be no need
for the writer to transport himself back to the past any more than the Greek

writer does who uses the Greek Imperfect.

Another difficulty with Ewald's explanation of the change from one form
to the other is that the writer is made to shuttle backwards and forwards
with every change of form. This, we noticed earlier, applies to Lee's theory
also. In our diagram, events (2), (3), and (4) are in the wayyqtl form; in
actual fact qtl and w^eqtl forms can be found alternating with wayyqtl. The use
of qtl forms must mean, on Ewald's interpretation, that the writer has reverted
to the absolute present to describe these particular actions/events.

The term relatively-progressive cannot be used with the same sense to
describe the consecutive Perfect and the consecutive Imperfect. In the case
of relative Imperfects, the action is relative to the preceding action; in
the case of relative Perfects the action is relative to the standpoint of the
writer, and not the preceding action. In the case of progressive Imperfects
there is a progression from the previous action 'then being realized'. The
actions, as it were, flow into one another. In the case of progressive
Perfects there is no such progression. Completed events are simply placed
one after the other; see the diagram. Advancement is made by accretion rather
than by progression.

1.3.2.6.4   The Semantic Difference between the Simple Imperfect and the
             Consecutive Imperfect

In 1847 Ewald took Lee to task for saying that when the Imperfect
is used to express the duration or repetition of an action, the simple
Imperfect, when so used, is equivalent to the consecutive form. Ewald replied:

> ...he [Lee] commits the further mistake of confounding two things
> which are altogether different, both in form and in signification.
> It is very easy to see that the two ideas he did (עָשָׂה) and he
> was doing (יַעֲשֶׂה) are quite distinct. But the form also of
> the imperfect is entirely different in both cases: when the
> imperfect denotes duration and repetition of an action, it
> always preserves its simple primitive form; when it is combined
> with vau consequutivum to express an event once past, it is
> always shortened or lengthened, and put into the form I have
> called voluntative. (1847:385)

Now, if the consecutive Imperfect always implies, either in its shortened
or lengthened form, past and finished action, how can it properly be called
an Imperfect tense? (See Lee's scholarly reply to Ewald, 1847 :79ff.)

Ewald's statements here are incorrect in a number of particulars. Firstly,
the consecutive Imperfect is not 'always shortened', since וַתִּבְכֶּה and she

<u>wept</u> occurs alongside וַתֵּבְךְ, וַתִּבְגֶּה alongside וַיֵּבְךְ, וַיִּשְׁתֶּה along-
side וַיֵּשְׁתְּ, וַיִּגְלֶה and וַיֵּצֶל, וַיִּצֶנֶה and וַיֵּצֶן, וַיַּעֲשֶׂה and
וַיֵּשׁ, וַיִּרְאֶה and וַיַּרְא, וַיִּרְבֶּה and וַיֶּרֶב, etc.[1] Secondly, there
is no semantic difference between the 'simple primitive form' (<u>i.e.</u> the
long form) and the apocopated form in the above examples. We even have a
duplicated verse in Jeremiah, namely, 10:13 and 51:16, in which we find
וַיַּעֲלֶה נְשִׂאִים and וַיַּעַל נְשִׂאִים meaning, 'and he makes the mist rise'.
It is clear also from these examples that the shortening is not due to the
prefixed ·וַ,[2] but to style, or variety, or some other such reason. Thirdly,
not every Imperfect can have an apocopated form. The following allow a
shorter form: the Hiphil of all verbs and almost every theme in ל"ה verbs,
and the Qal of ע"ע, ע"ו/י, פ"א, and פ"ו/י verbs. It is indeed
strange if the difference between the two forms is semantic that this shows
up only in <u>weak verbs</u> on the whole. It is also strange that if the Imperfect
is said to denote incomplete action <u>in any time sphere</u> why is it restricted
to durative and repetitious action in the <u>past</u>? Why could it not denote
a <u>single</u> action in the past as the <u>wayyqtl</u> form is said to do? We in fact
find that this is the case in Jud. 2:1 'I brought you [אַעֲלֶה] up from Egypt';
Jud. 6:5 where יַעֲלוּ and וַיָּבֹאוּ refer to a specific event; see also Ex.
33:7; Num. 35:20; Jos. 8:30. Only after examining the 774 simple <u>yqtl</u> forms
used of past events would a scholar be in a position to say that <u>none</u> of
these refer to <u>single</u> past actions/events (see Append. 1, Table 4).

Summary of Criticisms

The chief difference between Ewald and Lee was that Lee spoke in terms
of <u>Relative</u> and <u>Absolute</u> TENSES, while Ewald spoke in terms of Relative and
<u>Absolute</u> ASPECTS. Both used the shuttle idea to explain the presence of the
verb forms in every time sphere. Ewald's theory, therefore, suffers all the
weaknesses of Lee's theory (<u>q.v.</u> 1.3.1.3).

Whether primitive man conceived of everything under the two grand and
opposite aspects of Complete/finished and Incomplete/non-existing is very
difficult to prove.

<u>Yqtl</u> is said to denote incomplete action in any time sphere, therefore
it cannot be used to describe past completed historical events. The simple
<u>yqtl</u> form is used to describe past completed actions (see p. 35 above).

The heavy prefixed ·וַ is said to be made up of אָז 'a particle of time
referring to the past' plus the conjunctive וְ. It is equivalent to the

augment $\acute{\varepsilon}$- in the Greek Imperfect tense. This has not been proved. There is
no precedent in the Hebrew language for the assimilation of a strong consonant such as ץ, and Ewald makes no attempt to justify his conjectured form.

If ·וֹ is a particle of time referring to past time, then wayyqtl must be
a TENSE form. The form should never be found referring to the present or the
future, yet it is found used in both these spheres.

Wayyqtl is said to be a relatively-progressive action. The action is
progressive or incomplete, and is relative in relation to the preceding action
and not in relation to the absolute standpoint of the writer. If this is so
why is yqtl prefixed with a particle (way-) denoting absolute past time?

The term relatively-progressive is used in two different senses. The consecutive Perfects denote completed action, not progressive action. They are
finished actions in relation to the standpoint of the writer, not in relation
to the preceding action, as is the case with the consecutive Imperfects.

The Perfect form in itself cannot denote completed action since this would
not be true of the stative Perfects. The idea of completed action can apply
only to active verbs.

Yqtl is said to denote non-existent action. It is difficult to see how
non-existent action could be construed as incomplete action.

If yqtl indicates unfinished action then it cannot indicate finished
action in any time sphere, yet it is used on hundreds of occasions to denote
finished action in the past (without any prefixed waw).

* * * * * * *

Following the publication of Ewald's grammar in 1835 his ideas became
very popular. These are found in T. K. Arnold's grammar (1851:97); August
Dillmann applied his ideas to Ethiopic (1857), as did Th. Nöldeke to Syriac
(1880).[1] Justus Olshausen produced the first part of his own grammar in 1861,
which was popularized by G. Bickell. Bickell's work was in turn translated
into English by S. I. Curtiss in 1877. Wm. Wright followed Ewald's view in
his Arabic grammars (1862; 1874-5; 1896-8:vol. II, pp. 1-24). M. M. Kalish,
while retaining the older terms Past and Future, defines these in accordance
with Ewald's view (1862-3:vol. i, p. 278). He follows Ewald's earlier view
(1835:539) that ·וֹ is the remnant of an ancient form of הָיָה . The original
combination seems to have been הָוָה יִקְשׁר it was or happened that he bound;

the future יִקְשֹׁר having been chosen on account of its dependence on אָז
(1875:109). F. Böttcher is said by S. R. Driver (1892:72) to have been the
first to introduce the term waw consecutive into Hebrew grammar as early
as 1827. It has not been possible to confirm this remark. The slight difference between Ewald and Böttcher revolves around terminology. Böttcher
sees the contrast between the two verb forms in the terms das Perfect and
das Fiens (1866:§§587, 589, 939ff., 969ff.). Böttcher built his case on two
observations: form and function. From form he argued:Inasmuch as the Prefix-
form has the pronominal elements prefixed to the root, it denotes that the
act is viewed in its beginning, or is coming into being; the other form has
the personal elements suffixed and hence denotes that the act is completed
and past.[1] From function he argued that since 1 Kings 6:1 reads יִבֶן and the
parallel passage in 2 Chron. 3:1 reads(לִבְנוֹת)וַיָּחֶל Then Solomon began to build,
that therefore יִבֶן must mean the same thing.

J. P. N. Land's Hebrew grammar (1869) was translated from the Dutch into
English by R. L. Poole in 1876. His views are those of Ewald though he does
not acknowledge this (see pp. 147-8). F. Hitzig was a pupil of Ewald, so it
is not surprising to find him propounding his mentor's views (1870). He preferred to use the term waw relativum.[2]

* * * * * * *

1.3.3 The Inductive-Relative Theory of Isaac Nordheimer

Isaac Nordheimer died at the age of thirty-three (1809-42) in
the same year that saw the passing of his friend Gesenius. He learnt his
Hebrew through his Jewish grandfather, and at thirteen took up his Rabbinic
and Talmudic studies. From 1832-4 he studied Oriental languages at the University of Munich where he received his degree of Doctor of Philosophy. He is
said to have studied the works of Gesenius and Ewald (E. Robinson, 1843:385);
but as Ewald did not produce his new theory on the HVS until 1835, the year
Nordheimer left for New York, it would seem that Nordheimer knew only of
Ewald's 1827 grammar.

In 1836 Nordheimer met a young printer called William Turner, who was
later--forty years to be precise--to produce his own distinctive theory on
the HVS. Turner became a private pupil of Nordheimer in order to learn Arabic,
being proficient in Hebrew, Latin, German, and other modern languages already.

Together they planned to print an Arabic grammar, but this was changed and a Hebrew grammar produced instead. The manuscript was written out from Nordheimer's notes and dictation, as he was not sufficiently at home in the English language to prepare the work himself. Turner revised the work and saw it through the press. The first part appeared in Sept. 1837, and the whole volume in Feb. 1838. His Syntax appeared in 1841, a few days before his death. Turner took on the task of producing a Hebrew concordance begun by Nordheimer, and took up his teacher's post at the Union Theological Seminary.

The Relative Tense theory put forward by Nordheimer was first suggested by N. W. Schroeder in 1766, as we have seen above (1.2.2). The theory was comparatively unknown until Nordheimer produced the classic exposition of it in his Syntax (1841).

1.3.3.1   The Relative Tense Theory

Nordheimer stated that there were only two tenses in Hebrew, a Past and a Future. Since there is no Present tense in Hebrew, the province of one tense ends where that of the other begins, and as the point of their mutual coincidence is the time of narration, either one of them (qtl or yqtl) may be employed to predicate an event at the time of its occurrence. The choice of form will depend on whether the writer's attention is more particularly directed to the commencement of the action in the past, or to its continuance in the future (1841:159).

Basically yqtl denotes 'an action yet to take place', and qtl 'an action that is past' (p. 183). Consequently, he calls the simple form of these tenses the Absolute Future and the Absolute Past (p. 159). The consecutive forms, on the other hand, are called secondary tenses or the Relative Future and the Relative Past.

The tenses, Relative and Absolute, fit together as follows:

> Time considered abstractedly,...may be said to consist of a constant flow or succession of moments, whose beginning and end are lost in eternity. This uninterrupted and endless series of instants may not unaptly be compared to a straight line continued ad infinitum, which is not susceptible of specification in its whole extent, but which by the assumption of a point in any part of it is immediately converted into two lines branching off from such point in opposite directions (p. 169).

He then illustrates his view with the following diagrams:

```
A           C           B        He says:
├───────────────────────┤
      ⋙─────────➤            Let us suppose AB to be an indefinite
                             straight line proceeding from left to
                             right, and representing an indefin-
                             ite extent of time. If we now assume
```
in it a point C to represent the present, that portion of the line extend-
ing from C in the direction of A will represent past time, and that from
C in the opposite direction of B will represent future time. From this
we see that the times called past and future are purely relative, and
depend for their determination on the position of the moment called the
present; so that on shifting this last they may be mutually converted,
the past into future, and the future into past time. Thus, to return to
our illustration, if C be taken as the present, CA will represent all

```
                                        past, and CB all future time: but if
A      d      C      e      B           we shift this point back to d, the
├──────┼──────┼──────┼──────┤           portion of time Cd, which before was
                                        past, will now be future; and by
```
advancing it to e, the portion of time Ce will be converted from future
into past (p. 156).

The rest of his theory is simply the working out of his basic principle.

   We have already demonstrated the weaknesses of this approach to the HVS
(see 1.2.2.1). It remains here to point out two difficulties with Nordheimer's
presentation and interpretation of that principle. He states: 'When an absolute past form is used to denote present time, a following relative past [i.e.
wayyqtl] does so likewise' (p. 171). The same applies when the absolute past
form (qtl) is used in prophesy to predict a future event, the following relative past (i.e. wayyqtl) will likewise bear a future signification, e.g. Isa.
5:14, 15, 25; 9:5. We saw earlier that future wayyqtl forms could not be
accommodated in Ewald's scheme. It is strange that yqtl, which in itself
indicates future, when it has the prefixed ·1 becomes a relative past tense,
but if it follows a verb with a future meaning becomes a future once again.
On this principle the form of the verb is no certain guide to the relative
or absolute tense required. We are thrown back on to the tense required in
translation.

   The second difficulty springs from the first, namely, the tenses are
not so much relative as inducted. So although Nordheimer's theory appears to
follow Schroeder's view, it is in fact a mixture of the Relative Tense theory
and the Tense Inducted theory (1.2.3), and as such it partakes of the weaknesses of both.

* * * * * * *

1.3.4 The Nascent-Complete Theory of S. R. Driver

Between Nordheimer's Inductive-Relative theory and S. R. Driver's theory, first published in 1874, we have only one small contribution to the subject of the tenses that warrants our attention. This is the work of John William Donaldson, a one time Fellow of Trinity College, Cambridge, who wrote a work entitled, Maskil le-Sopher, published in 1848. He regarded the Jewish Conversive theory as 'childish' (p. 28), and Jewish teachers as wanting in authority (p. 48).

He appears to have read Gesenius and Ewald (and possibly Lee, p. 23) on the subject of the tenses (p. 1), but he was dissatisfied with their explanations: Hebrew does not have tenses but only differences in regard to the time occupied by the action. He calls the Suffix-form the primary tense, and the Prefix-form the secondary tense. The primary tense denotes a transient or speedily completed action; the secondary tense denotes a continuous action. However, both forms are really indefinite tenses, because Hebrew has no absolute means of stating that the commencement of the action is not completed or past. They are in effect indeterminate tenses, which imply a relation to some point of time other than the present (p. 23).

The primary form denotes SINGLE acts, while the secondary denotes SETS of acts, including repeated and continuous action. The former will represent the point, the other the line as a series of points (p. 28).

His explanation of the consecutive use of the forms is interesting:

> An observation of the practice of the ancient Hebrew writers shows that the use of the tenses is in strict accordance with this definition and explanation [of them]. And when they appear together in the same sentence, we find that the following rules are attended to. (I.) If the primary tense precedes, it designates the completion of the antecedent act necessary to the commencement of the continuous state indicated by the secondary tense which follows. (II.) If the secondary tense [yqtl or wayyqtl] precedes, it signifies the continuous period up to the completion of the act designated by the primary tense which follows. (p. 28)

He applies his theory as follows, taking Gen. 1:1-5 and 2 Kgs. 9:1-3:-

> In the beginning God created (as one act, בָּרָא) the heavens and the earth, and the earth was (at the moment of creation, הָיְתָה) without form or fulness, &c.: and God proceeded to say (וַיֹּאמֶר); Let there be (as a commencement of a continuance, יְהִי) light, and there proceeds to be (same word) light: and God sees (still the same continuance, וַיַּרְא) the light that it is good, and God goes on to divide (וַיַּבְדֵּל) between the light and the darkness; and God proceeds to name (וַיִּקְרָא) the light, day: and the darkness he finished by calling (as a termination of the first

day's creation, אְרָק) night.

(2 Kgs. 9) and Elisha <u>called</u> (completion of antecedent act, אָרָק)
one of the sons of the prophets, and <u>proceeds to say</u> (וַיֹּאמֶר)
to him: Gird up thy loins, and take this flask of oil in thy hand,
and go (imperatives) to Ramoth-gilead: and <u>thou hast come thither</u>
(antecedent act supposed to be completed, וּבָאתָ); then look out
(imperative) Jehu: and <u>thou hast gone in</u> (antecedent act completed), then make him stand up (imperative) from the midst of
his fellows: and thou <u>hast caused him to enter</u> (וַהֲבֵיאתָ) a
chamber, and <u>hast taken up</u> (וְלָקַחְתָּ) the flask of oil, and <u>hast</u>
poured out (וְיָצַקְתָּ) above his head, and <u>hast said</u> (וְאָמַרְתָּ),
thus <u>has said</u> (as a single act אָמַר) Jehovah, I <u>have anointed</u>
<u>thee</u> (מְשַׁחְתִּיךָ) to be King for Israel, and <u>thou hast opened</u>
(וּפָתַחְתָּ) the door, and <u>hast fled</u> (וְנַסְתָּה); and thou <u>dost not</u>
<u>tarry</u> (which is the forbidden continuation, תְחַכֶּה). (p. 28-9)

All the preceding verbs are in the primary form, because they refer to single
acts, considered as necessary antecedents to the imperatives and the secondary forms. In the execution of the commission all the narrative verbs are in
the secondary or continuous form.

This explanation of the tenses is in some ways similar to those of Ewald
and S. R. Driver and does not need to be treated separately on that account.

Driver's theory is very close to Ewald's Perfect-Imperfect theory. The main
difference between them lies in their interpretation of the <u>yqtl</u> form. Ewald
called it the <u>Imperfect</u> or incomplete action, Driver regards this meaning
as secondary (1892:1 n. 2), and <u>Nascent</u> or incipient action as its primary
meaning. When it comes to the consecutive forms Driver sometimes explains
these by the standpoint principle (Lee's theory) and sometimes by the inductive tense rule (Gell's theory). The following are the main points of his
Nascent-Complete theory. (References are to his 1892 edition.)

1.3.4.1   The Functions of Yqtl and Qtl

The two facts, says Driver, on which the whole theory of the
Hebrew tenses has to be constructed are:

> (1) that the Hebrew verb notifies the character without fixing
> the date of an action, and (2) that, of its two forms with which
> we have here more particularly to deal, one is calculated to
> describe an action as <u>nascent</u> [yqtl] and so as imperfect; the
> other to describe it as <u>completed</u> [qtl] and so as perfect. (p. 5)

The justification for these two meanings lies in his belief that 'the tenses
mark only differences in the kind of time, not differences in the order of
time: <u>i.e.</u> they do not in themselves determine the <u>date</u> at which an action

takes place, they only indicate its <u>character</u> or <u>kind</u>' (p. 3). By 'kind of
time' he means that an action may be contemplated according to the fancy of
the speaker, or according to the particular point which he desires to make
prominent. A speaker may wish to lay stress upon the moment at which the
action begins, in which case he will use the <u>yqtl</u> form, or he may wish to
stress the period over which an action extends, in which case he will use
the participle, or he may wish to lay stress upon the action as finished
and done, in which case he will use the <u>qtl</u> form; these are differences in
the kind of time (p. 2). In modern linguistic terms these differences in the
<u>kind of time</u> are called <u>aspects</u>.[1] It is one of Driver's firm contentions that
the line of demarcation between the two tenses is as clearly and sharply
drawn as between the aorist and the imperfect in Greek (p. 48). The two forms
always preserve their own proper force, 'which must not be lost sight of
because difficult of production in another language, or because the genius
of our own tongue would have been satisfied with, perhaps, some more obvious
mode of expression' (p. 48).

We might illustrate the three stages in any action that dominated the
thinking of the Hebrew writers as follows:

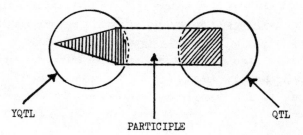

The difference between the Participle and <u>yqtl</u> is that the former indicates
<u>mere</u> continuance without progress, while the latter indicates continuance
with progress, or progressive continuance (pp. 27, 35).

1.3.4.2   The <u>Yqtl</u> alone

The terms used by Driver to describe the <u>yqtl</u> aspect are:
(1) Nascent (beginning to exist or develop); (2) Incipient (beginning to
exist or become manifest); (3) Inchoative (that which begins, or expresses
beginning); (4) Inceptive (noting the beginning, commencing); and (5) Egress-

ive (tending to issue forth). He says of this aspect:

> by thus seizing upon an action while nascent, and representing
> it under its most striking and impressive aspect (for it is just
> when a fresh object first appears upon a scene that it exhibits
> greater energy, and is, so to speak, more aggressive, than
> either while it simply continues [i.e. the participle] or after
> it has been completed [i.e. the qtl aspect]), it can present it
> in the liveliest manner possible—it can present it in movement
> rather than, like the pf., in a condition of rest. The action
> thus exhibited as ready or about to take place may belong to the
> past, the present, or the future;....(p. 27)

The yqtl form, then, expresses an action not as done, but only as doing (p. 29).
One and the same event may be described either as nascent, or as completed,
depending entirely upon the fancy of the speaker/writer. The time at which
an action occurs is not latent in the verb form, though a past event will
naturally be a completed one, and a future event an unfinished one. In themselves the verb forms are ambiguous as regards tense. The only reliable
criterion is the context.

> The context, intelligently apprehended, constitutes the differ-
> entiating factor which fixes the signification of the tense....
> a reference to the context—to the whole, of which it is itself
> an inseparable part—makes clear the relation subsisting between
> them, and reduces the ambiguity to a minimum. (p. 48)

It remains now to show how the yqtl aspect is used in each time sphere.

(1) In present time. Just as the English present is used to describe single
and frequentative actions, so also with yqtl used in this sphere (p. 36). In
fact, the use of the present in English to denote acts which may be or are
repeated is more common than its use to describe single actions, and agrees
in a remarkable manner with yqtl used in the same time sphere (p. 37).
Although qtl may also be used to denote personal habits or attributes and
general truths, all of which yqtl conveys, it is used by viewing these as a
completed whole. The forms are not interchangeable. Driver cautions us:

> Yet, however we translate, it must not be forgotten that a differ-
> ence still exists in the words of the original, and that each
> tense possesses a propriety the force of which is still percept-
> ible, even where it cannot be reproduced; it is simply the imper-
> fection, in this respect, of our language, its deficiency in
> delicacy that necessitates our obliterating the lights and shades
> which an otherwise constructed instrument is capable of express-
> ing. (p. 40)

(2) In future time. In this sphere the action has not yet begun to take place
at all, but its beginning to do so is contemplated in the future—nearer or
more remote, as the context and sense demand (p. 33). It is used of the future because it is emphatically τὸ μέλλον, and this is just the attribute

specially expressed by yqtl. The idea of frequentative action in the future is not immediately suggested by the form, for as Driver noted in his first edition: 'Where the future is spoken of, the force of the imperfect is exhausted by the idea of futurity which it conveys' (1874:26); or as he puts it in his last edition:

> The idea of reiteration is not prominent in this case, because the occurrence of the event spoken of is by itself sufficient to occupy and satisfy the mind, which does not look beyond to reflect whether it is likely to happen more than once:....
> (1892:28)

Where yqtl is used to relate single events in the future alongside qtl forms it must never be forgotten that each seizes upon and brings into view a different phase of action (p. 36).

(3) In past time. When yqtl is used to describe a single event/action in the past, and so not capable of explanation as a frequentative, the effect is to present in strong relief and with especial liveliness the features of the scene. The writer changes his real standpoint for an ideal one which places him in the times he is describing. The English Historical Present tense is the nearest we can get to the Hebrew idiom; an on-the-spot reporting of events. Where, however, the form is capable of explanation as a frequentative action no such vividness or change of standpoint is involved, for as Driver noted in his first edition:

> ...where the past is spoken of, its force is not exhausted, and therefore its presence not accounted for, if it connote the mere continuance of an event. The latter is a function performed by the pf.: the imperfect...must have been chosen in order to suggest in addition some feature accompanying the occurrence, in other words to connote and specify the mode or manner of occurrence. And this feature may be either that of incipiency, of reiteration, or...modality. (1874:26)

The yqtl form is also used for the subjunctive, potential, concessive, conditional, etc., in any time sphere (p. 41). Basically, however, the yqtl aspect is used in two senses, these are:

(1) Nascent action. Where a single action is being referred to the writer seizes upon its beginning, its coming into being, and pictures it to the mental eye. In the case of past events the writer changes his standpoint and takes up a 'present in the past' position.

(2) Frequentative action. Where an action is repeated in any time sphere the standpoint of the writer must necessarily lie outside the events being referred to. He views action objectively, because an event ready or about to take place would be likely and liable to occur more than once in the

nature of things; hence the additional idea of 'recurrency'. In any case
the gradual realization (or incipiency) and the repetition (or freq-
uency) of an action are regarded by language as nearly akin (pp. 27-8,
30).

1.3.4.3   The Qtl alone

Driver's view is very little different from that of Ewald. Qtl is
used as equivalent to (1) the Greek aorist, (2) the Greek Perfect, where the
action continues into the present and may, therefore, be translated by the
Present tense, (3) the English Past Perfect, (4) the immediate past, generally best translated by the present, (5) the English Present in the case of
verbs expressive of state or condition, whether physical or mental (In itself
qtl enunciates simply the completion of an act: it is by way of accommodation
to the usage of another language that the meaning is made more definite by
translating it sometimes as a Perfect, or Aorist, or Present tense.). It is
also used to express (6) general truths; here again the idiomatic rendering
in English is by means of the Present, (7) the pluperfect.

The most remarkable use of qtl is, undoubtedly, its use to indicate
actions the accomplishment of which lies indeed in the future. In such cases
the action is regarded as having actually taken place in the mind of the
speaker. This form is very frequent in promises, decrees, etc. An extension
of this use is the prophetic perfect. Here the writer places himself so far
into the future that he describes 'future' events in the qtl form as he looks
back toward the absolute present. Often a series of qtl's is interspersed
with the simple yqtl forms, as the prophet shifts his point of view, at one
moment contemplating the events he is describing from the real standpoint of
the present, at another moment looking back upon them as accomplished and
done, and so viewing them from an ideal position in the future.(p. 18f.).[1]

Qtl is also used to express the subjunctive, conditional, concessive,
imperative, precative, etc.

1.3.4.4   The Wayyqtl Form

Wayyqtl is used predominantly to connect together a series of
past events into a consecutive narrative (hence the term waw consecutive);
but it is also used of present and future events. The principle on which

yqtl is used in this way is not, after what was said in 1.3.4.2, hard to find. Yqtl represents action as <u>nascent</u>: accordingly, when combined with a conjunction (·וֹ) connecting the event introduced by it with a point already reached in the narrative, it represents it as the <u>continuation</u> or <u>development</u> of the 'past' which came before it. וַיֹּאמֶר is not so much <u>and he said</u>, as <u>and he proceeded-to-say</u> (<u>cf</u>. Donaldson, 1.3.4).

Because <u>yqtl</u> depicts action as incipient, in strict accordance with what appears to have been the primitive meaning of the form, Driver says:

> ...it is just in virtue of this, its original meaning, that, in coalition with ·וֹ , it grew up into a fixed formula, capable of being generally employed in historical narrative. That a series of past facts should ever have been regularly viewed in this light (a supposition without which the construction before us remains unaccountable), that in each term of such a series the salient feature seized upon by language should be not its character as past, but its character as nascent or progressive, may indeed appear singular: but the ultimate explanation of it must lie in the mode of thought peculiar to the people, and here reflected in their language. (p. 73)

This explains the <u>origin</u> of the use of <u>yqtl</u> to describe past events. The way the form is used historically in the three time spheres is as follows:

(1) In past time. <u>Yqtl</u> is the predominant verb form used in prose narrative. Because the form <u>wayyqtl</u> became one of the commonest and most frequently occurring forms, Driver thinks:

> ...it is probable that a distinct recollection of the exact sense of its component parts was lost, or, at any rate, receded greatly into the background, and that the construction was used as a whole, without any thought of its original meaning, simply as a form to connect together a series of past events into a consecutive narrative. (p. 73)

Remnants of the original meaning can still be felt where the particles אָז , טֶרֶם . צַר , etc., immediately precede the verb. But in general, the use of ·וֹ in the historical books, renders it inconceivable that it should have suggested anything except the idea of a <u>fact done</u> (p. 94).

(2) In present time. Sometimes a past action, or its results, continues into the writer's present; in which case it is often best to translate by the Present tense, <u>e.g.</u> וַיִּהְיוּ שָׁם 'and <u>they are</u> there unto this day', Josh. 4:9. Wayyqtl is also used where the event spoken of has not actually been accomplished, as in Jer. 38:9 וַיָּמָת 'and he is like to die' (AV); 'Ebed-melekh sees Jeremiah's death as inevitable, as actually taking place. Wayyqtl may also be used to express a general truth, 1 Sam. 2:6.

(3) In future time. In the description of future events, wayyqtl is used upon
exactly the same principle as qtl, i.e. it represents them as simple matters
of history. There are two contexts in which it is used: (1) where it is preceded by wᵉqtl (prophetic perfect), and (2) where it is not so preceded.
On the first Driver wrote:

> Just as elsewhere the impf. with ·ְו marks a continuation of the
> preceding tense, so here, too, it is employed if a writer desires
> to pourtray a future scene or series of events, as though they
> were unfolding themselves before his eyes, in the manner of
> ordinary historical occurrences. (p. 92)

The conjunction ·ְו simply shows that the action to which it is prefixed is
a continuation or development of the preceeding verb, which happens to be a
prophetic perfect; though it is a fact that this conjunction was so appropri-
ated by the universal custom of the language to the description of actual
fact (p. 119).

On the second he notes that where the prophet changes his real standpoint
for an ideal one he may continue the situation described in the preceding
sentence using wayyqtl forms. To quote Driver:

> The ·ְו in such cases also represents the event, often very aptly,
> not merely with the certainty of the prophetic perfect, but as
> flowing naturally out of, being an immediate consequence of, the
> situation described in the preceding sentence. (p. 93)

In the case of Isa. 9:5 the AV translates 'and the government shall be' (וַתְּהִי),
whereas the Hebrew is really speaking about a fact done (pp. 93-4). The action
of a wayyqtl verb is not seen by the Hebrew writer as an independent action,
but rather, as a dependent one, the sign of which is the prefixed ·ְו .

1.3.4.5   The Wᵉqtl Form

Wᵉqtl occurs in two forms which must not be confused, since the
slight change in form is indicative of a difference in grammatical value. The
two forms are:
(1) Qtl with waw consecutive and ultima stress where possible, and
(2) Qtl with waw conjunctive
The former is distinguished by its (a) syntactical position, and (b) change
of tone position.

We saw earlier that wayyqtl inevitably followed the simple qtl form as
its constant companion. Where the union of ·ְו and yqtl was broken, the qtl
form took over. Exactly the same phenomenon occurs in the case of wᵉqtl; where
wᵉ becomes separated from qtl, the verb regularly lapses into the yqtl form.

The qtl consecutive, therefore, is the direct antithesis of the yqtl consecutive.

The qtl consecutive can be distinguished from qtl conjunctive by an alteration of the tone which constantly attends and accompanies the former (p. 115). And slight though the change may appear, וְקָטַ֣ל can never be substituted for וְקָטַ֣ל without introducing a material modification of the sense. Driver cautions:

> However difficult it may appear to find a satisfactory explanation of this waw consecutive with the perfect, one thing is perfectly clear, and ought most carefully to be borne in mind: a real difference of some kind or other exists between the use of the perfect with simple waw, and the use of the perfect with waw consecutive, and the external indication of this difference is to be found in the alteration of the tone which constantly attends and accompanies it. (p. 115)

The material difference in meaning between the two forms is as following:

(1) The qtl conjunctive. Qtl keeps its own individuality and meaning. Its action is absolute and unqualified, indicating completed action in the past.

(2) The qtl consecutive. Qtl loses its own individuality and meaning. Its action is relative and limited in application.

Because the qtl consecutive usually follows the simple yqtl form as its constant companion (pp. 114, 145), it invariably assumes the various meanings that that form has acquired, i.e. single action in the present and future, and frequentative action when used in the past (pp. 143-5, 139). In some cases no yqtl verb precedes the qtl consecutive, just as sometimes no qtl precedes the wayyqtl verb, yet the qtl consecutive must not be taken in an absolute or unqualified sense. Driver explains:

> But the perfect with waw consecutive is also found without being attached to any preceding verb from which to derive its special signification: from constant association with a preceding imperfect it became so completely invested with the properties of the latter that, though not originally belonging to it but only acquired, it still continued to retain and exhibit them, even when that in which they had their proper seat was no longer itself present....it has, in fact, grown so like its partner as to be able to assume its functions and act as its substitute.
> (pp. 139-40)

The meaning of the qtl consecutive will in each context be determined by the preceding or dominant verb, usually the yqtl verb. If yqtl is future, so will w^eqtl be; if yqtl is past it will also be frequentative, and so will w^eqtl be. Whatever meaning the preceding verb has this is conducted to the following qtl consecutive. Qtl subordinates its sense to the preceding or dominant verb (pp. 118, 120-1, 123, 125, 140). Driver put it thus:

> Whatever, therefore, be the shade of meaning borne by the first or 'dominant' verb, the perfect following, inasmuch as the action it denotes is conceived to take place under the same conditions, assumes it too: be the dominant verb a Jussive, frequentative, or subjunctive, the perfect is virtually the same. To all intents and purposes the perfect, when attached to a preceding verb by means of this waw consecutive, loses its individuality: no longer maintaining an independent position, it passes under the sway of the verb to which it is connected. (p. 118)

An action described by the qtl consecutive is regarded as completed, but only with reference to the preceding verb, only so far as the preceding action necessitates or permits it. It is the peculiar syntactical position occupied by qtl, as regards the dominant or principal verb, that causes it virtually to assume the particular modal phase of the latter. If, for instance, the principal verb involve will, would, or let..., the subordinate qtl consec- utive verbs must be understood in the same tense or mood; in other words, as governed by the same auxiliary, cf. 2 Kings 5:11 (p. 123-4). If the preceding verb is an imperative, the qtl consecutive meaning is wholly determined by the meaning of the dominant verb, in this case an imperative, hence it will assume the function of an imperative (p. 125).

After yqtl, in any of its senses, the qtl consecutive will be found with the same meaning, thus (1) after yqtl as a pure future, Gen. 12:3; 18:18. (2) After yqtl as a jussive or cohortative, Gen. 1:14 and 31:44. (3) After yqtl denoting would or should, Amos 9:3. (4) After yqtl as a frequentative, whether of present or past time, Gen. 2:24 and 2:6. It may follow a prophetic qtl (p. 126) and consequently have a future meaning. Sometimes after a fact has been stated summarily by a qtl form, we find it succeeded by qtl consecut- ives indicating frequentative actions, and not single actions which would be indicated by conjunctive qtl verbs (pp. 129, 143-5). The consecutive qtl verb וְהָיָה will consequently have either a future or frequentative sense (p. 146). The conjunctive qtl verb וְהָיְה will denote a single action in the past, e.g. Gen. 38:5 (p. 161). Only the context can determine when וְהָיָה is to be taken in a consecutive sense or in a conjunctive sense since the form itself does not admit a change of tone position (pp. 125, 127 n.2, 131). A change of tone represents a change of meaning (p. 116), and since tone changes are syn- tactically conditioned, analogy, in the absence of any tone shift, will leave the reader in no doubt one way or the other (p. 125).

These are the main points of Driver's theory.

1.3.4.6.   Criticisms of Driver's theory

        Firstly, the nascent <u>yqtl</u>. It is a self-evident fact that Heb-
rew does not have any means of distinguishing between punctual, durative,
iterative, habitual, and other aspectual distinctions, morphologically.[1]Instan-
ces may be found where a verb in the <u>yqtl</u> form is given all these aspectual
distinctions in a modern translation. Clearly, these distinctions are not
native to Hebrew otherwise they would be distinguished in the morphology of
the verb. It is also a self-evident fact that Hebrew verbs are not aligned
to a triple division of time. Instances occur where a <u>yqtl</u> verb is translated
by all three tenses, past, present, and future. Clearly, these distinctions
are not native to the HVS, otherwise ways would have been found to distinguish
these tense categories unambiguously. Whether an action is punctual or durative
will depend upon the nature of the action and the context in which it is used:
the Hebrew verb forms <u>cannot</u> supply this information; similarly with tense
distinctions, and those between single and frequentative actions.

        It is Driver's view that any action may be viewed from three different
stages in its development. For example, the mode of action in נָקַר (Job
30:17) and תְּנַקֵּר(Num. 16:14) is identical since the root means <u>to pierce</u>.
We are told that the Philistines took Samson and 'put out his eyes' (וַיְנַקְּרוּ,
Jud. 16:21, RV). If we slow down the action and look at its component parts
the initial stage of this operation can only be described by a circumlocut-
ion in English, such as: <u>they are about to pierce</u>....; the middle stage by:
<u>they are now piercing through</u>....; and the final stage by: <u>they have pierced</u>....
It is Driver's view that Hebrew is able to mark these three stages in any
action: thus <u>yqtl</u> marks the first stage (the nascent or incipient stage); the
participle marks the mere continuance of the action begun; and <u>qtl</u> marks the
completion of the operation.

        The first thing we might say about this definition/view of <u>yqtl</u> is that
it is too narrow. Like the Conversive <u>future</u> and Ewald's <u>incomplete</u> it cannot
indicate <u>complete</u> <u>actions</u>, not necessarily completed actions. For example, in
Proverbs 30:17 we read: 'The eye that mocks [תִּלְעַג]a father,/ that scorns
[וְתָבֻז]obedience to a mother,/ will be pecked out [יִקְּרוּהָ]by the ravens of
the valley,/ will be eaten [וְיֹאכְלוּהָ] by the vultures.' It can hardly be the
case that only the commencement of these actions are in view; the actions are
complete in themselves though they may be often repeated. The vultures could
hardly <u>begin to eat</u> an eye that had not yet been plucked, but was only in the
process of being plucked. Each of the <u>yqtl</u> verbs presupposes the completion

of the previous action.

It is Driver's firm conviction that since qtl is used to narrate single events in the past, the use of the simple yqtl form in the same past sphere must have been chosen 'in order to suggest some additional feature characteristic of the occurrence, which, in the case before us, is the fact (or possibility) of its repetition' (p. 29). Even if we accept that repetition or frequentative action is a characteristic feature of the past yqtl verb it follows that such repetitious actions are made up of individually complete actions. For example, Gen. 29:2, 'for out of that well they watered [יַשְׁקוּ] the flocks'. It is most unlikely that the writer intended by this yqtl form to mean: 'for out of that well they used to begin to water the flocks'. Clearly, then, it is inappropiate to describe frequentative actions as nascent actions.

Yqtl is also said to describe future action. It is difficult to see how a form which was chosen to present action in its most impressive and striking aspect, presenting action in movement rather than, like qtl, in a condition of rest, should come to convey non-existent action. J. Strong took up this point in his short note on Driver's 2nd edition of his Treatise; he says:

> It is not an adequate explanation...to say that the event is "preparing to take place, or developing" (p. 24). There are usually no signs whatever of its occurrence; it is not merely or properly incomplete; it is not yet even begun, except in the mind of the writer. Surely the fundamental import of the form in question cannot be so disguised or varied, in this very common use of it, as not to be distinctly recognizable. The attempt to translate the verb, in these exceedingly numerous instances, as an incipient act would be preposterous, and the author accordingly passes over this very important usage with a few general and vague remarks (p. 25); not even illustrating it by a single example! (1885:107)

It might even be argued that nascent action is too narrow a view of an action for it to be a fit medium to describe a total event made up of a number of individually complete actions, e.g. 2 Chr. 28:15, 'they clothed them, gave them sandals, provided them with food and drink, and anointed them' (וַיַּלְבִּשׁוּם וַיַּנְעִלוּם וַיַּאֲכִלוּם וַיַּשְׁקוּם וַיְסֻכוּם וַיְנַהֲלוּם). Clearly, it was not the writer's intention to describe partial actions; each action is complete and presumably sequential, otherwise the captives were being clothed, shod, fed, and anointed, all at the same time, if these verbs are given a nascent translation. On the use of wayyqtl to describe past events G. R. Driver writes:

> Equally unsatisfactory is the current explanation of this construction itself. It is that in the first case 'the imperfect

represents action as nascent: accordingly, when combined with a
conjunction connecting the event introduced by it with a point
already reached by the narrative, it represents it as the continuation or development of the part which came before it.'....
yet every action, whether incomplete or complete, is in some
sense nascent or emergent, i.e. it has arisen out of certain
precedent conditions which will have been described by a preceding verb in the narration of the story. At the same time the
nascent act described as such by the imperfect may in itself be
complete and ought therefore from that point of view to be described by a perfect tense. (1936:86)

Even if we accept the view that wayyqtl connects an event introduced by
it with a point already reached by the narrative this does not make for good
story-telling, as there would be considerable over-lapping of ideas. For
example:

Strictly speaking this
is what we would get
if each wayyqtl was
joined to the point
reached in the
narrative.

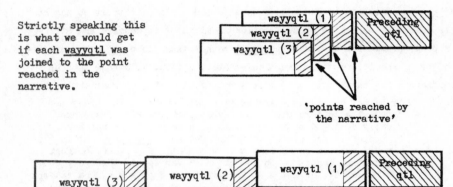

'points reached by
the narrative'

If, however, we join the complete nascent acts together this is how it would
look. Each wayyqtl assumes the completion of the preceding wayyqtl action as
its point of development.

Again, if yqtl indicates nascent action, by implication it must also
mark the transition from one action/state to another. רָעֵב means 'to be
hungry'. Is the subject of יִרְעַב in Prov. 6:30 entering into a state of
being hungry? 'Men do not despise [לֹא־יָבוּזוּ] a thief, if he steal [יִגְנוֹב]
to satisfy his soul when he is hungry [כִּי יִרְעָב].' Surely the point here is
that the man is so famished that unless he gets something to eat he is in
danger of exhaustion or death, hence the pity shown to him. (The RSV rules
out any pity shown to the hungry man.) How does one enter into רָדַם 'to
be silent'? To do so implies that one passes from a non-silent into a silent
state. Is this what the Hebrew writer intends to bring out when he uses the

yqtl form? Or is he simply telling us that the subject 'is hungry', 'is silent'? Once the idea of entering into a certain process or development is introduced we are forcibly reminded of the corollory action: movement from one state into another.

Again, there are certain verbs, which, if put into the yqtl form would indicate the opposite state to that implied in the verb itself. For example, if yqtl indicates that the subject is only entering into the state of being innocent (נקה), it is implied that he is not yet in that state. The opposite meaning will likewise be implied in the yqtl form of the following verbs, to be naked (גלה); to finish (גמר); to be dark (חשך); to be exhausted (דלל); to extinguish (דעך); to lack (חסר); to be impure (טמא); to sit (ישב); to be able (יכל); to be poor (רוש); to be sleepless (שקד); to be bereaved (יתם); to complete (כלל); to commit adultery (נאף); to be clear (צרח); to be modest (צנע); to lie down (רבע); and, to be unjust (רשע).

While Driver accounted for the use of yqtl to describe past events on the basis of his nascent meaning, he realized that that meaning alone was insufficient to convey a fact done. Consequently he is compelled to conclude: 'But in general, the use of ·ן in the historical books, renders it inconceivable that it should have suggested anything except the idea of a fact done' (p. 94). One might question, therefore, whether it ever existed to convey a nascent description of a past fact. If the idea of nascency was lost or disguised when past facts needed to be related (pp. 96, 73), it is a wonder that it still remains when used alone, or after the particles, אָז, טֶרֶם, צַר, etc.[1] The presence of אָז in the following examples shows that it neither (1) determines the time sphere in which the action took place, nor (2) whether the action is nascent (describing a single event) or frequentative (describing more than a single occurrence):

אָז יְדַבֵּר

> Then spoke Joshua to the Lord in the day when the Lord gave the Amorites over to the men of Israel; (Jos. 10:12)
>
> Then he will speak to them in his wrath...saying, I have set my king on Zion, my holy hill. (Ps. 2:5)

The context gives the action a past and a future tense respectively. In both contexts a single action is described.

אָז יִקְרָא

אָז תִּקְרָא

> Then Joshua summoned the Reubenites, and the Gadites, and the half-tribe of Manasseh, (Jos. 22:1)
>
> Then you shall call, and the Lord will answer; (Isa. 58:9)

אָז יַעֲלֶה / At that time Hazael king of Syria went up and fought against
Gath, and took it. (2 Kgs. 12:18 (Eng. 17), 16:5)

יַּ֫עַל־ \ And a mist went up from the earth, (Gen. 2:6)

Concerning the latter Driver remarks:

> In strictness, יעלה expresses only a <u>single</u> event as beginning or
> ready to take place; but an action of which this may be predicated
> is in the nature of things likely to happen more frequently, and
> thus the additional idea of 'recurrency' would be speedily super-
> induced upon the more limited original signification of the
> imperfect. (pp. 27–8).

Again, only the context, not the time sphere, determines whether יעלה denotes
a single or frequentative action. If it is frequentative in Gen. 2:6 then the
following <u>wqtl</u> must also be given a frequentative sense, not that it <u>expresses</u>
recurrency as such, but rather, it views the actions collectively—as one
action, or one result/consequence. Whether the action in Gen. 2:6 is frequentative or single is a matter of individual interpretation; grammatically it
can be either (2 Kgs. 12:18 is an example of <u>single</u> action in the past).
It may well be that the single event (יעלה)—the concrete example—is preferred to the abstract idea of reiteration.[1] The concrete is put for the
abstract throughout the Hebrew language.

אָז יַעֲלוּ / Then bulls will be offered on thy altar. (Ps. 51:21[E.19])

וַיַּעֲלוּ \ The the Philistines went up and encamped in Judah, (Jud. 15:9)
Only the context shows that the verbal idea is different. As the forms stand
isolated from their contexts they could refer to any time, and could be interpreted as either 'to offer', or, 'to go up'. Similarly, יַעֲלוּ in Jud. 6:5 and
1 Kgs. 6:8 are pasts, but futures in Isa. 60:7, Ezek. 38:18 and Lev. 2:12 (= 'to
offer'). Driver notes that <u>yqtl</u> is seldom used for future frequentative action
as 'the force of the imperfect is exhausted by the idea of futurity which it
conveys' (p. 64 above). This is not the case in Ps. 51:21 above.

תֵּלֵךְ   And if you will walk in my ways... (1 Kgs. 3:14)

אָז תֵּלֵךְ   Then you will walk on your way securely, (Prov. 3:23)

וַתֵּלֶךְ   And you have walked in the way of Jeroboam, (1 Kgs. 16:2)

All these actions are durative. The prefixes וְ , אָז , do not determine the
mode of action of the verb, that is determined by the use made of the verbal
idea in a given context. The particle אָז does not determine the time sphere
in which the action may take place, <u>cf</u>. Exod. 15:1.

Then they said among the nations, 'The Lord has done great
things for them, (Ps. 126:2)

אָז יֹאמְרוּ
יֹאמְרוּ

And whenever any of the fugitives said [יֹאמְרוּ], 'Let me go
over,' the men of Gilead said [וַיֹּאמְרוּ] to him,...(Jud. 12:3,
cf. Ps. 41:6; Hos. 7:2; Isa. 8:20; 2 Sam. 5:8; and 1 Sam. 19:24).

It is Driver's contention that wayyqtl can refer only to single actions, and
yqtl to frequentative past actions. Where the context does not permit a frequentative meaning the action is a vivid present, and the writer has changed
his standpoint to a 'present in the past'. If יֹאמְרוּ is a vivid present
then so must וַיֹּאמְרוּ; if the former is a frequentative, then the latter
is also; if the former is nascent, the latter is too; if the former is complete, the latter is too.

Driver noted that wayyqtl may also be used to describe future events (p. 67
above). Future events are naturally non-past events, so in these cases the
writer has changed his standpoint with the initial prophetic qtl and the
following events introduced by ו֩ are subsequent to it (pp. 81, 97, 32). The
suggestion of Driver's that the prefixed ו֩ was employed to 'throw the action
into the past' is therefore not strictly correct (pp. 96-7, 73, 79). The
tenses are relative, not absolute, says Driver on p. 5, but even this is not
precise enough, for the most that the conjunctive ו֩ can indicate is that the
action to which it is attached introduces an action that is subsequent to the
preceding one, hence its employment in past, present, and future, contexts.
And hence it is that wayyqtl must sometimes be translated, 'and he shall...'
(for examples see 1.2.1.1, and Driver, §§81-2).

Secondly, the consecutive forms.[1] We saw above that the qtl consecutive
loses its individuality and takes on the meaning of the dominant verb (usually
the immediately preceding verb). In these cases it is difficult to see how
qtl can indicate completed action, yet we are assured by Driver that

> The meanings assumed, however divergent, do not in reality
> involve any contradiction: a fundamental principle can be
> discovered which will embrace them all—a higher unity exists
> in which they meet and are reconciled. (p. 47)

Obviously this statement must be limited to the context in which it was said,
as it cannot be said of the consecutive constructions.

In the case of the qtl consecutive a completed action is out of place
if it assumes all the meanings of the simple yqtl form (p. 125ff.). Driver
takes a different view of the consecutive qtl when it follows a prophetic
qtl. He does not regard the wqtl forms following such a prophetic qtl as

further instances of prophetic qtls, but rather as qtl verbs which have lost
their own individuality and have consequently taken on the meaning of the
dominant verb, in this case, the prophetic qtl. The proof of this, he argued,
lies in the syntactical position of the following verbs and the ultima position of the tone where possible (p.67 above). He gives no examples of a
prophetic qtl with a prefixed waw.

The consecutive qtl is much wider in its use than simply indicating
future action. Where a simple yqtl occurs in a past narrative it may be followed by the consecutive qtl, in which case it will take on the meaning
assigned to the simple yqtl (usually a frequentative one, sometimes as a
'vivid present in the past').

The inducted tense solution advocated by Driver to solve the difficulties connected with the consecutive qtl was not a new one. It was put forward
by P. Gell in 1818 to circumvent the Conversive theory. The result is the
same when it comes to translating the form so that Driver could write:

> The preceding remarks...will also shew in what sense we are justi-
> fied in still applying to the former term waw conversive; in
> virtue of the limitation imposed by it upon the perfect, it
> changes or modifies the application of the verb, so that the
> area covered (e.g.) by וְהִכָּה is by no means coextensive or
> identical with that represented by the broader הִכָּה.(1874:
> §109 Obs., omitted in 3rd ed.)

There appears to be no difference between Driver's view of the consecutive
qtl assuming the meaning of a preceding jussive yqtl, and the application
of the Conversive theory/Waw Inductive theory to the same situation (cf.
Driver, §113 (2)).

* * * * * * *

Probably S. R. Driver more than any other Hebrew scholar has influenced
the English-speaking world in its understanding of the Hebrew 'tenses'. (It
would probably have been better if Driver omitted the term 'tenses' altogether in his work.) He, more than any other scholar, popularized Ewald's
Complete-Incomplete or Perfect-Imperfect theory.

Reactions have ranged from Benjamin Douglass'consternation when he first
read Driver's book: 'This is opening a wide door. It is giving too much to the
enemy' (1885:3), to the view that 'The whole treatment presents a picture
strongly characterized by complexity, obscurity and artificiality, a system
which it is difficult to imagine as developing and existing in the minds of

any language group.' (F. R. Blake, 1951:1).

From the appearance of Driver's theory in 1874 until Hans Bauer's Conservative Waw solution in 1910 it is clear that the views of Driver and Ewald
dominated the grammars. However, there were still strong supporters of the
Jewish Conversive theory around, such as B. Davies (1880:xxiii), W. R. Harper
(1883), J. Kennedy (1889:76), T. Bowman (1882:139, 141), and Tregelles (p. 54f.).

There were also supporters of the Relative Tense theory, such as W. H.
Green (1880:294. He appears to fall back on the Conversive theory, p. 128),
J. Strong (1885-6), M. S. Terry (n.d. [1885] :190), W. G. Ballintine (1885-6),
and A. B. Rich (1874:121ff. He follows Nordheimer who suggested that the imperative was derived from the yqtl form (1841:II, 193-4), and not vice versa.[1]).

We find Ewald's view appearing in the following grammars, W. H. Lowe
(1887:19, but cf. pp. 29, 47 for Conversive view), H. L. Strack (1883. He
followed Nordheimer's view on the significance of the pronominal elements
with the verb forms (p. 89).), F. E. König (1881-95. He did not fully acquiesce in the terms Complete and Incomplete in his Syntax, 1897:§129-134). König
was the first to refute Bauer's hypothetical nomen agentis form qatāl (1911:
719-20). Other supporters were H. Ferguson (1881, 1882), W. H. Bennett
(articles in 1885-6), A. Müller (1882), A. S. Ballin (1881:71ff.), S. Sharpe
(1877:15, 18), C. J. Ball (1877:69), A. B. Davidson (1894), and Paul de
Lagarde (1889. He regarded the imper. as the oldest form of the verb, cf.
pp. 12, 22, 76.). B. Stade also followed Ewald's view. He considered the
wqtl = past in the Pre-exilic passages as corruptions.[2]

* * * * * * *

1.3.5   The Factual-Descriptive Theory of William Turner

Turner was the young printer who became the friend and associate
of Isaac Nordheimer in 1836. He was perfectly acquainted with Nordheimer's
Relative Tense theory having seen it through the press for him. Nothing in
Turner's theory could be said to have been culled from the other's theory.

The essence of Turner's theory is that qtl expresses the action or state
as the attribute of the person or thing spoken of; the yqtl form expresses
or represents the verbal action as in or of the subject, the produce of the

subject's energy, the manifestation of its power and life, like a stream
evolving itself from its source (1876:368, 377). Whereas the first represents the act or state of the verb as an independent thing: the Factual;
the second expresses the same act or state as a process, and one that is
passing before our very eyes: the Descriptive (his terms, p. 384).

1.3.5.1   The Origin and Meaning of the Qtl Form

          Turner follows Lee's suggestion that the noun is prior to the
verb (cf. Lee, 1828:78-9). He regards the Semitic verb as really nothing
else than a nominal or adjectival term of attribution (p. 365). He adduces
the following facts in favour of this view. (1) A complete sentence may be
formed without a verb. (2) The verbal forms in Hebrew are almost either
absolutely identical with nominal forms, or differ from them in vocalization.[1] (3) The verbal forms share with nouns in their ordinary inflections.
Thus the third person of qtl, קָֽטְלָה , has a feminine ending in –ā– or
–at after the ordinary analogy.[2] The same person in both forms takes a plural
ending in –ūn or –ū, the ordinary plural ending of nouns in Arabic, traces
of which exist in Hebrew also. In like manner the he locale of nouns is paralleled in form and significance by the he paragogic of verbs. The he usually
indicates in nouns the object towards which movement is directed.[3] As appen-
ded to the 1st person yqtl forms it marks the striving of the agent towards
the object (pp. 378-9). (4) These verb forms often interchange with the
infinitive, another fact which vouches for their nominal character.
          On the strength of these arguments he bases his case that the verbal
forms in question are primarily nouns. This being the case the qtl form is
'directly derived from a verbal or participial noun', i.e. קֹטֶל , קָטֵל ,
and קָטַל (p. 367); and the yqtl form has been moulded on the imperative
and infinitive construct which express the idea of the verb in the most bald
and abstract manner of which the language is capable (p. 371).[4] His footnotes
refer one to Lee's Grammar for the arguments and evidence. But whereas Lee
argued that the nominal qtl indicated past action, Turner interprets the
same form as an attributive fact (in the case of transitive verbs) or attribution (in the case of intransitive verbs). In this way he avoids the problem that we pointed out with regard to Lee's Past tense designation, since
the stative verbs cannot be so designated. He also avoids Ewald's Complete
which likewise is inappropriate to stative verbs. Turner preferred the term

Factual because this does not say anything about complete or incomplete, or past, present, or future; it simply states a _fact_ as the attribute of the person or thing spoken of (p. 368). He sees no essential difference in the circumstance that in the one, קָטֵל, קֹטֵל, a quality, in the other קָטַל an activity, is apposed; since the apposed activity is not represented as an energy which the subject puts forth, but as a thing which marks what he is, which forms an element in his name, and stands as a distinction of his name (pp. 368-9). While acknowledging that the difference in vocalization, קָטַל, קֹטֵל, קָטֵל, was symbolical and suggestive at the formative stage,[1] he thinks it improbable that 'we shall ever be able to project ourselves so thoroughly into their modes of thought and of expression as to recover and define with certainty what these ideas were' (p. 369). In his estimation, however, the participial base sheds light on the original meaning of the qtl form.

Another factor that sheds light on its meaning is the composition of the form. He observes that the personal pronouns are suffixed, not prefixed, and this draws from him the comment:

> Now, according to the ordinary law of collocation in Hebrew, exemplified, e.g., in the construction by apposition and by annexion, and also in the joining of substantives with adjectives and of verbs with adverbs, the defined word precedes and the defining follows. Hence in קָטַלְתִּי, קָטַלְתָּ, etc., the verbal root must be regarded as holding the foremost place in the thought of the speaker, as well as in the composition of the word. It is the action as a fact which is prominent, and in it the agent is regarded as involved. (p. 370)

He then goes on to make the following distinction between the participle and the qtl verb:

> We perceive here the difference between such verbal formations and those looser statements in which an unattached pronoun and a verbal noun are used. We feel that הֹלֵךְ אָנֹכִי is not precisely equivalent to הָלַכְתִּי, and the difference seems to me to consist mainly in this, that in the former the emphasis lies on the person who goes, in the latter on the fact of his going. (p. 370)

In Turner's estimation the position of the personal pronouns determines the relative importance and prominence of the two portions of the word. Thus, while in the qtl form the verb is the defined and leading element, to which the subject is subordinated, in the yqtl form the subject takes the leading place, and the verb with its action is presented as that by which the subject is distinguished and in which its power is manifested (p. 376-7).

Turner admits to finding this form less easy to analyse than the other. For an explanation of the form and position of the personal pronouns he explores two possibilities. (1) The verb form as it stands may be a nominal form. Here he notes Ewald's suggestion that nouns with prefixed yodhs are an old formation, common to Arabic, Phoenician, Himyaritic, and to Hebrew (<u>e.g.</u> יְהוָה , יַעֲקֹב , יִשְׂחָק , יִשְׂרָאֵל , etc.), and Dietrich's statement that this formation--

> was originally representative of abstract terms, especially sen-
> sible attributes, whereby at the same time the bearer of such
> attributes is indicated, being employed less for things without
> life than for things with life or conceived of as living, and
> very frequent for the names of animals and plants. (1846:373)

On this line of research Turner arrived at the meaning for <u>yqtl</u> as one who manifests personal qualities, <u>i.e.</u> the abstract property of the root is rep-resented as embodied in some living or personal existence, and so to speak, energised and made alive.

(2) The second possibility he explores was put forward by Donaldson who wrote:

> It is, indeed, difficult to believe that when ־י—עִבְרִ signifies
> "a Hebrew <u>man</u>," and יָה—עִבְרִ "a Hebrew <u>woman</u>," while כֹּתֵב—יִ
> means "<u>he</u> is writing," and הּ—כֹּתֵב "<u>she</u> is writing," these par-
> allel forms are not due to the same principle of phonology.
> (Quoted from <u>Maskil le-Sopher</u>, 1848:26)

According to this analogy, says Turner, the <u>yqtl</u> form indicates the personal or active performing of that which the root denotes.[1] It is the verbal noun which expresses <u>doing</u>, and that not statically as a characteristic of the subject, but dynamically as resulting from the subject's life and energy (p. 375). Either or both of these possibilities compel him to regard the <u>yqtl</u> form 'as expressing distinctively the element of personal life and activity' (p. 376). Whereas in the <u>qtl</u> form it was the act that was made prominent, he now finds that in <u>yqtl</u> it is the actor; the form describes a process, like a stream evolving itself from its source.[2] He sets out the stark contrast in meaning between the two verb forms as follows:

> It might be said that the first [qtl] is the more abstract, the
> second [yqtl] the more concrete,--the one the more objective, the
> other the more subjective;....Perhaps the most proper words which
> our language affords for the expression of the distinction are
> these,--the Factual and the Descriptive. The one makes statements,
> the other draws pictures; the one asserts, the other represents;
> the one lays down positions, the other describes events; the one
> appeals to reason, the other to imagination; the one is annalistic,
> the other fully and properly historical. (p. 384)

When it comes to explaining the form of the cohortative Turner finds a ready analogy in the noun with <u>he</u> locale suffixed to it. He bases this on the argument that the two verb forms have been derived from nouns, though he is aware of the obvious resemblance of the <u>yqtl</u> form to the imperative and infinitive construct in which 'we have the action of the verbs set forth in an entirely indefinite and abstract way, and as a thing of thought only, not of reality' (p. 371).

To explain the shortened form of the jussive, he argued for a parallel between the absolute noun and its construct form and the Prefix-form and its jussive form: both are shortened for the same reason, <u>i.e.</u> haste is made append as quickly as possible to that which is to be defined its defining element, and to bind them vocally into one whole. The jussive expresses what is determined by something else, and is thus united with it by the shortening of the form into one compound phrase (p. 381).

1.3.5.3   The Consecutive forms

He considers the <u>yqtl</u> form in the consecutive construction to be no different in meaning from its use without the prefixed ·ו. He accounts for the daghesh by adopting Schultens idea (1737:424) that it is compounded of the conjunction and the article, <u>i.e.</u> ·הַ} (p. 382).[1] He adopts this suggestion because it is in harmony with his research that a nominal significance continues to inhere in these verbal forms. He meets the objection that the article ought to be on the following word since it is the defining word (in his understanding of the construction), by pointing out that there are exceptions with nouns, and adding that the different circumstances 'are doubtless sufficient to account for the different construction' (p. 382). In fact he can justify why the article <u>ought</u> to be prefixed to the verb in this case:

> The annexion [of the article] is of necessity more loose and free in the one case than in the other; it is not a definite thing, but an action proceeding from a certain agent in certain circumstances, which in this case the article points to, and doubtless the only mode of unambiguous definition, at least when the verb stands first, is that of prefixing it to the verb itself....Just as when prefixed to nouns it points to a certain individual or property, marking it out for special notice, so is it when thus prefixed to the verb. It points to the action as that it is which is passing before our eyes. (p. 382-3)

Unfortunately he does not give an example of how he would translate the consecutive <u>yqtl</u> construction, nor in what way the simple <u>waw</u> prefixed to <u>yqtl</u>

would differ from it.

He considers the particles אַף, טֶרֶם, צַר, etc., to have the same force
as the demonstrative הֵן. They do not have any conversive power (pp. 390,
363). These introductory particles not only link events into a series of happenings but call attention to each as it passes under review. Probably the
introductory phrase, and so, with the Historical Present forms the most exact
translation of which the English language is capable of to express this Hebrew mode of description (p. 390). History, as presented in the OT, becomes
thus like the unrolling of a panorama, and every scene is pointed at as it
makes its appearance and passes by. He regards וַיְהִי as equivalent to an
introductory particle, because it serves the purpose of clearing the ground
and preparing the stage for the display of the scenes which follow (p. 390).[1]

As regards the consecutive qtl construction and the use of qtl for the
present and future, Turner follows a consistent line of application for these
forms. He lists three main categories (apart from its frequentative use in
the past); these are: (1) In certain forms of expression in which the living
source from which action proceeds is obscured or concealed, e.g. in cases
where passive or neuter forms are interchanged with active. He noticed that
frequently when the latter were yqtl the former were usually in the qtl form
(p. 395). In this category he placed Ewald's observation that לֹא requires the
qtl form in clauses which contain negative attributes, as in Ps. 15:3–4.
(2) The emphatic use of qtl (pp. 395–404). He makes the following subdivisions: (a) To make a simple fact prominent and emphatical. (b) To state general truths, habits of mind and character, and the like. (c) The stative
usage, or statements relating to condition, mental states, etc. These verbs
do not express any energy or process, but render emphatic the state itself
which the verb denotes. (d) The prophetic qtl, the statement of what is yet
future on its factual side, not as the contemplated issue of a process but
as the object of such an intuition as that by which we image the past. (e)
Emphatic asseveration, promises and threats. (f) Commands, counsels, and
entreaties. (g) To express a strong wish or desire.[2] (h) In questions. (i) In
hypothetical statements. (j) When the flow of narrative, or the issuing of
promises (couched in yqtl forms), is broken up by the insertion of the subject or object or some other part of speech at the commencement of a separate clause, the qtl form is used under these syntactical circumstances. The
reason for the employment of qtl in these circumstances is because the fact
comes at the beginning of the clause and the qtl form is the recognized form

to emphasize it.

The third main category covers the explanatory statements which occur in the course of a narrative described in the consecutive yqtl style.

However, he is aware that there are many situations where the yqtl form is found where we might have expected the qtl form. He does not jump to the conclusion that therefore the forms are interchangeable or equivalent in sense, as many grammarians have done before and since his day. By carefully applying his new understanding of the basic difference between the two forms he opens up new possibilities for resolving many difficult texts.

1.3.5.4   An Assessment of Turner's Theory

Turner had the theories of Driver, Ewald, Lee, Nordheimer, and Donaldson, to contend with when he put forward his uncomplicated solution to the HVS in 1876. In the same year Sir W. Martin put forward a similar theory in passing, but this does not appear to have been noticed by later writers on the subject.

The starting-point for Turner's reconstruction of the growth of the HVS is the suggestion (Lee and others) that the verb forms have developed from nominal bases. He accepted Lee's analysis in particular, concerning the origin of qtl and yqtl; but instead of seeing the resultant forms as Past and Present tenses, he saw them as pointing to an objective (qtl) and a subjective (yqtl) view on the part of the writers/speakers. Any event, he held, whether past, present, or future, can be described as a fact, and accordingly it would be presented in the qtl form; or else the speaker may choose to present the same event (or series of events) as the personal activity of the participant(s), and record it in the yqtl form.

Because these two forms have such divergent functions the speaker is free to employ either of them at any moment to advance the story or event in the most telling way. When the Hebrew prophet wishes to relate events lying in the future, the fact that he uses the qtl form indicates that he is more interested in the results—the facts of the new situation—than in the manner they were arrived at. On the other hand, the Hebrew historian, who already knows all the facts of his story, shows by his choice of yqtl forms that he is interested in the actual forging or shaping of the facts of history: history is presented as it actually happened. With this, Lee, and to some extent, Ewald,

would agree. Thus the real difference between Lee and Turner is very slight.
While the former thinks that the action of yqtl is always in the present,
either absolutely or relatively, the latter pictures the person or agent in
actual performance of the deed. In both cases the action is seen as emerging
or emanating from the subject. On the other hand, the difference between
Ewald and Turner on this point is that Ewald wants to see incomplete action
in the yqtl event, whereas Turner does not think this is what the writers
have in mind. Where all three overlap is not difficult to discover since
a 'live' presentation must necessarily take place in the 'present', and a
present action has the appearance of being an incomplete action.

From this conception of the relationship between the action and the actor
it was a natural step for Turner to see the jussive and cohortative as secondary formations derived from yqtl. (The yqtl form was moulded on the imper. and
infin. (p. 370-1).)

With his new insight into the radical difference between the two verb
forms he rejected the idea that the forms could be interchanged with no dis-
cernible difference in meaning. He illustrates this in the following manner:

> Occasionally...statements of existing condition stand side by side
> with others representing a change in that condition...and thus
> give rise to those contrasted modes of expression which have
> seemed to Gesenius and others to establish...their own tense-
> theory regarding the forms....Thus Gen. xvi. 8, Whence camest
> thou? [אֵי־מִזֶּה בָאת] and whither <u>wilt thou go</u>? [וְאָנָה תֵלֵכִי]
> Ex. x. 14, Before them there were no [לֹא־הָיָה] such locusts as
> they, neither after them shall be such [לֹא יִהְיֶה]....In such
> passages, the reference, in so far as it exists, to past and
> future time is, I conceive, secondary and constructive. What is
> essentially and primarily contained in the words is, on the one
> hand, an emphatic statement of fact, and on the other hand, a
> description of what is to be superadded to or come forth from
> this fact through the purpose and energy of some living person.
> (pp. 397-8)

Granted his new insight the following concession is puzzling:-

> It is, at the same time, to be freely granted that there are
> many instances in which in our apprehension, there exists no
> apparent reason why the one form rather than the other should
> be employed, as <u>e.g.</u> why the question, Whence comest thou? should
> sometimes appear as מֵאַיִן תָּבוֹא, and sometimes as מֵאַיִן בָּאת .
> A wide border-land in which the forms freely interchange must,
> on every conceivable theory, be acknowledged. (p. 405)

Ewald saw very little difference in the two questions (<u>Syntax</u>, 1879:8), likewise Müller (1882:4); but others have tried to bring out a difference between
the two forms (<u>cf.</u> W. Martin, 1876:14, and J. Strong, 1885b:230).

The verb forms have been determined by the actual situation then prevailing, for in Gen. 16:8 Hagar was resting when the angel asked her, 'Whence camest thou? (אֵי־מִזֶּה בָאת). It would have been inappropriate to have used the yqtl form since that would have implied that she was going somewhere at that moment; though it is possible that Hagar could have been viewed as on a journey, and her present situation ignored.

Joseph uses the qtl form in Gen. 42:7, 'Whence came ye?' (מֵאַיִן בָּאתֶם), because at that precise moment it was obvious they were not on a journey, but had arrived. Notice, however, the difference in Jos. 9:8, 'Who are you? And where do you come from?' (וּמֵאַיִן תָּבֹאוּ). It is obvious to Joshua that these men are on a journey, that is their present activity. Joshua's question is: From where did you start out on your journey? He does not know yet that he is the goal of their journey; but this comes out in the choice of verb form they use: 'From a very far country your servants have come, בָּאוּ not וַיָּבֹאוּ, implying that they had finished their journey and had reached their destination. Again, in Jud. 17:9 the yqtl form is the appropriate one to use on this occasion, because Micah chances to meet a Levite passing by his place. He asks, 'Whence comest thou?' (מֵאַיִן תָּבוֹא). If he had asked: מֵאַיִן בָּאתָ , 'From where have you come?' it would have implied that Micah's home was the Levite's destination. But the Levite's answer shows that this was not the case—'and I go to sojourn where I may find a place (וְאָנֹכִי הֹלֵךְ)'. The use of the forms would seem to suggest that where a person has arrived at his destination, that he has finished his journey (or a stage of it), is it appropriate to ask: מֵאַיִן בָּאתָ. Only when one meets someone in the course of his travels is the question מֵאַיִן תָּבוֹא appropriate; because at that precise moment he is still engaged in that activity, hence the yqtl form.

There are a number of unsatisfactory elements in Turner's theory. The first has to do with his philosophical view of language. Concerning the HVS he says:

> These verbal forms correspond to the two leading questions of intelligence,—What? and How? The first interest of the under-standing is the knowledge of facts, the second is that of causes;— the first inquiry—What exists? and the next, How has it come into existence? We first know things by themselves, in an isol-ated and unconnected way, and then we know them in their depend-ences and relations, as links in an evolving chain, or as stages in an unceasing process. The one aspect of human knowledge is presented by the Hebrew Perfect, and the other by the Imperfect ....Thus the distinction...is...more primitive and profound, than that of the time of the action in any of its aspects.
> (p. 384)

But one could accept his theory without having to accept his philosophical interpretation of it. If his views concerning the origin of language were correct we would expect to find two 'tenses' at the heart of every modern language.

Secondly, he has overlooked the close affinity between the participles (apart from the Base/Qal form) and their respective Prefix-forms in all the other themes (Piel, etc.), in all the other Semitic languages. He has concentrated on the similarity of the qtl form and the Base or Qal participle without demonstrating the morphological connection historically.

Thirdly, he explains the origin of the verbs from nouns with a similar morphology. This may be the case with the qtl form as he has demonstrated, but the case for yqtl being formed from a nominal base is not convincing. In some cases it could be argued that personal names have been formed from yqtl verbs, e.g. Isaac (cf. Gen. 21:6), and Israel (see p. 129 below).

Fourthly, he regards the imperative as older than the yqtl verb form, and the latter to be moulded on it. This can hardly have been the case (see p. 171 below).

Fifthly, if the nearest equivalent to the yqtl is the English Historical Present tense we are still left with a relative and an absolute use of the yqtl and the qtl forms, which brings us back to the standpoint principle and the ambiguity that that theory involves. וַיִּקְרָא may refer to the future or the past (see 1.2.1.1).

While Turner has given us a new insight into the two verb forms, and into the yqtl form in particular, we are still left with the problem of the tense of any given action. When do we take the action or fact in a relative sense and when in an absolute sense? How do we distinguish between prospective and retrospective actions? The problems inherent in Turner's theory have been pointed out already in Lee's theory (cf. 1.3.1.3).

* * * * * * * *

1.3.6   The Factum-Existens Theory of J. A. Knudtzon

Up until the middle of the 19th century comparative Semitic studies revolved around Arabic, Aramaic, Hebrew, and Ethiopic. There was no parallel to the consecutive constructions in Hebrew to any significant extent, though each language had the qtl and yqtl forms. With the discovery of the Assyrian/Akkadian language in 1841, and the publication of its literature in the 1850's, it was not long before scholars were regarding it as the oldest Semitic language (cf. E. Hincks, 1866:480, who described it as the 'Sanskrit of the Semitic languages'.). However, it was soon also discovered that Assyrian had no active qtl form.[1] Nöldeke, in his much acclaimed essay, 'Semitic Languages', wrote:'Assyrian differs in many respects from all the cognate languages. The ancient perfect has wholly disappeared, or left but few traces' (1886:650). He completely rejected the idea that Assyrian was the 'Sanskrit of the Semitic world', declaring it 'unworthy of a serious refutation' (p. 642). He took it as a matter of course that a comparative grammar of the Semitic languages ought to be based upon Arabic. The suggestion that Assyrian had lost the qtl active was immediately challenged by G. Hoffman:

> If the Babylonian system does not know of a postfigiertes Perfect, does it signify a loss, or is this Perfect a new formation already in Canaan deriving from a participial-adjectival form?
> (1887:605)

Similarly, Wellhausen comments: 'It is not necessary to suppose that the Assyrian has lost the Perfect; perhaps it never possessed one despite the fact that all the sister languages possess it' (1887:968).

But long before Nöldeke wrote his essay the debate over which verb was the oldest had begun. In 1878 Paul Haupt was struck by the remarkable similarity between Ethiopic and Assyrian: between two languages geographically remote from each other. Consequently he regarded anything they had in common as belonging to Common Semitic. He explained the vestiges of the Perfect in Assyrian—not as remnants but—as the beginnings of the Perfect in Assyrian, and the West Semitic (WS) qtl was considered a new formation derived from the participle. The oldest verb form, in his opinion, was the Assyrian Present iqátal, and the Ethiopic Imperfect yĕqátĕl (p.ccxlvi). The shorter forms, iqtul in Assyr., and yĕqtĕl in Ethiopic, are derivatives of the longer forms. He pointed out that the Assyrian language had undergone no significant change over the centuries covered by the extant literature, and concluded from this that therefore it could not have lost the Perfect without trace.

It was well known, however, that the Egyptian language, which could be
traced back as far as the earliest Assyrian inscriptions, showed evidence of
the qtl form in its Pseudo-Participle,[1] but no evidence or remnants of the yqtl
form. A. Erman suggested that 'the Egyptian simply lost the Imperfect, because
it has preserved its Perfect form...in a drastically limited way' (1900:345).
In Neo-Egyptian it has been reduced still further 'before our very eyes' notes
Bauer (1910:8). On the one hand, we appear to have a very stable picture in
the Assyrian language, marking one end of the archaic spectrum, while on the
other hand, we have the swiftly developing Egyptian language in which we can
observe the last stages of its 'Semitic' forms being discarded.

Virtually all scholars of this period regarded the active qtl form as
the youngest to be formed. Later, however, the priority swung round in favour
of the qtl form, compare G. Bergsträsser (1929:9-14), G. R. Driver (1936:
28ff.), and T. W. Thacker (1954:157). The evidence for qtl being the youngest
form was stated by Wellhausen :

> Everywhere the Imperfect conveys the impression of greater original-
> ity; it is more opaque, irregular, and, one might say, it
> appears to be more verbal. All moods derive from it. In the dia-
> lects its form is much better established and varies far less
> than the Perfect form. In Hebrew it still overlaps the sphere of
> the Perfect. (1887:968)

F. Prätorius has no doubts about the matter, he says:

> The Kushitic favours the priority of the Proto-Semitic origin of
> the preformative conjugation, i.e., the Semitic Imperfect; the
> Kushitic favours the idea that the Perfect is an internal Semitic
> formation, as the apparent Perfect of Kushitic seems to be an
> internal Kushitic formation. This supposition seems to be even
> more probable as the Berber language seems to point to the same
> conclusion. (1892:332)

R. E. Brünnow agrees with this and adds:

> One could even obtain further evidence for it [the priority of
> yqtl] such as the fact that the suffix formation still continues
> to grow in the Semitic area into modern times...whereas new for-
> mations by prefixes do not occur anywhere. A method of formation
> which is still alive must, in any case, be younger than one which
> has ceased to be active. (1893:132)

H. Zimmern, likewise, regarded the qtl verb as a secondary form (1898:99).
It would not be a profitable venture to follow the numerous discussions on
this particular topic, nor the effect Darwin's theory had on discussions
relating to the development of language.

If Paul Haupt was the first to approach the HVS from the historical-
comparative point of view, then J. A. Knudtzon was clearly the next to make a
significant contribution in this area.

Knudtzon produced a thesis in 1889 entitled <u>Om</u> <u>det</u> <u>saakaldte</u> <u>Perfectum</u> <u>og</u> <u>Imperfectum</u> <u>i</u> <u>Hebraisk</u> ('On the so-called Perfect and Imperfect in Hebrew') which was a review of the way the two Hebrew verb forms had been dealt with in the grammars from the time of Ewald onwards.

In his own explanation of the forms he comes closest to W. Turner's view, but the influence of Haupt and S. R. Driver can be clearly discerned especially in his 1892 article.

1.3.6.1   The Original 'Present' Perfect

In 1892 Knudtzon set out his views on the HVS in <u>Z.A.</u> vol. 7, pp. 33-59, and it is to this article that the following page references apply. References to his thesis will be made clear with a prefixed T.[1]

He sums up the various usages of the Perfect-Permansive under the concept of the <u>present,</u> because originally it indicated state. The perfective or completed/past meaning of the Perfect is a development from this original state meaning. The analogy he uses is that of the Greek Perfect which not only has reference to a past action but also to a present state (p. 34). This is how he accounts for the aorist function of the <u>qtl</u> form. He does not envisage any fundamental difference between the stative and the active <u>qtl</u>. The stative <u>qtl</u> does not indicate a state which has been arrived at, but indicates something present, at hand, not a present event or something which has happened. It is very close to the adjective which no one regards as a state which has happened.

The active <u>qtl</u> developed very naturally from this 'present at hand' meaning, since 'he is old' easily changes to 'he has become old'; 'he is clothed' to 'he has clothed himself'; 'he is a murderer' to 'he has murdered' (p. 35, T.114-9). Basically, then, <u>qtl</u> described a state which was not thought to have happened. The writer simply describes a present fact, hence his term 'Factum' or 'Fact' in place of Ewald's Perfect.[2] He regards the active <u>qtl</u> as a departure from the original state idea; the Assyrian Permansive (/stative) has retained the original function of the form having never developed an active <u>qtl</u> form. Both the active and stative 'states' belong to the present.[3] The one has arisen from a <u>nomen</u> <u>agentis,</u> the other from an adjective (<u>i.e.</u> the stative <u>qtl</u>); both originally described a present state (p. 48).

1.3.6.2   The Original 'Present' Imperfect

He does not accept that the characteristic of the yqtl verb is incomplete action (p. 48), nor that it designates something present in relation to the present time of the speaker. Rather, yqtl describes the present of the speaker irrespective of whatever sphere of time he might be in—past, present, or future (p. 49, T.120-6). It presents us with the happenings themselves, whereas qtl verbs refer to their having happened (p. 55). In this sense, therefore, they are not interchangeable, at least they were not interchangeable in the very beginning. The yqtl expresses something presenting itself, something emerging, hence in this verbal form some sort of movement is involved. That the movement does not lie in the verb itself, otherwise verbs describing state would not appear in the yqtl form, suggested to Knudtzon that it might lie in the relation of the action to the perception of the speaker (p. 57). It might be illustrated as follows: At a given moment, a man is confronted by something which makes an impression on him, this sets his heart in motion (or the agitation may arise in his own heart through suddenly remembering something) and he gives expression to this impression by means of the yqtl verb-form. Most frequently the thing presenting itself to him and agitating his spirit will itself be something moving (i.e. an action). Movement creates movement and this is portrayed and conveyed in the yqtl. He regards the yqtl form as eminently suited to express one's inner emotions and feelings, and anything which impresses us; thus the awareness that God is great will be expressed by the yqtl form: יִגְדַּל יְהֹוָה (Mal. 1:5). He argues that because yqtl expresses movement it is unsuitable when one wants to express in words something present, whether it is in front of one, or only in one's consciousness, but which has not encountered or aroused the mind at that moment or entered into an interrelation with a definite case in which it may have happened. For this reason qtl verbs formed from adjectives (qati/u/l) and nomina agentium (qatal) are used to predicate the 'fact' which has come into being. This solution explains the origin of the qtl forms and their original function; because, reasons Knudtzon, 'it is more natural that something descriptive should be expressed rather than the present' (p. 58).[1]

Knudtzon, however, did not give the priority to yqtl. He followed Paul Haupt and suggested that the Assyrian iqátal was the first, with iqtul a close second.[2] Indeed, these two forms shared the same present meaning (emerging action) initially. Yqtl was used to relate past experiences including the (externally) present . In Assyrian a longer and shorter form arose but at the beginning there was no difference in meaning. Later, however, with the devel-

opment of the future Knudtzon suggests that the two forms divided the functions and tense spheres between them. The present and the future were expressed
by the original iqátal (the fuller form) and the past by iqtul (the shorter
form). He notes that apart from the Qal form the only difference between the
longer and shorter form is that one has an -i- vowel and the other an -a-
vowel before the final root consonant. These vowels came to indicate the past
and present/future tenses respectively (p. 50).

Knudtzon does not say what happened to the fuller (iqátal) form in Hebrew. He simply notes that it has only one form, yiqtol, with its original
meaning. It would appear, then, that the two forms coalesced in Hebrew but
did not become totally confused. He notes that the shorter form (iqtul) was
used for the past, and this has its counterpart in the consecutive yqtl construction in Hebrew. He regards wayyqtl as a definite past tense as it gradually lost its distinctive meaning and became indistinguishable from wqtl with
a past tense function (p. 51). Wayyqtl even took over the present meaning of
the qtl form, e.g. 'The Lord sitteth as king for ever' (וַיֵּשֶׁב) Ps. 29:10.
He does not think there are very many wayyqtls that have retained their
original present function (p. 56). This is very little different from Driver's
view of the form.

1.3.6.3   An Assessment of Knudtzon's Theory

Knudtzon's work marks a new approach to the problems of the HVS,
the historical-comparative approach. Up until his era the problems of the HVS
were looked at in comparative isolation from the rest of the Semitic languages.
He appears to have been the first to suggest that the wide range of functions
given to the yqtl form in Hebrew go back to a 'present' yqtl. In suggesting
this universal present function for the proto-Semitic yqtl or rather iqatal,
he is following Turner's idea who called it the Descriptive because the form
presents the subject performing the action of the root verb, the result of the
personal energy of the subject. Knudtzon's idea, while embracing Turner's
idea, goes much deeper into the psychological relationship between man and
his world. The yqtl form expresses dynamic thoughts and actions. Historical
events are portrayed as dynamically as they actually happened. It is the
form to convey the dramatic, the unfolding, the actual happening. This comes
to the same thing as Driver's nascent interpretation.

It would appear that the two main tenses in Hebrew, the past and present/

future tenses were originally denoted by two <u>yqtl</u> forms, <u>iqatal</u> and <u>iqtul</u>, as attested in Assyrian. In time the first and longer form became indistinguishable from the second and shorter form, and this is the situation, says Knudtzon, that we find in the Hebrew language today. In this way he can explain why <u>yqtl</u> is used to describe past events; it is the proto-Semitic <u>iqtul</u> form (the shorter form). In this way also he can explain why <u>yqtl</u> is used to describe pres./future events; it is an apocopated form of the proto-Semitic <u>iqatal</u>.[1] However, it is difficult to see how <u>iqtul</u> developed from <u>iqatal</u>, even though the two sets of themes may contain forms which are almost identical morphologically. The difficulties become even greater when it becomes apparent that Knudtzon's <u>iqatal</u> should read <u>iqáttal</u>, and the tone on <u>iqtul</u> should be placed thus <u>íqtul</u>.

Another difficulty with his proto-Semitic reconstruction is his suggestion that PS has two forms with identical 'present' functions, and only later did the one (<u>iqatal</u>) take the pres./fut. tense and the other (<u>iqtul</u>) come to be used almost exclusively for past events. Instances where <u>wayyqtl</u> have a present or future meaning in the OT are interpreted as remnants of the original 'present' function of <u>yqtl</u>. Instances such as אָז יָשִׁיר 'Then Moses sang...' are likewise remnants of the PS stage.

Two interesting points are brought out in Knudtzon's work. The first is his observation that if the <u>yqtl</u> form denotes movement then that movement does not lie in the verbal root otherwise stative verbs would not be found in the <u>yqtl</u> form. This would seem to suggest that the form itself does not favour one mode of action more than another, and hence his rejection of the terms Incomplete and Imperfect for this form may be valid. His own term is <u>Exsistens</u>, or Existence, but this is not exclusive to <u>yqtl</u> actions, for in a sense his Factum (which places the <u>state</u> before our eyes) is an existent fact.

His second contribution is his treatment of the active and stative <u>qtl</u> verbs. His decision not to divide the <u>qtl</u> category into two categories (active and stative) is consistent with his treatment of the <u>yqtl</u> category. The verbal roots may be divided into these categories, but he thinks the <u>form</u> itself denotes the fact of a happening or state. The <u>form</u> does not tell one whether the action is complete or incomplete, active or stative, this information is carried by the vowel changes.

* * * * * * *

1.3.7   The Waw Conservative Theory of Hans Bauer

We saw how Knudtzon postulated two Prefix-forms in PS to account for the wide range of tense functions in the Hebrew yqtl (or Imperfect). Bauer, probably taking the suggestion from Knudtzon, used the different bases for the qtl (or Perfect), i.e. adjectives and nomina agentium, with their different modes of action to trace the wide range of tense functions in the Hebrew qtl form.

Other scholars had been making various comparisons between the Assyrian and Hebrew verbal systems, but Bauer's theory in 1910 was by far the most complicated attempt to work out the probable stages of development of the Semitic verbal system.

Before examining Bauer's theory it would be appropriate to look at his objections to S. R. Driver's theory, since as he says—

> It was in the studying of this book [Driver's Treatise] that the conviction bore in upon me that we are here presented—not with a solution but rather—with a further problem..., the explanations of the author,...cannot possibly offer the last word on the subject. (1910:23)

Following his criticisms of Driver we shall examine the principal new nodal points in his own work in order to appreciate his solution.

1.3.7.1   Criticisms of S. R Driver's Theory

With respect to Driver's Imperfect he says:(1) It is inappropiate to refer to future actions, or actions not yet begun, as incomplete (p. 24, cf. SRD §21). (2) If yqtl denotes nascent action, it becomes impossible to reconcile this with the pluperfect meaning assumed by some Jewish grammarians (but see SRD, p. 88.) and many modern exegetes for a number of cases (p. 27, cf. SRD §76).[1](3) The assumption behind the term 'waw consecutive' that the action is to be considered as 'the temporal or logical consequence of an action referred to immediately before' can be disproved by the fact that eleven biblical books commence with the wayyqtl form and there can be no question of a connection in every case with the preceding book (p. 38). There are also cases where the most emphatic consequence can be found, yet no wayyqtl form follows because the waw is separated from the verb by a short insertion, e.g. Gen. 41:30-1, 'the famine will consume [וְכִלָּה] the land, and the plenty will be unknown [וְלֹא־יִוָּדַע] in the land' (p. 38, cf. Jer. 22:26). (4) Bauer rejects the suggestion that the reason for the use of the nascent yqtl form to describe past events lay in the mode of thought of the Hebrews with the following 'weighty consideration':

> Does it not seem exceedingly strange that the supposed switch
> of the narrative viewpoint can occur only after the particle
> wa (not wᵉ), and that even the shortest insertion (e.g. the
> negative lō') when separating the waw from the verb form, has
> the effect that the action is no longer understood as being in
> progress but can only be conceived of as completed? (p. 26)

Bauer comes to the conclusion that the syntax is responsible for the verb
form because there is no difference in meaning between the Imperfect consecutive and the simple Perfect with past meaning (p. 38). [1]

(5) Bauer contends that there is no uniform function for the Imperfect form.
The language, he says, has been credited with a miraculous play of fantasy
and with all kinds of intricately complicated thought processes, in order to
iron out the inconsistencies and contradictions in the use of the tense forms. [2]
He firmly believes that there is no common denominator by which the dispar-
ities can be bridged (pp. 19, 25, 28, 47).

(6) He objects to the abrupt switches of standpoint in Driver's theory
because this gives the discourse the character of something wavering and
unsteady, whereas to accept his theory that the consecutive tenses are old
archaic tenses presents us with a serene and uniform portrayal, in which old
and new forms of depiction are merely blended according to the free judgment
of the poet (p. 35).

Of these objections only (1) and (4) would give Driver any trouble.
He makes similar objections to Driver's understanding of the Perfect form.
He rejects the idea of a uniform function for the Perfect. The psychological
explanation, whereby something is considered to be past when in reality it is
still future, comes in for severe censure (pp. 28, 29). He firmly rejects
the idea of a prophetic Perfect (p. 34). He shows that the concept of
'completed action' is inappropriate for many verbs denoting bodily states (p. 13),
states of mind (p. 33), activity expressions (p. 33), verbs in proverbs and
dictums, and in subordinate clauses (p. 34). [3]

Bauer's real objection, then, is that Driver and others have assumed
that the relationship between form and function is a uniform one. Bauer, on
the other hand, contends that each form has two functions, or, to put it
another way, each function has two forms. They could hardly be more opposed
in their approach to the chief problem of the HVS.

1.3.7.2   The Principal Nodal Points in Bauer's Theory

The first nodal point is that there is no uniform relationship
between form and function in Hebrew. The reason for this is that the Perfect
form may belong to an older style (proto-Semitic or Assyrian), or to the
younger West Semitic style. According to the context it can have either a

present/future meaning (=PS style), or a past meaning (=WS style). Similarly with the Imperfect: in the older style it has a past meaning; in the younger style it has a present/future meaning. His first new hypothesis, then, is that Hebrew is not a unified language in the way Assyrian (=ES) is; it is a Mischsprache.[1] It is composed of two historically different tense systems.(pp. 19, 45).

The second nodal point is the suggestion that the West Semitic Perfect consecutive qataltá must be present in ES. He, therefore, formally identifies qataltá with the Assyrian ikášad (pp. 20, 30).[2]

The third nodal point is that the Imperative is the oldest form of the verb. The Imperfect must, therefore, be older than the suffixed Perfect because its morphology is closer to the Imperative (p. 7).

The fourth nodal point is that the Indo-Germanic languages originally had only the two time orders of Present and Past; the Future was formed by the combination of an auxilary word and the Present tense, e.g., 'I will go'. He argues:

> We must dismiss the conclusion...that the Semitic languages
> necessarily express categories of time or action other than our
> own. Otherwise one would have to assume that the temporal perspective
> of the ancient German, which stands on practically the same level
> as the Semitic, were incommensurable with our own modern way of
> thinking. Nobody, however, would want to draw such an absurd
> conclusion. (p. 49)

In the following sections we shall outline the way in which the verbal systems of East and West Semitic developed from a proto-Semitic origin.

1.3.7.3 A Diachronic-Synchronic View of the Development of the East and West Semitic Verbal Systems.

In the table below we have outlined Bauer's view of the way the proto-Semitic verbal system evolved. Down the left-hand side of this table are the letters A to L, and along the top the stages of development are marked with the numbers 1 to 8. We shall use these co-ordinates to refer to specific developments in our analysis. Each stage, i.e. each vertical column, gives us a synchronic view of the various diachronic developments. Bauer views these developments as taking place very gradually and over a period of thousands of years (p. 4). He draws an analogy with geological developments concerning which geologists have come to the conclusion that the same forces which are moulding today's layer have been operating continuously in the past, creating and destroying mountains. Likewise,' argues Bauer, 'it has become one of the most fruitful principles of linguistics to make the same factors which we see

LINE	PROTO-SEMITIC BASIS: Adjectives *qat/i/ul	Verbal Form *qutul	Noun Agentis *qatil	PROTO-SEMITIC DEVELOPMENT 1	2	3	PRE-HISTORIC DEVELOPMENT 4	5	6	7	8	Historical Situation	BIBLICAL HEBREW (Proto-Semitic / West Semitic; Archaic style / Younger style)
A				Primitive Nouns etc.	Primitive Nouns etc.	Primitive Nouns etc.	Nouns etc.	Nouns etc.	Nouns etc.	Nouns etc.	Nouns etc.	COMMON	Nouns etc.
B		qutul		Primitive Personal Pronouns	Younger Personal Pronouns	Historical Pronouns Dominant	Historical Personal Pronouns	Historical Personal Pronouns	Historical Personal Pronouns	Historical Personal Pronouns	Historical Personal Pronouns	COMMON	
C				Imper/Inf	Imper/Inf	Imper/Inf	Imper/Inf	Imper/Inf	Imper/Inf	Imper/Inf	Imper/Inf	COMMON	Imper/Inf
D				Jussive	Jussive	Jussive	Jussive	Jussive	Jussive	Jussive	Jussive	COMMON	Jussive
E				Jussive	Jussive	Jussive	Jussive	Jussive	Jussive	Jussive	Jussive	COMMON	Jussive
F		yá-qutul		yáqtul Universal	yáqtul Universal	yáqtul Universal minus Pres Part	yáqtul Form(Past)	yáqtul Narrative Form(Past)	yáqtul Narrative Form(Past)	Narrative Form(Past) yáqtul	Narrative Form(Past) yáqtul	WEST	yiqtól (Past)
G						Pres Part	Narrative Form(Past) yáqtul	yáqtul takes over Pres Part functions	qatála takes over Pres Part yáqtul(past) yáqtul	Pres Part yiqtól (v^eyaqtul)	Pres/Put yiqtól (v^eyiqtól)	WEST	yiqtól (Pres Part)
H						Pres Part yákóšad	Pres Part yákóšad	Pres Part yákóšad	Narrative Form(Past)	Impf Consec wayyiqtol	Impf Consec wayyiqtól	EAST	Impf Consec
J	(a) ← Non-Perfective → (b) qatal ← Perfective →			Pres Part kašad-tá	Pres Part qatal-tá	qatal-tá	Pres Part qatáltá	Perf Consec w^eqatáltá	Perf Consec w^eqatáltá	Perf Consec w^eqatáltá	Pres/Put qatáltá	WEST	Perf Consec; qatáltá (Pres Put)
K						qatal-tá	Past qatáltá (v^eqatáltū)	Past qatáltá (v^eqatáltū)	Past qatáltá (v^eqatáltū)	Past qatáltá (v^eqatáltū)	Past qatáltá (v^eqatáltū)	WEST	qatáltá v^eqatáltū (Past)
L	qat/i/ul			Permansive kašiq Stative kabid	Permansive kašiq Stative kabid	Permansive kašiq Stative kabid	Permansive kašiq Stative kabid	Permansive kašiq Stative kabid	Permansive kašiq Stative kabid	Permansive kašiq Stative kabid	Permansive kašiq Stative kabid	EAST	Stative kabid

A Diachronic-Synchronic View of Bauer's Theory
Regarding the Origin of the Semitic Verbal System

in the present life of languages responsible for the origin of these languages'
(p. 3). He suggests that 'all uniformity in language...is the product of
evolution and therefore secondary' (Grammar, 1922:§35d).

Using this table as our outline we shall go through each of the
eight stages of development noting Bauer's comments and arguments.

1.3.7.4 Stage 1 : The Universal Yaqtul Verb

If we dissect yaqtul into its component parts, we have a primitive
personal pronoun ya- and the verb q(u)tul. Originally, Bauer thinks, there were
only four primitive pers. pronouns: 'a-, na-, ya-, and ta- (p.8; §29b"). He
regarded these prefixed pronouns as very primitive because in the second and
third persons there is no distinction between gender and number. The prefixed
ta- was used for masculine and feminine singular and plural subjects indiscriminately, whereas the younger suffix pronouns removed the ambiguity completely,
i.e., -ta and -ti in the singular, and -tumu and -tinna in the plural. The
other component—qutul—served simultaneously as infinitive, imperative, and
finite verb in general, e.g., 'to rise', 'Rise!', and 'you rise' (ta-qutul).

Bauer gives two main reasons for thinking yaqtul is the oldest
finite verb form. (1) The imperative belongs to the more original strata of
the language, therefore that form of the verb will be older which stands
closest to it. This is commonly agreed to be the Imperfect. (2) The Imperfect
exhibits in its older layer a richness of vocalization similar to the imperative, and just as we would expect according to the analogy of other languages
(p. 7). He agrees with R. E. Brünnow (1893: 132) that a method of formation
which is still alive must be in any case younger than one which has ceased
to be active. In the case of Neo-Syriac dialects new suffix forms still continue to grow whereas new formations by prefixes do not occur anywhere (p. 6).

Since qutul was the original verb form, Bauer considered it irrelevant to talk in terms of tenses; being an all-embracing universal tense it
expressed both objective (Driver's 'kind of time') and subjective (Driver's
'order of time') relations. In short, it was a universal multi-functional
verb, denoting no time in particular, merely action (p. 10); for this reason
Bauer preferred to call it an 'aorist' verb form (p. 24). In this respect,
Bauer argued, it resembled the Chinese and probably also the Indo-Germanic
verb in being timeless (pp. 35, 46, §35g).

A synchronic view of stage 1 shows that there was only one finite
verb form (yaqtul) for relating events (F1).

1.3.7.5   Stage 2 : The Development of the Suffix Personal Pronouns

If we dissect qataltá into its component parts these are qatal
and -tá. And since the components of a compound form must be older than
the compound form itself, therefore the suffixed pronominal elements must
be older than the form qataltá, see B2.

1.3.7.6   Stage 3 : The Present Participle Qatal

It is generally recognised, says Bauer, that the form of the
Semitic Perfect grew up from the combination of a verbal noun with the personal pronoun (p. 12), i.e., qatal-tá = a killer--you.(At this stage the pronoun carried the tone throughout, i.e., tá-qutul and qatal-tá [p. 37].)The
close combination of the verbal noun with the pers. pronoun was gradually
and inevitably felt to be a finite verb.

Bauer recognised, however, that the verbal noun qattāl (or qatāl
as he preferred to write it [p. 12]) could have denoted the time sphere of
a Present Participle or a Past Participle, depending on the mode of action
inherent in the nomen agentis. He thinks it highly unlikely that the new
verb form (qatala) could have denoted both perfective and imperfective action.
Inevitably the form would become identified with one or other of these modes
of action, and this is what happened. Qataltá became a Present Participle,
with functions similar to those of the conjugated participle in Syriac
(pp. 17-18).[1] The effect of this new verbal form on the multi-functional
yaqtul is best expressed in Bauer's own words:

> The entry of the verbal form qatala into the organism of the language
> results at the same time in terminating the timeless character [i.e.
> the universal time] of the Imperfect. As the newcomer settles and
> extends itself in a part of the territory in which hitherto yaqtul
> was the long accustomed sole ruler, the latter withdraws into the
> region which is left unoccupied. Only now...does it have any mean-
> ing to speak of tense....In this way the problem...reduces itself,
> roughly speaking, to a simple subtraction solution. Whereas we can
> denote the area of application of qatala with a relative exactness
> in a positive way, the territory of yaqtul can really only be
> determined negatively, i.e., as the remainder of the original time-
> less and thus universal function, in as far as it has not been taken
> over by qatala. (pp. 15-16)

If we look at stage 3 synchronistically we can just begin to see a division
into East and West Semitic. With the emergence of the Present Participle
kašadtá at H3, yaqtul at EFG became a Past Participle (=E3), and apparently
did not undergo any further shifts in function, as can be seen at H8 and E8
respectively (see p. 18). Likewise we can begin to see the WS verbal system

emerging at J3 and F3, where the same thing has happened as in ES. If we assume for a moment that Assyrian had a <u>suffixed</u> Present Participle (<u>i.e.</u> kašadtá) at H3, then East and West Semitic were indistinguishable at this point in time of their development.

Bauer suggests that it was during the settling-down stage, when it depended upon the individual whether to use <u>qatala</u> or <u>yaqtul</u> for the Present Participle sphere, that Babylonian-Assyrian separated itself off from the common language (p. 18). The subsequent development of these two forms, compared with the proto-Semitic, was relatively small, argues Bauer. The unsettled relationships of the PS language have merely consolidated themselves by the fact that <u>ikšud</u> has been completely ousted from the present (imperfective) sphere, and <u>ikašad</u> has become the sole governing form in this sphere (p. 20).

Bauer rejects Barth's suggestion that the growth of the Assyr. Permansive provided the occasion for the change to the prefix form. His own suggestion is unclear, it reads:

> I would like to suggest an alternative explanation. If we assume that Assyr. did originally conjugate *<u>kašad</u> like the <u>qatal</u> conjugation, then the prefixing and affixing flexions coincide even in this case in the third persons of the Reflexive stems (I.2 and IV) according to the Assyrian phonetic laws: *<u>iktašad</u> and *<u>yaktašad</u> both become <u>iktašad</u>...; *<u>inkašad</u>, *<u>yankasid</u> become <u>ikkašad, ikkašid,</u> differing, therefore, only in the vowels of the second radical. It thus appears very likely that the coalescence which arose according to phonetic laws in the aforementioned forms, extended itself by analogy to the other persons and stems, the (secondary and rarer) present following the lead of the (original and more common) preterite. (p. 20)

Firstly, it is not clear what he means by 'affixing flexions' in Assyrian. The Permansive is the only affixed form in Assyrian. Secondly, the examples he gives are all prefix forms to start with. And thirdly, the present does not appear to have been the first to adopt the prefix form of conjugation which implies that originally it was a suffix conjugation, since the form <u>ikašad</u> is regarded as secondary by Bauer. It is possible to make sense of the phrase 'the prefixing and affixing flexions' if we assume that these stand for the Preterite and Present conjugations respectively in proto-Semitic, but applied or transferred to the equivalent conjugations in ES. If so, then ES did have the suffixed Present Participle <u>kašadtá</u>. and therefore stage 3 did actually exist at one time. We may conclude from this that East and West Semitic were indistinguishable at this stage. (See 1.3.7.15 for the probable source of Bauer's idea.)

At H4 kašadtá undergoes a morphological metamorphosis to emerge as
ikašad(or probably yakašad originally). Kašadtá.as a result,was ousted from
East Semitic completely.

It is not clear whether the Permansive belongs to stage 3, and is
therefore a proto-Semitic form, or emerged independently in East and West.
Concerning the origin of the Permansive/stative he says:

> We must think of the forms qatila and qatula as having arisen in
> a similar way to qatala. Proto-Semitic adjectives such as *'amuq
> 'deep', *salim 'prosperity', *jabis 'dry', first developed forms
> such as *'amuqta and *salimta and *jabista, by way of suffixing
> the personal pronouns. (p. 13)

He saw no semantic difference between qatila and qatula in the PS period.
He thinks that the sense of a continuing state may in the beginning have
been associated with a few qatul adjectives; this was developed further
through analogy. He also thinks that this applies to the forms qatilta and
qatalta. Originally they did not denote transitory states and actions
respectively. Certain verbs did denote these distinctions, but there was
no consistency between form and function in the PS period. The distinctions
between qatala and qatila on the one hand, and qatila and qatula on the other,
are not logically, but only historically, comprehensable. In other words, the
thematic vowels in PS were allophones not allophonemes.In a footnote on p. 15
he identifies the three forms (qata/i/u/la) with the entry of qataltá into
the language at stage 3.   Later, when he set out to account for ikašad
in ES he felt compelled to identify it with the WS qataltá because,'the
Permansive...does not enter into the picture because it contains a qatil and
a qatul but no qatal, and moreover, the full form of the affixes betrays its
recent origin' (p. 20, emphasis mine). It would appear that East Semitic did
not form the Permansives qatila and qatula until its inherited Present Participle suffixed form—qataltá—assimilated to the preterite prefix form (i.e.
qataltá becomes taqatal). So clearly in Bauer's mind Assyrian created the prefix form ikašad before it went on to develop the suffixed forms (qati/u/la).
Therefore, it would seem the forms qati/u/la do not belong to the PS language but were developed independently in East and West Semitic after ES split
off from PS. We have therefore placed the earliest appearance of the ES Permansive at L5, and the WS Statives a stage earlier, at L4; although if we
were to take Bauer literally and accept that the Stative entered the language
organism at the same time as qataltá, then it should appear at stage 3, which
would pose problems for ES.

The origin of the Permansive/Stative precludes their ever being considered as proper verbs; being PS adjectives they were unable to form participles or imperatives (pp. 13, 33, §35i). They never completely cast aside their nominal character (§35i).

In spite of the morphological difference between the two Present Participles in East and West Semitic at this stage, and the possibility that WS had developed its Stative forms, there is remarkable affinity in functions of their two main verb forms. Both divisions have confined yaqtul to the expression of past and completed action (see E4 and F4). And both have limited their respective Present Participles to the expression of present or incomplete action, and durative or habitual action whether this occurs in the past, present, or future (pp. 17, 22, 32). It was never used to denote perfective action (pp. 17, 21). It was the identity of functions that led Bauer to equate the Perfect consecutive in Hebrew with the ikašad form in ES. He noted the following similarity of functions: both can be used as imperatives (p. 31); as jussives (pp. 23, 31); to express a wish (p. 31); in legal prescriptions (p. 31); with a past frequentative meaning (pp. 21, 22, 31-2); present/future (p. 30, passim); they can continue a preceding yaqtul (p. 28); neither the Perfect consecutive nor ikašad are used for the pure present (p. 30). The sole basis, then, for his identification rests on the similarity of functions in their respective language groups (p. 20).

1.3.7.8 Stage 5 : The Past Participle Qatál

At this stage an unusual development occurred in WS in that we get a repeat performance of stages 3 and 4 with the introduction of the perfective qatálta. We noted earlier (1.3.7.4) that PS took up only the non-perfective aspect of the nomina agentium, i.e., the Present Participle qataltá. Now, however, WS took up the perfective side of the nomen agentis and formed a Past Participle qatálta. Because of the change of tone position qatálta was thought of as quite a different word from qataltá (p. 37). With the arrival of another past tense form, yaqtul 'was deprived of its narrative function and limited to its other, not precisely defined, applications, which we can define approximately as those corresponding to a Present Participle' (p. 18), i.e., with the arrival of qatálta (at K5) it took over some of yaqtul's past functions at G5, and forced yaqtul to take up a Present Participle function at G6, thereby creating another 'new' verb form.[1] This 'new' yaqtul form was also distinguished from the older one by a change of tone position, or as Bauer has put it:

It can be presumed that the shift in territory of the tenses
ran parallel in time with a change in accent, so that of the two
forms only the free standing ones were affected while the attached
forms [i.e., the consecutive forms] remained on at the old level.
(p. 37)

It is taken for granted that WS underwent a change of word-order so that
the verb came to the head of the sentence and thereby into association with
Bauer's 'conservative waw'. In ES, which Bauer equates with PS, the verb
usually comes last in the sentence with the conjunctive -ma suffixed to
the narrative preterite iqtul forms. The vertical line of dots between stages
4 and 5 marks this change of word-order.

1.3.7.9 Stage 6 : The West Semitic Yaqtúl Verb

This new verb form developed as a direct result of the emergence
of the perfective qatálta. Because of the change of tone position yaqtúl
was thought of as quite a different word from yáqtul, in much the same way
that the tone position in words such as présent and presént helps to
distinguish morphologically similar words in English (p. 37).

Bauer gives two explanations for WS yaqtúl = Present Participle.
If we go back to stage 2 there was only one multi-functional verb form—
yáqtul (mil'el tone). At stage 3 a new verb form appears (qataltá) and yáqtul's
semantic area is halved to denote perfective action only. At stage 5 another
qatálta form appears in yáqtul's remaining perfective area, and this development
forced yáqtul to move into the non-perfective area corresponding to the Present
Participle—the shift in territory being accompanied by a shift of tone. Bauer
thought that this non-perfective function may have been retained by yáqtul
long after qataltá took over its original non-perfective territory (p. 18, 25-6).
so, then yáqtul = non-perfective action before the introduction of qatálta, and If
therefore it is slightly misleading to link its non-perfective function to
the rise of the perfective qatálta at stage 5. His other explanation for the
non-perfective (Present Participle) function of yáqtul emerges in his explanation of the Jussive meaning in Assyrian, he says of the Jussive, it—

>...cannot be understood in terms of the preterite function of ikšud,
>but must fall within an earlier age when ikšud still retained the
>more comprehensive meaning of yaqtul which it has kept in the West
>Semitic languages. (p. 21)

It seems that he is referring to the WS yiqtol form which functions in all
time spheres as well as having a Jussive and an imperative function. Hence
his 'new' WS yiqtol = non-perfective action, is in fact a direct descendant of
the PS yaqtul = multi-functional verb.[1] He notes that wayyiqtol, just like the

PS <u>yaqtul</u>, is timeless, and is thus able to express all modes of time (p. 27). With the emergence of the new non-perfective <u>yiqtol</u> West Semitic possessed two <u>yiqtol</u> forms distinguished only by the position of the verbal tone, <u>i.e.</u> the archaic or universal <u>yíqtol</u>, and the younger West Semitic <u>yiqtól</u> with non-perfective functions. Later on, at Stage 8, the tone position of the archaic or preterite <u>yíqtol</u> shifted to conform with the younger form.

1.3.7.10   Stage 7 : The Consecutive Forms

Bauer envisaged two contemporary trends during this stage affecting the 'free' forms of the older or PS style. Firstly, the new WS perfective <u>qatálta</u> replaced the 'free' PS perfective <u>yáqtul</u> as the tense of narration (p. 18). And secondly, the new WS imperfective <u>yiqtol</u> replaced the free imperfective <u>qataltá</u>. However, in both cases each of the older forms 'kept back a number of lesser or greater areas within the territory seceded to the other', <u>i.e.</u> to the new forms (p. 19), so that they did not die out completely. In the Hebrew bible there are around 770 simple or 'free' Imperfects with past or perfective meaning, and approximately 2,700 'free' Perfects with present/future or imperfective meaning. The major evidence for the PS style, however, is present in the consecutive forms. These constitute the older or PS layer of Hebrew. At this stage they retained their original accentuation, <u>i.e.</u> <u>wayyíqtol</u> and <u>w^eqātaltá</u>. Concerning these PS forms Bauer says:

> An archaic style must be present in those combinations with <u>waw</u>, an inherited conventionally maintained habit of speech...which has been preserved in the fixed sentence structure. But only in this structure; as soon as the restricted speech context is in any way disturbed, <u>i.e.</u>, anywhere where a new insertion occurs, immediately a switch of functions takes place, and the modern style comes into its own. (p. 26)

Indeed, so fragile is this archaic syntax that if the speaker desires to make a negative statement by inserting the negative particle לא(!) he can only use the younger style. Bauer traces this phenomenon to the following linguistic law:

> Where the verbal form was tied closely to a particle the law of resistance to change has shown itself stronger than the drive toward change....In this the blind force of laws governing language is once again so appropriately revealed—laws according to which what is attached survives, and what is free floating goes on developing. (pp. 19, 36)

Archaisms are preserved in poetry and in elevated prophetic speech (pp. 33-5), yet its older style was sufficiently distinct that there was little room for ambiguity. He says:

> In raising his listeners up into a higher realm, the prophet chooses

the form qātal in its archaic meaning to make the events more
immediate; for his part the listener, as soon as he becomes
conscious of this elevated style, grasps the perfect no longer as
the tense of the past, but immediately present to the mind, as
present/future. (p. 35)

He regards the Imperfect consecutive as the equivalent of the Perfect qātal,
and therefore inter-changeable (pp. 26, 34).[1]The same thing applies in
the case of the Perfect consecutive and yiqtól (p. 28).

It is clear in Bauer's mind that the Hebrew language has simply
duplicated its older verbal system, 'a situation', he thinks, 'which reasoning
men would never have thought of...since it came about through the blind force
of linguistic laws' (p. 36).

1.3.7.11   Stage 8 : The Historical Situation

Once the younger forms became well established the tone position
of the older forms shifted to conform to their accentuation; so that the
archaic yíqtol and wayyíqtol assimilated to the younger pattern—yiqtól,
and the archaic qātaltá and weqātaltá (but not always in the 2nd pers. masc.
sing. or 1st pers. sing.) assimilated to the younger qātálta and weqātálta
without in any way indicating 'a shift in territory'. The cause of this
assimilation may have been the linking of two synonymous Perfects or Imperfects
(p. 38). These analogical developments could have been going on for a long time
any time after stage 4, but by stage 8 they were completed and very much the
norm.

In this outline of Bauer's theory we have concentrated on the
main aspects of his view since it is not possible to take up many of the
minor points and supporting arguments in a work of this nature. In the following
sections we shall look at the difficulties standing in the way of this theory
replacing that of Driver's theory.

1.3.7.12   A Critical View of Bauer's Theory

The chief problem Bauer is attempting to solve is how can the Perfect
have a past function on the one hand, yet have a present/future function on the
other hand? Likewise, how can the Imperfect have a present/future function and at
the same time have a past function?[2]He says that they cannot have both functions
and therefore we must look for a historical solution whereby two Perfect and
two Imperfect forms arose in the language (distinguished by the position of the
tone) each of which had either a pres/fut. or a past significance. He claims
to have found just such a historical solution, as we have outlined above. The
following are just a few of the difficulties with his approach, his presupposit-

ions, and some of his proposed stages of development.

1.3.7.13   The Priority of the <u>Yaqtul</u> Form

The main reason for thinking that this form, as opposed to the suffix-form, has the priority is based on the form of the imperative.[1] He rightly thinks that this mood belongs to the very beginning of human speech, and therefore if its form has not changed it must go back to the PS stage. This is a reasonable suggestion, and consequently his argument that that form of the verb which comes closest to it has the better claim to be the oldest finite verb form is likewise a reasonable deduction. When, however, he suggests that the pronominal prefix elements are older than the suffix elements, he is not on safe ground. He has also the problem of determining whether the vowel allomorphemes /ø/, /ĭ/, /ă/, /ŭ/, suffixed to the imperatives, belong to the earliest period of the language, or whether there was only one imperative *<u>qutul</u> which was ambiguous as regards number and gender. He is then left with the problem how the early speakers managed to circumvent the ambiguity. Similarly in the case of the primitive Imperfects, for here Bauer envisages only four primitive personal pronouns which were prefixed to the 'verb' <u>qutul</u>, viz., <u>'a—qutul</u>, <u>na—qutul</u>, <u>ya—qutul</u>, and <u>ta—qutul</u>.[2] The latter form <u>ta—qutul</u> is ambiguous as regards number and gender, since it may refer to all the second persons both singular and plural, and masculine and feminine, as well as the third feminine forms—singular and plural. Bauer does not explain how the early speakers resolved these ambiguities, as they must have done quite quickly. In the historical situation these are very clearly resolved by the final vowels, therefore the suggestion is hypothetical that there was an earlier period in the language when there was considerable ambiguity before the final vowels were introduced.

A further weakness is his assumption that the Imperfect must be older than the Perfect because its form is closer to the Imperative. It may be closer but which came first, the Imperfect or the Imperative? It does not harm Bauer's reconstruction whether the Imperative preceded or sprang from the <u>yqtl</u> form. It is only when the origin for the Imperative is sought for elsewhere that difficulties arise, see 1.3.8.31 and 1.3.9.15. It is true to say, however, that the majority of modern scholars who have written on the subject regard the Imperative as an abbreviated form of the Imperfect. The following is a selection from a host of scholars who view the imperatival form as an apocopated form of the Prefix-form: D. Gutman (1971:47, 75); S. Moscati (1969:136); M. M. Bravmann (1951-2:54-6); I. J. Gelb (1952:219f.); E. Y. Kutscher (1965:21-51); I. Nordheimer (1841: II, p. 193); A. B. Rich (1874:121); T. H. Robinson (Syriac: 1962:58); F. Rosenthal (Aramaic: 1961:45); W. Wright (Arabic: 1896: I, p. 61); T. Nöldeke (Syriac: 1904:141); A. Dillmann (Ethiopic: 1907:174); C. H. Gordon (Ugaritic: UT 1965:77). W. J. Martin made the observation that—

> In a situation when the person directly addressed is present there is no need to use a specific personal pronoun.... It would be easier to explain the imperative as a truncated form of the imperfective, than to account for the re-introduction of the pronominal element into the Akkadian relative.
> (1957:318)

As long a go as the time of Ibn Janah (1106) Jewish grammarians considered the imperative as essentially a part of the Prefix-form (cf. S. L. Skoss, 1955:15 n. 41). R. Gordis gives examples of archaic imperatives said to be derived from the Prefix-form (1937:107). If so, this would support Martin's point.

Bauer, of course, saw the connection between the imperative and yaqtul in the universal function of *qutul which may have been suggested on the analogy of the evolution of life from a single-celled organism.[1] Later on Bauer uses the geological analogy to explain the two layers in the Hebrew verbal system. This was an unfortunate model since the boundaries between older and younger rocks are sharply drawn. There may be gaps of centuries between two adjacent layers plus the fact that there is seldom any direct relationship between such layers. These factors make it unsuitable as a model for linguistic developments.

G. R. Driver (1936) objected to Bauer's view that the Imperfect was older than the Perfect. Bauer had suggested that the Imperfect 'exhibits in its older layer a richness of vocalization' which somehow meant that it was thereby older than the Perfect (see 1.3.7.4). Driver nullifies this argument with the observation:

> Bauer's argument that the varieties of the aorist and imperative are evidence of the priority of yaqtul and qutul as against qatil may be two-edged; for it may be argued with equal justification that every form, however manifold are the varieties of it even in the earliest period of the language, must at some time have been derived from a single simple form. (1936:15f., cf. p. 21)

Driver, however, did not appear to appreciate the strength of Bauer's first and main argument for the Imperfect's priority, namely, its closeness to the form of the Imperative (see 1.3.8.31).

In conclusion, then, even if Bauer is correct in seeing the Imperfect and the imperative in an original *qutul verb, he has not established
whether the imperative mood is older than the indicative or any other mood,
and consequently, he cannot rule out the possibility that a suffixed indicative form based on an equally old verb *qatal existed alongside the PS
imperative, or may even have preceded the indicative *qutul form. He can,
however, claim that his yaqtul form is as old as the imperative and consequently,
he has put forward a better case than Driver who also tries to link the suffix
(permansive) form with the imperative. With respect to the supposed universal
functions of Bauer's yaqtul form, we have shown that this fits in well with
a particular view of language development which is outside the scope of this
dissertation to deal with.

1.3.7.14   The Identification of ES taqátal with the WS qataltá
This was Bauer's second nodal point and it raises a number of difficulties for his theory. Firstly, did ES have the suffixed form originally and
only later replace it with the preformative form? If it did then we have evidence that ES could throw off PS formations without leaving any archaic remnants, and thus we have to leave open the possibility that it could have done
so on a number of occasions in the past, and consequently, no great weight
should be attached to omissions of features which may appear in all the other
Semitic languages. If on the other hand, ES from the very beginning used the
prefix form (taqátal), and WS used the suffix form, then it is not clear which
method of conjugation can claim the priority. If the suffix form is older, and if
ES never had the suffixed qatalta form, then we would have to conclude that
it was at this point in time that the split between East and West Semitic
occurred, which in turn means that the permansive/stative forms do not belong
to the PS level, but were developed independently in East and West Semitic. It
will also follow that whereas the stative forms in WS (i.e. qatila and qatula)
are secondary, the permansive forms in ES are primary forms. In view of the
fact that the Egyptian language retains the suffix form (Bauer, pp. 7-8), it
seems difficult to escape the logical conclusion that this form was in existence prior to the East-West split, unless, of course, we postulate that
Egyptian also developed it independently.

Secondly, Bauer postulates the form qatāl as the nomen agentis for
the active qatal form; but G. R. Driver says that his qatāl nomem agentis is

purely hypothetical (p. 15),[1] while E. König (1911:719-20) adds that not this but qātil is its true and normal type.

Thirdly, it is now clear that Bauer's iqátal should in fact be written iqáttal which further removes it from the WS qatala; so that he not only has to account for the doubled second radical but also for the switching around of the pronominal element and indeed the replacement of the older pronominal elements by the later ones. If the morphological difficulty involved only the position of the same pronominal elements then we could find parallels for this within ES, e.g., the conjunctive(-ma)is frequently found suffixed to the verb which is not the case in WS.[2] But here we have a change of pronominal elements plus the doubling of the second radical, hence there can be no question of a formal identification as these forms stand in their historical contexts.

Fourthly, he thinks that the functions common to the two forms are so identical that we must accept that they are basically the same 'tense'. He — clearly appears to have overlooked the fact, however, that while ES may use iqátal quite freely in descriptive narrative of past events, the WS (wᵉ)qātaltá always occurs in direct speech contexts, and predominantly of events which still lie in the future. Admittedly, S. R. Driver (1892 §113,4) and others speak of a Perfect consecutive used in a past frequentative sense, but in Driver's case he thinks these Perfects lose their individuality and pass under the sway of the preceding or dominant verb (1892:118, 139-40), even if there is no preceding verb present.(See pp. 75-76 for my criticisms of this view.)

Fifthly, Ethiopic has both the Suffix form (qatala) and the Prefix form (yeqáttel), the latter written yeqatel by Bauer (p. 44). Because the middle radical was not doubled Bauer suggested that it was a new internal Ethiopic development from qatala on the analogy of the duplicated stems where yeqattel stands alongside qattala, and yeqātel alongside qātala (p. 44). It does seem remarkable that both ES and Ethiopic hit upon the same verb form independently including a similar tone position. This similarity caused P. Haupt in 1878 to postulate that 'where the Assyrian and Ethiopic agree in forms (and words), we are dealing not with new formations...but with the primitive possessions of the Semitic family of speech. We therefore maintain:
1. The Assyrian Present (iqátal) and the Ethiopic Imperfect (yĕqátĕl) are no new formations, but the oldest verbal forms of the Semitic family of speech.' (1878:246). E Hincks, as early as 1855, noted the similarity between the Ethiopic and Assyrian forms (Oct. 1855:153), but he was cautious not to rely on such similarities as proof of a special connection between the two languages (1866:488). Not so cautious was Haupt who drew up 12 similarities and

declared that 'Next to Assyrian among the sister tongues stands Ethiopic'(JAOS 13 (1889):ccli;[1] cf. 1878:ccxlvi). It was Hincks who discovered that the middle radical of the Present was 'frequently doubled'. He considered this 'an abuse' (Oct 1855:153), and this opinion seems to have prevailed for the next one hundred years (cf. G. R. Driver, 1936:73). Hence, in the light of the fact that the second radical is frequently doubled, Bauer's explanation of the Ethiopic yeqáttel is considerably weakened, and the way is left open to identify it with the Assyrian iqáttal (but see W. Leslau, 1957:251-3 and 1.3.8.1(8) below).

1.3.7.15 The late development of the Permansive/Stative

According to Bauer (1.3.7.6) the adjectival forms qatilta and qatulta do not belong to the PS stage, but were formed independently in East and West Semitic after ES split off from the common language. This is a strange situation given Bauer's conjecture that qatal + tá was initially not a verb, but a nomen agentis plus a personal pronoun: it meant 'a murderer—you'. Only later was it felt to be a verb, which raises the possibility that during this intermediate period the personal pronoun could have been suffixed to adjectives as well as to nouns (e.g. šarráku 'I (am) king'), without them being felt to be verbs. But according to Bauer this did not happen, and for a good reason. According to his scheme the forms qatilta and qatulta could not be prior to iqátal (=qatalta in WS), because these forms could not be considered as proper verbs. Only when the nomen agentis (qatál) had become a verb could the other adjectival forms be patterned on its form. But this explanation fails to account for forms such as šarráku 'I (am) king', which could have stood alongside the nomen agentis forms such as qatálku 'I (am) a murderer' before these 'were felt to be verbs'. If for a moment we conjecture that the three forms qatala, qatila, and qatula, were developed simultaneously in PS it would imply that since ES had the qatila and qatula it must also have had the qatala form, and now it becomes clear why Bauer did not envisage a simultaneous development, because it would imply that East Semitic lost the qatala form, whereas he appears to think ES never had a suffixed nomen agentis form.

Although Bauer does not acknowledge the source of very many of his ideas, it would appear that he had read P. Haupt's article "The Oldest Semitic Verb-Form" (1878:ccxliv-ccli) very carefully. In his paper (1910:5) he mentions Haupt's article in order to reject his view that the Assyrian iqátal is the oldest verb form. However, Haupt not only suggested that Semitic formed its original verbs on the preformative pattern, but he provided Bauer with two other ideas. Firstly, he suggested that the variety in the forms of the Imper-

fect when contrasted with the Perfect indicated the greater antiquity of the
former (Haupt, p. ccxlix). Secondly, by comparing Bauer's puzzling explanation
for the change from qatalta to taqatal (see 1.3.7.6) with that of Haupt's
explanation, it becomes clear that Bauer is thinking of the Arabic forms. For
by placing the Arabic VIIth conjugation inqatala alongside the Imperfect
yanqatilu, one obtains a superficial resemblance in the 3rd person singular
forms (but not in the other persons). It appears to be Bauer's view that the
close resemblance in the case of the 3 pers. sing. forms in Assyrian
triggered the switch for all the other persons in the reflexive themes and
that this development spread by analogy throughout all the other themes.

1.3.7.16   The WS Perfective qatálta

We saw above (1.3.7.6) how Bauer mapped out the rise of the non-perfective qataltá in WS with its ES counter-part taqátal. However, if we accept his
scheme we are left with difficult transitions in its development. First of all
he acknowledges that the form qatal + tá was not a tense or time order, but
a mode of action order. He realized that in the early stages the aspects of
perfective and non-perfective action could not be imposed upon a verbal root,
but 'lie in the concrete meaning of the verb itself...to be more precise in...
the mode of action' (p. 16). At this stage, then, there were no time orders
as such, so that in this period of the development of PS the suffix -tá was
added to perfective and non-perfective nomina agentium such as 'the Overcomer--
you', 'the Freer of the Fatherland--you', where the action is completed and
therefore belongs to the perfective past. The situation was no different in
concepts such as 'a Wanderer--you', 'a Striver--you', and 'a Singer--you',
where the action is not completed but continues or is repeated. Bauer then
suggests that the combination of the nomen agentis and -tá were gradually
felt to be a verb, with the consequent result that 'it appears right away
improbable that two such opposed meanings could stand alongside one another
for so long within one verbal form' (p. 17). Yet we have seen that they were
able to stand alongside one another for probably centuries before they were
'gradually felt to be verbs'. Bauer thinks that the language dropped all the
perfective forms such as 'an Overcomer--you', 'a Murderer--you', etc., reserv-
ing the 'new' verb form for the non-perfective nomina agentium 'a Singer--you',
'a Wanderer--you'. We then encounter another difficulty at this point, because
ES either did not have the suffixed -tá in the period before the compound
qataltá 'was gradually felt to be a verb', or if it did it apparently switched
over to the prefix form as soon as the earlier form (qataltá) was gradually

felt to be a verb. Now if ES split off from the common language as soon as
qataltá was felt to be a verb, How could it have restricted itself to the non-
perfective if it was really a nomen agentis with prefixed pronominal elements?
And in WS how are we to account for the development that envisages perfective
and non-perfective remaining alongside one another in the pre-verbal state and
in the historical situation that we see in Biblical Hebrew, but apparently
not in an intermediate state? There is, of course, no evidence that a verbal
noun of the form qatāl ever existed in PS, and we have seen that the second
radical is doubled in ES, hence the assumption that qatala and iqattal go back
to a single PS form must be seriously questioned.

1.3.7.17   The WS Imperfective yiqtól

This form is held by Bauer to belong to the younger layer of WS
(1.3.7.9). Just as the younger qatálta was distinguished from the older
qataltá by the position of the tone, and hence were regarded as completely
different words, so he believes the same thing occurred in the case of the
new Imperfect; it was pronounced yiqtól whereas the older one was pronounced
yíqtol (or yáqtul). He regarded the form yiqtól as a new creation. He appears
also to think that its pres/fut. meaning is a new innovation in the WS system,
and is later than the emergence of the qatálta perfective form. We may trace
its rise as follows in Bauer's own words:

> In the West Semitic languages...the form qatala underwent a further
> development in which the entire stock of tense relationships was
> completely remoulded. It is here that the perfective meaning...
> asserted itself and carried over into the whole stock of [perfective
> nomina agentium] verbs. In this way the form became suited to serve
> as the tense of narration,...yaqtul as a result was deprived of
> its narrative function and limited to its other, not precisely
> defined, applications, which we can define...as...a present parti-
> ciple. (p. 18)

There are a number of interrelated problems here. Firstly, we have a stage
where the yaqtul form is the only verb in PS, but alongside it was the semi-
verbal form qatal + tá with perfective and non-perfective meaning. The perfective
was dropped from PS only to re-emerge in WS after the split when it took over
from yaqtul as the tense of narration. That the perfective nomina agentium
were never developed in PS is, a priori, hard to accept. Secondly, we have many
instances in biblical Hebrew where wayyiqtol is replaced by weqatal (cf. 2 Sam
6:16 with 1 Chr 15:29; 1 Kgs 3:11 with 2 Chr 1:11; 2 Kgs 19:26 with Isa 37:27),
but where it seems unlikely that wayyiqtol would be forced to take on a new
role or a new tense function. Thirdly, he has produced no analogies for his
proposed developments which might give them a measure of probability, espec-

ially given his assurance that the factors which we see operating in the life of present-day languages have been responsible for the origin of these languages (p. 3). It is hard to see how this interchangeableness would force wayyiqtol into the pres/fut. sphere.

Fourthly, he gives two sources for the new WS yiqtól. Firstly, it only appears after the perfective qatálta ousts yaqtul from the narrative function to which it had been restricted by the emergence of the non-perfective qataltá. Secondly, it would appear that the non-perfective qataltá did not completely take over all yaqtul's pres/fut. functions and it is this residual function that has been preserved in the WS yiqtól. If this is the case then the WS yiqtól cannot be regarded as a new form since it is a PS function.

1.3.7.18   The Change of Tone Position

Bauer glosses over the fact that whether the Perfect has past, present, or future meaning, the tone is always on the penultimate syllable in the case of the 1st and 2nd pers. sing. masc., which implies that the tone does not function as a tense discriminator. The same applies in the case of yiqtól, it can be either past, present, or future. This fact has been ignored by Bauer and his predecessors. Instead, he has constructed his theory around the observation that the 1st and 2nd pers. sing. forms usually have ultima tone when they have a pres/fut. meaning, and are preceded by the waw conjunction, but a penultima tone when they have a past meaning. No attempt was made to explain the contexts in which this occurs in Hebrew, since this is the only WS language in which it occurs. Its function in Hebrew has not been understood, yet it has been applied to all the WS languages. He does not explain why qātálnu never takes ultima tone in Hebrew. He suggests that it was the close association of qātal with waw that enabled wᵉqātaltá to retain its old meaning and intonation (p. 30). One wonders, then, why wayyiqtol lost its penultima tone but retained its old meaning.

Bauer had reasoned that the position of the tone distinguished the non-perfective qataltá from the perfective qatálta (likewise with yiqtol), yet it is quite clear that many perfective verbs have the ultima tone and many non-perfective verbs have the penultima tone; therefore, the tone position is irrelevant as a perfective/non-perfective marker. Yet it was precisely on this observation that Bauer introduced his tense opposition Pres/Fut. : Past. This highlights the danger of taking a phenomenon from one language and indiscriminately applying it, as a broad principle or characteristic, to a cognate group of languages. It would have been better had Bauer explained the conditions under which the change of tone took place in Hebrew, which, of course, no one has done satisfactorily to-date, and then he would have been in a better position to see if it could be applied to the PS stage of development. Until this work has been done any discussion on tone changes in PS must remain speculative.

1.3.7.19   The Two Layers or Styles in Hebrew

One of the reasons why Bauer objected to S.R. Driver's theory was that Driver and others held that the Perfect always referred to completed action and the Imperfect to incomplete action. Bauer retorted: 'the use of the Perfect for something future appears totally inconceiveable' (p. 29), and, 'a solution to the problem in question is altogether impossible, as long as we cling to the absolute perfect meaning of qatal' (p. 30). He argues that if the Hebrew writer expresses a completed action in his Perfect consecutive, then we are reminded all the time of our inability to feel our way into the Hebrew's conception, and there results a sense of unease, similar to that which we experience when faced with people whom we do not understand in certain points (p. 32-3). But Driver's switching from real to imaginary completed actions is not any less severe than Bauer's switching from pres/fut. to past within the same verb form. It is not always clear, if we accept Bauer's view, when the verb form we are faced with in the Hebrew text belongs to the older or younger layer, e.g., Num. 18:12 'All the best of the oil,...the firstfruits of them which they shall offer (יִתְּנוּ = younger layer) unto the Lord, them I have given (נְתַתִּים = older layer?) thee'. If נְתַתִּים means, 'them I will give thee', as it surely does then the Perfect here must belong to the older layer. See 1 Sam. 14:10; Jud. 7:9; 1 Kings 13:9; Deut. 17:4 and scores of other examples where the switch from old to young forms is debatable. In the example just cited it could be argued that נְתַתִּים reflected the mental decision of the speaker, and it is not such a strange idea as the English translation shows. In Driver's theory the Perfect means 'completed action', and it is left to the speaker to decide whether this is to be taken in a literal or idealized sense, which will not be difficult in its context. In Bauer's theory the Perfect could mean any tense whatsoever, because there is no way of differentiating between the younger and older forms (except in the 1st and 2nd pers. sing., and not always even with these, as Bauer realized, p. 38).

There appears to be an apparent contradiction in Bauer's view of the strain such a juxtaposition of two styles would exert in Hebrew. On the one hand he says:

> Unnatural as it may appear to us that a language in which ׀ means
> 'and' and תִּקְטֹל 'you will kill', does not say וְתִקְטֹל! but after
> the Proto-Semitic manner וַתִּקְטֹל; and that conversely the form
> קָטַלְתָּ 'you have killed' is not combined with ׀ , but one has to
> say for this in the old fashion וְקָטַלְתָּ —certainly neither this
> rule nor the hard force of compulsion implied within it ever con-
> sciously occurred to the Hebrew. Even in German we say 'du tötest'
> (תִּקְטֹל), but not 'dann du tötest', but rather with inversion 'dann
> tötest du' (וַתִּקְטֹל!). Just as few Germans have any conception of
> the inflexible rule of inversion, and yet handle it...with infallible
> competence, so too <u>mutatis mutandis</u> the same will have been the case
> with the Hebrews. (p. 36).

But on the other hand he says:

> When one considers, however, what a strain the juxtaposition of the
> two styles meant for the language, how a Proto-Semitic construction
> more or less constantly existed in fragile equilibrium, and switched
> over to the West Semitic construction whenever the context was dis-
> turbed: if one considers further how every language is continually
> occupied in casting off useless irregularities, then the disappear-
> ance of the consecutive tenses can be explained even without direct
> Aramaic influence. (p. 37)

One the one hand the Hebrews are said to be unconscious of the hard force of
compulsion latent in the two styles, yet on the other hand the two styles are
said to be in fragile equilibrium.

1.3.7.20 Concluding Assessment of Bauer's Theory

Bauer set out with the specific task of offering the student of
Hebrew an alternative explanation of the HVS to that presented by S. R. Driver.
We have examined seven areas of his alternative explanation and found too many
difficulties with it to consider it a viable alternative to Driver's explanation.
We have pointed out the difficult transitions required by Bauer to get from his
single universal verb form to the complex situation we have in Hebrew and the
other Semitic languages. It is precisely these transitions and the presuppositions behind them that stand in the way of his explanation being accepted as the
definitive solution to the problems of the HVS which Bauer held it to be. Four
points in Bauer's theory stand out.

Firstly, there is his original suggestion that the WS Perfect consecutive
was none other than the ES <u>iqatal</u>, or rather PS *<u>yaqatal</u>. Having made this
identification and confident that <u>iqatal</u> never had a perfective meaning he
concluded that the meaning of <u>qatala</u> in the PS period must have been close
to the present participle throughout the whole Semitic community. The metamorphosis of <u>qatala</u> to <u>iqatal</u> (or vice verse) is probably the greatest

difficulty in his reconstruction.

Secondly, Bauer has no doubts but that the HVS is a tense-orientated
system. He is astonished that anyone could think that the temporal perspective of the Semites were incommensurable with 'our modern way of thinking'.
In this regard he finds himself in sympathy with the Jewish Conversive Theory.
They were right but for the wrong reasons. There was no actual transfor-
mation of the forms into their opposite tense; there was no mysterious
power in the prefixed waw. He saw his contribution as giving the Conversive Theory a better foundation, a better explanation, after the severe
criticism it received following the publication of the epic work of Driver
and Ewald on the subject.

Thirdly, Bauer suggested that as the imperative belongs to the original
stratum of language, then that form of the verb will be older which stands
closest to it morphologically. Granted that this is so, that in itself does
not exclude the possibility that a form not at all close to the imperative
may have preceded it. And secondly, what is the evidence that the imperative
is a primary form in the historical languages, and not a secondary or derived
form?

Lastly, Bauer could have greatly strengthened the various steps he took
in his reconstruction of the stages of the development that PS went through
had he illustrated those steps using linguistic laws that are shaping today's
languages. He had justified his reconstructions on the grounds that, 'it has
become one of the most fruitful principles of linguistics to make the same
factors which we see in the present life of languages responsible for the
origin of these languages' (p. 3). Or again, using a geological analogy,
geologists 'have come to the conclusion that the same forces which are
moulding today's layer have been operating continuously in the past'. The
fact that Bauer did not choose to do so may mean that either he knew of no
parallel for his proposed transitions, or that the linguistic law at work
in his reconstructions was a new discovery. If the latter proves to be the
case, then Bauer is in danger of circular reasoning; if the former, then
he should have given analogies from modern languages.

Despite the difficulties which we have noted above, Bauer's work became
the foundation and framework for future work on the subject using the historical-comparative approach, chiefly the work of G. R. Driver and T. W. Thacker.

* * * * * * *

1.3.8   The Composite Language Theory of G. R. Driver

The striking fact Driver noted about the Hebrew language was that
it had far more duplicate forms than any other Semitic language (1936:105), and
that every phenomenon of Hebrew usage finds a parallel idiom in one or other
of the Semitic languages (p. 124). Given that 'the speech of a people normally
reflects its origin' (p. 151), Driver wrote:

> ...the Hebrews must have been a mixed nation, drawn principally
> from the neighbouring Semitic races but containing also a certain
> amount of foreign blood....It will then be natural to find some-
> thing of this heterogeneous origin reflected in the Hebrew lang-
> uage. (p. 151)

He held that the two main strands in the Hebrew language were Akkadian and
Aramaic. A third strand was Amorite ('something between Aramaean and proto-
Arabic') of which hardly anything is known (p. 151). Hebrew tradition pre-
serves a recollection of a Babylonian element (Gen. 11:27--12:9), and an Aram-
aean background (Deut. 26:5). Ezekiel speaks of an Amorite as well as a
Hittite (non-Semitic) strain in the Hebrew people (Ezek. 16:3, 45). Hence
Driver argued:

> ...if indeed the mixed origin of the Hebrews is accepted, much
> will have been brought into their language by the various racial
> elements (Accadian, Amorite and proto-Arabic, Aramaean, Phoenic-
> ian and Canaanite [plus 'the Ḥabiru...a mixed horde of robbers
> composed of refugees and outlaws from the surrounding nations,
> largely Semites, lying between the Elamite mountains and the Med-
> iterranean sea' (p. 151)]...) which must have gone to the for-
> mation of the Hebrew race, and many of the peculiarities of Heb-
> rew will be survivals from the diverse dialects of these peoples.
> (p. 107)

Driver argues in his work (=PHVS) that since the syntax and accidence
exhibit clear evidence of a composite origin (cf. pp. 73, 98-107), this is a
strong argument in favour of his thesis that the HVS itself is also derived
from a twofold source, i.e. an Eastern and a Western (p. 107). His chief contention was that 'the constructions with strong wāw go back to the Akkadian,
while those with weak wāw go back to the Aramaean element in the Hebrew language' (p. 152). At the same time, he cautions, it must not be supposed that
Hebrew is a pure and simple mixture of Akkadian and Aramaic as known within
historical times; there must be a proto-Semitic element in it, a primitive
and purely Hebrew nucleus must also have been a component part of it (pp. 107,
151). Nevertheless, there is 'a clearly defined twofold strain, Akkadian on
the one side and Aramaean on the other' in the Hebrew language (p. 152). Though
traces of these two strands appear in other Semitic languages he argues:

The reason why more [traces] have survived in Hebrew than elsewhere is that it is nearer historically to the source and therefore less homogeneous; the elements composing it have not had as much time to become welded into a perfect unity. Further, the people seem to have been more obviously heterogeneous in origin and therefore less ready to use a single language; for it can hardly be doubted that each unit must have clung to its original dialect well after the formation of the literary language.... Moreover Hebrew, as compared with Accadian or early Aramaean, is far too smooth and free from anomalies or variations from any fixed or definite standard; such a state of affairs can only be the result of an artificial levelling away of all inequalities of style....the language of the Old Testament reflects...not so much the roughness and vigour of a speech just becoming classical as the polish of the study. (p. 152)

From these quotations it is clear that there are two separate or distinct issues. On the one hand (if we leave Hebrew aside for the moment), two different verbal systems have developed within the Semitic group of languages, i.e., an Eastern (or Akkadian) and a Western (or Aramaean) system. On the other hand we have the relationship of the Hebrew language to these developments. In the first part of this review of Driver's theory we shall set out his view on the way the Eastern and Western verbal schemes developed, and in the second part we shall set out his arguments for the relationship of Hebrew to these two schemes.

1.3.8.1   Stage 1 : The Priority of Qátil with Universal Functions

In sharp contrast to Hans Bauer's theory that yaqtul originated before qatil and qatal (1.3.7.4) Driver argues for the exact opposite development. He remarks that Bauer's 'assumption that yaqtul was originally timeless and therefore universal' lacks direct support (pp. 20, 33 n 2). Analogy, he suggests, shows that what is simplest is earliest. Therefore, he argues, qatil 'is on the surface the simplest form of the verb from which all other forms have been demonstrably developed'(p. 26). In the following table we have set out the various stages of development through which the Eastern and Western schemes have evolved. It is to be noted that the first five stages—since they are common to all the Semitic languages—belong to a time when there was no division into East and West Semitic; but by stage 6 a sharp distinction occurs with the rise of the past qatál-form and the present-future yiqtól-form in the West. To the right of stage 7 we have shown the Eastern and Western elements that make up the composite nature of the Hebrew verbal system.

The first verb form to develop was qatil. It is really a noun (p. 74) or adjective (pp. 26, 75) in origin, and originally was stative or intransitive (pp. 76, 29). At times it was necessarily used in a transitive sense (p. 29),

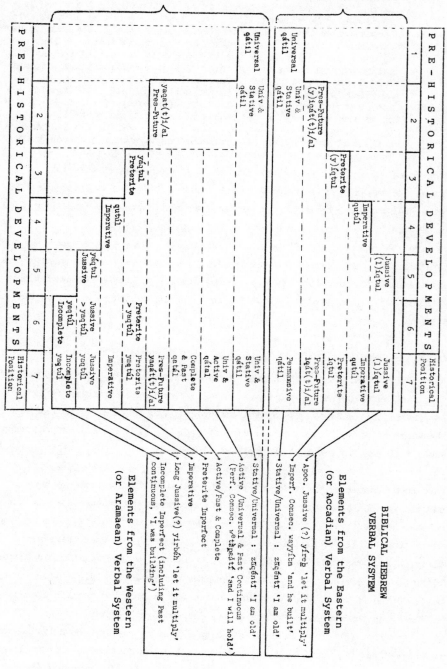

Diagram of G. R. Driver's theory showing the composite nature
of the Hebrew Verbal System

but this was rare (pp. 52, 80-1, 106, 112). Because this form was originally
used to describe   pure   states it referred most often to the present, sometimes to the past, and only occasionally to the future (pp. 112, 116, 149).
Even when qatil comes near to a tense describing an already completed act
it never loses entirely the fundamental idea of a state which properly underlies it (p. 80). In reference to past time, then, qatil generally describes
an already complete and finished state as more or less permanent (p. 113),
and in relation to present or future time it always describes a more or less
lasting condition (p. 125, cf. p.128). Although Driver stated on p. 112 that
qatil refers most often to present time, nevertheless he argues (pp. 28-9)·that
because qatil expressed properly state which had of necessity arisen in time
already past at the moment of speaking, this would make it imperative that the
lang-
uage would require a present-future tense before that of a preterite. He notes
that this new present-future tense (yaqáta/il) 'took over that sphere which
qátil occupied only by an extension of its proper function, namely the description of present and future time' (p. 29 cf. p. 82).

Another term used by Driver on occasions to embrace the functions of this
early verb form is the designation 'universal sense' (pp. 28, 80, 94, 112, etc.).
It is not clear whether this designation is intended to cover or include only
the functions outlined above, or whether other functions are to be assumed under
this designation. From a statement on p. 112 it would appear that the term
'universal' refers to universal time, i.e. past, present, and future time, and
also to 'universal' functions, i.e. active, passive, or stative, transitive and
intransitive states or events, complete or incomplete action. The 'universal
sense' intended by Driver appears to coincide with the Akkadian permansive
'tense'(pp. 43, 48), which never developed the active qatal-form (pp. 81-2,
120). Where qatal forms do appear in Akkadian he thinks they are 'probably
incorrect' (p. 112 n 2). He suggests that the reason why Akkadian did not
develop the qatal form was because that language introduced case-endings which
indicated whether the force of qatil in a specific case was active or passive
(p. 81). In the West the case-endings had disappeared before the evolution of
the classical language, and it was therefore imperative that, if the noun could
give no indication of the construction, the verb should do so. Consequently an
active qatal was developed out of qatil by a change of vowel based on the
accordance of the nature of the vowel with the meaning required to be expressed
(p. 82).

It was at this point that a system of vocalization originally purely
phonetic became semantic. The proto-Semitic (or Akkadian) permansive had -a-

in the first and -i- in the second syllable. The -a- may be presumed to have
been selected as the strongest vowel to give body to the primitive qtl. Con-
trariwise the -i- seems to have been chosen as the weakest vowel merely to
serve what may be called a segolate function, i.e. to facilitate the pronunciation of qatl which, as it stands was not easily pronounced by Semites; thus
the softest vowel came by chance to be the sign par excellence of state, and
on the other hand, the hardest vowel, namely -a-, was generally chosen when
the need for a distinct form to describe activity as distinct from state came
to be felt, whether in the perfect qatal or the present-future yaqat(t)al formations. Thus -i- is to -a- as stativity (or passivity) is to activity; they
stand at opposite ends of the pole, and the choice of opposite vowels to denote
opposite ideas may be described as polarity, though the phenomenon itself is
not due to polarity (p. 45, cf. p. 72).

So far we have sketched Driver's view of the origin, function, and vocalization of qatil. In what follows we give the main reasons why he considered the
suffix-form originated before the prefix-form and before yaqtul in particular.
Firstly, analogy suggests that what is simplest is earliest. In Greek the present is prior to the future which was developed before any past tense (pp. 26,
29). The uninflected qatil is clearly not as complex as ya+qtul, and compound
forms cannot be older than their constituent parts. Driver regards qatil as
the simplest form and the one from which all other forms have been demonstrably
developed (p. 26). The Greek language appears to have evolved first a present
(the shortest verb form) then a future and lastly a past tense. In Homer the
future forms are clearly marked, while the augment of the past is optional (as
indeed it remains to the end in the pluperfect tense),(p. 29).

Secondly,   It would seem a priori likely that primitive man would be
             occupied rather with present and future than with past events,
             i.e. with the needs of daily life rather than with history,
             and it would therefore be natural to expect that, so soon as
             the ambiguities of the universal usage of qatil came to be
             felt, the first requirement of the early Semites would be a
             present-future tense. (p. 28)

Knudtzon's argument that the imperfect is prior to the perfect-permansive because it is natural for 'something presenting itself' (i.e. yaqtul)
to be expressed before something 'present' (i.e. a state) is rejected by
Driver on the grounds that:

             This argument rests on the assumption that human beings began by
             observing in the first instance what most forcibly drew their attent-
             ion and then went on to look at the accompanying circumstances; but
             reflection seems to show that in actual fact a man only sees what
             comes towards him as it arises out of a background which he has

already observed. (p. 25) ....In other words, forms describing a
permanent or unchangeable state are antecedent to those applied to
the description of temporary states [the prefix-forms], since the
use of such forms necessitates reflection in order to realize that
the state so described is changeable....and to reflect as well as
to relate and to compare are the predominating marks of a later
age, while naïve and unconscious experience...become ever more
characteristic of the earlier period the further back one goes.
(p. 26)

The fact that qatil expressed properly state would make the need of a present-
future more urgent than that of a past tense which is the last to evolve (p.29f.)

Thirdly,   the uses to which qatil is put are of almost universal range...and
these must reflect a period of time antecedent to the development
of yaqatal and yaqtul which both have a strictly limited reference;
for, indeed, it is hardly conceivable that subsequently to the
evolution of these two tenses another neutral form of universal
application overlapping them can either have grown up or been
created. (p. 28)

Fourthly, in Akkadian nouns and adjectives can be inflected in the same
way as the suffix forms,[1] so that at times it is impossible to say whether any
given form is a noun or a verb (e.g. whether šaknāku means 'I am' or 'have
been appointed' or 'I am an appointee'), shows that qatil goes back to a very
early period of time when the noun or adjective on the one hand and the verb
on the other hand were still imperfectly distinguished. This impression is
strengthened by the fact that qatil exhibits a mixed inflection being purely
nominal and primitive in the third person but developed and pseudo-verbal in
the first and second persons (see p. 26). It also follows that if the uninflected qatil is prior to the inflected first and second persons then it must
also be prior to the inflected yaqtul form.

Fifthly, a form with an afformative is probably older than one
with a preformative inflection, since it conforms to a general rule of the
Semitic languages that the predicate precedes the subject (p. 27).

Sixthly, pronominal suffixes are more primitive because they are less worn
away than those of the prefixes. Time must be allowed for the process of
attrition and coalescence, and the combined form must be subsequent in point
of development to its component parts (p. 27).

Seventhly, the prefix ta- of the feminine third person in taqat(t)al
and taqtul, is explicable only as having arisen out of qat(i)lat (where it
is a nominal ending) on the false analogy of the prefix ta- expressing the
2nd masc. person in taqtul, in the same way as the n- of qatalnā has been
transferred, so to say, to the beginning of naqtul. Likewise the plural ending
-ū in yaqtulū can be explained only as having arisen through the false analogy
of the permansive plural qat(i)lū and not vice versa (cf. pp. 27, 39, 75-77).

Eighthly, since awareness began with the description of permanent states (qatil) and moved on to the description of temporary states (iqattal),
and finally blossomed in the ability to relate, reflect, and to compare experiences (yaqtul and qatal), this is reflected in the evolution of the verb forms
themselves. If we assume that the form qátil-ta (in which the nominal precedes
the pronominal element) is already in existence, it will be readily conceded
that the obvious and indeed only possible way of creating a new form out of
the same given elements is to invert them, i.e. ta-qátil. This development is
assured by the fact that the accent in both forms falls in the same place (pp.
26, 29). The fact that both Akkadian and Ethiopic have this form with an accented
middle syllable cannot be accidental.[1] Also the diverse uses of the form in these
two languages argue great antiquity in that they describe what is actually
(externally) present which must be regarded as prior to forms expressing what
is appearing (whether from outside or within) to a person as coming into being,
such as the West Semitic imperfect tense as seen in the Hebrew yiqtol form
(pp. 30-1). In any case, it is difficult to see how yáqtul can have arisen
directly out of qátil in view of the position of the accent in the two forms
(for the origin of yaqtul see 1.3.8.4).

Ninthly, Driver disagrees with the argument that the wide diffusion of
yaqtul (or the prefix-form) in the Hamitic languages proves the priority of
that form over the suffix-form. First of all it does not follow that it is therefore older than qatil; and secondly, against this presupposition must be set
the fact that Egyptian has nothing corresponding to yaqtul while it has a pseudo-
participle of great antiquity corresponding closely with qatil (p. 20).

Tenthly, 'It seems a priori likely that forms descriptive of facts are
more primitive than those expressing modes' (p. 19).

> ...it is probably necessary to regard the imperative qutul
> as posterior in time of development to the permansive qatil
> ...for not only are there traces of the permansive even in
> the second person performing the function of the imperative,
> which it would hardly have taken over if there had already
> been an imperative in use, but also the -u in the plural
> second person can only be explained as being derived by
> false analogy through the preterite from the permansive....
> (p. 28)

In putting forward his view that qatil was the first verb form to evolve he
was not saying something new. He notes that F. Hommel had put forward this suggestion in 1890 (in ZDMG 44 pp. 535-48), followed by F. E. König (ZDMG 65 [1911] p.
720) and G. Bergsträsser (1929, II, 9-14); though the suggestion appears to have
originated with Ernst Heinrich Meier (1813-66) in his Hebräisches Wurzelwörter-
buch in 1845 (cf. F. Burgess, JSL NS 3 (Jan. 1853) p. 434).

1.3.8.2   The Origin and Function of Qatal

We have seen how qatil became the first verb form to develop and
how its characteristic -i- vowel came by chance to denote state or stativity.
Because qatil primarily described a state formed in past time, but which
could extend into the present (though the form began its existence as a general present participle, see p. 23), and because it rarely extended to future time (for examples see p. 116) or active-transitive events (see p. 22),
it was only natural that the first new form would supply the deficiencies of
qatil. The deficiencies were met in different ways. In Akkadian an entirely
new verb form emerged, namely iqát(t)al, whereas in West Semitic qatil underwent an internal vowel change.to emerge as qatal (probably accented qátal).
The choice of vowel in both new verb forms was due to polarity, i.e. -i- and
-a- stand at opposite ends of the vowel scale just as stativity and activity
stand over against each other (pp. 72, 81). Only with the introduction of the
-a- vowel did the -i- vowel come to denote stativity. Before this the -i-
vowel had no such meaning, hence it is that a number of qatil verbs remained
in West Semitic with active and even transitive meanings (pp. 46-9).[1] The truly
verbal qatal 'he has killed' came into existence beside the properly nominal
qatil. Driver follows Ungnad's suggestion that the process had been hastened
or facilitated by the Hebrew rule that -i- in a closed accented syllable
becomes -a- and also by the analogy of verbs with a hard guttural as medial
or final consonant (p. 46).

Driver suggests that the reason why Akkadian was able to employ qatil
both transitively and intransitively was that originally the mere presence or
absence of an object sufficed to indicate whether the force of qatil was passive
or active, and for this purpose the case-endings of the noun were sufficient.
However, in the West the case-endings disappeared, hence it was necessary that,
if the noun could not obviate the ambiguity, the verb should do so; hence the
emergence of qatal (pp. 81-2).[2]

Initially in West Semitic qatil and qatal were universal in meaning, being
applied indifferently to past, present, and future states and events (p. 112).
Qatil, however, settled down to denote state, whereas qatal denoted primarily
acts and actions. Qatal (and iqatal in Akkadian, p. 88) took over the active
and transitive functions of qatil (p. 82). Yet because qatal had its origin
in qatil--

> it retained enough of the old universal sense of the original qatil
> ...to be also employed not only for the description of facts which
> have formerly taken place but are still of constant recurrence and
> hence are matters of common experience (namely, to perform the func-

tion of a gnomic aorist) but also with reference to future events, although this use was in practice confined to poetic and...prophetic language and certain legal phrases. This usage however was rare and almost, if not quite, died out at a relatively early date. (pp. 82-3)

In contrast to H. Bauer (1910:12, 17-18), F. W. M. Philippi (B.A.S.S. 2 [1892] p.371[2]), and P. Haupt (JRAS NS 10[1878]p. ccxlvi), who attempt to separate the Accadian qátil from the Hebrew qātál, Driver maintains that it is safe to assume that a primitive qatil lies not only behind verbs descriptive of states but also behind those expressing activity (p. 22); consequently, he would maintain, the change of vocalization does not mark qatal as an independent original verbal form, rather it is the result of an extension of meaning in the originally nominal or adjectival qatil (p. 22). In support of this view he draws upon Knudtzon's work (ZA 7[1892]pp. 33-48) who attempts to show that the permansive and perfect forms are identifiable in respect of their functions (p. 22).

The following is a brief summary of the old universal functions which qatal continued to hold alongside its obviously past tense or complete mode of action.

(1) The Present. Driver is firmly convinced that this was the basic meaning or functional time sphere in which qatal emerged, and this being so, it follows that it described the present or 'actual' but not necessarily the 'complete' (p. 23). He points out that the perfect in 'the heavens are higher (gabᵉhû) than the earth' (Isa. 55:9) means not that the heavens have become but that they are higher than the earth (p. 23).[1] Under the present he would include gnomic sentences and legal or semi-legal phrases which are apt to be survivals from an older stage of language (p. 88). Also states or actions which began in the past but continue into the present (p. 115); mental or spiritual states whose origin is past but whose effect is present; states or actions which are in course of being performed as the speaker speaks, e.g. 'I lift up (hărîmôtî) my hand'; and consequently it is used of states or actions which have become habitual whether in the case of individual persons or in universal propositions. It may also serve to indicate a state or an act of which the accomplishment has not yet taken place but is regarded as inevitable 'Behold! we do/shall perish (gāwa'nû)'.

(2) From this last it is but a short step to the use of the same form as a purely future tense whether of state or of action. Where it occurs in Hebrew it is usually found in conjunction with -u-, the old nominal conjunctive (p. 113). In practice, however, the future use is confined to poetic and the kindred prophetic language and certain legal phrases (p. 82). He rejects the

suggestion that the 'prophetic perfect' is simply the ordinary past perfect
used to impart to descriptions of the future 'a forcible and expressive touch
of reality, and reproduces vividly the certainty with which the occurrence of
a yet future event is contemplated by the speaker' (p. 87). He acknowledges
that the prophets may use the past perfect in this way but that this is not
the origin of the 'prophetic perfect' is suggested by the fact that it occurs
in numerous passages where there is no such 'vividness' and where it would
be out of place: for example, in questions such as 'how long wilt thou have
refused (mē'antā)?' In any case there is a different accentuation of the old
universal perfect which distinguishes it from the later past perfect. The
proto-Semitic, Akkadian, and Hebrew 'prophetic perfect', are all accented
on the vowel following the first radical in the case of the 1st and 2nd pers.
sing., namely, (wᵉ)qᵃtáltā (p. 89). The same applies in the case of the 3rd
pers. fem. sing. qᵃtᵉlā and 3rd pers. masc. pl. qᵃtᵉlū (p. 21). From this
Driver concluded:

> The accentuation of the Hebrew verb, then, in the construction with
> consecutive wāw is that of the primitive Semitic speech as exhibited
> in the Accadian language and must therefore be regarded not as a
> peculiarity invented by the Hebrews but as an archaism surviving
> from the common proto-Semitic speech. (pp. 89-90)

The fact that the future perfect (i.e. the old universal qati/al) is sometimes
used without a prefixed wāw yet with a different tone position (i.e. qātáltā
instead of the expected qᾱtaltā) in the Hebrew bible must be attributed to the
Massoretes

> who, having lost the true pronunciation, obliterated these natural
> distinctions, as they did almost all differences of dialect, and
> so introduced hopeless confusion where there had formerly been per-
> fect clarity. The ear conveyed these niceties of a living speech
> to the hearer, but the eye gave no hint of them to the scholar in
> his study. (p. 97)

We can take it for granted that where a perfect form has a future meaning it
is a survival of the old universal permansive-perfect (pp. 147-50).

(3) Where the perfect form has clearly a past/complete meaning it is virtually certain that we have here the Aramaic or Western perfect (p. 88) i.e.
qatál. However, where examples are found in past time in reference to habitual
states or actions lasting over a considerable time, these are survivals of the
universal qáta/il and are not to be confused with the Western qatál, for example, 'and he[Abraham] was believing (wᵉheʾĕmìn) in Yahweh' (Gen. 15:6), where
the perfect is the universal one and not the single completed action of the
Western qatál (cf. pp. 113ff. and 129ff.).

(4) Where the perfect has an imperatival function this belongs to the univer-

sal or proto-Semitic qáti/al (p. 118). It also follows that the imperative (qutul) is a later development which took over the imperatival function from the permansive-perfect, otherwise how can one explain the use of the second person performing the function of an imperative if there was an imperative form already in use? (p. 28).

(5) Where the perfect has a precative or optative meaning here again we have remnants of the universal qáti/al (pp. 147-50, 94).

In essence, then, Driver is saying that there are two distinct forms of the perfect, one Eastern (proto-Semitic or Akkadian), accented qátil, and one Western (Aramaean), accented qatí/ál. The latter has only the meaning of single completed action in the past, whereas the former has all the other functions except completed past action (pp. 15, 88, 138-9, cf. 96-7). He suggests that only 'some such hypothesis...seems capable of meeting satisfactorily all the difficulties presented by this complex system' (p. 88, cf. 93-4). He concurs therefore with Bauer's argument that there can be no solution to the complex Hebrew verbal system on the theory that the perfect has only one basic function (i.e. completed action)(p. 15). The simplest solution, he suggests, is to assume that the two forms were confused over the centuries (p. 91), and if this is the case then only an historical approach to the problem can unravel the path(s) of development (pp. 88-9). He points out that all the Semitic languages—except Akkadian—have the two forms of the perfect (see pp. 81, 88, 89 n 1, 95, 106, 112, 116, and 148), but only in Hebrew is the old differentation of the tone retained.[1]

1.3.8.3   Stage 2 : *Yaqát(t)al—The Second Verb-form to Develop

Because primitive man was occupied with the present and the future he soon felt the ambiguities of the universal qatil which properly denoted state which had arisen before the time of speaking. The first requirement, therefore, would be the need for a present-future tense with active meaning (p. 28f.). Although qatal emerged in the West with an active and universal sense, it was rare and almost, if not quite, died out at a relatively early date. This was inevitable, for while the conception of a form of the verb having a universal range is possible in regard to the description of a state, it is not so easily compatible with the description of an act; hence qatal in the West became a pure tense restricted almost entirely to past time (p. 83), and describing completed action in past time (p. 88).

While the argument put forward above for the appearance of a present-future before a past or preterite is more or less subjective, yet it can be reinforced by another of a purely objective nature derived from the formal evolution of the new tense. If it be presumed that such a form as qátil-ta is already in existence, it will be conceded that the obvious and indeed only possible way of creating a new form out of the same given elements is to invert them; the result is ta-qátil. Note that the tone in both forms falls in the same place (p. 29).

The choice of the hard -a- vowel in the new form (iqátal) was made for the same reason as in the Western qátal, namely, as the opposite of the soft -i- which had become identified with stativity (pp. 81, 54). Another example of polarity has already been referred to, namely, whereas the pronominal elements follow the stem in the permansive-perfect (due to their nominal origin) they are prefixed in the Present (=iqatal) due to polarity (p. 40).

For these reasons, and the fact that this new form appears in Akkadian, Ethiopic, and the Tell el-'Amarna tablets, it would appear that this form was once common to all the Semitic languages. The presence of this form in the 'Amarna tablets is an argument in favour of supposing it once existed in but was lost from Hebrew before the historic period (p. 106), a view put forward by H. Torczyner in 1912 (in Z.D.M.G. 66, p. 88). Driver suggests that had the new form survived in Hebrew it would have been indistinguishable from the Piel and this probably accounts for its disappearance (p. 83).

Just as qatil-ta and ta-qatil are formally so close to one another, so their meanings are in essence quite close since both at bottom mean 'you (are) in a killing (state)'. The basic difference between them can be seen on two levels; first, qatil predominated in the past sphere and where this extended into the present, whereas iqatal dominated in the present and future spheres; second, while qatil became more and more restricted to describing states, iqatal took over its transitive functions (pp. 29, 118). Besides, it took over or else shared with qatil the function of prohibition and mild command (p. 120). The distinction between the third verb form—yaqtul—and iqatal is clear: the former describes a single momentary act in the past, whereas the latter describes what is incomplete, whether past, present or future, and ought properly on this account to be termed the Imperfect (p. 127, cf. p. 137f.).

1.3.8.4   Stage 3 : *Yaqtul—The Third Verb-form to Develop

In the transition from states to tenses the last tense to evolve is the past tense (pp. 29-30). It is therefore reasonable to suppose that the development of the preterite yaqtul followed that of the present-future iqat(t)al; and this can be formally proved.

> Starting from the fact that in qátilta an afformative and in
> taqáta/il a preformative conjugation already existed and given
> once again the same data, the sole course now open for the creation
> of a third tense was by the modification of one of these forms. Neg-
> atively, it is difficult to see how yáqtul can have arisen directly
> out of qátil in view of the position of the accent in the two forms.
> Positively, the fact that taqáta/il is not a form partly nominal
> and partly verbal describing a state but a proper tense expressing
> something of the same nature as that which the latest form is re-
> quired, namely activity, shows why it was preferred for modificat-
> ion; thus the new form has prefixed, not postfixed, inflections.
> (p. 30)

The reason for the -u- vowel in the preterite is clear once the priority of
the present iqat(t)al is conceded:[1] as the soft -i- was chosen as the characteristic vowel of the original stative, so the hard -a- was chosen as its
opposite, i.e. to that of the active, which was the next form in order of development; the only remaining vowel was -u- which, as different from that of
the stative and the active, was the only choice left for the last or preterite tense (p. 54). The fact that we also have yaqtal forms, i.e. with -a-
instead of -u-, can be explained on the principle of opposites; since qatil
and yaqtal are opposite in form—though both are stative—the -a- vowel 'is
unavoidably used in the imperfect tense of intransitive verbs as the vowel
furthest removed from the i > ē of the perfect tense' (p. 72).

   Driver rejects Bauer's suggestion that yaqtul had a universal function
initially (p. 20), if only on the grounds that it is inconceivable that a
preterite and a jussive—however close the resemblance may be formally—
can have a common origin; for strong asseveration cannot be regarded as an
effective link between the two ideas, since the description of past events
differs in kind toto caelo from a command which in its very essence relates
to future time (p. 19f.). From its very inception yaqtul indicated a single
momentary action in the past or already begun in the past (pp. 110, 125-6,
132-44), irrespective of the mode of action of the verb (p. 110). There is
no difference between the Western waw+perfect (=past) and the imperfect
consecutive tense in Hebrew and the preterite in Akkadian (p. 94).[2] It never
has a nascent meaning (pp. 33, 91, cf. pp. 108-10, 120-1, 125-8). It is
properly an aorist in historical narrative and for this reason ought to be
called the Aorist tense (p. 127). Even when it appears to refer to present
actions there is always an element of past time present (p. 137). Where it
appears to have a habitual or customary meaning this is because a concrete
actual happening underlies a general assertion or truth (pp. 135, 137). Hence
the imperfect always refers to an actual event in history (p. 125) so that
it is incorrect to assign a present sense to it (p. 135). In contrast to the

universal qátal (the perfect consecutive in Hebrew), which denotes incomplete or frequentative action in the past, yaqtul denotes completed action in the past (pp. 120, 126, cf. p. 135). A final argument in support of a preterite meaning is that this can be the only meaning in certain personal names. Thus Jacob was called Ya'ᵃqōb 'he grasped the heel'; so also Yiśrā'ēl 'God contended'; Yōsēp (Joseph) 'He added' because 'Yahweh added (yōsēp) to me another son' (Gen. 30:24), not 'Yahweh add to me another son' as this would make nonsense, since the child was already born (p. 143).

This preterite yáqtul has to be distinguished from the later Western yaqtúl, since the former has the tone on the first or initial syllable whereas the latter has the tone on the final syllable; the latter never has a preterite meaning. Remnants of the preterite yaqtul have remained in all the Semitic languages (for examples in Arabic see pp. 95, 120, 139, 142; Ethiopic and Mandaic p. 145, cf. p. 19 and 31 n 3; Aramaic pp. 120, 142, 19; Moabite p. 120 and Tell el-'Amarna p. 106) where the original distinction has been obliterated in every case except Hebrew (pp. 91, 120). Akkadian alone has preserved the preterite as a narrative tense (p. 120), and the original accentuation (p. 90), hence it is that we find that the Hebrew imperfect consecutive has preserved the primitive intonation yáqtul because the narrative yaqtul form was borrowed direct from Akkadian. This primitive accentuation is best seen in the ה"ל verbs where the accent in way-yíbn 'and he built' is in the same position as in the Akkadian íbni 'he built'. Occasionally the same weak verb occurs in the form way-yibnéh 'and he built' but this is due to confusion with the later imperfect yibnéh 'he was building'.[1] This confusion shows that at an early stage the true distinction between the Eastern preterite yáqtul and the Western yaqtúl (past continuous) had been forgotten owing to the similarity of the two forms. In other words, the accentuation of the preterite wayyiqtól 'and he killed' was due to the model of the imperfect yiqtól 'he was killing', with which it was incorrectly identified (p. 90f.). He rejects the suggestion of his father (1892:75-77) that the drawing back of the tone in the imperfect suggests its connection with what precedes as a 'purely superficial observation which does not explain the phenomenon' (p. 85); it is 'too artificial...to be in the least degree convincing' (p. 86).

The suggestion that two yaqtul forms underlie the many functions of the imperfect in most of the Semitic languages—two forms which differed only in the place of the tone—did not originate with Driver but with M. Lambert in 1893 (R.E.J. 26, pp. 49, 52-4). Likewise the idea that yáqtul was derived from yaqátil through the elision of its medial vowel (even though it bears the tone) can be traced back through J. A. Knudtzon (1892:49-50) to P. Haupt (1878:247).

1.3.8.5   Stage 4 : The Imperative

It is unlikely that the imperative qutul is older than the universal qáti/al, partly because it seems a priori likely that forms descriptive of facts are more primitive than those expressing moods, and partly for reasons connected with inflection (p. 19). That the universal qatil retains traces of an imperative function in the second person makes it probable that it is anterior to the imperative, for it is hardly likely that qatil took over this function if there had already been an imperative in use (p. 28). Likewise, the suffixes of the later imperative, -ī; -ū; and -nāh, can only be explained as being derived by false analogy through the preterite form, which in turn took the -ū ending from the suffix qat(i)lū form where it is of nominal origin (p. 28, 41). The fact that iqatal has also imperative functions would suggest that the imperative is posterior to it (p. 120).

The analogy of other languages suggests that the shortest possible form of the verb will be required for the expression of a command; for thus an abrupt tone will be given to it. It is natural, therefore, to find that the Semitic imperative form in its simplest state consists of the radical consonants without any preformative or afformative element; but it is distinguished from the simplest form of the universal qatil, with which it is externally identical, by two things, namely the position of the tone and the nature of the vowels (p. 32). The reason for the different tone positions is that in the statement of a fact for which the universal qatil is used, it is necessary to give full weight to the root which predicates something of the subject, hence the tone is placed on the first syllable of this form; the abruptness of a command on the other hand is indicated by the speaker hurrying on to the last syllable, which thus receives the tone, while the first syllable is almost unsounded. The reason for the different vowel in the second syllable of the imperative is that it followed the same principles, whatever these were, that determined the second syllable of the imperfect yaqtul; so although the second vowel of the imperative form is identical with that of the preterite tense, it must not be supposed that the former follows or is based on the later, since there are insuperable semantic objections to connecting these two forms. The first vowel of the imperative, which was of little importance except as a helping vowel, was simply assimilated to the second (p. 32).

1.3.8.6   Stage 5 : The Jussive and Cohortative

The Jussive and Cohortative, being moods, must be later than the

G. R. DRIVER   130

descriptive tenses (p. 19), and being clearly inflected on the analogy of the
preterite they must be later developments (p 28). That the jussive and the
preterite forms do not go back to a single universal yaqtul is evident from
their meanings; for semantically it is impossible to see any connection between
their usages. It is impossible to conceive any transition of sense whereby
ikšud meaning 'he captured' can have come to mean also 'let him capture', or
vice versa. Akkadian usage shows clearly that the preterite tense in no sense
can be said to denote nascent or emergent action, which might have formed a
transition link. The only way out of this difficulty, suggests Driver, 'is to
assume that the preterite ikšud is formally independent of the jussive or
precative ikšud and that it has arisen spontaneously from a different origin'
(p. 33). We have already seen (1.3.8.4) that the preterite was developed
from yaqát(t)al and the -u- vowel was chosen because it was the only one left;
the jussive, however, arose from the inadequacy of the imperative qutúl in
the second person, hence it was felt necessary to prefix the pronominal element to the imperative. A similar thing happened to produce the cohortative.
In both forms, however, the loss of the unstressed vowel in the first syllable
of qutúl resulted in the forms yáqtul and áqtul, in which the tone was thrown
back on to the pronominal elements in accordance with the proto-Semitic rules
regulating the free tone or accent (pp. 33-4). These rules also account for
the apocopated jussive forms which F. W. M. Philippi (B.A.S.S. 2[1892] p. 376)
thought qualified them to be regarded as primitive forms. Another reason which
may be responsible for the initial stressed syllable in the jussive and the
cohortative is —

> that the almost unsounded vowel in the first and the stress on the
> second syllable would have further withdrawn the sound from the begin-
> ning of the word and made the resultant form almost unpronounceable;
> further, the third and first persons as distinct from the second
> person (which is virtually implied in all imperative forms and is
> therefore left unexpressed in most languages) required to be emphas-
> ized and so was put first to draw attention to it. (p. 34)

By postulating an independent origin for the jussive Driver solves a problem
which until his time had not received a satisfactory explanation—a problem
which is raised in its simplest and acutest form in the Akkadian language. There
ikšud means 'he captured'; but how can likšud (< lū ikšud) mean both 'he surely
captured' and 'let him capture', and how can the same form underlie both ūl (lā)
ikšud 'he did not capture' and ai ikšud 'let him not capture'? The answer is
simple, they do not; the same form had two unrelated origins (p. 33). Examples
of the jussive usage in the major Semitic languages are given on p. 124.

The origin of the emphatic -a(h) commonly attached to the preterite shows

that it has in itself no optative or cohortative force, though it is often found
with the younger West Semitic imperfect. Originally it imparted special emphasis to statements of fact, whether the reference is to past or present or future time, and in optative clauses. In time it was simply an appendage, added
even when there was no special emphasis in accordance with the rule that terminations tend with the passage of time to lose their force (p. 77). It is significant that all the instances of the Hebrew -āh referring to past time are in
poetical passages (S. R. Driver, 1892:58-9), where archaisms are a priori likely (PHVS: 78). P. Haupt (J.A.O.S. 13 [1889] p. cclxiv) gives examples where
in wishes and similar clauses the Akkadian -a corresponds with the Hebrew
cohortative -āh.

So far we have noted five clear stages of development which are common to
all the Semitic languages. These five stages resulted in five verbal forms: a
universal qatil which was deprived of all its functions to finish up as a
stative permansive; a present-future iqát(t)al; a preterite yáqtul; an imperative qutul; and the jussive yáqtul (and the so-called cohortative). However,
West Semitic underwent further developments which resulted in some duplication
of its tenses; these will be the subject of the next section.

1.3.8.7   Stage 6 : The West Semitic yaqtul

In West Semitic yaqtúl denotes incomplete action (cf. p. 95) which
cannot be more opposed to the proto-Semitic yáqtul which denotes complete
action; therefore Driver rejects the attempt to reconcile these 'contradict-
ory usages of yaqtul(u)...on the assumption, often far-fetched, of a common
underlying sense such as that of nascence or emergence' (p. 91). He suggests
instead that 'the development of qātal as a tense describing completed action
in past time caused yiqtōl...to become the tense of every kind of incomplete
action' (p. 89).[1] He further notes that in Akkadian and Ethiopic, which employed
yaqati/al to describe incomplete states or acts, there was no need of an
imperfect yaqtúl. The new imperfect was evolved only in those languages in
which qatil and especially qatal served as purely perfect tenses describing
what is complete in past time, and there it served to make good the deficiency
or loss (cf. p. 83f.) of yaqattal (p. 121). Indeed, the presence of the twofold
inflexion in the present iqat(t)al and ya/iqatal in the Tell el-'Amarna letters
is an argument in favour of supposing that the present once existed in but was
lost from Hebrew before the historic period (p. 106).

By the time, then, that Biblical Hebrew had been evolved, the form
(y)iqat(t)a/il had become obsolete and only (y)iqtul survived amongst

the Western Semites. Yet just as the Acc. iqata/il and the corresponding Eth. yeqatel did not have precisely the same force,...so
the various derivatives of the primitive yaqtul did not all perform
the same functions; for the Acc. iqtul is a preterite tense but the
true Hebr. yiqtōl describes incomplete action whether past or present or future. (p. 84)

The idea that yaqtul(preterite) was manoeuvred into the present-future (incomplete) sphere following the development and intrusion of the perfect qatal
was first suggested by Bauer (1.3.7.8).[1] Among the functions attributed to
this new imperfect is that of customary action which Bauer had maintained
belonged to the older strata of the language (1.3.7.9). Driver also attributes gnomic—and since yiqtol describes what is merely future in time—wishes,
intentions, and mild commands, when it may be,and often is,indistinguishable
from the jussive both in form and meaning (p. 123).

The assimilation of the tone in the jussive and the preterite to that of
the younger yiqtól took place before the historic period (pp. 91, 96-7, 143,
145).

So far we have discussed the origin and growth of the two verbal systems
in the Semitic family of languages. Thus the Eastern system is identical with
the Akkadian verbal system, while the Western covers all the other Semitic
languages. It is Driver's theory that the Hebrew verbal system consists of two
verbal systems—the Eastern (=Akkadian) and the Western (=Aramaic). In the next
section we shall look at the four factors which support this view.

1.3.8.8   The Evidence that Hebrew is a Composite Language

It must be remembered that the Hebrew we have is contained mainly
in the Massoretic Text, and when we compare it with Akkadian or early Aramaic
it is noticeable that it is far too smooth and free from anomalies or variations from any fixed or definite standard. Such a state of affairs can only be
the result of an artificial levelling away of all inequalities of style. In fact,
the language of the OT reflects, though not in all respects and with notable
exceptions, not so much the roughness and vigour of a speech just becoming
classical as the polish of the study (p. 152). We have had cause on numerous
occasions to note examples where the Massoretes have introduced confusion into
the Hebrew text, either in the vocalization (pp. 52, 66, 67, 70, 100, 106 n 1,
140) or the place of the tone in the consecutive forms (pp. 90, 96-7, 140, 143)
or through some other misunderstanding (pp. 147, 150). Hence the Hebrew language as now presented and represented in the Hebrew Bible is more of a literary
or stylised language, having been progressively pruned of its uncouth and

archaic expressions by a long line of Massoretic scholarship which came to
an end around A. D. 700. Nevertheless many expressions and remnants of dialects
did escape the keen eyes of the Massoretes which makes it doubly important that
modern scholars ought to be careful not to fall into the same error as their
Jewish predecessors in emending every unique word or phrase out of existence
as a parallel idiom may be found in one of the other Semitic languages (p. 152).

1.3.8.9   The Hebrews were a Mixture of Peoples

That diverse strands of nations and tribes have gone into the making
of the Hebrew nation is clear from the Hebrew writings themselves. Hebrew tradition preserves an account of Abraham's coming from the Babylonian city of Ur,
a stay in Haran, and a nomadic life in Palestine (Gen. 11:27-12:9). The Deuter-
onomist makes definite mention of an Aramaean strain in the Hebrew people
(Deut. 26:5). Ezekiel speaks very definitely of an Amorite as well as a Hittite
(non-Semitic) strain in the Hebrew people (Ezek. 16:3, 45)(p. 151). So according to their own traditions the Hebrews must have been a mixed nation.

1.3.8.10   The Hebrew vocalization is a Mixture of East and West Semitic

The choice of the thematic vowel in the verbal forms had been a problem
for which no satisfactory solution had been found until Driver propounded his
solution. He suggested (following M. Lambert, J.A. 15 [1890] pp. 169-74) that
there were two principles governing the final vowel. In the East the phonetic
principle prevailed, while in the West the semantic principle prevailed (pp. 62,
71). Lambert (op. cit.) divided the Arabic consonants into three main classes:
Group 1 : Surds   w, b, f, m,   s, d, q, j, š,   h, h,   (prefer the -u- vowel)
Group 2 : Grêles   m, l, n, r   t, d, z, z, s,   ', ',   (prefer the -i- vowel)
Group 3 : Claires   t, d, t, h, k, ġ,   (these take indifferently -a-, -i-, or -u-).
Driver noted that 63 intransitive verbs in Hebrew were vocalized yiqtol instead
of yiqtal according to Hebrew rules. On examination, however, the striking fact
was revealed that 56 of these 63 verbs had a b, p, m, h, g, k, q, in the second
or third place of the root, 'and these are the very letters which have been
found in those Assyrian verbs which have been improperly vocalized with u in
the present or preterite tenses ' (p. 64). Hence the vocalization of these
Hebrew intransitive imperfects is due to the nature of the consonants in the
final syllable; they therefore follow the Akkadian/Arabic phonetic principle
(p. 64, cf. p. 73).

He also noted a similar phenomenon in the case of intransitive perfects
which have been vocalized qātal instead of according to the normal Hebrew rule

qāṭēl, but in this case the -a- vowel is due to the Western semantic principle whereby active intransitive verbs are assimilated to the active transitive forms (pp. 47-8). Cases where an intransitive perfect can take either -i- or -a- in the final syllable will naturally belong to two distinct layers in the language, and the qāṭēl form will be older than the qāṭal form (pp. 48-9).

One example from the 'Amarna Tablets helps to illustrate the transition between the vocalization of the Akkadian imlik and the Hebrew yimlōk, namely, the form imluk. Here the -u- in imluk is caused by the influence of the -k- having prevailed over that of the -l-; whereas in the Akkadian form the -l- has prevailed over the -k- and hence the -i- vowel (p. 62).

1.3.8.11   The Hebrew Vocabulary is a Mixture of East and West Semitic

That the Hebrew vocabulary is composite is apparent from the presence in it of numerous synonyms. For example, the four negative particles reflect different sources, inasmuch as the Hebr. lō' is identical with the Acc. lā and the Aram.-Arab. lâ, the Hebr. 'al with the Acc. ûl and the Sab. 'l, the Hebr. bal with the Phoen. bl, and the Hebr. 'î with the Acc. ai or ē and the Eth. î-;....(p. 98)

This point is strengthened by the numerous examples of synonyms and duplicate forms in Hebrew which Driver has presented on pp. 99-104. Lastly,

1.3.8.12   The Hebrew Verbal System is a Mixture of East and West Semitic

The suggestion that Hebrew is a composite language presents no diffi- culties when one considers that the correspondence from Tell el-'Amarna exhib- its clear traces of two verbal systems drawn from distinct yet cognate languages but so interwoven as to constitute a peculiar composite dialect (p. 106). In it there exists side by side a double inflexion of qatil or qatal in the forms nasrāku and nasrāti, and a double inflexion of the preterite iqtul and yiqtul (yaqtul). In each case the first form is Eastern, while the second is Western. What is, however, even more important is that this duplication is not confined to the inflexion of the tenses but extends to the meaning of the two forms which occur also in Hebrew. For in these same texts qatil and qatal cover the whole range of meanings possessed by the corresponding forms in Akkadian and Hebrew. So too iqtul and yaqtul exhibit the meanings both of the Akkadian preterite iqtul and of the Hebrew imperfect yiqtōl.

A glance at the diagram on p.118 illustrates the two sources from which Hebrew acquired its duplicate system of tenses. The constructions with strong or conservative waw (p. 96) go back to the Akkadian verbal system, while those with weak or conjunctive waw i.e. the simple forms, go back to the Aramaic verbal system (p. 152). Hebrew inherited these two systems through a merger

of many Semitic languages spoken by the diverse elements which went into the
formation of the Hebrew people, and not to the fact that Hebrew went simultaneously through the same stages of development as the other Semitic languages in various countries and at various times (p. 105). Although Hebrew
adopted and ultimately reduced 'the ingredients of the composite speech' (p. 105)
to a more or less homogeneous language, it was never quite able to assimilate
the Akkadian or archaic elements. This is apparent when one considers that
the consecutive forms required to be marked, either with the conjunctive
waw or some particle or other, and were therefore 'felt to be in some way unnatural or improper,'i.e. not indigenous in the language (p. 96). Indeed the
reason why the initial long -ā- in qātáltā did not become šewa as in qᵉtaltém
was that it was felt to be archaic and therefore the expected shortening did
not take place in these cases. The form was 'taken over, as it were, bodily
into Hebrew' (p. 90 n 1) from the proto-Semitic verb where a full vowel occurred
in the first syllable as can be seen in the Akkadian qátlāta. It follows then
that the Hebrew qātál is an imperfect synthesis of Eastern and Western forms;
for the long -ā- reflects the accented -a- of the Akkadian qátil and the tone
on the short -a- corresponds with that on the Aramaic qᵉtál (p. 90 n 3). There
can be no doubt, however, that in an earlier stage of the spoken language the
older forms (i.e. the consecutive tenses) were distinguished from the younger
or Western forms by a different pronunciation/intonation relics of which can be
see in wᵉqàtaltá where the secondary tone marks the more primitive accentuation,
and in the weak imperfect consecutives forms such as wayyíbn as opposed to the
later wayyibnéh (pp. 90, 96-7). The Massoretes unwittingly assimilated the older
tone position to that of the Western style (op. cit.), though it is possible
that the forms were confused at an early stage of the language (p. 91) as these
forms hardly outlived the Babylonian exile (p. 96, cf. p. 137f.). It is also
probable that the present-future yaqattal was once a feature of the HVS but
that it too disappeared at an early stage (pp. 83-4, 106, but cf. p. 89 where
it is possible that Hebrew failed to develop this form).

A Detailed Criticism of Driver's Theory

First we shall look at his four arguments that the Hebrew language
and people are composite, and then we shall examine his view on the historical
development of the Eastern and Western verbal systems.

1.3.8.13 A Mixture of Peoples

Firstly, we should notice that the evidence presented by Driver
is rather meagre; it also ignores the major traditions of the Hebrews about

their origin. Secondly, it is difficult to see how Deut. 26:5 refers to an Aramaean element in the Hebrew nation when it refers to an <u>individual</u>, and the <u>father</u> of the Twelve Tribes at that who <u>spoke</u> Hebrew (Gen. 31:47).

Thirdly, the references in Ezekiel refer to Jerusalem—not to all Israel. This should immediately make us cautious about using them in the way Driver has done. Closer examination of the text shows that they occur in an allegory possibly based on the cruel practices of the Canaanites. It would appear that baby girls born to prostitutes were simply abandoned in the open fields where they were probably born. Where the prostitute was a non-Semite (Hittite) and the father of the child a Semite, there might well be differences of skin colour, or racial features, etc., which would make it difficult for such children to be accepted as part of the local community. The chances of her survival were probably lessened by the preference for male children generally in the East. The infant girls who did survive would in all probability end up making a living like their prostitute mothers, hence the proverb (16:44): 'Like mother, like daughter' (RSV).

Jerusalem in her youth was bare, naked, and polluted (like the prostitute's abandoned baby), but Jahweh had pity on her and washed her, etc. (beautifully illustrated in finding and caring for a prostitute's abandoned baby). Yet for all his care she grew up a harlot (16:28, 30, 32, 34) patterning the life of the prostitute's daughter, hence the retort: 'You are the daughter of your mother' (16:45, RSV). Could it be that Ezekiel came across such an abandoned baby and recognized from its physical appearance its origins, or knew the mother, and this incident suggested the form of his prophesy against Jerusalem? Or did the prophesy of stripping Jerusalem bare and leaving her naked as at the beginning, because of her harlotry, find a ready analogy in the abandoned prostitute's daughter? In either case, however, we should be cautious about pressing the the allegorical details of the prophesy—which was delivered in the sixth cen- tury B. C.—into a reconstruction of the origin of the Israelites.

1.3.8.14   A Mixture of Vocalization Systems

That Akkadian (or Eastern Semitic) is said to share with Arabic (or Western Semitic) the phonetic principle of vocalization (p. 73) is enough to show that the so-called phonetic principle is not the exclusive possession of East Semitic. The phonetic principle can be seen in Hebrew, Syriac, and Ethiopic, where the guttural consonants take the vowel -a- exclusively (pp. 51, 44 n 7).

That Akkadian (East) shares with Arabic (West) the semantic principle of vocalization shows that this principle is not the prerogative of West Semitic. In other words Driver's contention that 'one principle [phonetic] has prevailed in the East, another [semantic] in the West' (p. 62) is misleading. We give his own evidence for both principles in Akkadian. He gives examples of the phonetic principle in operation on pp. 46, 48 where he says, 'Here, then, there are two distinct principles at work, the one (proto-Semitic) Eastern with its exclusive preference for qatil even in an active or transitive sense, the other Western with its retention of this form for stative verbs and its increasing tendency towards qatal for all active verbs.' But on p. 54 he notes that the transitive sense of qatil is rare, and that the form was originally stative (see 1.3.8.1) He gives other examples of the phonetic rule in Akkadian on pp. 69, 71, 57-8.

The evidence for the semantic principle in Akkadian goes right back to the universal qatil where it denoted only a state; the transition to states began with the introduction of iqatal. '...thus the softest vowel came by... chance to be the sign par excellence of state....Contrariwise, the hardest vowel, namely a, was generally chosen when the need for a distinct form to describe activity...came to be felt...' (p. 45). Even in the four active per-mansives mentioned by Rowton (1962:235), which occur hundreds of times in Akkadian literature, the context alone determines whether they are active or stative (p. 238). Driver notes that all Akkadian verbs fall into one or other of the following three schemes:

qatil	iqatal	iqtul
qatil	iqatil	iqtul
qatil	iqatil	iqtil

yet he is forced to admit that

> neither scheme, either that resting on the meaning [the semantic or Western principle] or that resting on the sound [the phonetic or proto-Semitic principle], has been entirely carried through, and it is often difficult to see why the one rather than the other has been preferred in any given case....in other words, why is sometimes the meaning and sometimes the sound the effective cause of the vocalization? (p. 56)

Indeed, he is not sure 'whether the meaning or the nature of the consonants is [to be] considered originally to have been the predominant influence in determining the vocalization' (p. 58). He even points out examples of Akkadian roots which have 'the two types of inflexion, that dependent on the meaning and that dependent on the consonants, fully developed, and this suggests that many more, if not all of them, may have had double sets of tense-formations but that examples of all their forms have not yet been found' (p. 59). Finally he says, 'The result of this examination of the forms of the Akkadian and Hebrew verbs is to show that several principles underlie the vocalization as found in extant texts'

(p. 72), and proceeds to give us a diagram showing three principles shared by Hebrew and Akkadian (p. 73) and presumably by all the other Semitic languages. In the light of his own results it is difficult to see how Hebrew borrowed the phonetic principle from the Akkadian strand, and the semantic principle from the Aramaean strand when both principles are present in both strands. A mixed system of vocalization is common to all the Semitic languages; and what is common can hardly be called borrowed.

Driver's acceptance of Lambert's classification of the Arabic consonants is another weak point in his argument for the phonetic principle determining the second vowel of the verb forms. For a more scientific approach to the classification of Arabic consonants see J. H. Greenberg (1950:178), and especially for the rules determining the patterning of the root morphemes. These rules would suggest that the chances of one of Driver's 'surds' occurring as the third radical in the case of Hebrew's 1890 roots are one in two. Of the remaining 50% with no 'surd' in the third position it was found that one in two of the second radicals will be a 'surd'. Now if 'surds' are supposed to prefer the -u- vowel then we can have no difficulty in accounting for the -u- vowel since the chances of a 'surd' in either second or third position are 75 in 100 (or 75% of all roots), especially when we can assume that this preference or influence 'may be either progressive [i.e. the surd in second position can overrule the influence of a grêle or claire in the third position] or regressive [i.e. the surd in the third position can overrule the influence of a grêle or claire in the second position]' (p. 46, cf. pp. 53, 56). If one then adds to this the rule that grêles and claires may also influence the second vowel either progressively or regressively one has a 'phonetic principle' that is so all-inclusive, or general, that it can 'explain' the choice of the final vowel in the various pseudo-verbal or verbal forms in the Semitic languages.

In one case Driver has actually created a difficulty which in reality may not exist; this concerns his division of the Hebrew perfect into intransitive (i.e. qātē/ōl) and transitive (i.e. qātal) verbs. This was an unfortunate division because he discovers that there are intransitive qatal forms in Hebrew (p. 48), and a number of intransitive verbs vocalized—'incorrectly according to meaning'—yiqtōl (p. 63). This unfortunate division is surprising in view of the following statement: 'Further, when the distinction is made in the Semitic languages, it is not between transitive and intransitive but rather between active and stative verbs, as Lambert...has shown' (p. 82 n 2). He also notes that the so-called accusative particle אֵת follows both transitive and intransitive qatal forms (pp. 52, 64, 65, 66). Once it is realized that the -a- vowel denotes activity and the -i- vowel stativity then it can be seen that there is no need to invoke Driver's 'phonetic principle' to account for the 'wrong' vowel in these verbs. Indeed, Driver weakens his own case for a mixture of vocalization systems in Hebrew with the statement:

> Clearly, then, in Accadian the phonetic principle is still strong, while in Hebrew it exercises, except in the case of guttural verbs, but little influence, having given place in most cases to the semantic principle. (p. 71)

The fact that both the phonetic and the semantic principles are at work in all the Semitic languages to some extent, as Driver has ably demonstrated, is sufficient evidence to lead us to be cautious about the extent of borrowing in Hebrew of either of these principles.

1.3.8.15 A Mixture of Vocabulary

It is interesting that while Hebrew has four negative particles, which are assumed by Driver to have been derived from four or more Semitic groups which went into the making of the Hebrew people, Akkadian has three of them. It is also significant that in his tables of duplicate forms on pp. 99–104 the same duplicate forms are found in other Semitic languages. Although these tables are not intended to be exhaustive, they are on that account open to misinterpretation as regards extent and degree of duplication in Hebrew when compared with the other Semitic languages.

It is interesting that when the 'Amarna scribes borrowed Akkadian vocabulary they usually retained the Akkadian spelling. Thus we find iqatal alongside ya/iqatal, and iqtul alongside ya/iqtul (p. 106). Why do we not find Akkadian and Aramaic spelling patterns in Hebrew? Is it that the Massoretes have artificially excised all such spelling differences (for Driver's view on this possibility see pp. 106 n 1, 140)? Or could it be, as G. E. Mendenhall has pointed out (1947:1), that the 'Amarna scribes...

> were not writing in the Canaanite language but were trying (with varying success) to write Akkadian. Consequently, it is difficult to isolate the verb forms and usages which can be regarded as Canaanite, since forms which look like Canaanite having the preformative yi- instead of Akkad. i- may have Akkad. vocalization.'?

In any case, the fact of the matter is that there is very little evidence (if any) of Akkadian or Aramaic spelling patterns in the Hebrew of the O.T. While this fact in itself does not undermine Driver's theory, when taken with the fact, again ably demonstrated by Driver, that duplicate forms are common to all the Semitic languages to some extent, then the theory is weakened considerably.

1.3.8.16 A Mixture of verbal systems

Driver's strong point that Hebrew has a duplicate system of tense/
aspects (based on the fact that 'the same phenomenon has repeated itself
twice on Palestinian soil, and this agrees with the known facts of history
in that country' (p. 98)) has been considerably weakened by recent doctoral
work on the North-West Semitic verbal system. W. L. Moran (1950) has shown
that Byblos has a qatal form with all the meanings of the Hebrew simple Perfect and Perfect consecutive. It also has a yaqtul form with all the meanings
of the simple Imperfect and Imperfect consecutive in Hebrew. T. L. Fenton has
discovered the same phenomena in Ugaritic (1963), and I. D. Marcus (1971) has
confirmed these observations. In Ethiopic we have the only other Semitic language with the yeqabber form. It also has the West Semitic qatal form.

The conclusion seems inescapable: if Hebrew is a composite language then
Ethiopic has a better claim to such a description, and the recent work on the
Ugaritic verbal system in particular shows that Hebrew cannot be a composite
language, unless, of course, all the North-West Semitic languages are composite.
More will be said on this matter in the main section of our criticisms which
follow.

In conclusion, then, Driver has not presented a convincing case that the
Hebrew people, vocalization, vocabulary, and verbal system are composite.
Further work and discoveries in North-West philology since Driver's day point
away from his hypothesis and toward an appreciation of the Hebrew language as
a distinct dialect within the North-West group of languages. It is also true
to say that modern scholarship is not as wholesale in its disparagement of the
work of the Massoretes as Driver was, and much of Driver's hypothesis is
dependent upon this disparagement being well-founded.

Major Difficulties in Driver's Theory

In this first section we shall simply itemise the difficulties as briefly
as possible before commencing a more detailed look at the weaknesses of his
solution.

1.3.8.17

Driver has not put forward very convincing evidence to support
his view that qatil had universal functions originally. The starting point
of his whole reconstruction of the PS verbal system rests on the hypothesis
that qatil had universal functions. The examples given by Driver where qatil
is said to refer to future events or states have been challenged by I. D.
Marcus who concluded: 'Driver's assertion that the stative originally

had a universal force—past, present, and future, and thus an optative force
is not borne out by the examples. Neither his examples of the stative having
a future meaning nor those of the stative having an optative meaning without
the particle lū are very convincing' (1971:12).[1] He also points out that of
the 450 examples of stative verbs in Rowton's article only one is held to have
a future meaning (1971:15). D. H. Madvig declares that, 'The significance of
the permansive is primarily stative; consequently it is used principally in
description. It has no intrinsic time reference; this aspect must be derived
from the context.' (1966:84). W. L. Moran had already reached this conclusion
concerning the Perfect in the Amarna letters from Byblos in 1950, but surprisingly few Hebraists have noted his work and discovery.

1.3.8.18 If qatal were a universal form and denoted past complete/incomplete,
as well as future/present tenses, then how can it be said that its past
incomplete function is older than its past complete function? Yet Driver on p. 83
does not see how qatal could retain its universal range of functions if it
primarily described an act, hence he assumed it lost its universal sense (except
in archaic material and phrases) and became a pure past tense. It is difficult
to see how qatal could retain its universal functions in Hebrew or any other
N. W. Semitic language unless it was in use for a considerable time to become so
well established that the form could take on a specialized function such as
'a pure past tense' and yet maintain the older, and in some cases opposite,
functions, e.g. qatal=complete alongside qatal=incomplete (cf. yaqtul=complete
alongside yaqtul=incomplete action).How can one have a universal act in the
past or the future? It was to meet this difficulty that Driver says its universal functions dropped away very quickly, but it still leaves the question
how it could have adopted universal functions in the first place if it felt it
necessary to drop them so soon afterwards.

1.3.8.19 Driver's suggestion that qatal cannot be a proto-Semitic verb form
because Akkadian did not develop it is difficult to accept when one considers
that in Egyptian the active-transitive use of the old Perfective (Pseudo-
Participle) is in Middle Egyptian merely a survival, but in Old Egyptian more
common (see A. H. Gardiner,[2] 1950:234-42). This would indicate, according to
Moran, 'that the active-transitive use goes back into the prehistoric period
and is perhaps as old as the stative-intransitive use' (1950:114 n 58). T. L.
Fenton rejects the suggestion that the West Semitic qatal grew out of the
stative, and gives it as his interpretation of the forms that 'The phenomenon
of the "stative verb", that is, a verb whose qtl form is qātēl and which has

an Imperfect of the type yiqtal, is a secondary development ' (1973:36).
It is difficult not to connect the Egyptian form with the West Semitic qatal,
and hence to trace the form back to a Hamito-Semitic stage, which is prior
to the Common- or proto-Semitic stage. The recent discovery of Eblaite, which
can claim to be the oldest Semitic language to be discovered so far, has the
active qatal form. If we place alongside this strong evidence the remnants of
a qatal in Akkadian (p. 112 n.2) the overwhelming conclusion is that qatal is
a proto-Semitic, if not a Hamito-Semitic, form. It is possible that Driver
has unconsciously followed the trend of his day and allowed the Akkadian language to dominate the proto-Semitic verbal system.

1.3.8.20   At 1.3.8.1 (3) Driver argued that qatil, and not yaqtul or yaqatal,
was the original verb form because 'it is hardly conceivable that subsequently
to the evolution of these two tenses another neutral form of universal application overlapping them can either have grown up or been created.' On this criterion, then, qatal must be prior to yaqat(t)al. And if he is right that yaqattal
and yaqtul developed in proto-Semitic before it split into East and West Semitic, then why does the universal qatal appear only in West Semitic? If a universal qatal developed after the evolution of yaqattal and yaqtul, then his argument for the priority of qatil is invalidated.

     But even more difficult is his explanation for the rise of qatal in West
Semitic but not in East Semitic. He postulates that the case endings were dropped
in'West Semitic'and this caused the verb to resolve the ambiguity by vowel
changes. For this to be the case we have first of all to allow enough time for
the case-ending system to develop, and then some time for its break-down, before
the qatal form is created, which it did in only one part of the Semitic world.
It follows that with the break-up of the case-ending system and the consequent
evolution of qatal in the West, East and West were clearly two separate dialects
at this point. How then is one to account for the fact that both East and West
developed yaqattal, yaqtul, the imperative, jussive, cohortative, etc., in the
same chronological order and morphologically identical?

1.3.8.21 A difficulty arises in his explanation of the rise of yiqtol=imper-
fect in the West. He places the rise of qatal before the evolution of yaqattal,
and the rise of the West Semitic yiqtol after the split with the East (which
must be dated after Stage 5, (cf. 1.3.8.7), yet his argument runs: 'the development of qatal as a tense describing completed action in past time caused
yiqtol...to become the tense of every kind of incomplete action' (p. 89). Now

presumably, the yiqtol that has become the incomplete yiqtol in the West is none other than the preterite yiqtol (developed at stage 3). How can a preterite yiqtol be converted into a present-future yiqtol? Indeed, how could a preterite yiqtol develop in West Semitic if it already had a preterite qatal? Were there two preterite tenses in West Semitic before it felt the need of an imperative (developed at stage 4)? And which came first—qatal or yaqtul? If qatal, then it could not have caused yaqtul to become a present-future, for the simple reason that it did not exist. If yaqtul, then what becomes of the 'universal qatal'?

1.3.8.22 The claim that 'the consecutive constructions are connected with the East-Semitic (Akkadian) and the ordinary construction with the West-Semitic (Aramaic) verbal system' [1] is not in keeping with Driver's findings. For example, qatal with universal meaning did not develop in East-Semitic, according to Driver, hence the Perfect consecutive is a West-Semitic construction. Also, yaqtul (preterite) is said by Driver to have arisen in the proto-Semitic period hence it cannot be an East- or a West-Semitic construction but belongs to Common Semitic. Moran has shown that both the Perfect and the Imperfect consecutive constructions as well as the ordinary constructions occur in Byblos (1950: pp. 38, 51), and Fenton has done the same for Ugaritic (1963: pp. 26, 35, 56, 77, 82, 86-7, 96; 1973: 34, 37).[2] If Hebrew is a mixture of Akkadian and Aramaic and came into existence at the time of the Conquest of Palestine, it cannot have derived its Perfect consecutive construction from Akkadian for the simple reason that it did not exist in Akkadian at that time.

1.3.8.23 If the universal qatal indicated past, present, and future, active and transitive meanings, then yaqattal cannot have been the first verb form to indicate Present-Future functions as Driver supposes, and it raises the question how yaqattal could have been formed in West Semitic as well as leaving unanswered the morphology of the form, i.e. why the doubled middle radical?

   He suggests that yaqat(t)al took over the active functions of the universal qatil, and presumably in the West it took over the active Present-Future meanings from qatal, i.e. those very functions which are said to constitute the Perfect consecutive, thus leaving qatal with the past function. Now since many scholars have shown that Hebrew, Ugaritic, and the Amarna correspondence from Byblos, show no distinct trace of a yaqattal form in these languages, it means that qatal having lost its Present-Future functions to yaqattal in remote antiquity regained these functions after yaqattal faded from these languages presuming of course that they ever had such a form.(See the definitive work of I. D. Marcus, 1971:75f. who was unable to find a genuine yaqattal form in the N. W. group of Semitic languages. Compare also G. Mendenhall, 1947:5 and T. Fenton, 1963:115f. The form is not even mentioned in Moran's thesis.[1]).

1.3.8.24   In the Semitic languages where the Perfect is used for the past and the future there is no distinction of tone between them to differentiate the two different time spheres. Driver admits that in order to hold that Hebrew shows a different tone position he has to assume that the secondary tone in the 1st and 2nd pers. sing. masc. once constituted the major tone position. In any case not all the 1st and 2nd pers. have even this secondary tone, nor is there an unambiguous connection between the movement of the tone in these forms and their meaning. No definitive work has yet been done in this area. (See Appendix 2 for a survey of work done on the phenomenon.)

Since none of the other Semitic languages makes any distinction between the Perfect consecutive and the ordinary Perfect, it is just possible that we are asking the wrong question concerning its meaning. A new meaning for the Perfect could avoid the 'tense' difficulty altogether. It should be noted that the tone differs from one language to another, thus Arabic qátala, but Ethiopic qatála, while Hebrew has qātál and Aramaic qetál; yet in all these languages when the Perfect is used alone for the future there is no change of tone. No valid arguments can be drawn from tone position as to the meaning of a verb form, only the context can show whether the action is to take place in the future or has already taken place in the past. There are over 200 examples in Hebrew where the simple Perfect has a future meaning. The same phenomenon occurs in Ugaritic including the dialect of Byblos.

1.3.8.25   Again, where the Imperfect is used for past and future actions in any Sem. lang. there is no difference in tone position. Again Driver has to resort to the apocopated Imperfects to find a different tone position. However, it is interesting that in no language is there any difference between the simple yaqtul used as a past and used as a present–future. Again this may not be surprising if the form does not indicate 'tense' relationships. It is only when tense–aspect relationships are imposed that peculiar difficulties are created for the HVS. A change of approach to the problem may eliminate these artifical difficulties.

It is a common failing with the historical–comparative approach to undervalue, or ignore, the fact that the simple Perfect and Imperfect forms make no tonal distinction when used in their opposite 'tense' or function in any Semitic language. On other occasions undue attention is paid to the shift of tone position with the consecutive Imperfects in Hebrew, without considering the possibility or probability of an alternative explanation, which an inductive study of the phenomenon might supply, for example, the apocopation of weak verbs such as the Lamedh Hē class of verbs.

1.3.8.26   Again, it is worth pointing out that in no Semitic language is there a difference of tone position between the preterite yaqtul and the Jussive yaqtul in the strong verb. If the historical languages feel no need to introduce a tone dististinction why should it be required in proto-Semitic? (See 1.3.9.16)

1.3.8.27   Driver thinks that the two qatal forms were distinguished by tone position, but he does not make clear whether the difference is between complete action (in the past, i.e. qatál) and incomplete action (i.e. the universal present-future meaning qátal), or between Past on the one hand, and Present-Future on the other hand. If it is the former distinction this cannot explain the two positions in qatil; if it is the latter it is unnecessary since qatil primarily describes a durative state in any time sphere.

   If yaqatal took over the active present-future meaning of the universal qatil, then yaqatil must have taken away the stative present-future meanings, where does that leave qatil? And if yaqtul took away the active past functions of qatil and yaqtal took away its stative past functions, what is there left for qatil to denote?

   These eleven difficulties, while not insuperable, nevertheless are the basic weaknesses in Driver's theory in its present form. It is appreciated that it is inevitable, given the nature of the historical-comparative approach, that many of the missing links in the development of language have to be bridged by scholarly conjecture. The following observations are not intended to denigrate this approach, but to focus attention on its Achilles' heel.

1.3.8.28   The striking thing one notices about Driver's theory is the number of a priori arguments used at the heart of his reconstruction of the HVS. Some of these are questionable, such as the priority of qatil because states precede tenses (p. 80ff.); that what is simpler is earlier (see 1.3.8.1(1)); that primitive man would be more occupied with the present and future than with the past (1.3.8.1(2)); that to reflect as well as to relate and to compare are the predominating marks of a later age (1.3.8.1(2)); that naïve and unconscious experience become more characteristic of the earlier period the further back one

goes; that the past tense is the last tense to evolve; that pronominal suffixes are more primitive because they are less worn away than the prefixes
(yet the prefixes in all the Semitic languages are identical, and show identical 'wearing' after centuries of independent development); that afformative
forms are older than preformative forms; that the prefix ta- in taqtul is
explicable only as having arisen out of qat(i)lat, where it is a nominal ending, and the -ū in yaqtulū has arisen from qat(i)lū (see 1.3.8.1); that the
evolution of awareness began with the description of permanent states and only
later moved to the description of temporary states (i.e. tenses); that forms
descriptive of facts are more primitive than those expressing moods; that the
Massoretes, having lost the true pronunciation, introduced hopeless confusion
where formerly there had been perfect clarity, i.e. they gave all the Imperfects milra' tone thus obliterating the distinction between the East Semitic
yáqtul and the West Semitic yaqtúl (1.3.8.2. p. 125 above); that the preterite and jussive yaqtul cannot have a common origin for their forms (1.3.8.4);
that the jussive and cohortative, being moods, must be later than the descriptive tenses (1.3.8.6.); that there can be no underlying connection between
the preterite and the present-future usages of yaqtul; and lastly, that there
is no semantic connection between the past and the present-future usages of
qatal in Hebrew.

Many of these a priori and a posteriori arguments are based on Driver's
tendency to assume that the Semitic verb forms express clearly definable
tense-orientated aspects. Right at the outset of his reconstruction of the
development of the PS verbal system Driver equated the complete: incomplete
opposition with the tense opposition, past: present-future. For example, PS
yaqt·l/complete began its existence as a preterite or Aorist tense, and,
according to Driver's reconstruction, it could not be used in any time sphere
but the past. He held that it never has a nascent meaning (pp. 33, 91; see
p. 128 above). It is quite probable that Driver may not have intended con-
sciously to understand the Semitic verbal system in terms of time, but
much of what he has written appears to imply such an understanding.

1.3.8.29   The Cohortative. In one way this verb-form crystallizes the cen-
            tral difficulty of the yqtl form in Hebrew, namely, how can
the same form have such diverse functions? Driver concluded that yqtl could

not cover both past and pres/fut. spheres and discovered another yqtl form
to cover one time sphere which relieved the burden from the other. However,
when we come to the cohortative we find that it is used to narrate historical
events and function as the first person indirect imperative. It also expresses
the direction of the will to an action and thus denotes self-encouragement,
resolution, wish, etc. How can the cohortative form cover such diverse functions? Is the solution to postulate another 'cohortative' form to share the
functional burden? For the distribution of cohortatives both without waw and
with weak and strong waw see Appendix 3.

Driver regards the simple cohortative form in 2 Sam. 22:38 as though it
were a preterite yqtl (p. 78), presumably because it is paralleled by a simple
yqtl form in the parallel passage (Ps. 18:38). If he were consistent he would
postulate two cohortative forms, one an old preterite and the other a more
recent and younger cohortative. It was precisely the same problem with the
jussive yqtl form that caused Driver to search for two yqtl forms to separate
the jussive function from the preterite function.

1.3.8.30   The Present/Future Yqtl in Hebrew. The recent work of I.D. Marcus
            shows that yqtl in Ugaritic has the same range of functions as the
Hebrew yqtl. It is the regular form in Ugaritic for narrating the past, and it
is frequently used to describe present and future actions (1971:99, 102). This
had already been pointed out by Madvig in his doctoral thesis (1966:74 n.1),
and before him T. L. Fenton showed that yqtl is the regular narrative form in
the literary texts where it even appears with a prefixed conjunction w- exactly
as in the parallel wayyqtl construction in Hebrew prose. Of the texts studied
he finds (1963:56, 82):

    561 examples of yqtl as a Past (largest category of usage)
    191   "   "   "   "   pure Future (second largest category)
    70   "   "   "   "   Past Continuous

Many implications could be drawn from these figures, suffice to note here that
if two yqtl forms are required in Hebrew, one from Akkadian and the other from
an Aramaic source, then Ugaritic and the other West Semitic languages must also
be composite languages; comparative Semitic studies do not bear out this possibility. Fenton interpreted his findings (above) to mean 'that yqtl has no
specific time-point reference, which enables it to be used as any "tense"....
In fact the use of yqtl in general statements is probably its most representative function' (1963:97).

1.3.8.31   The Imperative. Although Driver was aware of the morphological
            similarity between the imperative and the preterite yqtl, he says:

> ...it must not be supposed that the former follows or is based on
> the latter, since there are insuperable semantic objections to
> connecting these two forms; the identity is due merely to the
> application of the same principles, whatever these may be, in the
> determination of the vowel in both cases. (p. 32)

The only objection Driver has to connecting the imperative with yqtl is a semantic one. But this difficulty has been created by his own scheme of the development of the Semitic verbal system. See the diagram on p. 118 where he places
the rise of the imperative at stage 4 after the appearance of the preterite
yqtl at stage 3. He places the emergence of the pres/fut. yqtl at stage 6 and
the jussive at stage 5 which means that they were not formed or in existence
when the language (PS) required a distinct form for the imperative.

    Driver notes that the shortest possible form of the verb will be required
for the expression of a command. The analogy of other languages suggests that
it is the shortest form of an already existing longer form, i.e. that the form
of the imperative is a derived or secondary one, and not a primary form as
required by Driver's reconstruction. In English the imperative is identical
with the Present tense, as it 'has no imperative as a separate grammatical
category, that is to say, no verb-use which is necessarily imperative in meaning' (M. Joos, 1968:35). A. T. Robertson on the Greek imperative says: 'An
early imperative was just the non-thematic present stem' (1919:327).[1] Similarly, R. W. Funk writes: 'Like the subjunctive and optative, the imperative
is built on the appropiate tense stem, less augment' (1973:339).[2] Greek has
three forms of the imperative but each is based on its own appropriate indicative tense stem, they are the Present, Aorist, and Perfect tenses (Funk, op.
cit. p. 339).

    For most scholars the jussive or else the pres/fut. yqtl form forms the
basis for the form of the imperative.

1.3.8.32   The Qtl form. In Driver's reconstruction of the proto-Semitic
            verbal system he assumed that qatal was derived from qatil and
since qatil was held to have universal functions he thought qatal must have
had these also. We saw under 1.3.8.18 the insuperable difficulties with this
reconstruction. We saw under 1.3.8.22 that his statement that the consecutive
qtl construction was an East Semitic or Akkadian form was incautious. We now
know from recent work that the consecutive qtl is not confined to Hebrew.

In the dialect of Byblos 33 examples of qtl used for future action were found. Of these 24 were found to be preceded by the conjunction 'and' (u), thus paralleling the Perfect consecutive in Hebrew. Other examples were found where qtl was preceded by u and the meaning indicated past action. Another 122 examples were found of the simple qtl form with a present meaning. From these facts it was concluded that: (1) the qtl form cannot be a tense in the true sense of the word; (2) the qtl form in itself does not express the completion of an action or state; and (3) in every case the context determined the time sphere of the action; lastly, (4) the qtl form merely states the fact of an action, but it says nothing about the mode of action, or whether the action was customary, iterative, completed or incompleted (see Moran, 1950).

These findings support the view of many 19th century scholars who termed the qtl form 'Factum'. They also weaken Driver's statement that the consecutive qtl construction was not indigenous to Hebrew (cf. p. 90 n 1). If wqtl is not indigenous to Hebrew, but imported with an 'Akkadian strand' of the population, then consistency should lead him to postulate the same for Ugaritic, Arabic, etc.

Lastly, Driver calls the presence of the consecutive forms, particularly the consecutive qtl, in the Hebrew language 'archaisms'. The facts are as follows:

	Past	Present	Future	Others	TOTALS
wayyqtl	14,202	307	30	432	14,972
wyqtl	71	195	438	631	1,335
yqtl	774	3,376	5,451	4,698	14,299
wqtl	484	545	2,932	2,417	6,378
qtl	10,830	2,454	255	335	13,874

Now even if we allow for the possibility that the RSV has not correctly translated each form in a few cases, the fact remains that wayyqtl is the most common verb form in the OT. In what sense it can be said to be archaic, given these facts, is difficult to say. Perhaps Driver's statement that these forms were 'felt' to be unnatural may well reflect his own feelings for these forms, in the light of his own reconstruction, rather than the feelings of the Hebrew writers themselves.

1.3.8.32   Conclusion

Driver's theory dsiplays a good deal of acumen and learning, and has taken into account the not inconsiderable amount of literature on the subject. The originality of his work on the tenses lies in his rearrangement of the order of development of the verbal forms. While the solution may be Driver's

the approach is Bauer's. For example, both scholars commence their reconstruction of the HVS with the same basic premise, namely, form and function
are not uniform. They could not accept the possibility of double or opposite
functions inhering in each of the Hebrew simple verb forms. Each, then, started
out with the premise that behind the simple forms lay twin forms which were
originally differentiated by the position of the verbal tone. Bauer resolved
the issue by postulating two layers, an older (Akkadian) and a younger one
(West Semitic). Driver resolved the issue by postulating an original, or PS,
verbal system which was retained alongside a later, radically different,
verbal system (i.e. Aramaic).

Another point of similarity between the two approaches is the way both
scholars attributed a specific mode (or tense) to an early form and supposed
that this then dominated and determined the way forward as regards the rest
of the reconstruction of the development of the PS verbal system. In Bauer's
case he argued that yaqtul was the first real verb which had universal functions.
Everything else depended upon this premise. Driver, on the other hand, argued
that qati/al was the first verb, and everything that followed depended upon
this premise. As a direct consequence of Driver's choice Bauer's yaqtul is
restricted to single events in the past from the outset of its existence as
a verb form.

Lastly, both scholars regard the Akkadian verbal system, if not actually
PS itself, then the nearest thing to it. It will be interesting to see whether
the discoveries at Ebla shed any freash light on the question.

Neither the permutation of Bauer nor that of Driver is without merit,
but both suffer from the following weaknesses:
(1) Too great a degree of speculation at every stage in the reconstruction
of the PS and Hebrew verbal systems.
(2) A misunderstanding of the function of the tone shift in Hebrew and the
use made of this dialect phenomenon in the reconstruction of the PS verbal
system.
(3) The imposition of tense categories on the HVS in Bauer's case, and the
conscious or unconscious alignment of these tense categories with specific
Hebrew verb-forms in Driver's case.

* * * * * * *

1.3.9   The Comparative Egypto-Semitic Theory of T. W. Thacker

In 1954 Thacker published his book entitled, 'The Relationship of the Semitic and Egyptian Verbal Systems'. He treats the Egyptian and Semitic verbal systems separately before comparing their relationship. We shall not examine the Egyptian system except where it is necessary to make clear the relationship of Semitic to its Hamito-Semitic origins.

As regards the origin and development of the Semitic narrative forms Thacker makes no apology for the fact that he considers the Akkadian verbal system to have preserved almost intact the proto-Semitic system (pp. 118, 228, 322). The West Semitic system is held to be late and differs considerably from PS. On the other hand the Egyptian system of sdm.f forms resembles most closely the Akkadian system of preformatives and is therefore closer in that respect to the proto-Semitic forms than the corresponding forms of the West Semitic equivalents (pp. 228, 322). In support of this view he can cite four areas of agreement between the Semitic preformative conjugation and the Egyptian sdm.f formation, they are: (1) the stage of evolution; (2) the number of forms to be evolved; (3) the functions assigned to each form; and (4) the general structural pattern of those forms which correspond to one another in function.

The general outline of his view of the history of the Semitic verb-forms is as follows. In PS there was initially only one verb, this was the Permansive (Sem.)/Old Perfective (Egy.) qátil. Next to develop was the yáqtul form which took over the active aspects of qátil leaving it to denote the opposite, i.e. the stative aspect. Yáqtul was the exact counterpart to the now stative qátil form. Both were tenseless at this stage. The next stage saw the development between complete and incomplete action with the emergence of the yaqáttal form. These three forms were common to all the Semitic languages in their early stages, but as time went on two major changes occurred in the West Semitic group. The first of these consisted of a new form being introduced, namely, the Perfect qātál (p. 228). The yáqtul form up until the emergence of qātál served as the narrative (preterite) form; the new form to a large extent took over the function of the preterite yáqtul form in Hebrew, and to an even greater extent in Arabic, Aramaic, and Ethiopic, where this use is very rare, being confined to certain constructions and idioms.

The second major change to occur in West Semitic arose out of the above development, namely, it discarded its yaqáttal form because of its similarity to the intensive theme (i.e. Pi'el)(p. 189). The yáqtul form was in process

of being ousted from the WS system because qātál was taking over its preterite function. It was at this stage that the redundant yqtl (or an archaic PS
yqtl?) supplanted the functions of the disappearing yaqáttal form (p. 189).

On the origin of the WS qātál he makes two points. Firstly, it took its
form from the stative qátil by changing the -i- of the second syllable to -a-.
Secondly, the pattern for this change was the Present yaqáttal. On his view,
then, the WS Perfect was the latest form to be evolved (pp. 105, 323, cf. 237).

From this outline it can be seen that the WS development is quite complex,
for although it may look as though the WS yaqtúl had derived its present/future
meaning from the PS yaqáttal which in turn took it over from the PS universal
yqtl, it is Thacker's view that it derived its function from the universal
active proto-Semitic yáqtul (pp. 188, 236-7). The distinction between trans-
itive-active and intransitive-stative verbs by means of a vowel change began
with the yaqáttal form (p. 190, cf. p. 105 n.2).

With this understanding of PS verbal system as seen by Thacker we shall
examine the origin and development of each form in detail. The table on p. 154
shows the order of priority of the forms and the shift of function that they
went through in the course of their development.

1.3.9.1   The Origin of the Infinitive Absolute(Sem.)/Second Infinitive(Egy.)

The infin. abs.(Sem.) and the second infin. (Egy.) are the oldest
verb-forms in their respective languages. They thus agree in priority of
evolution. Both were universal forms, having both nominal and verbal functions. When employed as verbs they had no limitation of voice, mood, aspect,
or person. Both were incapable of inflexion and neither could be classified
as a noun, though they both had tendencies towards nominalization. They thus
agreed in employment and syntax.

The most ancient form of the PS infin. abs. was probably qatál and that
of the Egyptian sec. infin. was probably sꜥ⸗dám.[1] Both forms would thus have
the same characteristic vowel, i.e. -á- between the second and third root
consonants. The assumption is that they were essentially identical in structure. Later on their paths of development diverged, the Egyptian form gave rise
to various secondary forms while the Semitic form did not. Indeed, only in
Hebrew did the infin. abs. survive in its PS function, in all the other Semitic dialects the form became nominalized. In Egyptian it became more and more
a noun, but not wholly so.

PROTO-SEMITIC BASES		PROTO-SEMITIC STAGES OF DEVELOPMENT					HISTORICAL SITUATION		
(qṭl qṭl qṭl)		Ia	Ib	Ic	II	III	IV	V	VI
qaṭál	East→	Universal	Universal	Infin.Abs.	Infin. Abs.	?			
qaṭál	West→	Universal	Universal	Infin.Abs.	Infin.Abs.	Inf	(Hebr)	(Hebr)	(Hebr)
qátil	East→		Universal	Uni.Stat.	Uni.Stat.	Stative	Stative	Stative	Stative
qátil	West→		Universal	Uni.Stat.	Uni.Stat.	Stative	(Rare)	(Rare)	(Rare)
qᵉṭíl	East→			Imper	Imper	Imper	Imper	Imper	Imper
qᵉṭíl	West→			Imper	Imper	Imper	Imper	Imper	Imper
yáqṭul	East→				Uni.Act	Preter	Preter	Preter	Preter
yáqṭul	West→				Uni.Act	Preter	(Hebr)	(Hebr)	(Hebr)
yaqáttal	East→					Present	Present	Present	Present
yaqáttal	West→					Present	Pres(?)	Pres(?)	(Ethiop)
yaqṭul	East→						Jussive	Jussive	Jussive
yaqṭul	West→						Jussive	Jussive	Jussive
qaṭál	East→							Perfect	Perfect
qaṭál	West→							-----	-----
yaqtíl	East→							-----	-----
yaqtíl	West→							-----	Present

A Diachronic-Synchronic View of Thacker's Theory
Regarding the Origin of the Semitic Verbal System

1.3.9.2 The Permansive/Old Perfective

If the infin. abs./sec. infin. was the most ancient verb-form possessed by both languages it was very soon accompanied by the Permansive (Sem.)/Old Perfective(Egy.). This form is the oldest inflected one in both languages. They were both universal forms in their initial stages, and both have preserved something of their primitive character into historical times.

As regards the origin of the form it would appear that all the forms of the simple theme can be divided into three groups according to the base from which they are derived as outlined in the preceding table. They are:

(1) q́tl or sḋm;   (2) qt́l or sd́m;   (3) q́tt́l or sḋ́mm.

Bases (1) and (2) are the simplest and the most ancient, and both were initially uninflected and had universal meaning. Form (2) was the basis of the infinitive absolute, and form (1) was the basis for the later Permansive/Old Perfective. With the advent of nominal inflexions there was a desire to inflect the 'verb'. The base 'chosen' was q́tl/sḋm probably because a form accented on the vowel following the first root consonant would be more economical in vowels and would ensure that every element in the stem would be fully enunciated. Naturally the form was given the nominal inflexions, the only ones available. The new form thus acquired not only the external features of a nominal form but also its meaning. It was treated in all respects as a nominal form.

Although the proper sphere of the form was initially the description of state it was compelled to assume the role of an active verb when an inflected form was required. It thus became an inflected form of universal application. Since it was the only inflected verb-form it had to cover the whole range of verbal usage. It could serve as a finite form of a perfect participle. As a finite form it could be active, passive, or stative. It could be rendered by the past, present, or future tense as the context demanded; it was therefore inherently timeless and unrestricted as regards aspect. It was in every respect a form of universal application without limitation of any kind (p. 94).

1.3.9.3 The Imperative

This was derived from the same base as the infin. abs., namely, qt́l, because the abruptness of a command favours a form accented on the last syllable. It was inflected for number and gender, the terminations being borrowed from the Permansive (pp. 157, 320). The vocalization of the imperative was determined by that of the preterite yqtl in the case of Akkadian and the Prefix-form in the case of WS, though there was no ultimate connection between them and the imperative (pp. 156-7, cf. G. R. Driver, 1936:32-3).

The place of the accent is most likely to have been on the last syllable since the speaker would naturally hurry on to the final syllable and the first syllable would suffer severe abbreviation as a consequence. In any case its vowel was unimportant at this stage (p. 158).

On the origin of the form Thacker thinks that since the Permansive was employed as an imperative it is most unlikely that the imperative proper antedates it or evolved at the same time as it (p. 157). It was, however, a form which would have been required at a very early stage of development and its lack would have been felt before that of a narrative verb-form. As an inflected form it is presumably second to the Permansive in priority of evolution (p. 157, see Stage Ic).

Although the base form of the imperative is the same as the infinitive it did not originate in a nominal form since it is exclusively verbal in character. It is almost certainly of an interjectional origin, as is its vocalization (p. 157).

1.3.9.4   The Preterite yqtl

The possession of only one inflected verb-form would obviously be a great handicap to accurate expression and would often lead to ambiguity. It is Thacker's contention, and indeed the heart of his thesis, that the origin of the Semitic narrative forms cannot be found by an internal examination of its own forms but only by a comparative study with the proto-Egyptian forms; for prior to the evolution of yáqtul the only inflected narrative verb-form was the Permansive qátil. This form had universal functions but its proper sphere was the expression of state and passivity.

The explanation of the prefixed position of the pronominal elements is as follows. In Egyptian the primitive word order was subject followed by the verb. In conformity with the nominal character of the Old Perfective this was X sdm (where X represents a masculine nominal subject). Although there is no direct evidence, says Thacker, that Semitic ever had this word order (i.e. that it put the uninflected verb before the subject irrespective what number or gender the subject was), on the Egyptian evidence it is almost certain

that it too had this primitive word order. It went out of use in Semitic due
to analogy and foreign influences (pp. 234-5). The thinking behind this suggestion is that action is held to be the opposite of state; it is dynamic and
forceful whereas state is motionless and at rest. Some degree of emphasis will
therefore rest upon a word which describes activity and action. It will follow
that in the majority of contexts where the emphasis is on the subject the latter
will be in a passive state. On the other hand, where the emphasis rests on what
the subject is doing, i.e. the predicate, the position of the emphasized word
will normally be at the commencement of the sentence in both languages. This
resulted in a sterotyped syntax where the verb preceded the active subject,
but followed if the subject was passive. Unfortunately both these word orders
were lost in Semitic and the subject was allowed to precede the active verb if
it were emphatic. This rule was extended still further in Semitic so that even
the pronominal subject was brought to the beginning of the sentence. The result
of all this was that one got the logical inversion: as qátil X is to X qátil
so is ta + qátil to qátil + ta. For the 3rd masc. sing. pronominal element
ya was created. However, Egyptian has preserved the old rigid word order and
so has preserved the first two links which time has removed from the Semitic
chain, and this explains how the Semitic dialects came to have their pronominal elements prefixed (pp. 240, 235, 320).

The prefixed pronominal elements were characteristic of the new verb-
form and they were accordingly accented. The now unaccented vowel following
the first root consonant was elided (*ta+qátil > *taqátil > *tágatil) and the
vowel -i- changed to -u- (*tágtil > tágtul).

The function of yáqtul was universal and active as opposed to stative
(pp. 236, 320). It is the ancestor of the Akkadian preterite and the WS yiqtol,
one group (ES) having specialized its functions in one direction, the other
group (WS) in another direction (pp.320, 322).

Morphologically it can be shown that the Egyptian s͡d꞊m͡f form and Semitic
yáqtul are related. The accent in PS was initially yaqátil but later transferred to the prefix in order to emphasize the modification of meaning (p. 236).
The Egyptian s͡d꞊m͡f has preserved the accentuation of its parent since the
suffixed pronouns were not sufficiently heavy to draw the accent to themselves.

Semantically the derivation of yáqtul/s͡d꞊m͡f from qátil/s͡dm is impec-
cable (p. 236). Initially it was a form whose only limitation was that it was
active. As qátil properly expressed any kind of state situated in any time
sphere, so yáqtul originally described any kind of action in any time sphere

(p. 236). In the later stages of proto-Semitic (Stage III on the table) it probably had become almost exclusively indicative (p. 237) with a strong tendency towards the description of completed action. In the historical period (Stage IV) its functions have been developed in various directions. Akkadian has fostered the late PS trend and has specialized it into the form for the narration of completed events, i.e. past action. In WS, however, yaqtul has been developed into the form for the description of incompleted action, though many remnants of the late PS tendency to transform it into a form describing past events lingered on (p. 237). Since both forms are morphologically identical and both are narrative forms one may legitimately postulate that in an earlier stage of PS, i.e. at Stage II, the universal form could describe any action (p. 188). Since another interpretation for the origin of the WS yaqtul Pres/Fut. is possible the WS forms will be examined separately later on. It is sufficient to note here that since yáqtul/preterite is found in all the Semitic languages it is undoubtedly primitive (p. 186), whereas yáqtul/pres-fut. is confined to WS.

With the emergence of the universal yáqtul form the evolutionary pattern begins to emerge, namely, a protracted process of limitation of function. The Permansive, although nominal in origin and best fitted to describe states, was compelled to assume a universal character (Stage Ib). The existence of the infin. abs. helped to share the verbal load to a limited extent; the evolution of the imperative form deprived qátil of its imperatival function to a large extent. The further evolution of an active universal yáqtul took away qatil's active narrative function leaving it free to operate in its natural sphere—the description of states (p. 322). At this stage in the evolutionary development the contrast was between stative and active, but with the introduction of the yaqáttal/s⌐=d⌐m•m⌐f form a further limitation of function developed and a different contrast introduced.

1.3.9.5   The Yaqáttal Form

Thacker thought that it was most improbable that the first requirement of the primitive Egyptians and Semites would be an active present/future form (p. 230), since that would involve a double step. It would demand that the transition from state to action and from timelessness to present/future was made in one step. The language of both peoples shows that they were con-

scious not so much of time as aspect. Also the very pattern of the form
shows that it is more closely allied with action since the repetition of one
of the root consonants could describe repeated action or continuous activity
quite effectively, whereas to ascribe tense to the form is not so readily
apparent. In Thacker's opinion this precludes any direct connection with qátil
which has no doubled consonant. He offers two possibilities for its origin
(p. 238). The Semitic stem may have been derived from the universal yáqtul
form before the elision of the vowel following the first root consonant (i.e.
*yaqátil). Or alternatively and more probably it could have been derived from
a nominal base such as qattāl and conjugated on the model of yáqtul because of
its active character (p. 238). The accentuation of the Egyptian form makes it
unlikely that it was derived from its perfective śd⸗m‿f. Perhaps it was derived
from a nominal base with the third radical doubled. The Semitic form has -a-
as its characteristic vowel. This is very fitting for an active form as is also
the choice of -a- between the second and third radicals.

Stage III shows the effect of this new narrative form on the existing active universal yáqtul form. There were two immediate effects, firstly, it was
used only when it was desired to stress the continuity or incompletion of an
action, but inevitably it encroached on yáqtul's sphere. The result of this
tendency was that yáqtul became polarized to narrate actions the opposite of
the new form, namely, completed action (pp. 237, 330). Secondly, the new form
altered the balance of verbal contrast from active versus stative to complete
versus incomplete (pp. 175, 186-7). The yaqáttal/śd⸗m‿m‿f verb was the first
to indicate action of a special kind. It was also the first to introduce the
distinction between transitive/active and intransitive/stative by means of
vowel changes. Already in Akkadian iqattul occurs with some intransitive
verbs. There is nothing to suggest that thematic vowels occurred with qátil
and yáqtul in PS; they are not found in Akkadian. The yaqáttul form was thus
probably PS (pp. 180, 105 n. 2).

1.3.9.6   The Jussive

Three forms inflected by prefixed elements were evolved at the
PS stage as a result of the deficiencies of the Permansive and the imperat-
ive. Two were indicative narrative forms and the latest to be formed was the
Jussive (Sem.)/Prospective (Egy.). Since this form is common to Semitic and

Egyptian it must be primitive (p. 186). The quality of the vowels and the accentuation are secondary as they have been assimilated in the case of Akkadian to the preterite vocalization and accentuation, and in the case of WS to the yaqtúl/pres-fut. (pp. 183-4). Since the jussive in East and West Semitic is morphologically and semantically the same it may be assumed that they have a common PS ancestor, the primitive accentuation of which was very probably on the last syllable, thus yaqtúl. The accent shifted to the first syllable at a later stage of PS in accordance with the rules of accentuation then in force (p. 184).

For the origin of the jussive Thacker sees only one possible source—the imperative. The only other contender was the preterite yáqtul but he can see no obvious transition between ikšud 'he captured' and ikšud 'let him capture'. One must, therefore, assume that the two forms are formally independent. The jussive was created by prefixing the requisite pronominal elements to the imperative on the analogy of the Present/Future and Preterite forms. The unstressed vowel of the first syllable of the imperative was elided giving yaqtúl (pp. 189, 230). This theory of the origin of the jussive form receives 'powerful Egyptian support' according to Thacker (p. 169).

1.3.9.7   The West Semitic Qatal

In our review of the origin of the PS qátil and to some extent in our review of the yaqáttal form we touched briefly on the origin of the WS qatal. There we noted that its form was taken from the very ancient qátil form, and its pattern of vowels by analogy with the yaqáttal form (p. 105 n.2). At the PS stage qátil could and did function as a finite verb. As such it was not restricted to stative functions (p. 94). In the early WS speech the transitive functions of qátil were developed until it became the form descriptive of completed action and finally ousted the preterite yáqtul in this sphere (p. 105). All the Semitic languages (except Akkadian) developed this new form. Why this should have come about is not clear, unless it was felt that a form with postfixed inflexions provided a better morphological contrast to one with prefixed inflexions. In any case the vowel of the second syllable was changed to -a- and received the accent to draw attention to it. The fact that Arabic is accented qátala is doubtless because the laws of accentuation in force in that language make it impossible to hold the accent on the open second syllable with its short vowel and compel it to advance to

the first syllable. By analogy the -i- of the intransitive qatil(a) was
accented, but Ethiopic and Arabic have not taken this second step and have
preserved the primitive accentuation of the form (p. 106).

Despite their divergent functions the Akkadian Permansive and the WS
qatal(a) are derived from the same PS original, and initially qatal enjoyed
the same universality of employment as the Akkadian qátil form (pp. 94, 107,
cf. pp. 90, 118). The fact that the Egyptian Old Perfective and the Akkadian
Permansive stand very close to each other in function and have no counterpart to the WS qatal(a) points to the conclusion that the latter is a development peculiar to the West (p. 118).

1.3.9.8   The West Semitic Yaqtul

Two questions need to be asked about this form. Firstly, is the
WS yáqtul form primary or secondary? And secondly, is the function of the
form primitive or derived?

On the first question Thacker notes that if the form yáqtul denotes continuity its structure is not ideally suited to express this whereas the form
yaqáttal is; therefore the form yáqtul = continuity is not likely to be a new
creation but much more likely to be an adaptation of an earlier form. If so,
there are only two forms with which it could be equated, namely, yáqtul/pret-
erite, or yaqtúl/jussive. Due to the limited modal use of the latter Thacker
thinks it most improbable that it could be the parent. There remains then
only yáqtul/preterite (p. 188).

On the second question Thacker presents two different answers. Firstly,
he argues that its meaning is primitive, that it goes back to the universal
functions of PS yáqtul. Morphologically the PS yáqtul and the WS yáqtul are
identical and both are indicative forms (p. 188). Semantically he notes that
they are not the same but he feels that this is not an insuperable obstacle
to equating them. One may postulate, he argues, that in the early stages of
PS there existed a narrative form yáqtul capable of describing any action,
momentary or continuous, completed or incompleted (p. 188). It was the active
contrast to the stative qatil. This proto-yáqtul described any kind of action
in any time sphere, including the present-future (p. 236). He notes that it
was the result of emphasis that brought about the new yáqtul/pres-fut. meaning in WS. Describing the way the PS universal functions of yáqtul were
later specialized he says:

Its function was the narration of active verbal as opposed to
stative notions. It is the ancestor of the Accadian preterite
and the West-Semitic imperfect, one group having specialized
its functions in one direction, the other group in the other
direction. (p. 320)

When trying to account for the evidence put forward by Poebel that the
Akkadian íqtul had originally a present-future meaning (see p. 188) and that
Hebrew poetry contains many examples of the preterite yáqtul he is quite con-
tent to trace both these functions to the PS yáqtul and then explain the predominance of the preterite meaning in Akkadian as the later PS tendency.
He also argues that the WS present-future yaqtul is a specialized development of the proto-yáqtul active universal form (pp. 188, 237, 320). He nowhere draws the conclusion that the WS yaqtul/pres-fut. has an equal claim,
alongside the Akkadian preterite, to be considered a PS form and function.

The second explanation for the present-future function of the WS yaqtul
is that it derived it from yaqáttal when that form began to disappear from
WS (except in Ethiopic). He explains as follows: The Akkadian iqáttal and the
WS yaqtul express two fundamentally different notions, namely, incompletion
and continuity. However these two ideas merge in present time. He then poses
the question, Which is the primary significance of the Akkadian iqáttal and
the WS yaqtul? He argues that continuity, or at least repetition, which is
one of its aspects, is the primary significance. Repetition is indicated in
the reduplication of one of the root consonants whereas the idea of incompletion cannot be indicated by such mechanical means (p. 175).

Now, since yaqáttal is primitive WS yaqtul must be secondary because its
form has been adapted to convey the same meaning as yaqáttal.

The following two tables illustrate Thacker's thinking on the probable
historical development of the Semitic verbal system. The two PS forms are
yaqtul/completion and yaqáttal/incompletion

	COMPLETION	INCOMPLETION
(1) Akkadian....................................	yáqtul	yaqáttal
(2) Ethiopic....................................	qatala	yaqáttal
(3) Aramaic, Arabic, & Hebrew.................	qatal(a)	yáqtul

Now if qatala in the WS languages is secondary and has replaced the PS yáqtul
(preterite function) the table can be reconstructed giving the PS situation:

	COMPLETION	INCOMPLETION
(1) Akkadian.................................	yáqtul(1)	yaqáttal
(2) Ethiopic.................................	yáqtul(1)	yaqáttal
(3) Aramaic, Arabic, & Hebrew.................	yáqtul(1)	yáqtul(2)

This results in line (2) being identical with line (1), but line (3) is impossible since there is no distinction between the two forms. If one WS language, namely Ethiopic, could differentiate between the two types of action it is most improbable that the other three languages of that group could not do likewise. Since the form yáqtul(1) is found in every line it is part of the primitive system. The form yáqtul(2) occurs only in line (3) and is thus the form that renders the reconstituted line (3) impracticable. It must be a new form which has been introduced into the scheme after the replacement of yáqtul(1) by qatal(a). If so, what form can it have supplanted? The only possible form is yaqáttal, which is found in lines (1) and (2). This gives us the following primitive scheme (p. 187):

<pre>
                                COMPLETION   INCOMPLETION
      Proto-Semitic............... yáqtul   yaqáttal
</pre>

The reason why WS (except Ethiopic) dropped its primitive yaqáttal form was because its form was proving to be inconvenient due to liability to confusion with the Pi'el theme (p. 189).

We appear to have two origins for the yáqtul/pres.-fut. meaning in WS. If its meaning is primitive the WS yaqtul = pres.-fut./incompletion goes back directly to the universal active yáqtul; if on the other hand its meaning is regarded as secondary then this has been derived from the PS yaqáttal. The two origins may be illustrated as follows:

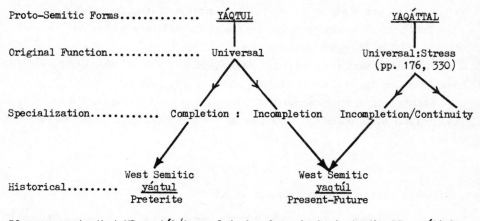

Proto-Semitic Forms.............. YÁQTUL   YAQÁTTAL

Original Function................ Universal   Universal:Stress
                                                          (pp. 176, 330)

Specialization........... Completion : Incompletion   Incompletion/Continuity

Historical........   West Semitic   West Semitic
                         yáqtul   yaqtúl
                        Preterite   Present-Future

If one accepts that WS yaqtúl/incomplete has been derived via the PS yaqáttal then PS yáqtul may have specialized to completed action in Akkadian, and its presence in Hebrew will be due to an Akkadian strand in the population (p. 189). It is possible, however, to harmonise these two views, see 1.3.9.14.

Assessment and Criticisms of Thacker's theory

Before examining his theory in detail in the following sections we shall note the influence of G. R. Driver's theory on Thacker's reconstruction of the PS forms and Thacker's modifications of his theory.

1.3.9.9   The Influence of G. R. Driver's Theory

The extent of Thacker's dependence on Driver can be gauged by the numerous footnotes to Driver's PHVS. Both men approach the problem of the Semitic verbal system from the same evolutionary standpoint. Driver traces the three main Semitic narrative forms to a universal qátil. The order in which they evolved was (1) qatil, (2) yaqátal(yaqáttal), and (3) yáqtul. Thacker accepts qátil as the starting-point of the Semitic verbal system and its priority. From it arose the narrative verb forms qátil and yáqtul, in Driver's scheme (1) and (3).

Both scholars are agreed that the Akkadian forms are the most primitive, and so both theories tend to deduce the primitive forms from an examination of that language's forms. Thacker in particular draws a very close parallel between the Egyptian and the Akkadian verbal systems and where these agree he regards those agreements as proto-forms.

Thacker follows Driver in thinking that Hebrew/WS had a proto-Semitic yaqáttal verb form (PHVS, p. 83). Both agree that it disappeared from Hebrew before the literary period due to possible confusion with the Pi'el theme.

Both men are agreed that the jussive is an independent form and preceded the rise of the WS yaqtúl/pres-fut. form.

Both agree that the imperative is an independent form. The suffixes have been formed on the analogy of the yqtl form.

Again, both scholars agree that there are two ethnic strands in the Hebrew population, Akkadian and Aramaic, and the HVS reflects this in its verb forms.

1.3.9.10   Thacker's Distinctive Contribution

Thacker diverges from Driver's theory on two major issues. Firstly, he disagrees with Driver over the origin of the yaqáttal form. He cannot see how it could have been derived from qátil because this form cannot account for the doubled middle consonant (pp. 168, 230, 184). Instead, Thacker suggests that PS yaqáttal evolved from a nominal base with a doubled root consonant.

Secondly, he differs over the priority of the verb forms. The priority of qátil is not disputed, but Driver holds that the next form to appear was yaqáttal. Thacker disputes this and argues that it was yáqtul derived from the first (qátil) verb form. He has two main criticisms of Driver's view. Firstly, to argue that the first requirement of the primitive Semites was an active present-future form involves a double step. It demands that the transition from state to action and from timelessness to present-future shall be made at one step (p. 230). This is most unlikely, comments Thacker, since the Semites were not conscious of time so much as aspect. Secondly, he feels it would be wrong to assign a purely preterital function to the PS yáqtul as Driver is forced to do seeing he has placed the reflection on past events as a later sophisticated development. Thacker cannot see how one can possibly separate the WS yaqtul/pres-fut. from the preterite yáqtul since both go back to a universal form.

Another point of difference between them is that while Driver created yaqáttal from the universal qátil form, i.e. a verbal origin, Thacker saw its origin in a nominal form such as qattāl. Initially it indicated stress but later it took over the active present functions of the universal active yáqtul. Driver, on the other hand saw it as a pres-fut. from its creation. They differed on other minor points such as the origin of the pronominal elements, but these do not affect the central issue of the tenses.

From these differences with Driver the most important one is his suggestion that yaqtul preceded yaqáttal in priority. This enabled him to give universal active functions to it and so account for the wide range of functions it has in Hebrew in particular. In his reconstruction he is not particularly interested in WS because its verbal system is considered a later development. His main interest is to link the Egyptian and proto-Semitic verbal systems therefore he is more interested in the Akkadian verbal system in making his comparisons.

It is not surprising, therefore, to find only two references to the consecutive yqtl and he follows Driver's view in these. He makes one reference to the consecutive qtl (p. 94) simply to note its future function. He follows Driver in seeing in these constructions remnants of an Akkadian and an Arabic strand in the language (p. 179). As far as the HVS is concerned Thacker's approach is the same as Driver. The explanation for the wide functions given to the yqtl and qtl is basically the same as Driver gave, i.e. duplicate forms with different functions derived from two ethnic sources.

1.3.9.11   Thacker's View of the Relationship of Semitic and Egyptian

He divides the simple forms of both languages into three categories based on the order of their evolution. The point he wishes to demonstrate is that both languages developed the same forms at the same time and in the same manner. The first two categories are as follows:

SEMITIC FORM		BASE : BASE		EGYPTIAN FORM
qatál	Infin. Absolute	qt l : sḏ m	Second Infin.	sḏ m
qátil	Permansive	q tl : s ḏm	Old Perfective	sḏ m
qᵉtúl	Imperative	qt l : sḏ m	Imperative	sḏ m

. . . .

Second Category

yáqtul	Preterite	q tl : s ḏm	Perfective	sḏ m f
yaqáttal	Pres–Future	q t l : s ḏ mm	Imperfective	s ḏ m=m f
yaqtúl	Jussive	qt l : sḏ m	Prospective	s ḏ m f

. . . .

The third category consisted of those forms that developed after Semitic and Egyptian became independent. Unfortunately this is where Thacker's three stages/categories prove to be too schematic for it does not take into account the fact that Egyptian has a causative theme similar to Semitic. He is no doubt right in his basic thesis that Egyptian and Semitic have too much in common that is ancient to deny them a common origin, but it does not follow that they went their own way after the second category of verbs were formed as the possession of the causative proves, unless one speculates that the causative theme was the earliest theme to evolve and the parting came after it had become established. The presence of the causative theme in Egyptian introduces the difficulty that the longer the languages developed together until the derived themes were formed the harder it is to explain why their basic forms are so distinct.

The forms in the two tables above certainly favour Thacker's thesis that Egyptian and Semitic have some affinity but the presence of the causative theme does not favour his evolutionary hypothesis concerning the growth of the Hamito–Semitic verbal system.

1.3.9.12   Thacker's Evolutionary Theory of Language Development

In this respect Thacker is in good company with Bauer and Driver. Both of these scholars set out to show that the PS language began with one verb, which of necessity had universal functions, though they disagreed as to the form of that first verb. The terminus was the historical position of the attested Semitic languages. Between these two points an evolving verbal system was devised using every available clue in the process, and guided by certain a priori arguments.

The chief disadvantage with this approach is that it is possible to advance more than one theory that is capable of explaining the evidence. Though one scholar may argue more plausably than another, there is inevitably always something speculative about the theories. Much of this speculation could be removed by drawing analogies with modern language development. The disadvantage pointed out here inheres to a greater or lesser extent in all the theories we have examined so far.

1.3.9.13   Hebrew: A Conglomerate Language

We have already noted Thacker's dependence upon Driver for this theory (cf. Driver, PHVS pp. 151-2). In Thacker's explanation of how Hebrew came to possess a preterite yqtl he gives the following account:

> It would seem that something like the following happened in early West-Semitic. The ever increasing and developing use of qatala to narrate action which took place in past time forced yáqtul, as a form descriptive of past events, into the background....In Hebrew its frequent though restricted employment is due to the Accadian strand of the Hebrew population. (p. 189)

In trying to explain why Hebrew comes to have the same 2nd fem. pl. termination as Arabic, namely, -na, he says, 'The Hebrew -na may be due to the Arabic strand in Hebrew' (p. 179). These kinds of arguments are difficult to prove or disprove. Just how sizable a 'strand' it would take to make its presence felt, never mind leave its mark on the language, is difficult to judge.

1.3.9.14   The Narrative Verb-forms

Firstly, the WS yqtl/incomplete. Thacker appears to give two different explanations for its function. His first solution is that it derived its meaning from the universal yqtl form, and is on that account primitive.[1] His second explanation is that it derived its incomplete meaning from a different PS base, yaqáttal, and is on that account a new and secondary form.

The first explanation is Thacker's, the second is a modification of Driver's view. Taking Thacker's modification of Driver's view first, i.e. that the WS yqtl is a new, secondary form, we may note that both scholars agree that this new form appeared after the rise and replacement of the preterite yqtl by qatala (p. 187). It was precisely this development, Driver argued, that caused the preterite yqtl to take on the new function of describing incomplete action: 'the development of qātal as a tense describing completed action in past time caused yiqtōl [preterite]...to become the tense of every kind of incomplete action' (see 1.3.8.7). Thacker, however, drew back from accepting this polarity solution. He accepted, nevertheless, Driver's view that the WS yqtl was a new, secondary form (pp. 186, 187). 'It must' he says, 'be a new form which has been introduced into the scheme after the replacement of yáqtul(1) by qatala' (p. 187).

It is not clear, however, whether this new, secondary form is the same as Driver's, namely, the preterite yqtl which has been made redundant, having been supplanted by the newly created perfect qatala (p. 186),[1] or whether, and this is the second possibility, 'new' means new life for an archaic yqtl/incomplete which had lain dormant, or had been used in a specialized manner, but which, nevertheless, had survived continuously from PS times.

If the former is the case, then Thacker has made a significant improvement on Driver's polarity solution with respect to the origin of the incomplete function in the WS yqtl verb-form. For whereas Driver viewed the origin of the incomplete function of the new (but in reality, the now redundant preterite) yqtl form as due to polarity, Thacker suggested that the new form supplanted the yaqáttal function in WS (p. 187), even though he was aware that: 'The Accadian present and the West-Semitic imperfect both express two fundamentally different notions, namely, incompletion and continuity' (p. 175). Driver, by contrast, made no provision for the transfer of the yaqáttal functions when this form died out in WS (as both scholars agree it undoubtedly did). Following on from this, if by 'secondary' both scholars mean that the form of the new WS yqtl/incomplete is in fact the preterite yqtl, which had been made redundant as a result of replacement by the new perfect qatala and has now been filled with a new meaning which it did not have before (namely, incomplete action or yaqáttal functions), then these terms are being used correctly.

However, if the latter is the case, namely, that the origin of the WS yqtl/incomplete goes back directly to a PS universal yqtl which had survived continuously in a dormant or specialized usage from PS times, but which was brought into prominence due to the replacement of the preterite yqtl by qatala, then the WS yqtl/incomplete cannot, strictly speaking, be called a new or secondary form.

One way in which the conflict regarding the origin of the WS yqtl/incomplete function might be resolved would be to postulate the origin of the WS yqtl from the PS universal yqtl. The explanation for its later predominance could be linked with the disappearance of the yaqáttal form in WS. The WS yqtl did not derive its 'incomplete' function from yaqáttal, but the disappearance of that form allowed it to expand into its sphere of functions. This development, of course, cannot be directly correlated to the changes that took place in the 'complete' sphere of functions. For there the development of qatala and its encroachment upon the preterite function of yqtl was one of simple subtraction. There would be no question of the displaced or supplanted preterite yqtls taking on the 'incomplete' function due to polarity (Driver's solution).

Because the WS yqtl did not derive its form from the displaced preterite yqtl (Driver's solution), but goes straight back to PS yqtl, and because it did not derive its function from a disappearing yaqáttal, but rather from PS yqtl, it would be very inappropiate to deem it a 'new' or 'secondary' verb form.

The main difficulty with this alternative explanation for Driver's and Thacker's solution is that they have made the WS yqtl form the youngest and latest to develop, whereas on this view the form ought to be considered a primitive form alongside the preterite function.

The dilemma in Thacker's reconstruction is that if the function of the WS yqtl is secondary and new (i.e. that it has taken over yaqáttal's function), then there is no contradiction in his statement on p. 187 that this verbal form is limited to three WS dialects, and is not found in Akkadian. If, however, the function is primitive (i.e. it goes back directly to PS yqtl), then there is a contradiction, because of the evidence of this verbal form in Akkadian and PS (p. 188).

Secondly, yaqáttal in Hebrew. Under 1.3.9.8. we saw how Thacker substituted yáqtul for qatal(a) in the second table which left only one odd form in the table, namely, yáqtul(2). Given the form in which he presented his reconstruction the logic of his conclusion is perfectly justifiable: behind yáqtul(2) must have stood the yaqáttal form. However, on this same

method he could have gone the other way and substituted qatal(a) for the
Akkadian line 1, table 1. This, of course, was not an attractive alternative
given his stated position that Akkadian was the nearest thing to PS, and
also his ready acceptance of the qatala form as a late WS development. The
evidence for the qatala form in Eblaite in 2250 BC will require a re-evalu-
ation of this long accepted premise. No certain evidence of a yaqáttal form
has been found in WS (see 1.3.8.23), nor in Eblaite to date. It will be
interesting to see what fresh light Eblaite may throw on the development
of a yaqáttal theme in the 23rd century BC.

Thirdly, the WS qatal(a). In a footnote on p. 105 Thacker argues that
the distinction between transitive and intransitive verbs by means of a vowel
began with the form yaqáttal.(Stage III, p. 154). Qatala is a purely WS development most probably on the analogy of yaqáttal: 'The West-Semitic perfect is
a secondary West-Semitic development which has no counterpart in Akkadian....'
(p. 118). Yet on p. 105 he traces its origin back to the qátil form (following Driver, PHVS p. 82):

> In the early West-Semitic speech the transitive functions of qatil
> were developed until it became the form descriptive of completed
> action and it finally ousted the preterite yaqtul in this sphere.

This development presupposes the existence of a PS qatila with active,
completed action functions at Stage III. Now if the active, completed and
incomplete functions were transferred to yáqtul and yaqáttal respectively,
this would explain why Akkadian does not have an active qatila function at
Stage III. But it also constitutes a problem, for at this stage in the development of the PS verbal system, according to Thacker's reconstruction, the
Akkadian and West Semitic verbal systems are identical. Only after Stage IV
do East and West Semitic go their own way (p. 240).

The difficulty can be partially overcome by postulating another stage
in Thacker's scheme, i.e. a Stage IIIb. This stage would allow for (a) the
vowel change qatila to qatala, and (b), the transference of the universal
active functions of qatila to qatala. This development would then explain
and account for the universal functions of qătal in Hebrew (i.e. the Perfect
consecutive, etc.) and the qătal/past, completed action. However, this modification to Thacker's scheme still leaves the problem of three active verb
forms in proto-West Semitic, yaqtul, yaqáttal, and qatala, the first two of
which have already deprived qatila of its active functions at Stages II and
III respectively, and before these could be transferred to qatala at Stage
IIIb. (The earliest appearance of qatala is after yaqáttal (p. 105) at Stage
III.)

1.3.9.15   The Imperative

On a number of occasions Thacker made the point that the terminations of the imperative have been borrowed from the Permansive-Perfect (p.
320). The imperative is by its very nature addressed to the second person.
In the following table the 2nd persons of both the Permansive/Perfect and
yqtl are given.

Language	Qtl	Yqtl	Imperative
Akkadian:	qabrā́ta	táqbur	qúbur
	qabrā́ti	táqburī	qúburī
	qabrā́tunu	táqburū	qúburū
	qabrā́tina	táqburā	qúburā
Hebrew:	qābártā	tiqbór	qᵉbṓr
	qābárte	tiqbᵉrī́	qibᵉrī́
	qᵉbartém	tiqᵉrū́	qibᵉrū́
	qᵉbartén	tiqbórnā	qᵉbórnā
Aramaic:	qᵉtálte	teqbór	qᵉbór
	qᵉtálte	teqbᵉrī́n	qᵉbór
	qᵉtaltṓn	teqbᵉrū́n	qᵉbór(un)
	qᵉtaltḗn	teqbᵉrā́n	qᵉbór(en)
Arabic:	qabárta	táqburu	ʼúqbur
	qabárti	táqburīna	ʼúqburī
	qabártum(ū)	táqburūna	ʼúqburū
	qabártunna	táqburna	ʼúqburna
Ethiopic:	qabárka	téqber	qéber
	qabárki	téqberī	qebérī
	qabarkúmmu	téqberū	qebérū
	qabarkén	téqberā	qebérā

With the exception of Aramaic, which would give the impression of having one
imperative form for all persons of the imperative, in every case the imper.
form is in fact the corresponding person, number, and gender of the yqtl form
minus the initial t- which is redundant semantically as every 2nd pers. of
the yqtl form has it in common. What is common, and therefore redundant, will
be discarded in an effort to say the word as quickly as possible, as in the
abruptness of a command. We have placed the 2nd persons of the qtl form along-

side the yqtl and it is clear that its terminations have not been used in the imperative forms. The four phonemes used to distinguish the imperative forms are: ∅ (zero, masc. sg.), -ī- (fem. sg.), -ū- (masc. pl.), and -ā- (fem. pl.). These are identical with the yqtl forms. Note especially the forms underlined and in particular the Hebrew and Arabic fem. pl. forms. There can be no reasonable doubt that the form of the imperative in each language is derived from the longer yqtl, in other words it is the 2nd persons of the yqtl but uttered as quickly as possible; it is not an independent form as Driver and Thacker assume (cf. 1.3.7.13).

If the imperative is a derived form in every Semitic language and derived from the indicative yqtl form how does this affect Thacker's theory? In the first place he put the development of the imperative among the top three most ancient PS forms (see table p. 154). If, however, the imperative is derived from yqtl then yqtl must precede the imperative on the priority scale. The situation then becomes difficult for Thacker's reconstruction because he will need either a universal yqtl or the WS yqtl/pres-fut. to come before the imperative. If the imperative is a quickened form of the universal yqtl then how can that same form be used of past events? The other alternative he has is to let qátil serve as the PS imperative (as he has already stated did happen at the very beginning of the PS language) and place the present or historical imperative after the rise of yqtl/pres-future. But since Akkadian does not have this development, according to Driver and Thacker, we are left with the problem of how the Akkadian developed its imperative from a preterite yáqtul. If the label 'preterite' could be removed from the Akkadian íqtul and the form given a meaning from which an imperative would be a natural extension then we would be on the way to recovering the meaning of the Prefix-form in the Semitic languages.

1.3.9.16   The Jussive

From the table of forms below it will be observed that the place of the tone on the jussive is the same as in the yqtl. In Hebrew and Aramaic yqtl and the jussive have both ultima tone, in Arabic, Ethiopic, and Akkadian yqtl and the jussive have both penultima tone. In no language do we get a mixture of tone positions; what the yqtl is the jussive is.[1] Yet Thacker goes along with Driver's suggestion, that though there is no distinction now between yqtl and the jussive there must have been a distinction in proto-

Semitic (p. 238). The obvious and simple reply to this is that if these languages do not require that distinction <u>now</u> what reason do we have for thinking
that they needed it <u>then</u>?

Just as we saw that the imperative has been derived from <u>yqtl</u> so also in
the case of the jussive (and cohortative). This dependence can be seen in the
fact that in every language the position of the tone and the morphology of the
jussive is <u>identical</u> with its respective <u>yqtl</u> form in every language. This can
hardly be a coincidence.

Language	Qtl	Yqtl	Jussive	Yaqáttal	Imperative
Hebrew	qātál	yiqtól	yiqtól		qᵉtól
Aramaic	qᵉtál	yiqtúl	yiqtúl		qᵉtól
Arabic	qátala	yáqtulu	yáqtul		'úqtul
Ethiopic	qatála	yéqtel	yéqtel	yᵉqáttel	qétel
Akkadian	qátil	yáqtul	yáqtul	yaqáttal	qútul
Egyptian	sádm	sédmet	sedmét	sedémmet	sdém

The accentuation of the Egyptian forms is conjectured by Thacker (p. 221). In
Coptic the tone is on the last syllable where possible.[1] Its 'causative in T',
which is held to be the last remnant of the Egyptian Prospective (= Semitic
jussive), and its narrative forms all agree in having the tone <u>on the same</u>
<u>syllable</u> (p. 226). The same phenomenon occurs with the Semitic jussive and its
narrative forms; the tone of <u>yqtl</u> and the jussive is <u>always</u> on the same syllable.
Thacker, however, has placed the tone of the Egyptian jussive on the last syllable and the narrative form on the initial syllable. Since the position of
the tone is conjectured in these forms to what extent has the positioning
been influenced by his presupposition that at an earlier stage the universal
<u>yqtl</u> differed from the jussive only in the position of the tone? See the table
on p. 154 where Thacker gives <u>yáqtul</u> for the preterite and <u>yaqtúl</u> for the
jussive. This is not in keeping with the observable facts in the historical
languages none of which introduce a distinction of tone position, not even
Akkadian. It would thus appear that in Common Semitic there was no distinction
either. Now since the position of the tone is identical for the imperative,
jussive, and <u>yqtl</u> forms, and since we have already established that the imper.
is a derived form, it seems reasonable to suggest that the jussive is also a
derived form from <u>yqtl</u>. If this is so then the jussive must be traced back to
a PS <u>yqtl</u> from which it and the imperative could be easily developed by extension. The fact that Egyptian has the equivalent (if true) must mean that the
jussive was created <u>before</u> Egyptian split off from PS. Diagrammatically the

dependence of the imperative and the jussive on the yqtl form was as follows:

Long Form   Intermediate Form   Shortest Form

| Narrative yqtl | ---------------> | Jussive | ---------------> | Imperative |

It is apparent that the jussive is none other than a quickened yqtl
(yašmíd > yašméd). It is a variation on the same form to impart urgency or
polite persuasion. Its form is 'half-way' between the narrative yqtl and the
imperative. Semantically this is also its position. It is not quite an imperative (the shortest form), nor is it a narrative form (the longest form). It
partakes of both which is reflected in its intermediate form. The jussive
and the imperative are derived from the yqtl form and this possibility opens
up new alternatives in any future work using the historical-comparative
approach.

Conclusion

Thacker has shown that Egyptian and Semitic have remarkable similarities
and that these are basic to them. In particular he has shown that the place
of the tone in relation to the initial syllable of the verb forms is identical
(except for the Jussive, but see 1.3.9.16) in both languages. Our concern was
not to trace the agreements between Egyptian and Semitic to some common origin,
but rather to trace the relationship of the HVS to the PS verbal system in
order to throw light on the meanings of the Hebrew 'tenses'.

It is only fair to Thacker's work to point out that his main aim was not
to throw light on the HVS, unlike the other theories we have examined. Indeed,
little or no attention has been paid to the central issue in his work which
was to trace the probable development of the Egyptian and proto-Semitic verbal
systems from a common origin. It was not our task, therefore, to evaluate the
Egyptian evidence (but see 1.3.9.11 above). For the purpose of the present
work we have simply extracted Thacker's reconstruction of the proto-Semitic
verbal system from his work. In the light of our examination of his reconstruction the following observations can be made:-

(1) His view of the HVS and the PS language follows Driver's closely with a
few, but significant, modifications.

(2) Because of this reliance on Driver's work Thacker's reconstruction is
    open to some of the same criticisms of that theory (cf. 1.3.8.32).

However, despite this reliance, Thacker has made two significant points that
deserve notice. Firstly, in place of Driver's polarity solution for the origin
of the WS yqtl/incomplete function, and also his explanation for the origin
of the form (i.e. that it was adapted from the ousted preterite yqtl in WS),
Thacker has suggested that both form and function go back to the PS universal
yqtl. This seems a better explanation as the form and function in question is
found in Akkadian (p. 188).

Secondly, although Driver is reputedly known not to have thought of the
Hebrew verb forms as expressing time, this point is not made clear in his
work (PHVS), particularly where he appears to suggest that yáqtul from its
inception was a preterite tense (see 1.3.8.4). It is quite probable, as we
have suggested elsewhere, that particular tenses were aligned or associated
with specific aspectual distinctions, and this accounts for some of the
difficulties in Driver's reconstruction. Thacker, by contrast, leaves us in
no doubt that the PS verbal system was not a tense but an aspectual system
(p. 230). Any indication of time by means of a verb-form came very late in
the history of the Semitic languages, and then the description of events
from this standpoint is usually only partial (p.322).

On the specific matter of the problem of the 'tenses' in Hebrew Thacker
follows Driver's view. As Thacker did not see the 'tenses' as a problem,
neither did he see the need to challenge Driver's position on this issue.
For this reason his work cannot be faulted; it was not an issue in his book.
His work must be assessed, and rightly so, on the relationship of the Egyptian and Semitic languages, and the probability that they go back to a common
origin. We might just add that nothing we have found in his reconstruction
of the PS verbal system would preclude this possibility.

                        * * * * * * *
                          * * * *
                            *

T. W. THACKER   175

1.3.10 An Evaluation of the Six Approaches to the Problems of the HVS

Under Sections 1.2 – 1.3.9 we have examined ten individual theories
which attempted to provide a guide or solution to the HVS. These ten theories
represent six different approaches. In what follows we will attempt to give
the basic outline of each approach and evaluate the proffered solution in the
light of the following facts, which also constitute the main problems of the
HVS.

Firstly, every tense ('order of time') in the English language is
required to translate the five Hebrew verb forms, namely, qtl, wqtl, yqtl,
wyqtl, and wayyqtl.

Secondly, every mood (except the imperative in the case of wayyqtl) is
required to translate the five Hebrew verb forms.

Thirdly, both aspects or modes of action ('kind of time'), i.e. Perfect
and Imperfect, are required in the translation of the five Hebrew verb forms.
For the Imperfect the 'Present', 'Future', and 'non-Past modal' provide many
examples. For the Perfect the 'Past', and 'Past-modal' provide many examples.
(see Appendix 1).

Each theory not only has to contend with these facts, but they also raise
other difficulties in the light of other facts not included above. Further,
they create new problems in the course of their own reconstructions. Reference will be made to these as they arise.

Note: The page references throughout the following section are to the
present work and not to the author's work unless specifically stated.

1.3.10.1 The Tense Solution or the Waw Conversive Theory

This solution originated with the Jews. We traced the evidence
for it back to the 10th century beginning with Japheth ha-Levi's Waw 'ătîdî
or 'Waw of Future'. David Kimchi (1160-1235) called it Waw haššārût or 'Waw
of Service', Dunash called it Waw 'otepet or 'Waw Oblique'; but finally the
term Waw hippuk or 'Waw Conversive' became the standard term for the phenomenon. The term may have been coined in the time of Elias Levita (1468-1549).

This solution is still popular in Jewish grammars (p. 21). Christian
Hebraists in the Medieval and Reformation Periods on the whole accepted
this explanation. In the 17th and 18th centuries it came in for some harsh

criticisms but remained the only practical solution until the middle of
the 19th century. It was the solution accepted by Gesenius. The explanation
became less popular in time because, no doubt, of the growing number of inexplicable exceptions to the rules that had been drawn up (pp. 10-11), and the
appearance of new explanations for the waw conversive phenomenon, principally
those of Ewald, Lee, and S. R. Driver. We have drawn attention to the inexplicable exceptions to the conversive rule on pp. 20-21, the chief of which were:-

(a) The use of wayyqtl in present and future situations (Append. 1, Table 3).

(b) The use of yqtl and wyqtl of past events (Table 4).

(c) The use of qtl (without a prefixed waw) of future events (Table 2).

The explanation of qtl and wqtl used in future events was said to lie
in the observation that 'the matter is as clear as though it had already
passed, seeing that it has already been decreed' (p. 8). Long after the
Conversive Theory had been abandoned by Hebraists this explanation was retained and incorporated into the new theories.

The Conversive solution failed because it tried to fit the HVS into
the tense structure of another language. In attempting to do this the form
and distinctiveness of the HVS was lost. The defenders of the Conversive
solution argued their case from the absolute necessity to convert the Hebrew
verb forms in translation.

The attempt to mould the HVS to a tense-oriented system resulted in the
gap between the Semitic and Indo-Germanic modes of thought being considerably narrowed, if not obliterated. As a consequence Hebrew was considered
to be either a primitive language with a crude tense system, or else it was
so closely identified with the verbal system of the translation language
that it almost became that language's verbal system written in Hebrew script.
This attempt, plus the initial presupposition that the HVS was a tense system,
constituted the basic weaknesses in this solution, and accounted for its
unpopularity, if not demise, at the turn of the century.

1.3.10.2   The Relative Tense Solution

The first to put forward this solution appears to have been
Julius Bate in 1751. He suggested that Hebrew had only two tenses, the
Present (including the Past) and the Future. He did not expand on this idea
or even refer to relative tenses as such. The first to do so was probably
Nicolaus Wilhelm Schroeder in 1766.

This solution did away with the need to convert the tenses since the two forms, qtl and yqtl, were given tense significations which were used in both an absolute and a relative sense. While the theory was accepted, disagreement arose as to the tense value to give to the two forms. The following permutations were put forward:

	YQTL	QTL
Schroeder, etc.	Future	Past
Weir	Future	Present
Lee, etc.	Present	Past

Schroeder's idea was supported by S. Johnson (1767), W. H. Barker (1773), A. Bayly (1773), G. Fitzgerald (1813), T. Keyworth (1825), T. Prosser (1838), W. Beeston (1843), W. H. Duncan (1848), W. Wilson (1850), J. G. Murphy (1850), and H. Craik (1863). One or two of these grammarians claimed to have discovered the idea independently, as did O. L. Barnes, who put forward this solution in 1965 unaware of its previous existence.

Weir's view has found no supporters since he produced it in 1849. Julius Bate put forward the nearest thing to it in 1751, but there is not sufficient evidence to show how he worked out his idea in practice.

Lee's idea was supported by T. Jarrett (1848), G. F. R. Weidemann (1849), H. M. Wheeler (1850), W. Paul (1852), who wrote a commentary on Genesis using this approach, and Robert Young (1862), who translated the entire OT on this principle. His translation has been reprinted to this day.

The weakness common to all three views is that the biblical writers are credited with the facility of being able to write all their accounts, be they historical or prophetical, from two standpoints. That is, they write either from the time in which they are living (the absolute standpoint), or from the time of which they are writing (the relative standpoint). It is claimed that the writer can alternate his standpoint from verse to verse and even from sentence to sentence. The switch in verb form indicated a switch in the writer's standpoint. The proponents of this view are well aware of the mental agility required on the part of the reader or listner to keep up with the writer or speaker as he shuttles up and down the time scale at will, one moment viewing events from a relative present position, the next viewing them from the absolute present position.

The main difficulty with this view is that there are a number of syntactical conditions and other factors which condition or dictate the form of the verb. For example Narrative and Direct Speech Styles have precise

rules governing the form of the verb; also chiastic structures will play
a part in the forms of the verbs. These factors are liable to create confusion as to the exact standpoint of the writer.

In some ways this solution faces all the difficulties of the Conversive
theory in that often the relative waw is missing. (In these cases recourse
is had to the Waw Inductive theory to get over the difficulty.) But most of
all it inherits the difficulties surrounding the idea of tenses in Hebrew.
The very fact that scholars have rung the changes on the permutations of the
tenses shows that these categories do not fit easily into the HVS.

One positive benefit of this attempt was that it recognised a bigger gap
between the Hebrew and the Indo-Germanic verbal systems which the Conversive theory had reduced to a minimum, or non-existent, level. The presence
of an Historical Present Tense in some languages, such as Greek and English,
helped to strengthen the theory behind the Relative Tense solution, whereas
the Waw conversive idea was unknown in any other language. Probably for
the reasons outlined above (pp. 23-4, 43, 59 (Schroeder); pp. 34-6 (Lee);
and pp. 40-1 (Weir)) this solution never really took hold in the universities and other places of learning.

1.3.10.3   The Waw Inductive Solution

This solution was put forward in 1818 by Philip Gell. In the
same year a similar idea was put forward by John Bellamy who attempted to
translate the OT on this principle. He understood the wayyqtl form to be
made up of the future yqtl form and a waw inductive prefixed to it. The
future form was chosen because the action was future to the first qtl verb;
it was translated as a past because the waw conducted the past tense of the
first verb to it (p. 25).

Gell took the view that there were only two tenses in Hebrew, a Present-Future (yqtl) and a Past tense (qtl). It would appear that he was unaware
of the two tense Relative and Absolute uses. He suggested that the tense of
the first, or governing, verb was inducted into the following verb which
retained its own tense subordinately (p. 25). He conceded, however, that
this principle did not apply to the qtl forms when used subordinately in
the prophetic writings for future events. He suggested, and this suggestion
was taken up into S. R. Driver's theory in 1874, that the consecutive qtl

loses its individuality in such cases and assumes the meaning borne by the first or dominant verb.

This concession points up the basic weakness of the theory. Gell held that his solution banished 'the barbarism of ן conversive' (p. 16). However, S. R. Driver held that the same solution shews in what sense the retention of the former term waw conversive can be justified, in that a limitation is imposed by the prefixed waw on the meaning of qtl. If this is indeed the case, then the Waw Inductive solution is a semantic refinement of the Waw Conversive theory.

This solution, like the Waw Conversive, had the effect of narrowing the gap between the Hebrew and Indo-Germanic verbal systems.

Although Gell's solution is little known it is the one most widely used when it comes to the translation of the Hebrew text. It has the distinction of being the most pragmatic solution ever put forward; it has all meanings for all forms.

1.3.10.4   The Aspectual Solution

This approach was adopted by John William Donaldson (1848), G. H. A. von Ewald (1827-79), and S. R. Driver (1874). Donaldson's version is not comprehensive enough to be applied to every type of genre in the OT. He set up the aspectual opposition, Single acts versus Sets of actions.

The main difference between Ewald and Lee's Relative Tense idea was that,while Lee thought of the HVS in terms of relative and absolute tenses, Ewald thought of them in terms of relative and absolute aspect/mode of action categories; but both took the idea of transportation of the writer to the site of the actual event(s) as their common principle. This latter principle was also used by S. R. Driver but to a lesser extent.

Both Ewald and Driver conceived of the HVS as being an aspectual system at first. Ewald made the distinction between Complete (qtl) and Incomplete (yqtl), whereas Driver made it between Perfect (qtl) and Nascent (yqtl). Both held that the observable trend in the language was towards a true tense system.

Both scholars acknowledged that in the case of the wayyqtl form the tense stage has definitely been reached. Ewald voiced the opinion that it 'exactly answers to the Greek aorist' (p. 52), while Driver argued that 'it

is inconceivable that it [wayyqtl] should have suggested anything except
the idea of a <u>fact done</u>' (p. 73).

Both men differ, however, in their understanding of the Perfect Consecutive form. Driver fell back on Gell's <u>Waw</u> Inductive solution and acknowledged that the Perfect did not indicate complete/past actions automatically
in this construction. In other words he rejected the Jewish understanding
of this construction. He reasoned that these Consecutive Perfects lose their
individuality and take on the meaning of the preceding dominant verb; consequently they could indicate incomplete action as well as future events.
This interpretation plus the introduction of tenses into the HVS constitute
the main weaknesses of Driver's solution.

Ewald, on the other hand, fell back on the Jewish interpretation of
the Perfect Consecutive phenomenon, where it is said to be used of events
which are regarded by the speaker as being already as good as accomplished
(p. 45).

Ewald's relative and absolute use of the two aspects suffers the disadvantages that we noted in the case of the Relative and Absolute Tense
solution with regard to the switch of forms and the positional present of
the speaker or writer. These disadvantages, plus the introduction of tenses
into the HVS, constitute the basic weaknesses of his solution.

One positive aspect of this approach, taken as a whole, is the impression that the HVS is somehow different from the Western mode of thought. The
introduction of tenses into the HVS, however, has the effect of considerably eclipsing or off-setting this impression.

1.3.10.5   The Factual - Descriptive Solution

William Turner belongs in a class of his own. The essence of
his theory was that the two verb forms point to an objective (<u>qtl</u>) and a
subjective (<u>yqtl</u>) view on the part of the speaker or writer. The <u>qtl</u> form
expresses the action (<u>qatal</u>) or state (<u>qati/ul</u>) as the attribute of the
person or thing spoken of. The <u>yqtl</u> form, on the other hand, expresses the
verbal action as in or of the subject, the produce of the subject's energy,
like a stream evolving itself from its source (pp. 77–8). Whereas in the
<u>qtl</u> form it was the act that was made prominent, in the <u>yqtl</u> form it was
the actor. He sets out the contrast in function and meaning between the

two forms as follows: Abstract (qtl): Concrete (yqtl); Objective: Subjective;
Factual: Descriptive; Statements: Pictures; Asserts: Represents; Reason:
Imagination; and Annalistic: Historical. Because there are no tenses and
no aspectual oppositions he avoids most of the criticisms levelled at the
other solutions. He saw no distinction in meaning between the forms in their
simple and consecutive appearance in the OT. Hence he avoids any hint of
conversion or a relative use of the forms.

It has not been easy to detect weaknesses in Turner's solution as far
as the theory is concerned. Unfortunately he did not give any examples of
how he would apply this theory in practice to the consecutive yqtl construction, nor in what way the simple waw prefixed to yqtl would differ from it.
It is not altogether clear how his view of the qtl consecutive differs from
that of the Jewish understanding.

Certainly, without a tense framework to guide his thinking, the Western
mind finds Turner's solution very difficult to grasp, and hence to appreciate,
and even more difficult to apply to the Hebrew text. Thus he has opened up
an appreciable gap between the Hebrew and Indo-Germanic verbal systems.
We have noted in evaluating the other solutions that the degree to which
the Hebrew verbal system was brought into line with the familiar Indo-
Germanic mode, the more problems it raised. Turner has provided a solution
that does not attempt to bridge that gap. He does not explain the HVS in
tandem with any other verbal system, but explains its own distinctive mode
in its own right.

1.3.10.6   The Historical-Comparative Solution

Those who have used this approach with the specific aim of
throwing light on the development of the Semitic and Hebrew verbal systems
were J. A. Knudtzon (1889-92), Hans Bauer (1910), G. R. Driver (1936), and
T. W. Thacker (1954).

This approach analysed the basic problem of the HVS as one of duplicate
functions inhering in the same verb form. It was thought that in the historical
languages this situation was clearly anomalous, if not improbable; therefore
a solution had to be sought in the historical development of these languages
which could account for the phenomenon.

In the case of the qtl form, Knudtzon traced its Incomplete/Pres.-Fut.

and its Complete/Past functions back to an original qatil, which indicated
a present state. This original meaning was retained as the Stative or Permansive in the Semitic languages. The emergence of the active qtl/Past came
later. Presumably the Pres.-Fut. qtl in Hebrew goes back to the original
present qatil state, although Knudtzon does not say so in as many words.
Bauer either hit on the same idea independently of Knudtzon, or else
took over this solution from Knudtzon. G. R. Driver and T. W. Thacker also
trace the two functions of qtl back to a universal qtl. They account for the
presence of the two functions in Hebrew by assigning the qtl/Past to 'the
Aramaic strand in the population', and the qtl/Pres.-Fut. to 'the Akkadian
strand' in the Hebrew population. Originally these two qtl forms were distinguished by the position of the tone.

In the case of the double functions inhering in the yqtl form, Knudtzon
traced these back to an original yaqatal/Pres.-Fut. (the long form), and a
later(?) yaqtul/Past (the short form). It would appear that what happened
in Hebrew was that these two forms coalesced in the shorter form, but their
meanings did not become totally confused. Bauer accounted for the double
functions of yqtl by postulating a universal yaqtul which retained various
aspects of its functions in different languages. The Pres.-Fut. aspect he
held to be a later development, hence its appearance in WS but not in ES.
Driver agreed with this latter part of Bauer's view, but he argued that
yqtl never had a universal function; it began life as a preterite tense and
remained so in Akkadian. The younger yaqtúl/Pres.-Fut. arose when qtl/Past
took over the preterite function of the older yáqtul form. Originally these
two yqtl forms were distinguished by the position of the tone.

A disadvantage with this approach was the tendency to
align or couple particular tenses with particular aspects, e.g. Incomplete
with Pres.-Future, and Complete with Past. This was understandable, since
it was assumed that when yqtl was used to relate present or future events
it was referring to incomplete actions, and likewise when used of past events
qtl indicated completed actions. This assumption is not always justified.

Knudtzon, Bauer, and Driver regarded the wayyqtl form as a true preterite tense in the historical Hebrew language. Following the Aspectual
Solution, they viewed the language as developing from an aspectual/mode of
action opposition to a tense-oriented system. Not surprisingly they differ
over the extent to which this development has taken place historically.

The introduction of tenses into the HVS inevitably leads to a narrowing of the gap between Hebrew and Indo-Germanic verbal systems. The whole development of the HVS is seen as the development of one universal verb to the complex situation in the HVS which itself is viewed as developing into a fully-fledged tense system. This approach leaves itself open to criticisms and censure on many points. However, it is possible to accept an historical approach without having to accept the method or the results of these experimental reconstructions.

1.3.10.7   Concluding Observations

We have examined six different approaches to the problems of the HVS. Two of these would appear to have some contribution to make in a future attempt on the intractable problems surrounding the HVS. The two are William Turner's Factual - Descriptive solution and the Historical-Comparative approach of Knudtzon-Bauer-Driver-Thacker.

Turner's view is interesting because it is the only solution that places a real psychological gap between the Hebrew and Indo-Germanic modes of thought. The general assumption in the other solutions has been either to view Hebrew as a tense system, or as a rudimentary, crude, or elementary tense system in a developing state. These assumptions are due no doubt to the fact that all the solutions put forward in the period under review have been the work of 'European' scholars. One wonders what assumptions non-European scholars (Chinese, Indonesian, Japanese, etc.) would unconsciously adopt in their approach to the HVS. We must keep the possibility in mind that European scholars have unconsciously, and understandably, looked for the familar in the HVS. Every care must be taken in future studies of the HVS not to approach it with any preconceived ideas regarding the nature of its verbal system. Turner's solution has avoided the natural tendency observed in all other solutions to align the HVS with his own native language. In this he is virtually unique, and this is his valuable contribution to future studies in this area. To say that, however, does not mean that his solution must be endorsed as the final answer to the HVS.

The other solution which could make a valuable contribution to future research in the HVS is the Historical-Comparative approach. Of all the methods tried this one would seem to offer the best chance of getting as close to a solution of the HVS as it is ever possible to get. A number of modifications could be made which would turn this method into a more objective, scientific approach. For example, the principles and methods governing language development ought to play a larger part in tracing the evolution of PS and the HVS. Too much emphasis was placed on the historical and not enough on the comparative aspect. The terms ought to be reversed and the future approach labelled as the Comparative-Historical approach.

Another modification that ought to be made to the Historical-Comparative approach is that instead of leaping back to Proto-Semitic forms in one leap, perhaps a less ambitious step should be taken first, namely, measures should be taken to draw up a Common Semitic paradigm of the verbal system, and from this CSP principles of change and methods for forming the various verb forms (imper., Jussive, and other Prefix-forms) could be worked out more objectively.

In the Comparative-Historical method greater emphasis ought to be laid on Ugaritic and Byblian studies for comparative purposes, especially the work of I. D. Marcus, T. L. Fenton, D. H. Madvig, and W. L. Moran.

Perhaps the most important shift of emphasis in the future should be placed on a thorough study of the two styles of syntax observable in Hebrew, Ugaritic, and Byblian literature. The Narrative and Direct Speech Styles in Hebrew were never investigated by any scholar in the period under review. Likewise, the position of the verbal tone had never been properly studied as a subject in its own right. Another area of research is the inexplicable use of the Cohortative form to relate historical events. Add to this the need to investigate the parallel passages where changes of verb forms occur, and it will be realised that a good deal more preparatory work will have to be undertaken in the future before we are in a better position than our predecessors to put forward a viable alternative to the theories of S. R. Driver and Ewald which dominate present-day Hebrew grammars and commentaries. Just as the Waw Conversive theory was a stop-gap solution until other theories were put forward, so these 'new' theories ought to be similarly regarded until a more objective and scientific solution is found. For the present, then, we recommend Turner's objective approach, the Comparative-Historical method, and no one solution.

* * * * * * *
* * *

APPENDICES
NOTES
ABBREVIATIONS
BIBLIOGRAPHY
INDEX

APPENDIX 1

TABLE 1

w^{e}qtl forms*

BOOKS	Past	Present	Future	Non-past Modal	Past Modal	Imperative	Juss/Cohort	Non-verbal	TOTALS
Gen	17	26	125	7	5	15	12	1	208
Ex	29	7	227	21	1	254	5	24	568
Lev	8	24	89	41	–	520	6	25	713
Num	22	28	68	23	3	247	4	24	419
Dtr	10	54	141	112	2	248	2	55	624
Jos	5	85	34	18	–	38	–	5	185
Jud	14	2	43	14	–	19	1	6	99
1 Sm	44	4	78	30	–	38	9	7	210
2 Sm	25	4	43	23	–	14	2	4	115
1 Kg	22	5	69	28	–	52	5	7	188
2 Kg	36	3	41	5	4	26	–	1	116
Isa	28	57	371	5	–	5	3	18	487
Jer	35	38	413	9	8	46	4	6	559
Ezek	31	46	627	33	11	66	1	14	829
Hos	2	3	60	1	–	–	–	1	67
Joe	1	2	23	2	–	–	–	1	29
Amo	8	7	80	3	1	–	–	2	101
Ob	–	–	15	–	–	–	–	–	15
Jon	–	1	–	2	–	–	–	–	3
Mic	–	10	45	–	1	–	–	1	57
Nah	2	2	9	2	–	–	–	2	17
Hab	–	3	1	–	–	–	–	–	4
Zep	–	–	21	2	–	–	–	3	26
Hag	5	–	8	1	–	1	–	–	15
Zec	–	–	120	7	–	6	–	16	149
Mal	–	13	25	1	–	3	1	2	45
Pss	20	18	16	5	2	3	4	2	70
Prv	7	21	8	–	11	4	–	–	51
Job	12	23	14	–	1	1	–	–	51
S–S	1	3	–	1	–	–	–	–	5
Rut	2	1	4	1	–	16	2	–	26
Lam	3	–	1	–	2	1	–	–	7
Ecc	23	14	–	–	5	–	3	3	48
Est	8	4	–	1	1	–	3	–	17
Dan	16	1	71	–	1	–	–	–	89
Ezr	5	2	–	2	–	–	–	–	9
Neh	7	6	7	1	2	–	1	–	24
1 Ch	11	1	19	3	1	5	–	2	42
2 Ch	25	27	16	1	1	19	2	–	91
	484	545	2932	405	63	1647	70	232	

6378

TABLE 2

qtl forms*

BOOKS	Past	Present	Future	Non-past Modal	Past Modal	Imperative	Juss/Cohort	Non-verbal	TOTALS
Gen	804	58	6	4	11	2	5	1	891
Ex	463	29	7	1	1	–	–	2	503
Lev	158	12	6	9	1	1	–	3	190
Num	369	32	1	6	10	–	–	1	419
Dtr	486	35	5	3	5	1	–	1	536
Jos	400	23	2	2	1	–	–	1	429
Jud	410	23	6	2	6	1	–	–	448
1 S	577	41	4	2	3	–	–	2	629
2 S	447	43	1	4	3	–	–	3	501
1 K	593	44	3	1	2	–	–	3	646
2 K	570	61	3	4	2	–	–	4	644
Isa	646	300	57	2	7	3	3	8	1026
Jer	969	361	46	1	7	–	3	7	1394
Ezk	567	240	31	4	8	3	3	4	860
Hos	99	44	7	–	–	–	1	4	155
Joe	36	30	1	–	–	–	–	–	67
Amo	56	34	1	–	–	–	–	–	91
Ob	16	1	1	–	–	–	–	–	18
Jon	29	4	–	–	–	–	–	–	33
Mic	27	19	4	1	1	–	–	1	53
Nah	11	21	1	1	–	–	–	–	34
Hab	21	11	3	–	–	–	–	–	35
Zep	17	15	3	–	–	–	–	1	36
Hag	15	11	–	–	–	–	–	–	26
Zec	70	44	7	1	–	–	–	3	125
Mal	33	38	–	1	–	–	–	1	73
Pss	715	344	29	5	16	3	10	26	1148
Prv	70	114	5	–	3	–	1	3	196
Job	252	244	5	1	8	–	3	4	517
S–S	61	32	–	–	1	–	1	9	104
Rut	58	3	–	–	3	–	1	–	65
Lam	184	56	3	–	1	3	1	10	258
Ecc	121	27	2	–	1	–	2	2	155
Est	139	7	–	–	6	–	–	–	152
Dan	93	5	3	–	–	–	–	–	101
Ezr	72	2	–	–	–	–	2	–	76
Neh	223	5	–	–	1	–	–	1	230
1 C	357	13	–	1	3	–	–	1	375
2 C	596	28	2	–	4	–	2	3	635
	10830	2454	255	56	115	17	38	109	

13874

*As translated by the RSV

TABLE 3

wayyiqtol forms*

BOOKS	Past	Present	Future	Non-past Modal	Past Modal	Imperative	Juss/Cohort	Non-verbal	TOTALS
Gen	2096	3	-	3	2	-	7	1	2112
Ex	855	3	2	-	-	-	-	30	890
Lev	188	-	-	-	-	-	-	1	189
Num	730	2	-	1	-	-	-	15	748
Dtr	239	8	1	-	1	-	-	7	256
Jos	564	7	-	1	-	-	-	22	594
Jud	1110	1	-	1	1	-	-	23	1136
1 Sm	1263	4	-	2	-	-	1	46	1316
2 Sm	1020	3	-	-	-	-	-	36	1059
1 Kg	995	5	-	-	-	-	-	37	1037
2 Kg	1162	2	-.	1	-	-	2	49	1216
Isa	192	49	5	1	3	-	2	4	252
Jer	451	20	2	-	1	-	1	5	480
Ezk	458	18	9	-	5	-	5	20	515
Hos	39	3	1	-	-	-	-	-	43
Joe	7	-	-	-	-	-	-	-	7
Amo	24	4	-	-	-	-	.	1	29
Ob	-	-	-	-	-	-	-	-	-
Jon	81	-	-	-	-	-	-	3	84
Mic	3	1	1	-	-	-	1	-	6
Nah	1	3	-	-	-	-	-	-	4
Hab	4	9	-	-	-	-	-	2	15
Zep	2	-	-	-	-	-	-	-	2
Hag	13	-	-	-	-	-	-	3	16
Zec	100	1	-	-	-	-	-	14	115
Mal	7	2	-	-	-	-	-	-	9
Pss	245	66	9	2	1	-	6	3	332
Prv	11	20	-	-	-	-	-	-	31
Job	172	63	-	-	3	-	-	20	258
S-S	2	-	-	-	-	-	2	-	4
Rut	132	-	-	-	-	-	-	1	133
Lam	22	7	-	-	-	-	-	-	29
Ecc	3	-	-	-	-	-	-	-	3
Est	157	-	-	-	-	-	-	4	161
Dan	96	-	-	-	-	-	1	2	99
Ezr	84	-	-	-	-	-	2	-	86
Neh	249	-	-	-	1	-	2	5	257
1 Ch	460	2	-	-	-	-	1	8	471
2 Ch	965	2	-	-	-	-	4	5	976
	14202	308	30	12	18	-	35	367	

14972

TABLE 4

yiqtol forms*

BOOKS	Past	Present	Future	Non-past Modal	Past Modal	Imperative	Juss/Cohort	Non-verbal	TOTALS
Gen	25	88	290	34	24	47	15	-	523
Ex	30	47	373	66	3	211	17	7	754
Lev	9	86	52	197	6	523	1	14	888
Num	32	96	111	82	7	290	15	5	638
Dtr	30	115	238	200	3	349	17	12	964
Jos	8	18	68	30	1	48	8	3	184
Jud	18	30	79	36	1	33	17	-	214
1 Sm	31	52	169	66	1	34	35	5	393
2 Sm	48	48	108	46	4	16	46	3	319
1 Kg	37	18	141	42	-	48	30	3	319
2 Kg	26	19	107	17	4	47	20	1	241
Isa	48	375	760	49	17	54	57	6	1366
Jer	26	251	562	29	30	80	42	7	1027
Ezk	45	98	573	35	25	28	10	22	836
Hos	11	53	129	20	3	7	4	3	230
Joe	1	22	25	1	1	3	6	-	59
Amo	5	28	70	15	2	6	-	1	127
Ob	2	-	10	1	10	-	-	-	23
Jon	2	2	6	3	2	-	4	-	19
Mic	-	31	90	1	1	6	3	1	133
Nah	2	8	22	3	-	-	-	1	36
Hab	12	27	25	1	2	2	-	1	70
Zep	1	6	41	3	-	-	1	-	52
Hag	-	3	6	2	-	1	-	-	12
Zec	1	23	99	13	-	6	9	2	153
Mal	-	5	20	7	1	1	2	1	37
Pss	163	621	523	96	53	115	259	21	1851
Prv	4	391	201	16	25	90	29	1	757
Job	88	561	235	52	96	8	55	20	1115
S-S	7	20	11	-	13	1	4	3	59
Rut	2	18	16	11	5	11	5	1	69
Lam	7	23	11	-	8	5	7	3	64
Ecc	3	108	48	5	19	16	6	1	206
Est	10	8	14	1	7	3	15	1	59
Dan	2	4	80	-	5	3	3	1	98
Ezr	3	1	4	2	3	3	6	-	22
Neh	9	13	31	3	15	8	11	1	91
1 Ch	8	10	38	7	11	7	10	1	92
2 Ch	18	49	65	8	15	23	20	1	199
	774	3376	5451	1200	423	2133	789	153	

14299

*As translated by the RSV

TABLE 5

w^eyiqtol forms[*]

BOOKS	Past	Present	Future	Non-past Modal	Past Modal	Imperative	Juss/Cohort	Non-verbal	TOTALS
Gen	–	9	46	18	–	–	9	–	82
Ex	–	2	11	30	–	3	3	11	60
Lev	–	1	2	–	–	1	–	2	6
Num	–	1	9	13	–	–	9	4	36
Dtr	–	4	15	16	–	1	9	–	45
Jos	–	–	3	2	–	1	2	2	10
Jud	–	–	5	14	–	1	10	2	32
1 Sm	–	–	16	20	–	–	16	1	53
2 Sm	4	–	7	15	–	–	12	–	58
1 Kg	1	1	9	14	–	–	11	3	39
2 Kg	3	1	6	20	–	–	17	–	47
Isa	27	28	43	22	6	3	15	2	146
Jer	–	16	35	10	3	3	19	–	86
Ezk	–	6	13	6	–	–	1	1	27
Hos	2	1	20	4	–	–	2	1	30
Joe	–	–	–	–	–	–	2	1	3
Amo	–	1	2	1	–	–	1	–	5
Ob	–	–	–	–	–	–	–	–	–
Jon	–	–	1	2	–	–	3	–	6
Mic	1	–	8	2	–	–	4	–	15
Nah	–	–	–	–	–	–	–	–	–
Hab	1	5	4	–	–	–	–	–	10
Zep	–	–	4	–	–	–	–	–	4
Hag	–	–	–	2	–	–	–	–	2
Zec	3	–	6	1	1	–	–	–	11
Mal	–	–	2	2	1	–	–	1	6
Pss	9	35	72	33	9	6	58	–	222
Prv	–	11	19	3	3	–	3	–	39
Job	12	52	26	6	22	1	4	–	123
S–S	–	–	1	2	–	–	1	–	4
Rut	–	1	–	4	–	–	1	–	6
Lam	–	2	2	2	1	–	2	1	10
Ecc	1	11	1	–	–	–	2	–	15
Est	–	–	7	–	–	–	4	–	11
Dan	1	1	28	–	–	2	3	2	37
Ezr	1	–	–	–	–	–	2	–	3
Neh	5	–	1	4	2	–	4	–	16
1 Ch	–	1	2	8	–	–	3	–	14
2 Ch	–	5	12	9	3	–	7	–	36
	71	195	438	285	51	22	239	34	

1335

APPENDIX 2

CONTENTS

We have noted already in this work that the shift of tone in the 1st and
2nd pers. sing. Suffix-form with prefixed _waw_ often played an important role
in the reconstruction of proto-Hebrew and even Proto-Semitic. It would be a
great step forward if the tone shift could be shown to have a semantic function
in Hebrew. Four hundred and fifty years ago E. Levita (_ca_. 1550) made the observation: 'An accent on the penultima shows that the _waw_ is copulative' (see p.
11 above).[1] S. R. Driver maintains that 'a _real difference_ of some kind or
other exists between the use of the perfect with simple _waw_, and the use of
the perfect with waw conversive, and the external indication of this difference
is to be found in the _alternation of the tone_ which constantly attends and
accompanies it' (1892:§106). Great use is often made of the tone shift phenomenon especially by those attempting an historical-comparative reconstruction
of Proto-Semitic, but to date no complete study of the phenomenon has ever been
made.[2] The present work is a complete investigation into the phenomenon of tone
shift respecting the 1st and 2nd pers. sing. _wqtl_ in the OT. Its findings have
never been put forward before and therefore constitute a new understanding and
interpretation of the phenomenon. Previously the problem has been considered
mainly from the phonological aspect—the syllabic conditions. Our investigation has shown that the tone shift is mainly syntactically conditioned and only
in certain cases phonologically conditioned.

In 1938 C. H. Gordon put forward the rule: '_The_ shift _occurs when, and
only when, (a) the penult is a closed syllable or (b) the penult and antepenult are both naturally long syllables_' (1938:323).[3] It is one thing to state
the conditions under which a change of tone may take place, it is quite another
thing to state _why_ that change takes place in any given case. Gordon has confused the conditions with the cause. There are literally dozens of examples
where his syllabic conditions are met but no change of tone occurs. Gordon
was not aware of the large number of exceptions to his rule and so to account
for the seven exceptions that did not fit into his rule he fell back on
the old observation that there is a 'tendency to shift the stress from the
penult to ultima when the following word commences with a laryngal' (p. 324).[4]
We have noted the consonant immediately following every 1st and 2nd sing. _wqtl_
in the OT and found that א occurs three times more frequently than ל which
is the second most popular consonant to follow these verbs. And if we take the
four laryngals (א, ע, ה, ח) together we discovered that 54% of all verbs will
have one or other of these laryngals following it.[5] This fact can hardly constitute a sound basis for Gordon's 'tendency' rule. There are not just seven

exceptions to his rule but scores of similar cases as well as examples where
no laryngal consonant follows the verb yet the tone moves to the ultima. There
are also scores of examples where a laryngal consonant does follow the verb
but the tone does not move forward to the ultima. These have either not been
noticed by Gordon or else he felt they could be explained by the two factors
which he has identified as counteracting the shift, namely (1) when a disjunctive tone occurs on the verb itself especially with the two major ones, Silluq
and Athnach, and sometimes with the lesser ones, and (2) when the following
word is accented on the first syllable (p. 324). We shall see in the course
of this section that these two factors are very imprecisely worded or/and
misunderstood by Gordon. We cannot accept, however, his basic premise that:
'It is the nature of the syllables that conditions the shift' (p. 321). Our
study does not support this premise; conditions are not the cause of the tone
shift as we shall show.

Our investigation of the whole phenomenon of tone shift in the 1st and
2nd wqtl verbs was approached from a much broader perspective than that of
Gordon and others who have investigated the phenomenon. In Section 2.1 we will
present the results of that approach; in Section 2.2 we shall demonstrate the
determining influence of the syntactical context on the position of the tone;
and in Section 2.3 we shall show how the syntactical context influences the
tone position of the 3rd pers. pl. forms of ע"ש , צ"יי , צ"י, and ל"ה verbs.

2.1.   The Tone Shift in the 1st & 2nd pers. sg. Wqtl Forms

On a first count of the 1st and 2nd wqtl in Mandelkern's Hebrew
Concordance the total number of forms came to 1761. Seven of these had no tone
as they were in construct with another word. Of the remaining forms it was
found that 1295 had ultimate tone and 459 had penultima tone. We have set out
the information concerning these two facts in the following tables. On the
left side we have noted the type of Massoretic accent on each verb and we have
noted whether a monosyllabic or polysyllabic word follows the verb. Both these
factors played an important part in discovering the cause of the tone shift.

It is not possible within the limits of this dissertation to give the
full evidence of our findings but five areas were chosen for detailed examination, these were:

(1) The tone and phonemic possibilities,

(2) The position of the tone in relation to the tone on the following word

TABLE A

An Analysis of the First and Second person Perfect Verbs with prefixed _Waw_ in the Old Testament according to Tone Position and Class of Verb

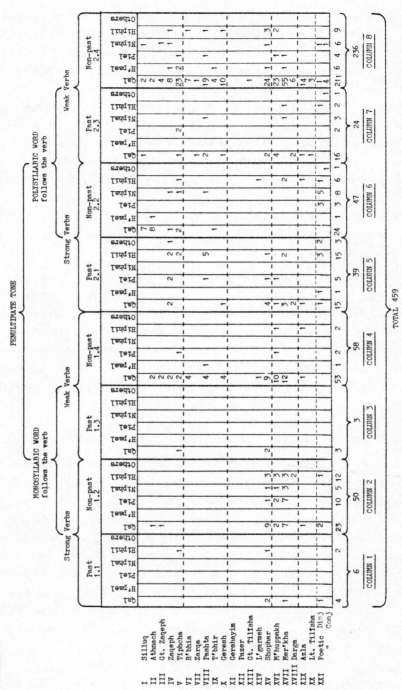

TABLE B

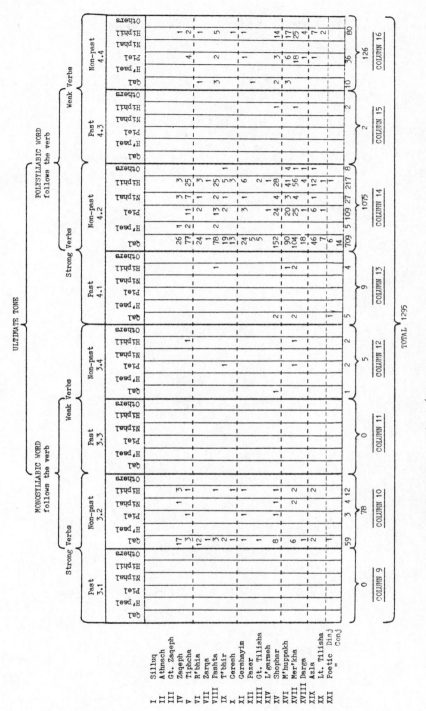

GRAND TOTAL : 1761 (459 penultima, 1295 ultima and 7 construct state)

(including the nasog 'aḥor phenomenon).

(3) The tone and syntactical relationships.

(4) The influence of the verbal tone on the consonant immediately following
the verb.

(5) The tone position with weak verbs and בוא.

In the following subdivisions we give the results of our investigation into
these five areas of special interest.

2.1.1.   The Tone and Phonemic Possibilities

         We noted the remarks of Levita and S. R. Driver that the tone is
used to distinguish between different meanings of wᵉqātaltī/-tā. On the statistical level they would appear to have a good case because out of a total of
1295 verbs with ultima tone 1284 have a 'non-past' meaning, or 99.15%, and out
of a total of 459 verbs with penultima tone 387 have 'non-past'/incomplete
meaning, or 84.65%. Of these 387 verbs with penultima tone 319 are ל"א and
ל"ה verbs in the Qal and Hithpa'el themes and it is well known these weak
verbs do not take ultima tone (there is only one exception, Lev. 24:5 וְאָפִיתָ).
This leaves only 68 cases which do not fit into Levita's observation. However,
it was our investigation into these 68 exceptions that led to the discovery
that the syntactical context was the determining factor in the position of the
tone on these verbs. This discovery was linked to the fact that wᵃtl verbs
with ultima tone are confined to Direct Speech Style; there are no cases of
ultima toned wᵃtls in Narrative Prose Style. Secondly, the syntax of wᵃtls
in Prose Style and Direct Speech Style is completely different and this has
influenced the position of the tone on these verb forms. It is not possible to
elaborate on this point here. Thirdly, Direct Speech Style differs from Prose
Style in most languages in pitch, modulation, expression, speed, animation,
etc., and Hebrew would hardly be an exception. The Massoretic accent system
would appear to capture this difference in the two styles slight though that
difference might appear at times. These broader considerations have not been
taken into account in previous studies on the problem of tone shift.

         The following points make it highly unlikely that the shift of tone posit-
ion/or non-shift has any phonemic status.

(1) The fact that one weak verb can undergo a shift of tone (Lev. 24:5) shows
that there is no phonetic difficulty preventing the shift, and analogy

with all the other weak verbs in the Piel, Hiphil, and Niphal themes would demand a change in tone position if the difference in tone position indicated a semantic difference. The fact that there is no change of tone position when the language can readily admit one weakens the argument for phonemic differences in the phenomenon.

(2) All strong and weak verbs take penultima tone when they end a sense-unit (either a sentence or a clause). If there is any phonemic significance in the position of the tone this must give way to the syntactical construction of the sense-unit. If the tone were truly phonemic this situation would be absurd.

(3) On the practical level if Levita were correct that 'An accent on the penultima shows that the _waw_ is copulative' i.e. the _qtl_ is a past, then how does one account for the exceptions where the verb has penultima stress yet the tense is non-past? Cf. Deut. 2:28; 1 Sm. 29:8; Ezk. 3:26; Is. 66:9; 2 Kg. 9:3; 1 Ch. 17:10; Ob. 10; 2 Sm. 9:10; Joel 4:21; 1 Sm. 23:2; Is. 8:17; Dt. 28:12; Ezk. 28:8; Jer. 38:10; 1 Kg. 2:31 (all the above have one of the minor disjunctives which can appear on the ultima syllable of the verb); Ex. 17:6; 1 Sm. 23:2; Jud. 6:26; Jer. 29:14; 1 Ch. 29:14; Lev. 25:21; Dt. 27:6; 1 Ch. 4:10; Jer. 10:18; Zch. 13:7; Dt. 23:14 (all these examples have a conjunctive tone and a polysyllabic word following them so that they cannot be explained on the nasog 'aḥor rule).

(4) Conversely, how does one account for the exceptions where the verb has ultima stress yet the tense is past? Cf. Am. 4:7; Dt. 17:4; Jer. 20:9; Lev. 26:41; Jer. 6:17; Jer. 12:3; 1 Kg. 19:18; Ezk. 29:7(2); Gen. 26:10.[1]

(5) Under certain syntactical conditions when an accented (disj.) monosyllabic word follows the verb the tone recedes to the penult position even though it is a non-past, e.g. Jer. 24:10 (וְנָתַ֣תִּי־ בָ֗ם); Lev. 25:35; Ezk. 39:27, 17:22. But there are other instances where the tone does not retract, e.g. 2 Ch. 6:36; 1 Kg. 8:46; 1 Sm. 16:3; Ex. 29:5, 40:3; Lev. 24:5; Dt. 7:25, 21:11, 23:14: Jer. 22:1; 1 Sm. 15:18; 2 Sm. 15:34. We have taken all the above examples from verbs with the conjunctive Shophar tone followed by Zaqeph on the monosyllabic word so that we are discussing like with like. We could do the same for other conjunctive signs on the verb but space does not allow this. However, if the tone position were phonemic we would have a chaotic situation here.

(6) In Appendix 4 we have tabulated over 100 examples where the same verb form has a past and a non-past signification, yet in no instance is there a difference of tone position to denote the supposed difference in meaning. These factors make it highly improbable that the shift of tone is phonemic.

2.1.2   The Position of the Verbal Tone in Relation to the Tone on the
         following word (including the nasog 'aḥor phenomenon)

There are two syntactical conditions that have an influence on the position of the verbal tone. The first is where a monosyllabic word follows the
verb, and the second is where a polysyllabic word follows the verb.

2.1.2.1   Where a Monosyllabic Word follows the Verb

         (1) Silluq on the monosyllabic word. If there is a conjunctive
sign on the verb it must be on the penult (7 examples = 7x); if there is a
disjunctive it may be on the penult (-x) or the ultima (1x).
(2) Athnach. If there is a conjunctive sign on the verb it must be on the
penult (5x); if there is a disjunctive it may be on the penult (-x) or the
ultima (3x).
(3)Zaqeph. If there is a conjunctive on the verb it can be on the penult (6x :
Ezk. 39:27; 17:22; Ecc. 9:16; Lev. 25:35; Jer. 24:10; 1 Sm. 3:13) or the ultima (11x : Jer. 22:1; 1 Kg. 8:46; 2 Ch. 6:36; Dt. 23:14; 21:11; 1 Sm. 15:18;
Lev. 24:5; Dt. 7:25; 1 Sm. 16:3; 2 Sm. 15:34; Ex. 40:3). In this study only
the strong verbs are considered which includes the Piel, Hiphil, Niphal, and
other non-Qal/Hithpael themes of א"ל and ה"ל verbs since these are considered strong verbs as far as their ability to take penult or ultima tone is concerned.
(4) Tiphcha. The conjunctive on the verb can be on the penult (10x : Ezk. 28:
25; 14:13; 35:11; Am. 1:4,7,10,12; Ezk. 30:14; Jer. 49:27; Am. 2:5) or the
ultima (7x : Ex. 29:43; 30:26; 40:7; 21:23; Jos. 15:19; Jud. 1:15, Ezk. 16:
60). A disjunctive on the verb may be on the penult (3x : all weak verbs) or
the ultima (14x : all strong verbs).
(5) R'bhia. The conjunctive on the verb is on the penult (6x : Dt. 14:26;
Ezk. 28:12; 35:3; 17:22; Ex. 25:12; Jer. 43:12). There are no examples of
ultima conjunctive tone and only one of ultima disjunctive tone (2 Sm. 11:
21).
(6) Pashta. Conjunctive on the verb can be penult (10x : Lev. 26:25; Hos. 8:14;
Ezk. 30:16; 32:8; Jer. 21:14; 50:32; Am. 1:14; Mal. 2:3; Lev. 26:36; 2 Sm. 6:
22) or ultima (4x : Lev. 19:34; 1 Sm. 2:35; Ex. 28:17; 26:33). Note: Pashta
has two conjunctives before it, M'huppakh and Mer'kha. When the verbal tone
is on the ultima it takes Mer'kha, when on the penult it takes M'huppakh.
M'huppakh is never found next to another toned syllable.[1]

(7) T'bhir. Conjunctive on the verb can be penult (6x : 1 Ch. 22:9; Dt. 28: 36; 16:2; Ezr. 9:13; Jos. 15:16; Jud. 1:12) or ultima (1x : Exod. 34:2).

(8) Geresh. Conjunctive on the verb can be penult (1x : Dt. 28:64) or ultima (1x : Nu. 31:28).[1]

It is clear from these results that only when the monosyllabic word following the verb has the major disjunctives Silluq and Athnach will the preceding verb have penultima tone (i.e. (1) and (2) above). In the case of the other disjunctives the retraction of the verbal tone is not automatic. We have examined each of the above lesser disjunctives (i.e. (3) to (8)) and found that where the monosyllabic word culminates its own sense-unit then the speaker telegraphs this by drawing back the verbal tone to the penult position, e.g., Dt. 28:36, שָׁם וַעֲבַדְתָּ 'and you shall serve there'. Compare this with Ex. 34:2 שָׁם לִי וְנִצַּבְתָּ 'and present yourself to me there' where the sense-unit is resolved in the word שָׁם and not in לִי. It is the tone position on the verb which helps us to see the syntactical unit. If one examines all the cases where the conjunctive tone is on the ultima syllable of the verb and this is followed by a monosyllabic word having a disjunctive tone it will be found that the sense-unit is not resolved in the monosyllabic word but in some other word beyond it. On the other hand, where a verb has a penult tone before a similar monosyllabic word it will be found that the sense-unit is resolved in this monosyllabic word. This interpretation of the tone shift solves all the exceptions that scholars have noted on the phonological approach to the phenomenon and it is our conclusion that an accented monosyllabic word following the verb does not in itself cause the verbal tone to retract to the penult position. Gordon was under the impression that any monosyllabic word would cause the verbal tone to retract. He criticises Bergsträsser over his treatment of 2 Kgs. 5:18 and in particular 'his failure adequately to reckon with nasog 'ahor' (p. 320). The example given is not a case where nasog 'ahor can operate: וְהִשְׁתַּחֲוֵיתִי בֵּית־ רִמֹּן.[2] Only when a disjunctive tone is on the monosyllabic word, not a conjunctive tone as here, may the verbal tone retract, but we have been careful to stress that this is never automatic except with Silluq and Athnach; in all other cases the syntactical relationship of the verb to the following words will determine the position of the verbal tone. The final decision rests with the speaker as there are no objective critera for determining the position of the tone in Direct Speech Style. We can replace Gordon's rule with the observation that ultima tone is possible for all verbs except those of the Lamedh Hē and Lamedh 'Aleph

classes in the Qal and Hithpaʻel themes provided analogy is not at work. This
last clause covers the exception in Lev. 24:5. Apart from the phonetic re-
straint[1] in the case of the weak verbs the position of the tone will be determined by the speaker's judgment on the syntactical relationship he sees between
the verb and its context.

2.1.2.2   Where a Polysyllabic Word follows the Verb

              Because a polysyllabic word will normally not be accented on its
initial syllable (e.g. לַיְלָה) the influence of its tone is hardly felt by the
preceding verb. We were thus unable to account for the position of the verbal
tone in any case as a direct result of the type of tone on the following word.

2.1.3   The Influence of the Verbal Tone on the Consonant immediately
            following the Verb

       It was noted that sometimes the second pers. sing. masc. wqtl caused the
initial consonant of the following word to take dagessation. This appeared to
be linked with the position of the tone on the verb, thus: וְאָכַלְתָּ שָּׁם (Dt.
14:26). The initial שׁ has a dagesh in its heart. It was found that the
dagesh was not inserted indiscriminately but followed very precise conditions
these are:

      Rule 1 : When the 2nd pers. wqtl has a disjunctive tone on the ultima
                or the penult syllable dagessation will not occur in the init-
                ial consonant of the following monosyllabic word.

      Rule 2 : When the 2nd pers. wqtl has a conjunctive tone on the penult
                syllable it will cause dagessation to occur in the initial con-
                sonant of the following monosyllabic word.

Dagessation does not occur when the 2nd pers. wqtl has a conjunctive sign on
the ultima syllable of the verb, nor does it occur with the 1st pers. forms.[2]
   The following Table shows the total number of verbs with a begad kepat
letter following the verb. It is interesting that out of a total of 115 verbs
with a disjunctive tone there is not a single case of a soft/aspirated letter
following the verb, hence Rule 1. The same rule applies to the second table of
קלף שׁשׂ consonants. Out of a total of 135 verbs with a conjunctive tone
Rule 2 holds good for 134 verbs. The apparent exception is 1 Sm. 23:2 but in

DETAILS OF THE VERB

Effect of the verb on the following consonant

DISJUNCTIVE

I	Silluq
II	Athnach
III	Gt. Zaqeph
IV	Zaqeph
V	Tiphcha
VI	R'bhia
VII	Zorqa
VIII	Pashta
IX	T'bhir
X	Geresh
XI	Gershayim
XII	Pazer
XIII	Gt. T'lisha
XIV	L'garmeh

CONJUNCTIVE

XV	Shophar
XVI	M'huppakh
XVII	Mer'kha
XVIII	Darga
XIX	Azla
XX	Lt. T'lisha

POETIC

Disjunctive
Conjunctive

(265 + 2 construct state)

TOTAL 267

TOTAL 251

Column headings (left group — CONSONANTS FOLLOW THE VERB):

MONOSYLLABIC WORD follows the verb
- PENULTIMATE — WEAK (1 pers / 2 pers), STRONG (1 pers / 2 pers); soft / hard
- ULTIMATE — WEAK (1 pers / 2 pers), STRONG (1 pers / 2 pers); soft / hard

POLYSYLLABIC WORD follows the verb
- PENULTIMATE — WEAK (1 pers / 2 pers), STRONG; soft / hard
- ULTIMATE — WEAK (1 pers / 2 pers), STRONG; soft / hard

Column headings (right group — CONSONANTS FOLLOW THE VERB):

MONOSYLLABIC WORD follows the verb
- PENULTIMATE — WEAK (1 pers / 2 pers), STRONG (1 pers / 2 pers); present / absent
- ULTIMATE — WEAK (1 pers / 2 pers), STRONG (1 pers / 2 pers); present / absent

POLYSYLLABIC WORD follows the verb
- PENULTIMATE — WEAK (1 pers / 2 pers), STRONG; present / absent
- ULTIMATE — WEAK (1 pers / 2 pers), STRONG; present / absent

fact the word is not a monosyllabic one hence Rule 2 which also applies
to the non-begad consonant table. Note that all the occurrences of dagessation occur with the 2nd pers. waṭl verbs with penultimate stress. Although we
have placed four examples of לְךָ֫ in the polysyllabic column it would appear
as if it is treated as a monosyllabic word,[1] if so, this leaves only two cases
of a genuine polysyllabic word following the verb which take dagessation,
namely, וְקָשֹׂתָ֫יו קְעָרֹתָ֫יו (Ex. 25:29) and וְשַׂדְתָּ֫ אֹתָם֫ בַּשִּׂיד (Dt. 27:3).

One can only marvel at the accuracy and consistency of the work of the
Massoretes in the application of the two Rules given above. There is no agreement on the significance of the daghesh in the following initial consonant.
J. D. Wijnkoop (JQR X, 1898, 511-2) thinks that the daghesh is placed in the
initial consonant to warn the reader not to double this letter. In O. O. Fletcher's translation of Baer's commentary on Proverbs (Hebraica 1, 1884-5, 145-
152) he shows that this is unlikely, though he does concede that it might have
this function, see §8 of his article where the last consonant of one word is
the same as the first in the following word. F. R. Blake's article (JBL 63,
1943, 89-107) has incorporated most of Fletcher's observations and examples
without materially improving on his labours. Blake thinks the daghesh is purely orthographic—a spelling device to denote a preceeding short unaccented
vowel. This solution can hardly apply to every case since sureq is found with
a daghesh following it, which must be a long vowel, and on the other hand
segol (ה.ֶ-), which is clearly a short vowel, is also followed by a dagheshed
consonant.

It would appear to us that in the case of the 2nd pers. waṭl forms the
daghesh in the following consonant closes the open syllable of the verb and
the long -ā- of the suffix -tā becomes the short -o- vowel, thus וַעֲבַדְתָּ֫ לֹ֫ו
would be pronounced wᵉ'abádto-lô without necessarily doubling the letter with
the daghesh. Otherwise how do we account for the fact that when the verbal
suffix has the tone no daghesh can appear in the following word?

2.1.4   The Tone Position with the Weak Verbs and בוֹא

It was noted that the weak verbs, i.e. ל"א and ל"ה, fell into
two groups, namely, those that did not change their tone position and those
that could change their tone position. To the former belonged all the Qal and
Hithpael verbs; to the latter belonged all the other verbal themes including
the root בוֹא in the Qal theme though in the following table we have included

it among the weak Qal verbs.

	PENULTIMATE TONE ON THE VERB	ULTIMATE TONE ON THE VERB
Weak Qal verbs	290 (97.32%)	8 (2.68%)
Weak non-Qal verbs :	28 (18.92%)	120 (81.08%)
Strong Qal verbs	68 (8.04%)	778 (91.96%)
Strong non-Qal verbs :	70 (15.42%)	384 (84.58%)
TOTALS	456	1290

Although we have listed 8 examples in the weak Qal ultimate column in fact seven of these are the root בוא which leaves us with the single exception of Lev. 24:5 (וְאָפִיתָ אֹתָהּ). So in fact out of 291 examples of ל"ה, ל"א verbs in the Qal/Hithpael category 290 have penultimate stress. But in the non-Qal/Hithpael category the percentages of penult and ultima stress show that they are regarded as strong verbs for the purposes of tone shift.

The Root בוא . This verb is unique among the weak Qal forms in that it is the only weak Qal verb that can alter the position of its tone freely.[1] The verb appears only in two themes (Qal and Hiphil) in the 1st and 2nd wqtl form. The statistics are as follows:

	PENULTIMATE TONE ON THE VERB	ULTIMATE TONE ON THE VERB
Qal :	14 (66.66%)	7 (33.33%)
Hiphil :	2 (6.45%)	29 (93.55%)
TOTALS	16	36

We may conclude, then, that not only must we consider the verb בוא as a strong verb for the purposes of tone shift, but that any shift in its tone is signi-ficant as far as the syntax is concerned.

2.1.5   The Tone and Syntactical Relationships

The following observations have been made from an inductive study of the use of the shift of tone position in Direct Speech Style.
(1) When a sense-unit ends with a verb the tone will invariably be on the penult syllable of the verb in the case of Silluq (Dt. 8:12: וְיָשַׁבְתָּ), Athnach (Isa. 14:4 וְאָמַרְתָּ), and Great Zaqeph (Dt. 32:40 וְאָמַרְתִּי). This shift of tone is syntactically conditioned and overrides any supposed phonemic signifi-cance.

(2) When the verb has any other disjunctive tone on its penult syllable it
indicates that the sense-unit concludes with the verb (Dt. 2:28 וְאָכַ֫לְתִּי)
or there is a slight emphasis on the verbal action (1 Sm. 23:2 וְהִכֵּ֫יתִי). The
rule would appear to be: When a natural or deliberate pause is made when the
speaker reaches the verb then the tone will retract to the penultimate syllable.[1] This rule accounts for the many exceptions to Gordon's syllabic rule.
(3) Syntactical verb pairs. Where two verbs are closely connected within the
same sense-unit the first will have ultima tone and the second penult (cf.
2 Kg. 9:3 וּפָתַחְתָּ הַדֶּ֫לֶת וְנַ֫סְתָּה) but more often the first verb will be a
simple Prefix form to which the second is paired (cf. Dt. 2:28, 1 Sm. 29:8,
32:2, Dt. 12:26, Ob. 10).
(4) Where a verb has ultima tone it can NEVER end a sense-unit. Ultimate stress
always implies that the verb does not end/climax/resolve the sense-unit. The
forward movement of the tone shows that the speaker's mind is on what follows
the verb (cf. Ezk. 29:3 דַּבֵּ֣ר וְאָמַרְתָּ֗ כֹּה־אָמַ֣ר , Dt. 13:15, 30:8, Gen. 6:21).
The rule would appear to be: A verb with ultimate stress cannot end a syntactical unit.

That the cantillation signs are servants of the sense-unit or syntax can
most readily be seen when a monosyllabic word follows the verb. Where the monosyllabic word concludes a sense-unit the verbal tone will recede to the penult position (see 2.1.2.1 above where we have given lists of examples where
the disjunctive on the monosyllabic word sometimes causes the verbal tone to
retract but sometimes it does not).

In the next section we shall demonstrate the determining influence of
the syntax of Direct Speech style on the position of the verbal tone.

2.2.   The Determining Influence of the Syntactical Context on the Posit-
            ion of the Verbal Tone

The Table on p. 175 has been divided into sixteen columns. In order that
we compare like with like we shall take examples from verbs with penult tone
and compare them with verbs having ultima tone in the corresponding column.
(1) Selected examples from Columns 2 and 10 compared: Non-Past.
The following examples demonstrate that when a disjunctive other than Silluq,
Athnach, and Great Zaqeph, occurs on a monosyllabic word following the verb
it does not automatically cause the verbal tone to recede to the penult pos-

ition.

Deut. 17:14   וִירִשְׁתָּהּ בָּהּ וְאָמַרְתָּ אָשִׂ֫ימָה

Deut. 23:14(13): וְחָפַרְתָּה בָּהּ וְשַׁבְתָּ וְכִסִּ֫יתָ אֶת־צֵאָתֶֽךָ

Deut. 17:14 ...and you possess it, and dwell in it, and then say...

Deut. 23:14 you shall dig a hole with it, and turn back and cover up...

    In Dt. 17:14 the speaker concludes the sense-unit with בָּהּ. It is also
well known that the last word in a major sense-unit receives special emphasis
which results in penultimate stress (where possible) and a lengthening of the
vowel where possible. Together these two factors prevent וְיִֽרִשְׁתָּהּ from having ultima stress,[1] so that here phonetic and syntactic factors merge harmon-
iously to determine that the tone _must_ be on the penultima syllable.

    In Deut. 23:14 we have the disjunctive Zaqeph sign on the monosyllabic
word following the verb which has ultima stress. Zaqeph is not as strong a
disjunctive as Athnach and hence it does not cut off the words from what follows, thought it may do so on occasions (see 2.1.2.1(3)). In this case the
speaker's mind is on the words following this smaller sense-unit and this
accounts for the ultima tone on the verb. Compare also:[2]

Eccles. 9:16   וְאָמַ֫רְתִּי אָ֫נִי Then said I...

Ezek. 17:22   וְשָׁתַ֫לְתִּי אָ֫נִי and I will plant it...

The conclusion we can draw from Exs. 1 & 2 is that ultima tone indicates post-
verbal interest and penultima tone interest in the verbal action itself or
to mark off syntactical units.

Deut. 14:26   וְאָכַלְתָּ שָּׁ֫ם לִפְנֵ֣י יְהוָה אֱלֹהֶ֑יךָ

Exod. 40:3   וְשַׂמְתָּ שָׁ֫ם אֵת אֲרוֹן הָעֵדֻ֑ת

Deut. 14:26 and you shall eat there before the Lord your God...

Exod. 40:3 and thou shalt put therein the ark of the testimony...

    In Dt. 14:26 the speaker's interest lies in the place (שָׁ֫ם) rather than
the thought that they are to eat _before the Lord_. The interest in the place,
then, causes the verbal tone to shift to the penult. In the case of Ex. 40:3
there is no emphasis on the place where they are to place the ark, hence the
disjunctive on the monosyllabic word does not affect the verbal tone position.
The speaker's interest lies beyond the monosyllabic word and this is reflected
in the position of the verbal tone.

Compare the following: Jer. 24:10 'And I will send among them' וְשִׁלַּחְתִּ֫י בָ֫ם
with Jer. 22:1 'and speak there this word' וְדִבַּרְתָּ שָׁ֫ם אֶת־הַדָּבָ֥ר הַזֶּ֑ה
Num. 23:3 'I will tell you' וְהִגַּ֫דְתִּי לָ֫ךְ with 2 Sm. 15:34 'then you will

; וְהֵפַרְתָּה לִי אֶת עֲצַת אֲחִיתֹפֶל: defeat for me the counsel of Ahithophel'

Ezek. 39:27 (בָּם וְנִקְדַּשְׁתִּי) with 1 Sm. 15:18 (בּוֹ וְנִלְחַמְתָּ); Deut. 28:36

(שָׁם וַעֲבַדְתָּ) with Ex. 40:7 (שָׁם וְנָתַתָּ); Jos. 15:16 (לוֹ וְנָתַתִּי) with

15:19 (לִי וְנָתַתָּה); 1 Sm. 19:3 (לְךָ וְהִגַּדְתִּי) with Ezek. 16:60 (לָךְ וַהֲקִמוֹתִי);

Ezek. 35:11 (בָּם וְנוֹדַעְתִּי) with Ex. 29:43 (שָׁמָּה וְנֹעַדְתִּי)

(2) Selected examples from Columns 4 and 12 compared: Non-Past.

We have already noted that non-Qal/Hithpael verbs are considered strong for
the purposes of tone shift (see 2.1.4).[1] We give a few examples to show that
the speaker determines the position of the verbal tone.

Mal. 2:3   וְזֵרִיתִי פֶרֶשׁ עַל־פְּנֵיכֶם

Exod. 28:17   וּמִלֵּאתָ בוֹ מִלֻּאַת אֶבֶן

Mal. 2:3   ...and (I will) spread dung upon your faces,

Exod. 28:27   And you shall set in it four rows of stones,

   In Mal. there is a slight pause on the word 'dung' and this causes the tone
to recede to the penult in the verb. In Ex. 28:17, on the other hand, there is
no such pause even though the same disjunctive appears on the following monosyllabic word, hence the ultima tone on the verb because the speaker's interest
is directed toward the resolving word 'stones'. Compare the following: Lev. 26:
36 (אֹרֶךְ וְהֵבֵאתִי) with Ex. 26:33 (שָׁמָּה וְהֵבֵאתָ)

(3) Selected examples from Columns 5 and 13 compared: Past.

In this section all the examples refer to past events which raises the question of what constitutes a Perfect 'consecutive' as distinct from the Perfect
'conjunctive'.

Hos. 12:11   וְדִבַּרְתִּי עַל־הַנְּבִיאִים

Am. 4:7   וְהִמְטַרְתִּי עַל־עִיר אֶחָת

Hos. 12:11   I have also spoken unto the prophets

Am. 4:7   and I caused it to reign upon one city,

In Hos. the speaker draws attention to the verbal action while in Amos the
verb is viewed as part of a sense-unit and the speaker hurries forward to the
concluding word 'one'. Compare the following: Job 7:4 (אָקוּם מָתַי וְאָמַרְתִּי)
with Jer. 20:9 (אֶזְכְּרֶנּוּ לֹא וְאָמַרְתִּי); Ecc. 8:15 (אֲנִי וְשִׁבַּחְתִּי) with
Jer. 6:17 (אֲלֵיכֶם וַהֲקִמֹתִי); Ecc. 2:5 (בָּהֶם וְנָטַעְתִּי) with Ezek. 29:7
(לָהֶם וּבָקַעְתָּ); 2 Chr. 19:3 (לִבָבְךָ וַהֲכִינוֹתָ) with 1 Kings 19:18
(בְיִשְׂרָאֵל וְהִשְׁאַרְתִּי); 2 Sm. 7:11 (cf. 1 Chr. 17:10) (לָךְ וַהֲנִיחֹתִי) with
Ezek. 29:7 (לָהֶם וְהַעֲמַדְתָּ).

(4) Selected examples from Columns 6 and 14 compared: Non-Past.

In these columns all the examples are followed by a polysyllabic word.

Deut. 2:28   וּמְכַרְתָּנִי וְאָכַלְתִּי וּמַיִם

Deut. 16:7   וּבִשַּׁלְתָּ וְאָכַלְתָּ בַּמָּקוֹם

Deut. 2:28   Thou shalt sell me food for money, that I may eat,

Deut. 16:7   And thou shalt roast and eat it in the place which...

1 Sam. 29:8   כִּי לֹא אָבוֹא וְנִלְחַמְתִּי בְּאֹיְבֵי

Lev. 22:32   וְלֹא תְחַלְּלוּ --- וְנִקְדַּשְׁתִּי בְּתוֹךְ בְּנֵי יִשְׂרָאֵל

1 Sam. 29:8   ...that I may go and fight against the enemies of my lord...

Lev. 22:32   but I will be hallowed among the children of Israel:

Compare the following: 2 Kgs. 9:3 (וּפָתַחְתָּ הַדֶּלֶת וְנַסְתָּה) with Deut. 23:14
(תָשׁוּב וְשַׁבְתָּ); Isa. 66:9 (וְהָפַרְתָּ בָּהּ וְשַׁבְתָּ); Isa. 66:9 (וְצָרַרְתִּי) with Dt. 30:8 (תָשׁוּב וְשָׁמַעְתָּ);
2 Sm. 7:11 (could be past)(וַהֲנִיחֹתִי לְךָ) with 7:12 (וַהֲכִינֹתִי אֶת־); Ob. 10
(וְנִכְרָתָּ) with 1 Sm. 10:6 (וְנֶהְפַּכְתָּ); Jer. 4:2 (וְנִשְׁבַּעְתָּ) with 1 Kgs.
17:3 (וְנִסְתַּרְתָּ); Ezek. 28:8 (וָמַתָּה) and Ex. 40:5 (וְשַׂמְתָּ); 1 Kgs. 2:31
(וַהֲסִירֹתָ) with Jer. 7:34 (וְהִשְׁבַּתִּי); 1 Chr. 29:17 (וְיָדַעְתִּי אֱלֹהַי)
with Dt. 4:39 (הַיּוֹם); Zech. 13:7 (וַהֲשִׁבֹתִי יָדִי)[1] with Jer. 23:3
(וַהֲשִׁבֹתִי); Jer. 10:18 (וַהֲצֵרוֹתִי לָהֶם) with Am. 9:9 (וַהֲנִיעוֹתִי);[2] Am. 1:8
(וַהֲשִׁבוֹתִי יָדִי) with Zech. 9:7 (וַהֲסִרֹתִי דָמָיו).

(5) Selected examples from Columns 7 and 15 compared: Past.

Deut. 11:10   תִּזְרַע אֶת־זַרְעֲךָ וְהִשְׁקִיתָ בְרַגְלְךָ

Gen. 26:10   וְהֵבֵאתָ עָלֵינוּ אָשָׁם:

Deut. 11:10   where thou sowedst thy seed, and wateredst it with thy foot,

Gen. 26:10   thou shouldest have brought guiltiness upon us.

Jer. 20:9   וְנִלְאֵיתִי כַּלְכֵל וְלֹא אוּכָל:

Lev. 26:41   אֵלֶךְ --- וְהֵבֵאתִי אֹתָם

Jer. 20:9   and I was weary with forbearing, and I could not stay. (RV 'I am...')

Lev. 26:41   I also walked contrary unto them, and brought them into the land
    of their enemies,

(6) Selected examples from Columns 8 and 16: Non-Past.

Compare the following all of which refer to future events yet the first reference has penult tone on the verb: 1 Sm. 23:2 (הַאֵלֵךְ וְהִכֵּיתִי) with 2 Kgs.
9:7 (וְהִכֵּיתָה); Joel 4:21 (וְנִקֵּיתִי) with Ezk. 39:25 (וְקִנֵּאתִי); Dt. 6:18
(וּבָאתָ) with 17:9 (וּבָאתָ); 2 Sm. 9:10 (וְהֵבֵאתָ) with Jer. 21:6
(וְהִכֵּיתִי); 1 Sm. 10:3 (וּבָאתָ) with Dt. 26:3 (וּבָאתָ); Dan. 10:14

(וּבָאתִֿ) with Gen. 6:18 (וּבָאתָֿ); 2 Kgs. 9:2 (וּבָאתָֿ) with 1 Sm. 20:19

(וּבָאתָֿ); Isa. 8:17 (וְחִכִּיתִֿי) with Ezk. 6:5 (וְזֵרִיתִֿי); Dt. 28:12(וְהִלְוִֿיתָ)

with Ezk. 36:30 (וְהִרְבֵּיתִֿי); Jer. 38:10 (וְהַצַּלְיָֿ) with 1 Sm. 15:3

(וְהִכֵּיתָֿה); Num. 27:13 (וְרָצְֿתָה אֹתָּה) with Lev. 24:5 (וְאָפִֿיתָ אֹתָֿה);

1 Sm. 23:2 (וְהִכֵּיתָֿ) with Ex. 3:20 (וְהִכֵּיתִֿי); Ezk. 38:15 (וּבָאתָֿ) with

Zech. 6:10 (וּבָאתָֿ); Lev. 25:21 (וְצִוִּיתִֿי) with Ezk. 13:15 (וְכִלֵּיתִֿי); 1 Chr.

4:10 (וְהִרְבֵּיתָֿ) with Gen. 26:4 (וְהִרְבֵּיתִֿי); Dt. 27:6 (וְהַצֵּלָיֿתָ) with Ezk.

26:3 (וְהַצֵּלֵיתִֿי); Dt. 23:14 (וְכִסִּֿיתָ) with Ex. 26:29 (וְצִפִּֿיתָ).

All the examples in the six categories pose insuperable difficulties
on Gordon's syllabic rule approach and on any attempt to link the shift in
tone position with a shift in meaning. The most that we can learn from the
change of tone position is that wqtl with ultima tone occurs only in Direct
Speech style, but penult tone also occurs in Direct Speech and is syntactically conditioned in exactly the same way that the ultima tone is conditioned.
We have noted already that the simple qtl does not undergo any change of tone
position, however, in the next sections we have examples where 3rd pers. pl.
qtl verbs show a change of tone position without a prefixed waw being present.
These examples will bear out our finding that the tone is syntactically conditioned.

2.3   The Tone Shift in 3rd pers. pl. Verb Forms

        Grammarians have noted that certain 3rd pers. pl. verbs with and
without prefixed waw sometimes show a change of tone position. So far as we
are aware no comprehensive study has ever been carried out on this phenomenon
let alone connect it with the problem of tone shift in the 1st and 2nd wqtl
forms. We have confined out attention to four categories of verb, namely, ע"ע,
ל"ה and , ע"ו , ע"י.

2.3.1   The 3rd pers. pl. Double Ayin Verbs (Qal)

        The facts are as follows. There are a total of 52 examples (first
count) of the 3rd pers. pl. without a prefixed waw. Of these 24 (or 46%) have
ultima tone and 28 (or 54%) have penult tone.[1] There are a total of 15 verbs
with a prefixed waw; 11 have ultima tone and 4 have penult tone. We shall

first of all examine those forms without a prefixed waw. There are three
roots in Group I that take both penult
and ultima, so these will form the natural starting-point for our investigation into the cause of the tone shift.

TONE POSITION

ROOT	Without WAW		With WAW	
	Ult	Pen	Ult	Pen
I { רבב	9	3	3	1
קלל	1	4	1	
דלל	1	1		
II { חתת		5	3	1
לעצ		1	1	
III { תמם		10		2
IV { רצצ			2	
חדר			1	
V { דמם		2		
רמם		1		
פסס		1		
VI { זכך	3			
ידר	3			
שחח	2			
שתת	2			
חרר	1			
צחח	1			
רכך	1			
	24	28	11	4

2 Sm. 1:23   קַלּוּ מִנְּשָׁרִים

Jer. 4:13   קַלּוּ מִנְּשָׁרִים

Here we have the same words but the order
is reversed. Both mean 'swifter than eagles'.
In the case of 2 Sm. the verb comes last in
the sense-unit and so it receives the disjunctive sign (Zaqeph). On the other hand in
Jer. קַלּוּ comes first in the sense-unit and
is resolved in the following word, hence
the conjunctive tone on the ultima syllable
of the verb. So clearly the syntax has
determined the position of the tone in these
two examples.

Isa. 38:14   ⅄ דַּלּוּ עֵינַי לַמָּרוֹם

Job 28:4   ⅄ דַּלּוּ מֵאֱנוֹשׁ נָעוּ :

Isa. 38:14 'My eyes are weary with looking
             upward.'

Job 28:4 '...they are minished, they are
          gone away from man.' (RV mg.)

We have given the RV mg. reading because it follows the Massoretic interpretation of the syntax and brings out the point that מֵאֱנוֹשׁ goes with the
following verb and not with דַּלּוּ which stands on its own as the penult tone
shows. In other words דַּלּוּ constitutes a sense-unit in its own right hence
the penult tone. In Isa. 38:14 the conjunctive tone on the ultima shows that
it belongs to a sense-unit consisting of three words and not just one as in
Job 28:4.

These are the two clearest examples where we can see the determining
influence of the context on the position of the tone. Of the 28 penult forms
only 7 of these are compulsorary having Silluq or Athnach with them (i.e. דַּמּוּ
(twice), רָבּוּ (three instances), תַּמּוּ and לַצּוּ). Of the 4 penult forms
with waw prefixed two are compulsorary (i.e. וָרָבּוּ and יָחְתּוּ). The other two have
the tone determined by the context, either to remain on the penult, which seems

to be the original position, or to move on to the ultima as the context may dictate.

2.3.2 The 3rd pers. pl. Ayin Yodh/Waw Verbs (Qal)

The facts are as follows. There are a total of 231 examples without a prefixed <u>waw</u>. Of these 214 (or 92.6%) have penult tone and 17 (or 7.4%) have ultima tone. There are a total of 85 verbs with prefixed <u>waw</u>; 70 (or 87.5%) have penult tone and 15 (or 12.5%) have ultima tone.[1]

		TONE POSITION			
		Without WAW		With WAW	
		Ult	Pen	Ult	Pen
I	בוֹא		98		29
	שׁוּב		11		16
	מוּת		15		11
	קוּם		10		5
	בּוֹשׁ		8		5
	פּוֹשׁ				1
II	גוֹל		11	1	3
III	סוּר		18	1	
	חוּל		2	1	
	נוּח		1	1	
	רוּץ		1	1	
	צוּף				
IV	שׂים	1	13	6	
	נוּע	3	2	3	
	רוּם	2	1		
V	פּוֹל		2		
	בּוּז		1		
	דִּין		1		
	זוּר		3		
	שׁוּת		3		
	טוֹב		2		
	אוֹר		1		
	גּוּר		1		
	לִין		1		
	מוֹט		1		
	מוּשׁ		1		
	נוּר		1		
	שׁוּשׂ		1		
	שׁוּשׁ		1		
	סוּף		1		
	צוּף		1		
	שׁוּט		1		
VI	נוּם	2			
	רִיב	2			
	דּוֹר	1			
	שׁוּח	1			
	פּוּק	1			
	דּוֹן	1			
	צוּר	1			
	רוֹשׁ	1			
	חוּר	1			
		17	214	15	70

In Group I there are six verbs which never take ultima tone when <u>waw</u> is prefixed; the reason is not apparent. In Groups II-IV we have the same phenomenon that we observed in the 1st and 2nd <u>wqtls</u>, namely, the tone moves to the ultima when the <u>waw</u> is prefixed to the verb. Groups II and IV are interesting for different reasons. In Group II when the <u>waw</u> is prefixed the tone may be on the ultima as in Lev. 26:36 וְנָסוּ מְנֻסַת־חֶרֶב 'and they shall flee as one flees from the sword', or on the penult as in Isa. 35:10 וְנָסוּ יָגוֹן 'and they have fled away—sorrow and sighing' (referring to a future situation). Group IV is interesting because here we have the verbs without any prefixed <u>waw</u> yet the tone can shift to the ultima. Compare Gen. 40:15 כִּי־שָׂמוּ אֹתִי 'that they should have put me (into the dungeon)' with Jos. 7:11 שָׂמוּ בִּכְלֵיהֶם : 'and put them among their own stuff'. In the former we have recorded direct speech in the latter narrative prose though in itself this does not account for the change. It would appear that some of the 41 roots listed seem to have a preference for penult or ultima tone. In the case of שׂים it would appear to be penult tone since we have other examples of direct speech which take ultima tone (1 Kgs. 2:15; Jer. 7:30, 42: 17, 44:12, etc.). If this is the case then it could account for the Vth and VIth groups of verbs which seem to prefer penult and ultima tone respectively. It is only in Group IV that we meet with some flexibility in the position of the tone. If we consider the root נוב it is translated as a past in Am. 4:8 (וָיָּשֻׁבוּ) and a future in Isa. 19:1 (וְיָּשֻׁבוּ) and Am. 8:12 (וְנָעוּ). It can hardly be argued that ultima tone signifies future action and penult tone past action, yet this is precisely what is held for the tone position in the 1st and 2nd wqtl verbs. In the following examples both verbs have the same tone position but the first is a past and the second a future event: compare Jer. 14:4 (בֹּשׁוּ) with Isa. 45: 16 (בֹּושׁוּ); Isa. 37:27 (וַיֵּבֹשׁוּ) with Isa. 20:5 (וָבֹשׁוּ); 2 Sm. 18:17 (נָסוּ) with Isa. 51:11 (נָסוּ); Ps. 78:34 (וְשָׁבוּ) with Jer. 31:17 (וְשָׁבוּ); Ps. 3:7(6)(שָׁתוּ) with Isa. 22:7 (שָׁתוּ); and Jer. 48:13 (בֹּושׁ) with Jer. 20:11 (בֹּשׁוּ).

The most that we can say about the tone shift in the 3rd pers. pl. ע"ו verbs is that where we have evidence of flexibility of tone position, as in Group IV, then the tone position is syntactically conditioned and not phonemically conditioned or even phonetically conditioned (Gordon). The same applies to the ע"ע verbs.

In the case of ע"ע and ע"ו/י verbs we have been able to isolate the following factors which influence the position of the verbal tone.
(1) The tone will be on the penultima—
- (a) When the verb forms its own sense-unit, see 2 Kgs. 19:36, Jer. 8:9,
- (b) When the verb comes last in its own sense-unit, see 2 Sm. 1:23, Job 28:4, Ps. 25:19, 35:15, Job 6:3.
- (c) When the verb is given the slightest emphasis at all, see Job 24:24, Ps. 12:2, Jer. 50:2 (cf. 8:9), Isa. 16:4.
(2) The tone will be on the ultima—
- (a) When there is a strong logical connection between the verb and the following word(s), see Lam. 4:7, Ps. 55:22(E. 21), Prv. 14:19,
- (b) When there is no special emphasis on the verbal action itself, see Isa. 38:14, 59:12, 24:6, Hab. 3:6.

All the above examples are without a prefixed waw. The same factors influence the position of the verbal tone when the waw is prefixed. Over and above these factors nasog 'aḥor will operate if the following monosyllabic word has a disjunctive tone and completes the sense unit, if it does not complete the sense-unit then nasog 'aḥor cannot operate even though the monosyllabic word may have a strong disjunctive tone on it. In other words nasog 'aḥor is not purely a phonetic but a phonetic-syntactic phenomenon.

The 3rd pers. pl. Lamedh Hē Verbs (Qal)

| | TONE POSITION | | | |
| | Without WAW | | With WAW | |
	Ult	Pen	Ult	Pen
היה	139	21	96	13
עשה	118	17	21	2
מחה	1			1
ראה	42	2	13	
בנה	10	1	10	
ענה	4	3	4	
עלה	18		8	
רעה	2		5	
רבה	5		4	
שתה	2		4	
המה	3		3	
פרה	1		3	
זנה	2		2	
תלה	2		2	
חיה	1		2	
חנה	3		1	
בכה	2		1	
אנה			2	
רדה			2	
אפה			1	
חעה			1	
ספה			1	
עטה			1	
חזה	2	4		
תעה	6	*1		
כלה	10	*1		
פרה	3	1		
מרה	2	1		
נשה		1		
שׁסה		1		
אבה	8			
בלה	4			
פצה	4			
שׁבה	4			
גלה	3			
חפה	3			
פנה	3			
שגה	3			
שׁוה	2			
יפה	2			
נאה	2			
נטה	2			
שלה	2			
גאה	1			
דמה	1			
כבה	1			
נצה	1			
רפה	1			
רעה	1			
שׁאה	1			
שׁעה	1			
	228	54	187	16

Because the form רבוּ could be either a Lamedh Hē, Double Ayin, or Ayin Yodh verb it seemed advisable to collect the Lamedh Hē verbs in order to see if it was possible to distinguish the roots by the position of the tone.[1] Out of a total of 485 verbs it was found that 70 took penult tone. When we examined these it was found that 68 of them had penult tone because:

(1) Nasog 'aḥor operated. This applied to the verbs without waw as much as to the verbs with waw (41 cases).

(2) The verbs were in construct with the following monosyllabic word and hence a secondary tone appeared on the penult (27 cases).

The only exceptions to the rule that all ל"ה verbs, with or without a prefixed waw, take ultima tone unless prevented from doing so by the two factors mentioned above are כָּלוּ (Ps. 37:20) and תָּצֻא (Isa. 16:8) (these are marked with an asterisk on the Table).[2] In the case of כָּלוּ: Silluq is the disjunctive tone but there are 48 examples of Silluq and Athnach, besides כָּלוּ :, and all of them occur on the ultima. We could conclude that since Ayin Yodh/ Waw verbs have a clear preference for ultima tone as is seen in the fact that all its verbs with Silluq and Athnach have penult tone, that therefore כָּלוּ is not a ל"ה verb but an ע"ו verb, i.e. √כּוּל 'to endure, sustain, contain'. However, in the context of the Psalm this does not make a very clear thought, and in any case the same verb occurs in the same sense-unit.

2.4   Summary and Conclusion

We have been able to show that the 1st and 2nd wqtl verbs are not alone in changing the position of the verbal tone. We have shown that some ע"ע and ע"ו verbs in the 3rd pers. pl. undergo a shift of tone without any prefixed waw. Obviously, then, the prefix waw cannot be the cause of the shift in these cases. When we examined these verbs we found that the shift of tone was determined by the logico-syntactical relationship of these verbs within their own sense-units. The fact that no waw was present when the tone shifted enabled us to isolate the real cause of the shift.[1] We next examined the same class of verb with prefixed waw. In some cases the tone shifted but in others it did not. Again, an examination of these verbs showed that the shift was syntactically conditioned. The initial position of the verb in its own sense-unit facilitated the shift just as a final position discouraged a shift. Our findings with respect to the ל"ה verbs showed that a rigid tone position prevailed with these verbs both with and without prefixed waw. Penult tone occurred in the case of verbs in construct and when nasog 'ahor operated.

When we came to examine the 1st and 2nd wqtls we noticed 68 cases which did not fit into Gordon's 'syllabic condition' rule nor into Driver's 'real difference' interpretation. On careful examination we were able to show that the tone was syntactically conditioned and was not linked with any phonemic change. We noticed that the ultima tone occurred only in Direct Speech discourses; it never occurred in Narrative Prose style. A major reason for this is that the position of wqtl in prose is distinctly different from its position in Direct Speech where it normally comes in initial position, and as we saw above this greatly facilitates the forward movement of the tone particularly in animated speech. Undoubtedly the tempo of speech will differ between the two styles and this will have some effect upon the position of the tone.[2] It would be very difficult to prove this in the case of a dead language like Hebrew though the cantillation signs might throw some light on the subject. Our findings, however, do not support the findings of other scholars that the shift in tone position is phonemic (Driver and most modern scholars in practice) or that it is determined by certain syllabic conditions (Gordon and others). Our chief conclusion is that the tone is syntactically conditioned and is non-phonemic.

* * * * * * *

APPENDIX 3

THE PREFIX FORM WITH SUFFIXED הָ - IN THE OLD TESTAMENT

(P = Prefix form;   VP = Prefix form + וֹ ;   WP = Prefix form + וֹ / וַֹ)

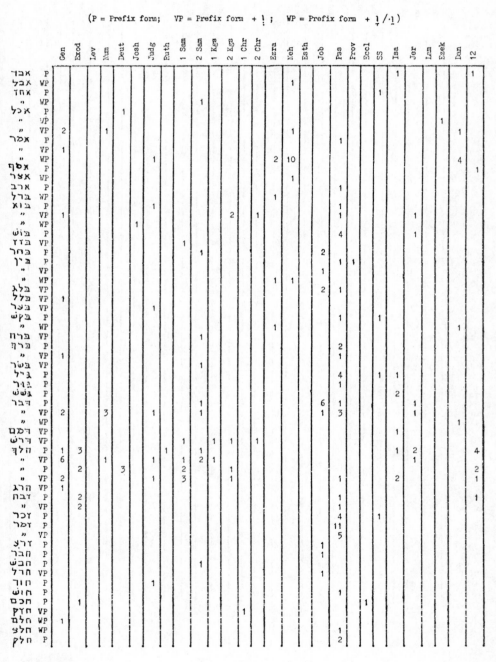

		Gen	Exod	Lev	Num	Deut	Josh	Judg	Ruth	1 Sam	2 Sam	1 Kgs	2 Kgs	1 Chr	2 Chr	Ezra	Neh	Esth	Job	Pss	Prov	Eccl	SS	Isa	Jer	Lam	Ezek	Dan	12
אבד	P																							1					1
אבל	WP																1												
אחז	P																					1							
"	WP					1																							
אכל	P				1																								
"	vP																									1			
"	VP	2		1													1											1	
אמר	P																			1									
"	VP	1																											
"	WP															2	10											4	
אסף	P							1																					1
אצר	WP																1												
ארב	P																			1									
ברל	WP															1													
בוא	P							1												1									
"	VP	1											2		1					1					1				
"	WP				1																								
בוש	P																			4					1				
בזז	VP									1																			
בחר	P							1													2								
בין	P																			1	1								
"	VP																		1										
"	WP															1	1												
בלג	VP																			2	1								
בלל	VP	1																											
בער	VP							1																					
בקש	P																			1			1						
"	WP															1													
ברח	VP									1																			
ברך	P																			2									
"	VP	1																		1									
בשר	VP									1																			
גיל	P																			4			1	1					
גור	P																			1									
גשש	P																							2					
דבר	P									1										1					1				
"	VP	2			3			1		1									6	1					1				
"	WP																			3							1		
דמם	VP																								1				
דרש	VP									1		1	1	1															
הלך	P	1	3				1			1														1	2				4
"	VP	6	2	1		1		1		1	2	1													1				
"	P		2		3					2			1																2
"	VP	2						1		3		1								1					2				1
הרג	VP	1																											
זבח	P		2																	1									1
"	VP		2																	1									
זכר	P																			4		1							
זמר	P																			11									
"	VP																			5									
זרע	P																		1										
חבר	P																		1										
חבש	P							1																					
חרל	VP																		1										
חוד	P						1																						
חוש	P																			1									
חכם	P		1																			1							
חזק	VP												1																
חלם	WP	1																											
חלץ	WP																			1									
חלק	P																			2									

		Gen	Exod	Lev	Num	Deut	Josh	Judg	Ruth	1 Sam	2 Sam	1 Kgs	2 Kgs	1 Chr	2 Chr	Ezra	Neh	Esth	Job	Pss	Prov	Eccl	SS	Isa	Jer	Lam	Ezek	Dan	12
חפש	P																									1			
חפר	VP																			1						1			
חשב	VP																			1	1				1				
טבע	P																		2	1	1			1					
ידע	P	1																		1		1		4					2
″	VP	2	1	1				1	1	1				1						1				4					2
″	WP														1									1					
רחל	VP	1									1									1				1					1
יכח	VP	1																						1					
יכל	VP																								1				1
ילל	VP	1																											
יען	VP										1																		
יסף	VP																1												
יעד	P																			1									
″	VP																1												
יצא	VP														1														
″	WP																1												
יצב	P	1						1																					
″	VP																												1
יצג	P	1																											
יעץ	VP																			1									
ירד	P	3								1										1									
ישב	VP						1																	1					
″	WP															1				1									
ישן	WP																			1									
ישע	WP							1												4				1					
″	VP		2																	1									1
כבד	**P**									1																			
כון	P	1	1											1															
כפר	**P**																1												
כרע	WP																			1									
″	VP	1																						1					
כרת	VP	1																											
″	P																												
″	WP							1																					
לבן	P	1																						1					
לון	P																					1							
לחם	VP							2		1		1																	
למד	VP																			1									
″	VP									1										1				1					
לקח	P	1													2									1					
″	VP																												1
″	WP								1																				
לקש	P							1																					
″	VP	1																											
מוט	P	1											1														1		
מלא	P	1																	5										
מלט	WP														1														
מרט	VP																			2	1			1					
נבט	P																			1	1								
נבע	P	2								1					1									1					
נגד	VP	2								1																			
נהל	P	1																											
נוס	P		1					1																					
נוף	VP																		1										

		Gen	Exod	Lev	Num	Deut	Josh	Judg	Ruth	1 Sam	2 Sam	1 Kgs	2 Kgs	1 Chr	2 Chr	Ezra	Neh	Esth	Job	Pss	Prov	Eccl	SS	Isa	Jer	Lam	Ezek	Dan	12
נוֹשׁ	WP																			1									
נכר	WP																1												
נסע	P	1																											
"	WP															1													
נצל	P																			1									
נצר	P																			1									
נפל	P										2			1															
"	WP																										1	1	
"	VP													1															
נקם	VP							1																1					
נתן	P				1							2																	
"	VP	6	1		1					1		3	1							2				2					
"	WP				1			1		1	1						3			2	1		1				1	1	
נתק	P																			1				1					
סבא	VP											1								1			1						
סבב	VP																1												
סגר	VP																		1					1					
סור	P		1																					1					
"	VP							2																					
סלד	VP									1									1										
ספר	P																			5									
"	VP																		1	1					1				
עבר	P				3	3		2		1																			
"	WP							1																					
"	VP										2													1					
עוד	VP					1														2				1			1		
"	WP																1												
עוף	WP																			1									
עור	P																		2	2									
עזב	P																1		2										
"	VP																							1					
עלט	P																					1							
עלץ	VP																			1									
עצר	P									1					1														
עמד	P																							1					1
"	WP																2												
ערך	P																		1										
"	VP																			1									
פון	P																			1									
פלט	VP																			1									
פלל	WP																											1	
פרש	WP													1	1														
פשע	P																							1					
פתח	P																			1									
"	VP																												1
"	WP	1																											
צוח	WP										1																		
צפן	P																				1								
קבץ	P																												1
"	VP									1																			
"	WP													1	1														
קוט	WP																			1									
קום	P							1												1			1						
"	VP	2																		1									1
"	WP																			1									
קדם	P									1										1									
קרב	P							1																		1			
"	VP																										1		
קשב	P																										1		
רדף	P									1																			1
"	VP									1																			

APPENDIX 3   213

		Gen	Exod	Lev	Num	Deut	Josh	Judg	Ruth	1 Sam	2 Sam	1 Kgs	2 Kgs	1 Chr	2 Chr	Ezra	Neh	Esth	Jct	Pss	Prov	Eccl	SS	Isa	Jer	Lam	Ezek	Dan	12
רוב	VP																			1									
רוץ	P																			1									
רוץ	P							2															1						
ריב	VP											1																	
שבע	WP																3												
שגב	P					1														2									
"	VP	1								1														1					
"	WP							1								1													
שיח	P																		1	6									
"	VP																			2									
שאל	P							1																					
"	VP	1																											
שאף	WP																			1									
שבר	VP	1																											1
"	WP																1												
שבת	P				1																								
שוב	P	1																											1
"	VP	2	1		1			1		1		1									1				2	2	2		3
"	WP																1			1									
שיר	WP																			1									
שיר	P		1					1												9				1					
שחת	P																								1				
"	VP																								1				
שכב	P																			2					1				
"	VP	1																											
שכח	P																		1	1									
שכל	P																			1				1					
שכם	P																			1			1						
שכן	P																			1				1					
"	VP																												
שלח	P				1										1														
"	VP		2							1	1	2																	
"	WP	1														1	2												
שלך	VP																1			1									
שלם	WP																1												
שלם	P																				1								
"	VP																			1									1
שמד	VP					1														1									
שפח	P																			2									
"	VP																			1									
שצא	P																			2					1	1			
"	VP		1		1															1						1			
"	WP																											1	
שמר	P																			2									
"	VP																			5									
"	WP																			1									
שסע	P																								1				
"	VP																												
שפט	VP							1																					
שקף	P																			1					1				
שקל	WP																2								1				
שרק	P																												1
שרק	VP	1																											

TOTALS

		Gen	Exod	Lev	Num	Deut	Josh	Judg	Ruth	1 Sam	2 Sam	1 Kgs	2 Kgs	1 Chr	2 Chr	Ezra	Neh	Esth	Jct	Pss	Prov	Eccl	SS	Isa	Jer	Lam	Ezek	Dan	12
(237)	P	15	12	-	5	10	-	9	2	6	12	3	2	3	1	-	1	-	18	82	7	1	9	14	7	1	1	-	16
(248)	VP	40	10	1	8	1	-	11	2	17	15	6	11	3	3	-	6	-	10	47	1	-	1	21	16	3	-	1	14
(97)	WP	3	-	-	1	-	1	5	-	2	4	-	-	1	1	16	29	-	6	11	-	1	-	-	2	-	3	10	1
		58	22	1	14	11	1	25	4	25	31	9	13	7	5	16	36	-	34	140	8	2	10	35	25	4	4	11	31

APPENDIX 4

Instances where the same q̲t̲l̲ verb has been translated by a Past
in one place and a Future in another place in the OT.

(The first reference is Past, the second Future.)

1	נָתַתִּי	Gen. 16:5/17:16
2	הָיְתָה	Gen. 3:20; 38:21/18:12
3	נָתַתִּי	Gen. 20:6; 27:37/23:13; 15:18
4	מְכָרוֹ	Deut. 32:30/Ex. 21:37
5	נִשְׁבַּר	Isa. 14:29/Ex. 22:9
6	נִשְׁבָּה	Gen. 14:14/Ex. 22:9
7	נִרְאָה	Num. 14:10/Lev. 9:4
8	מָאַסְתִּים	1 Sam. 16:7; 16:1/Lev. 26:44
9	דָּרַךְ	Deut. 1:36/Num. 24:17
10	נָתַן	Deut. 29:3/28:53
11	מֵת	Ex. 9:7/22:13
12	נָתַן	Deut. 9:11/28:52
13	בֵּרַכְךָ	Deut. 2:7/15:6
14	לָקַחְתִּי	1 Sam. 12:3/2:16
15	הָיָה	1 Sam. 2:11/1:28
16	בָּחַרְתֶּם	1 Sam. 12:13/8:18
17	פָּקַדְתִּי	Ex. 3:16/1 Sam. 15:2
18	נוֹתַר	2 Sam. 13:30/17:12
19	הָיָה	1 Kgs.3:12/3:13
20	אָמַר	Is. 45:18/45:24
21	הָלַךְ	2 Kgs. 21:21/20:9
22	מַתְנוּ	Num. 14:2/2 Kgs. 7:3
23	בָּאוּ	Is. 42:9/47:9
24	נָס	Jer. 46:5,21; 2 Sm. 18:17/ Is. 51:11
25	נִחַם	Is. 49:13; 52:9/51:3
26	רָחַץ	Lev. 22:6; 8:21/Is. 4:4
27	זָנוּ	2 Chr. 28:5; 34:16/Is. 35:2; 33:16
28	כָּלָה	Is. 24:13/32:10
29	הֵסִיר	Is. 36:7/18:5; 31:2
30	מָלַךְ	Is. 52:7; 2 Kgs. 23:36/Is. 24:23
31	הִגִּיַ	Jer. 43:6/Is. 28:2
32	הָיְתָה	Is. 1:21; 11:16/50:11; 64:9; 14:24
33	הִגִּיַ	Ezk. 7:12; Cant. 2:12/Is. 25:12
34	בָּזְזוּ	Jos. 11:14/Is. 33:23
35	חָשַׁח	Is. 26:5/25:12
36	הָיָה	Is. 39:2/32:14; 33:9
37	פָּקְדוּ	Num. 26:63,64/Is. 34:16
38	נִקְבְּצוּ	Ezr. 10:1; Is.49:18/34:15
39	חַתּוּ	Is.37:27;Jer.50:2/8:9
40	כָּרְתוּ	Jer. 34:18/46:23
41	נָתַתִּי	Jer. 35:15/31:33
42	הִשְׁכִּילוּ	Ps.106:7; Job 34:27/ Ps.64:10; Jer.20:11;10:21
43	הֹבִישׁוּ	Jer. 6:15; 8:12/2:26; 8:9; 50:2
44	נִשְׁמַע	Jer. 38:27; 8:16/50:46
45	מָלֵאתִי	Jos. 14:8/Jer. 31:25; Zch. 9:13
46	נִתְּנָה	Jer. 52:34/46:24
47	נָתַתִּי	Ezk. 15:6; 16:17; Gn.27:37/ Ezk. 11:21; 4:8
48	נְתַתִּיךְ	Jer. 6:27/49:15
49	נָתַתִּי מ	2 Chr. 16:8/Jer.25:31; Is. 34:2
50	בּוֹשָׁה	Jer. 49:23; 15:9/50:12
51	הָלְכוּ	Jer. 50:6/50:3
52	בֹּשׁוּ	Jer. 14:3,4; 48:13; Ps. 22:6; Jb. 6:20/Jer. 20:11; Is. 45:16
53	תָּקְעוּ	Ezk. 7:14/Jer. 6:3
54	בָּא	Jer. 15:9; 37:16; 39:1/ 25:31
55	רָצְשָׁה	Jer. 8:16; Jud. 5:4/Jer. 49:21
56	נִלְכְּדָה	Jer. 48:1; 38:28/48:41
57	הֻכָּם	Is. 27:7/Jer. 5:6
58	חֲשַׂפְתִּי	Jer. 49:10/13:26
59	הֹבִישָׁה	Hos. 2:7;Jl. 1:12/Jer. 46:24; 48:1
60	הֵבֵאתִי	Jer. 44:2/49:8

61	קְרָאוּ	Jer. 30:17; 36:9/31:6	96	שֶׁטַף	Lev. 15:11/Is. 8:18
62	רָעוּ	Ezk. 34:8/Jer. 6:3	97	בִּלַּע	Lam. 2:2,5/Is. 25:8
63	הַצַּלְתָּ	Ps. 56:14(13)/Ezk. 3:21	98	שִׁלַּחְתִּי	Jer. 24:5; 29:20/Is. 43:14
64	נָפְלוּ	Jer. 52:15/Ezk. 31:12; 27:34 Jer. 51:49	99	עָשָׂה	Is. 38:15/55:11
65	הָיָה	Ezk. 16:49/13:11; 15:2	100	הָיְתָה	Is. 11:16/14:24
66	כָּרְעוּ	Is. 46:2; Jud. 7:6/Ps. 20:9	101	רָאוּ	Is. 66:19; 39:4/52:15; 41:5
67	נָחַנִי	Gen. 24:27/Ps. 108:11	102	הַכָּבֵיד	1 Kgs. 12:10/Is. 8:23(9:1)
68	פִּזַּר	Ps. 112:9/53:6	103	גָּלָה	Is. 24:11; 1 Sam. 4:21,22; Hos. 10:5/Is. 5:13
69	פָּדָה	Job 33:28/Ps. 55:19(18)	104	כָּלָה	Is. 16:4/10:23
70	בָּנָה	Lam.3:5/Ps. 102:17	105	רִחַמְתִּיךְ	Is. 60:10/54:8
71	נִשְׁמְרוּ	1 Sam. 21:5/Ps. 37:28	106	נִחַם	Is. 52:9; 49:13/51:3
72	הֲבִישׁוֹתָה	Ps. 44:8/53:6	107	עֲשִׂיתֶם	Gen. 6:7/Is. 42:16
73	בָּזָה	Ps. 22:25; Ezk. 17:16,19; Num. 15:31/Ps. 102:18	108	נִשְׁמַע	Jer. 38:27; 8:16/49:21; 9:18(19)
74	נִרְאָה	Num. 14:10/Ps. 102:17	109	נָקְרָא	Am. 9:12; Ecc. 6:10/Jer. 44:26; 34:15
75	פָּנָה	Cant. 6:1/Ps. 102:18	110	עָבְדוּ	1 Sam. 4:9; Jos. 24:14,15/ Jer. 25:14
76	נִשְׁמְדוּ	Ps. 83:11/37:38	111	נִתְפְּשָׂה	Num. 5:13/Jer. 48:41; 50:46
77	רָאָה	Ps. 33:13; 114:3 /10:11	112	הִכֵּיתִי	Jer. 2:30/33:5
78	אָבַד	Job 4:7/11:20			
79	רָאוּ	Job 3:16/19:27			
80	נִמְלַט	Jer. 41:15/Prv. 11:21			
81	נִשְׁכַּח	Ecc. 9:5/2:16			
82	נִגְּרָה	Ps. 77:3/Lam. 3:49			
83	פָּקַד	Ruth 1:6/Lam. 4:22			
84	גָּלָה	Ps. 98:2/Lam. 4:22			
85	הַכִּיר	Deut. 33:9/Dan. 11:39			
86	כָּלָה	Is. 24:13; 16:4; 15:6; 1 Kgs. 6:38/Dan. 11:36; Is. 32:10			
87	נַעֲשָׂתָה	Dan. 9:12/11:36			
88	פָּרַץ	1 Chr. 15:13/2 Chr. 20:37			
89	נָטַתִּי	2 Chr. 7:19/2:9			
90	נָסֹגוּ	Jer. 38:22/Is. 42:17			
91	נִבְקְעוּ	Gen. 7:11/Is. 35:6			
92	שִׁלַּמְתִּי	Prv. 7:14/Is. 65:6			
93	מָלְאָה	Is. 34:6; 40:2/11:9			
94	אָפֵס	Is. 16:4; Gen. 47:15,16/Is. 29:20			
95	מָלֵא	Jer. 41:9/Is. 33:5			

NOTES

[NOTE: The first figure is the page number of this book and the figure after the hyphen is the superscript note number inserted in the text of that page: e.g. 18-12 denotes page 18, note 2.]

1-1 So Wm. Chomsky in 'How the study of Hebrew Grammar began and developed', JQR n.s. 35 (1944-5), 281-301.

2-1 Traditional grammar originated in Greece and was further developed in Rome and medieval Europe. The Arab grammarians drew upon the Syrian tradition and the Greco-Roman tradition in Spain. Hebrew grammarians were strongly influenced by the Arabs (see J. Lyons, 1968:18-19).

3-1 J. F. X. Sheehan in his thesis (1968:11-12) wrongly attributes this quotation to Japhet ben Qair who lived in the 13th century (mentioned on p. 304 of Munk's article, JA April, 1850).

3-2 For other weaknesses in Ḥayyuj's grammar see M. Jastrow, Hebraica III, 1886, pp. 172-74.

4-1 For other weaknesses see Jastrow, Hebraica IV, 1887, pp. 26-33.

4-2 This quotation is taken from The First Hebrew & Chaldaic Lexicon to the Old Testament, compiled in the tenth century by Menaḥem ben Saruḳ Selected and Translated from the original Hebrew by Herschell E. Filipowski....London, 1854:75 col. B lines 2-5. (Otherwise known as Menaḥem's Maḥberet.)

8-1 For the text and translation see A. R. R. Hutton, 1898:70-71, and Mason & Bernard, 1853:109-10.

8-2 For the text and translation see Mason & Bernard, 1853:115-16.

10-1 For the extent and quality of these translations see Rabin's thesis, 1943b:106-11.

10-2 For the text (ספר הבחור, fol. III, p. 2) and translation see C. Leo, 1818:226.

11-1 See C. J. Elliott's article, 'Hebrew Learning among the Fathers', Dictionary of Christian Biography, eds. W. Smith & H. Wace, London, 1880, vol. II, pp. 851-72.

11-2 For the text see Sheehan's thesis (1968:143 for photo-copy of original). For the translation see A. O. Schulz, 1900:10.

13-1 Ne quidem Deus tempus praeteritum in futurum convertere possit. This retort appears to have originated with Johann Justus von Einem in Methodus docendi linguas (p. 31), but this could not be traced or verified. He wrote sometime between 1714 and 1736.

13-2 The following are some of the ways the conjunctive ·ן has been interpreted:

(1) וַ or waw + definite article. First(?) suggested by Schultens, 1737:424. He was followed by W. Turner, 1876:381.

(2) הַ or waw + interrogative hē. First suggested by G. Chr. Storr, 1779:161. (See I. Eitan's article in AJSL 45 (1928-9), 143, where he notes that הַ sometimes becomes הַ with doubling of the following consonant.)

The above two explanations suspect that the doubling hides an assimilated ה ; the following suggest an assimilated Nūn.

(3) *וַאֲן > *וַנ . See J. P. Peters, 1887:113; I. Eitan, AJSL (1930), pp. 27-8 and D. Michel, 1960:47 n. 30. L. Köhler suggests * ṷan on Ugaritic evidence in his Lexicon in Veteris Testamenti Libros, Leiden, 1949, p. 247.

(4) *וַנ or waw + deitic particle (= original definite article according to Eitan, AJSL (1929), p. 141). See V. Maag, 1953:86-8; J. Hughes, 1970:13 n. 8.

The next two explanations suggest an assimilated Lāmedh.

(5) *הַל According to J. P. Peters (1887:113) the original form of the article in proto-Semitic was hal. This form has been aspirated in Hebrew, and the Lāmedh has been assimilated as in נ קָטַל from נ קָטַל. If the initial ה > ו then the waw in ־ו does not represent the conjunctive waw but the definite article.

(6) * וַל or waw + particle ל . First(?) suggested by Hubert Grimme, 1896:85f., 92. A. Poebel suggested ṷa 'and' and l(a) 'truly', 1939c: 118. Compare also G. M. Schramm, 1957:5-6.

The following explanation suggested an assimilated ד or ר .

(7) *וַאֲד According to Tafel & Tafel (Bibl. Sacra XIX [1862], 548) Ewald suggested this in his Ausfuhrliches Lehrbuch der hebräischen Sprache des alten Bundes (6th ed. 1862-3, p. 512 (§259), primarily because the conjunction is not simply 'and' but 'because' (Germ. da).

*וַאֲד Suggested by Ewald, 1879:19 (discussed on p. 48 above) and W. Harper, Elements of Hebrew Syntax, N. Y. 1906:84 n. 2. Peters suggested that the Hebrew adverb אָז went back to an archaic אָדֲי , Assyrian adi (1887:112).

The following two explanations suggested that a verb has been assimilated.

(8) הָוָה > וָה >־ו Probably first suggested by J. D. Michaelis, 1745: 52; cf. also W. F. Hezel, 1777:60f.; W. Gesenius, Lehrgeb., 1817: 294 (this view was later abandoned); G. W. F. Freytag, 1861:34; M. M. Kalish, 1875:109; R. Hetzron, 1969:9.

(9) הָיָה This was contracted to ־ו. First suggested by H. Scholze, Animadverss. de Aoristorum Graec. natura, Hamburg, 1735. For other early supporters of this view see A. O. Schulz, 1910:13f. Ewald accepted it in 1827 (p. 539) but later abandoned it. Compare also M. Stuart, 1831:85 n. 3; A. B. Rich, 1874:127; A. Duff, 1901:62 (וַיְהִי־הַיָה־וַיֹּאמֶר = καὶ ἐγένετο λέγει).

The next two explanations see in the heavy waw (־ו) a past tense augment or particle.

(10) ו is the equivalent to the past augment é- in Greek, so Ewald (see p. 48 above) and W. H. Green, 1880:130. Blake suggested that

ı became the sign of the past tense and ן of the present-future (1944:274, 294).

(11) **iͫ** This Egyptian adverbial particle or verbal auxiliary suggested to G. D. Young (1953:252) that ı (wa-) was an existential particle parallel to Egyptian **iͫ** and proto-Semitic *hawaya. Sheehan accepted this possibility, 1971:42.

The following four explanations see no significance in the dagesh of the heavy waw.

(12) *wā Considered by G. J. Thierry to be an interjection, 'there! this! look here!', OTS 9 (1951), 5-7.

(13) The conjunction is equivalent to the Akkadian suffixed -ma conjunction which is used in narrative prose, G. R. Driver, 1936:93 and C. F. Burney, 1919:210.

(14) The heavy waw is a phonetic variation of the simple or weak waw. ı becomes ן before an accented syllable (הָלְ֫כָה י֫וֹם) which points to a time when yiqtól had penult tone, i.e. yiqtol, and when ן was prefixed it became ן before the stressed syllable. Compare S. H. Siedl, 1971:17, 19, and E. S. Artom, 1965:9.

(15) The dagesh is an artificial creation of the Massoretes, so J. Jahn, 1809:465; S. R. Driver, 1892:72 n. 1; F. R. Blake, 1944:294; H. L. Eddleman, 1943:7; J. A. Knudtzon, 1892:51; and G. R. Berry, 1903:61. T. L. Fenton calls the phenomenon 'archaic waw-conservativum', 1973:38.

14-1   S. Lee (1851:470) states that the idea of Relative Tenses was taught by J. Robertson (Hebrew Grammar, 1758) who got the idea from W. Koolhaus (Dissertationes Philologico-exegeticae, Amsterdam, 1751). It has not been possible to verify this.

15-1   E. Rödiger revised the 14th (1845) to the 21st (1872), E. Kautzsch the 22nd (1878) to the 28th (1910), and G. Bergsträsser the 29th edition in 1929.

17-1   The most detailed explanation of the conversive waw and the conjunctive waw and the rules governing their use was that given by Granville Sharp in A Letter to a Learned Friend respecting some Particularities of the Hebrew Syntax, London, 1803:13-17. Since this work is rare we give a summary of his five Rules.

Rule I
        ı prefixed to future tenses converts them to perfect tenses; and when prefixed to verbs in the perfect tense it regularly converts them to the future tense....

Rule II
        When ı is prefixed to a verb, which immediately follows another verb of the same tense, without a prefixed ı , and in the same sentence, the ı in that case is merely conjunctive, and the second verb to which it is prefixed...must be construed according to its proper tense, whether future or imperative, and often also the perfect tense; but not always; as there are a few instances of exception....

Rule III
A prefixed **ו** does not affect or convert any verb in the imperative mood, nor any verb...in the future tense, which follow an imperative mood in the same sentence. But to perfect tenses the prefixed **ו** is conversive without hindrance from a preceding imperative verb.

Rule IV
After an interrogation, either of the emphatical **ה** , or of the interrogatory relatives **מי** or **מה**, the prefixed **ו** doth not influence any verb...of the future tense, or the present tense; but in perfect tenses the **ו** is regularly conversive, and is not influenced by a preceding interrogation.

Rule V
'If a future tense put for a praeterperfect tense' (which must be by having a prefixed **ו**) 'precedes a preter tense' (having also a prefixed **ו**,) 'the latter is merely copulative.'

This last Rule is a quotation from Elias Levita's grammar.

17-2   W. R. Hall has done the same for the LXX translation of Genesis and found that, 'The translators felt that both conjugations [qtl and yqtl] could express actions throughout the whole range of Greek tenses and moods' (1966:346-47).

18-1   The LXX translates **וקרא** by the Present καλεῖται.

18-2   Symmachus and Theodotian read the Future καὶ ἔσται also.

19-1   For over a hundred similar examples see Appendix 4

20-1   In a number of West African languages, including Yoruba and Igbo, there are no specific markers of past versus present tense, often they have markers to denote aspect. E.g. in Yoruba nonstative verbs have no marker if they have perfective meaning, and the marker ń before the verb if they have imperfective meaning (W. E. Welmers, 1973:345-7).

21-1   J. J. Curtis wrote: 'It seems probable that the idea of tense, coupled with an effort to explain the translations of the Septuagint and the Vulgate produced the "Waw Conversive" which for several centuries served to obscure the true nature of the verb' (1949:6f.).

21-2   G. Sharp, op. cit. (17-1), pp. 3-10, demonstrates the hold the Jewish Conversive theory had on Christian Hebraists from Buxtorf to his own day.

21-3   F. R. Blake, 1951:46; H. Levy, 1976:201ff.; J. H. Marks & V. M. Rodgers, 1955:38f.; I. J. Livny & M. Kokhba, 1973:48; and E. L. Carlson, Elementary Hebrew, Grand Rapids, Michigan, 1978, pp. 16, 43, 147. (Cf. Note 57-2)

21-4   For his treatment of the 'tenses' see pp. 335-44, 430-35.

24-1   The ablest exponent of this theory was I. Nordheimer (see 1.3.3. below). Other supporters of the theory were T. Keyworth, 1825:132; J. Prosser, 1838:xii; W. Beeston, 1843:59; W. W. Duncan, 1848:98; W. Wilson, 1850: ix; and H. Craik, 1863.

26-1   W. H. Bennett (1885-6) rejected the suggestion that WPs were dependent on a preceding Suffix-form. His work covers the Pentateuch only. M. Stuart had already voiced a similar objection in 1831:160.

26-2   Support for the Inductive theory came from C. Leo, 1836:243, and T. Connellan, 1827:10. Gell obtained his solution from reading G. Sharp's <u>Tracts</u>.

27-1   Compare O. L. Barnes' theory (1965) with that of J. G. Murphy (1850), and see 1.3.1.4.2 below.

28-1   Written by his daughter. The bibliography is not complete, <u>e.g.</u> the editions of his <u>Grammar</u>. For an evaluation of him see the article by R. S. Cripps, <u>BJRL</u> 35 (1952-3), 385-404.

31-1   Others who found an indication of difference of tense in the different positions of the root relative to the personal pronouns were E. Dowling, 1797:50f.; H. Ewald, 1870:§137; I. Nordheimer, 1838-41:I, p. 105; H. Steinthal, 1861:260; A. Dillmann, 1857:141; F. Böttcher, see p. 57 below; and W. Turner, 1876:376f.

32-1   B. Comrie put is as follows: 'Tense relates the time of the situation referred to to some other time, usually to the moment of speaking....in the absence of any specification of the time-point relative to which the time reference is made, this time-point is taken to be the present moment.' (1976:1-2)

34-1   The development of tense was seen by G. J. Theirry as follows: '...the speaker gives a whole series of short descriptions, of snap-shots, each independent of the other; his interlocutor sees the different scenes, each one painted before his eyes, as an immediate <u>present</u> fact, as a separate immovable picture. There is no question of a sequence of different scenes, no question of movies, one scene does not change into another....But when after a certain period the language was more and more rationalized, the element <u>time</u> rose before the consciousness of men....The row of immovable pictures became a moving film....The describer became a narrator.' (<u>OTS</u> IX (1951) 8-9)

37-1   Support for Lee's theory came from T. Jarrett, 1848:36; G. F. R. Weidemann, 1849:24; H. M. Wheeler, 1850:46-7 (partially); W. Paul, 1852; and R. Young in his <u>Literal Translation of the Bible</u>, 1862.

40-1   Barnes viewed the action as a Positional Present 'and Elohim is calling'. קרא (same verse) is a past event viewed from the same Positional Present standpoint 'while the darkness he had called Night' (1965:70).

42-1   <u>Cf.</u> note 31-1.

44-1   For the text see Sir W. Martin, 1876:4. This text is from J. Jahn's 3rd ed. 1809.

44-2   <u>Cf. Syntax,</u> 1879:249.

44-3   Unless otherwise stated the following page references are to Ewald's <u>Syntax of the Hebrew Language,</u> translated by J. Kennedy in 1879 from the 8th German edition, 1870.

48-1   See Note 13-2(7) and J. F. Smith's translation of Ewald's <u>Introductory Hebrew Grammar</u>, London, 1870:164.

48-2   See Note 13-2(10) and (11).

53-1   <u>Cf.</u> Notes 18-1 and 18-2.

55-1   <u>Cf.</u> T. Bowman, 1882:199-200 and H. Hurwitz, 1831. The latter notes that when the second root consonant happens to be either of the letters

ה, ק, ם, כ, ע, ר or ב it receives vocal sheva, thus וַיְּשְׁמֶה and אֶשְׁיָב (p. 138). See also p. 129 below.

55-2 This was S. R. Driver's explanation, 1892:76.

56-1 He was a pupil of Ewald.

57-1 Cf. Note 31-1.

57-2 Popular though Ewald's theory became there were not wanting supporters of the older Conversive idea in this period, e.g. B. Davies, 1880:xxiii; W. R. Harper, 1883; J. Kennedy, 1889:76; T. Bowman, 1882:139, 141; and S. P. Tregelles, n. d. (1882?), pp. 54-55.

62-1 B. Comrie, 1976; M. Joos, 1968; F. R. Palmer, 1974; G. N. Leech, 1976. The term 'aspect' is sometimes used in two different senses, i.e. (a) to denote how the speaker conceives of an action--the subjective view (cf. Landsberger, Islamica II (1926), p. 360 n. 1)--this is how Rundgren uses the term, and (b) to describe and denote how an action takes place--the objective view. This latter is better known as Aktionsart.

65-1 D. Michel noted that where a qtl verb refers to a future action, futurity is expressed by the context and not by the verb form per se (1960:90ff.).

70-1 Jenni has worked out the difference in aktionsart between the Pi'el and Hiphil themes. The former is unmarked while the latter denotes durativity to over-simplify his distinction (1968:52ff.).

73-1 J. A. Hughes made a special study of these 'archaic' remains in the prose passages of the OT (unpub. Ph.D Thesis, 1962). He worked on the assumption that Hebrew has a tense system, therefore where yqtl was preceded by אָז, טֶרֶם, צַד, etc., and referred to past events, he classed these as remnants of an archaic 'aorist'. Apart from Hughes' work no comprehensive study has been carried out on the effect these particles are said to exert on the following verb form. The following are the results of a cursory investigation into the particles אָז and טֶרֶם before the verb.

אָז occurs 105 times in the OT. In 12 cases no verb follows and once an imperative follows it, leaving 92 cases where a verb follows. We have followed the RSV translation of these 92 cases.

	Past	Pres	Fut	Others	TOTAL
אָז before the Prefix-form	20	2	29	7	58
אָז before the Suffix-form	31	2	1	-	34

These results would not appear to support the traditional understanding of the combination of these two forms, or Hughes' working hypothesis that אָז preserves the archaic yqtl. The construction אָז + yqtl is more often translated as a future than a past tense.

There are 35 cases where another particle occurs in combination with אָז e.g. מֵאָז, כִּי('-)אָז, אוֹ-אָז etc. These have been translated as follows:

	Past	Pres	Fut	Others	TOTAL
Prefix-form	1	2	9	1	13
Suffix-form	14	-	-	-	14

The other 8 cases are not followed directly by a verb. Adding the totals together we get:

	Past	Pres.	Fut.	Others	TOTAL
Prefix-form :	21	4	38	8	71
Suffix-form :	45	2	1	-	48

Out of 71 cases of אָז before yqtl only 21 times does the construction have a past meaning. In 50 cases the same construction is given a non-past meaning.

* * *

טֶרֶם occurs 55 times in the OT. In 3 cases no verb follows leaving 52 cases.

	Past	Pres.	Fut.	Others	TOTAL
Prefix-form :	23	19	3	-	45
Suffix-form :	7	-	-	-	7

If we examine the verb _immediately preceding_ the Prefix-form where it is given a Past meaning we find:

11 times it is preceded by wayyqtl which are translated by the PAST,
1   "   "   "   "   yqtl   "   is   "   "   "   "
8   "   "   "   "   qtl   "   are   "   "   "   "

(The other three cases begin a new thought.) Is it any wonder that טֶרֶם + yqtl is given a PAST meaning in these contexts? This is further borne out by an analysis of the 19 cases where the Prefix-form is given a PRESENT meaning.

2 times it is preceded by wyqtl which are translated by the future,
4   "   "   "   "   "   yqtl   "   "   "   "   "   future,
1   "   "   "   "   "   is   "   "   present,
1   "   "   "   "   qtl   "   "   "   "   "   future,
3   "   "   "   "   "   "   are   "   "   present,
1   "   "   "   "   "   "   is   "   "   imperative,

Twice an imperative precedes it; four times no verb immediately precedes that could be said to influence the translation; and once a Suffix-form with a past meaning is in the immediate vicinity but not directly related to the following construction.

If we were to analyse the influence of the preceding verb in the case of אָז + yqtl we would probably find a similar situation. The so-called conversive force of אָז and טֶרֶם depends on the fact that a corresponding tense (the past) precedes, with which it is co-ordinated.

74-1   G. R. Driver suggests that where wayyqtl appears to have a habitual or customary meaning this is because a concrete actual happening underlies a general assertion or truth (1936:135, 137).

75-1   For criticisms of Driver's interpretation of these constructions see G. R. Berry, 1902-4:60-69.

77-1   Lee linked the form of the imperative with the infinitive (1827:213), while T. W. Thacker linked it with the infinitive absolute (the inflected terminations being borrowed from the Permansive/Suffix-form), (1954:157, 320).

77-2   This view was rejected by S. R. Driver (1892:161 n. 1), while M. Lambert (1893:57) suggested that all 3rd masc. sing. forms should be emended as infinitive absolutes with <u>waw</u> conjunctive. J. Huesman (1956b:434) agrees with Lambert. A. Rubinstein, however, suggests that they are the intrusions of a late Post-Exilic milieu and before the OT text was fixed (1963:62-9).

78-1 Suggested by, among others, F. Böttcher (<u>Hebr. Sprachen,</u> Leipzig, 1866: §551); Lee (<u>Heb. Gram.,</u> 3rd ed., 1841:200); W. Wright (<u>Arab. Gram.,</u> 1874-5, I, p. 67); A. Merx (<u>Grammatica Syrica,</u> 1867:197); and A. H. Sayce (1872:127).

78-2 The ending <u>-at</u> can be seen in אֱלָךְתָ, Dt. 32:6, which is the regular form in Arabic, Ethiopic, and Aramaic, <u>cf.</u> Wright's <u>Arab. Gram.,</u> (1874-5 vol. I, p. 60).

78-3 Sayce suggests that: 'The idea of motion was suggested...to the primitive Semite, by dwelling upon the pure deep sound of <u>a</u> or <u>ha</u> by which the word was lengthened...beyond itself....From the substantive these terminations...were transferred to the verbs without losing their meaning' (1872:127).

78-4 <u>Cf.</u> Lee (1841:190); Donaldson (1848:19); Olshausen (<u>Lehrbuch</u>, Brunswick, 1861:527); H. Ewald (1835:§149); A. H. Sayce (1875:90).

79-1 On the symbolical meaning of the vowels see Ewald (1870:§149); Böttcher (1866:§§528, 590); Dillmann (1857:116); and A. H. Sayce (1872:72, 127; 1875:363). <u>Cf.</u> G. R. Driver, 1936:47-8.

80-1 The following are some of the suggestions put forward to account for the initial <u>yodh</u> in the 3rd pers. masc. sing. יִקְטֹל .
(1) Nominal origin. The verb form as it stands may be a nominal form (Turner's first possibility). Cf. Deitrich (1846:121f.)
(2) Nominal suffix but prefixed in the verb. (Turner's second possibility) <u>Cf.</u> Nordheimer (<u>Heb. Gram.,</u> I, p. 210); Schultens (1737:275); Storr (<u>Observationes,</u> 1779:143). אֶפְרָתִי 'an Ephraimite', or 'one belonging to...', Jud.12:5, <u>cf.</u> 10:3 and 19:11. See also Sayce (<u>JRAS</u> n.s. IX (1877), 49). Dillmann notes that in Ethiopic 'the ending <u>i</u> is for the most part used to form nouns indicating the agent from simpler personal nouns' (<u>Gram. d. Aeth. Sprache,</u>(transl. by J. A. Crichton, London, 1907) 1857:205).
(3) Deitic or demonstrative element. So Dillmann (<u>op. cit.,</u> 1857:198); Thacker (1954:177); G. R. Driver (1936:39); W. B. Stevenson (1936-7: 7-8).
(4) Demonstrative pronoun. G. J. Thierry (OTS IX (1951), 7) suggests iă = originally 'somewhere, elsewhere'. Dillmann (<u>op. cit.,</u> suggests *ija or *aja (p. 198).
(5) Personal pronoun. Wright suggests *<u>ya</u> 'one who' (<u>Arab. Gram.,</u> pp. 103-4, <u>cf.</u> pp. 294-5; <u>Comp. Gram.,</u> pp. 179, 182), as does Philippi (<u>ZDMG</u> 29 (1875), p. 171f.). Jahn (1809:177) and Lee (1827:206) suggest that as הִא was originally used for both genders (see espec. the Penta.) <u>yodh</u> stands for it. Others think it stands in place of, or is a contraction of, הוּא. <u>Cf.</u> F. E. König (<u>op. cit.,</u> I, pp. 148-9, 156-9); Olshausen (1861:452, 454); Gesenius (<u>Lehrgeb.</u> 1817:274-5); J. Kennedy (1889:76); B. L. Goddard (1950:4). For the interchange of ה and י see F. Prätorius, <u>Old Test. Student</u> II (1884-5), 25. For the initial <u>nūn</u> in Syriac

J. C. James (1920:129) suggests the development ‏ﬡ‎ > ‏נ‎ and shows
such a development in BH. G. Bertin (1882:113) thinks the origin
lies in a primitive substantive verb an (‏אָן‎) 'to be'. Others
think it is linked with the nûn in the personal pronouns, e.g.
‏אוֹנכִי‎, ‏אונתוׂ‎, ‏אנתָה‎ > ‏אתָה‎, etc., Turner, 1876:376. Ewald suggests (1870:§191[a])the yodh is 'weakened from ‏ו‎ or n'.

(6) Fragment of the verb ‏הָוָה‎ . Whereas in (5) the Prefix-form is made
up of the infinitive + abbreviated pers. pronouns, on this suggestion it is made up of the infinitive construct + abbreviated form
of the verb ‏הָיָה‎: ‏יִקְטֹל‎ = ‏קְטֹל‎ + ‏הוה‎ = is to kill. The first
to suggest this appears to have been Rudolf von Raumer in Gesammelte sprachwissenschaftliche Schriften, Frankfurt, 1863:470. Cf.
A. Merx, 1867:199; and G. Bertin, 1883:389-90. Böttcher regarded the
yodh is not a mark of the person but of the tense (1866:§925).

(7) A new derived root. Turner observes that the 3rd pers. masc. sing.
Suffix-form has no fragment of a pers. pronoun present, whereas
the other persons of the Suffix-form have them. Similarly, he argued
the 3rd pers. masc. sing. of the Prefix-form has no fragment of a
personal pronoun present. ‏יִקְטֹל‎ as it stands is the absolute form
of the verb; it is not a compound form. Dietrich appears to have
been the first to suggest this solution (1846:97ff.). Cf. also S.
R. Driver, 1892:7; A. Koch, Der semitische Infinitiv: Eine sprachwissenschaftliche Untersuchung, Stuttgart, 1874:7; A. H. Sayce,
JAOS IX (1877), 23-7, 30-2; and B. Stade, Lehrbuch der heb. Gram.,
1878:§478[c].

(8) Hamitio-Semitic analogies. See Benfrey, Verhältniss der aegyptischen
Sprache, Leipzig, 1844, pp. 15, 211f., 296.

80-2   D. Michel describes the difference between qtl and yqtl thus: Qtl has
an accidental character in relation to the subject whereas yqtl has a
substantial character. The former denotes voluntary actions...the
latter denotes something that 'belongs' to the subject and is manifested (1960:111f.).

81-1   Cf. Note 13-2.

82-1   Cf. G. S. Ogden's article (1971:451) where he notes the functions of
the verb ‏הָיָה‎ as (a) it posits the subjects existence, and (b) it
indicates transition from one sphere of existence to another. (This
article is a summary of his doctoral thesis.)

82-2   For a comprehensive treatment of the precative Perfect in the Semitic
languages see I. D. Marcus, 1970:3-33.

87-1   See Geldart (1874:25-34) for the debate whether the Permansive was to
be considered a verb or not.

88-1   G. Janssens points out (1972:49-50) that the Old Egyptian Pseudo-
Participle 'was used and inflected in the way of the Akkadian stative/
permansive'. It has mainly a stative/intransitive meaning. Cf. M. A.
Murray, 1905:58; and G. R. Driver, 1936:20 n. 2.

89-1   Cf. G. R. Driver, 1936:22-6. I would like to thank Rev. John Sturdy of Gonville & Caius College, Cambridge, for translating portions of this Danish thesis.

89-2   See Burney's reasons for rejecting this term, 1919:213.

89-3   Presumably Knudtzon would trace the Prophetic Perfect to an original present meaning, cf. Nordheimer, 1841, vol. 2, p. 165. Burney traces the Hebrew qātal to the Akk. permansive (1919:200-208). J. Barth, on the other hand, rejected this suggestion (1887:375ff.). According to Brockelmann (1907, G.V.G.S.S. vol. I, §52g) the change of i to a is a common phenomenon, which prompts G. R. Driver to view qātal as an extension of meaning in an originally nominal or adjectival form (1936:22). A. Poebel gives examples (O.Lz XIX (1916), 47-8) where the Akk. qatil has the same force as the Heb. qātal, e.g. maḥir 'he has received'. Cf. Akk. nadin and Heb. nātan 'he has given'.

90-1   While H. Bauer supported the priority of the yaqtul form he rejected this argument for it (1910:6).

90-2   In this he was followed by C. F. Burney (1919:203-4) and G. R. Driver (1936:30).

92-1   R. Meyer regarded the qtl form as an intruder in a Prefix verbal system where it took over some of yqtl's functions. He accounts for the pres.-fut. yqtl by postulating a durative *yaqattalu which coalesced with the Pi'el. For his contribution to the HVS see his Heb. Gram., Berlin, 1969, vol. II, p. 96ff., VTSupp. VII (1960), 309-17; and FuF XL (1966), 241-3.

93-1   The fullest treatment of the use of the Prefix-form as a pluperfect is probably that of D. W. Baker, 1973.

94-1   It is surprising, in the light of this observation, that Bauer did not pursue this point, because, instead of arriving at two verbal systems, he would have been forced to postulate two layers of syntax for the Hebrew language. Chiastic structures frequently require a change of word order which affects the verb form, see Lund (1930, 1933) and Ceresko (1975, 1976). Cf. 1.3.7.10 and f'note 128-2.

94-2   G. R. Driver acquiesces in this view with respect to the Imperfect consecutive forms (1936:15).

94-3   Bauer has in mind Böttcher's 'deeper psychological reason' (1866: II, pp. 114, 208) and Olshausen's interpretation of the Pf. consec. as 'a play of imagination', (1861:460). Ges.-K. (1910:§106) and S. R. Driver (1892:§13) held that something may be pictured in the speaker's mind as accomplished but which in reality may lie far in the future. This was also the view of the Jewish grammarians (p.8 above).

95-1   R. Frankena (1974) and Siedl (1971:46) agree with Bauer here. The former thinks Hebrew is a mixture of Akk. and Old Canaanite. The latter supports Bauer on the priority of the yqtl form (p. 7). Bergsträsser, on the other hand, rejected Bauer's two layers of usage for qtl and yqtl (O.Lz 26 (1923)257-260, 477).

95-2　　　According to Bergsträsser (1929:11 n. 3) M. Barth was the first to
make this identification. It was challenged by Haupt (1878:ccxlix) and
Knudtzon (ZA 6 [1892], 408ff.), but adopted by Brockelmann (GVGSS
§261).

98-1　　　First(?) suggested by G. C. Geldart, 1874.

101-1　　This suggestion was later taken and modified by G. R. Driver, see
1.3.8.7.

102-1　　This suggestion was put forward independently by T. W. Thacker, see
1.3.9.14 and 1.3.7.17.

104-1　　Cf. Note 128-2.

104-2　　For criticisms of Bauer's theory see G. R. Driver, 1936:9-15, and
A. Poebel's correspondence with Bauer in O.Lz vols. 19-22 (1916-19).
For criticisms of Bauer & Leander's terms for the verbs see G. J.
Thierry, OTS VII (1950), 145-46.

105-1　　This had been suggested earlier by D. H. Weir, 1849:309.

105-2　　Suggested earlier by A. J. Maas, Hebraica V (1889), 192-5.

106-1　　G. R. Driver rejected this development on the basis of usage (PHVS,
p. 94). The assumption 'that yaqtul was originally timeless and therefore universal lacks other support'(p. 20), Driver argued.

108-1　　Bergsträsser regarded Bauer's *qatal as an unprovable nomen agentis
(1929:13 n. 6).

108-2　　See PHVS p. 39 n. 5 where Driver notes that the deitic (h)a is found
suffixed to the noun in Aramaic but prefixed in Hebrew.

109-1　　JAOS 13 (1889). He was the founder of Assyrian Grammar and discovered
the Persian vowel system. (See bibliographical note by B. K. Lunn,
Trans. of the Dublin Univ. Oriental Langs. Soc., June 1962, vol. I/3,
p. 41).

110-1　　Knudtzon appears to have been the first to suggest that iqatal and
iqtul were originally one verb-form and only later changed the vowel
before the third root consonant (except in the Qal or Base theme) to
indicate past (iqtul) and present-future (iqátal) tenses (ZA 7 (1892)
p. 50; cf. p. 91 above).

121-1　　Cf. Burney (1919:205) for instances of adjectival and nominal forms
suffixed in the same manner as the Permansive.

122-1　　Greenberg noted: 'It is the very fact that two Semitic languages
geographically the most remote from each other, and otherwise with
very little in common that is not demonstrably Semitic Gemeingut,
share this particular formation that adds cogency to the thesis that
it is Proto-Semitic' (JAOS 72 (1952) 2).

123-1   A. Poebel (O.Lz 19 (1916) 47-8) and more recently and comprehensively
M. B. Rowton (1962:233-303) have pointed out numerous instances where
Akk. qatil has the same force as the WS qatal, e.g. sabātu 'to take',
leqū 'to accept, take', maḫāru 'to receive', and nasū 'to carry'. See
Note 89-3.

123-2   See Moran (1950:120 n. 86) where case-endings are still in use in
Amarna even though it has qatala. H. L. Ginsberg noted that the drop-
ping of case-endings was a late development and not even complete in
Phoenician (1970:107).

124-1   The same point is made by Moran (1950:34).

126-1   See Appendix 2 for a fuller discussion and explanation of this phenomenon.

128-1   J. H. Greenberg regarded this type of speculation as being 'as fruit-
less and outdated as the 19th century discussions concerning the relative age of the noun and verb in Semitic' (1952).

128-2   S. R. Driver asserted that, 'No fact about the Hebrew language is more
evident than the practical equivalence of ויקרא and ויקרא...ו (1892:99).
This view was shared by Knudtzon (1892:51, cf. p. 91 above) and G. R.
Driver (cf. p. 144 above).

129-1   Cf. p. 55 above.

132-1   A similar explanation had been put forward by Bauer, for which see
1.3.7.8, cf. 1.3.7.17.

133-1   Cf. R. L. Harris, 1950:33 n. 1.

142-1   Cf. also his article in JANES 2/1 (1969), 37-40.

142-2   Egyptian Grammar, London. See also 'Some Aspects of the Egyptian Language', The Proceedings of the British Academy, vol. XXIII, 1937
London), pp. 81-104, especially pp. 82-3 where he notes the following
characteristics of Egyptian, (a) the extraordinary preference for
nominal description over verbal narrative, leaning towards passive
rather than active forms, and (b) the striking logicality and self-
consistency of Egyptian syntax.

144-1   Cf. Appendix Note 4 of J. Weingreen, A Practical Grammar for Classical
Hebrew, London.

144-2   The Amarna Tablets exhibit a construction which resembles the Hebrew
consecutive qtl. Cf. W. L. Moran, JCS 2 (1948), 245, and C. H. Gordon,
Or 21 (1952), 123.

145-1   For a wider discussion of the issues see A. Bloch, 1963:41-50; J.
Cantineau, 1950:21-34; T. L. Fenton, 1970:31-41; A. Fitzgerald, 1972:
90-92; H. L. Ginsberg, 1938:3; A. Goetze, 1938:266-306, especially pp.
297ff.; C. H. Gordon, UT 1965:67ff.; E. Hammershaimb, 1941:105-10; Z.
S. Harris, 1939:49, 83; D. H. Madvig, 1966:80ff.; I. D. Marcus, 1971:

84ff., 93-5); and M. Martin, 1958:273ff.

For an example of yaqáttal in Punic see Berthier, 1955:115-16, and Février, 1958:31. V. Christian suggested that the doubled consonant was due to an assimilated nūn, i.e. *yagántal > yaqáttal, 1919-20: 733-34.

149-1 A Grammar of the Greek New Testament in the Light of Historical Research, Nashville. (4th. ed. 1934)

149-2 A Beginning-Intermediate Grammar of Hellenistic Greek, 3 vols., pub. by Society of Biblical Literature, USA, 1973.

153-1 The following system is used by Thacker to represent the structure of any form. The symbol ⌢ indicates any vowel without regard to its quantity and the symbol ∥ is used to divide syllables. An accented vowel or syllable is marked thus ⌢ .

167-1 This explanation was first put forward as long ago as 1910 by H. Bauer, cf. 1.3.7.9 above.

168-1 Thacker noted that yaqáttal with its doubled second radical is ideally fitted by its structure to express repetition or continuity, whereas there is nothing in the pattern yaqtul to suggest such a notion (p. 187f.). Since the latter is so used in West Semitic he reasons that it is probably an adaptation of an earlier form, either the jussive yqtl or the preterite yqtl. He eliminates the jussive form which left only the preterite yqtl (p. 188). The reader is left with the impression that WS took over the ousted preterite yqtl (Driver's view), presumably, because at this late stage in the development of the secondary WS forms there was no imperfect yqtl in PS (= ES).

This impression is strengthened by a later statement, 'Ethiopic alone has retained the present-imperfect yaqáttal. In place of it the other [WS] dialects have selected the preterite-imperfect and developed it into their imperfect' (p. 323).

Since, however, it is clear from the rest of Thacker's work that he viewed the incomplete function of WS yqtl as having been derived, not from yaqáttal but from the PS universal yqtl, his use of the terms 'new' to describe the emergence of the yqtl/incomplete in WS, and his use of 'secondary' to describe its function, are not intended to be taken literally.

The above statements can then be harmonised with Thacker's basic position provided that (a) yqtl, despite its pattern, did express the ideas of repetition, continuity, incompletion, etc., before yaqáttal was created and took over or supplanted, but not completely, some of these early functions; (b) the WS yqtl form is not an adaptation of an earlier form; and (c) the WS yqtl is traced back to a time when Akkadian and WS were still developing together, because of the evidence for this form and function in Akkadian (p. 188).

172-1 R. Hetzron attempted to prove that PS distinguished a perfect/preterite y'aqtul and a jussive yaqt'ul (1969).

173-1 Cf. e.g., J. M. Plumley's Coptic Grammar, London, pp. 12-13, 74-6. For other references to the tone in Thacker's work see pp. 116, 163, 219, 222-3, 227.

190-1   J. F. Gyles repeats this rule in his <u>Hebrew Grammar</u> (London), 1814, p.118.
        G. R. Berry notes that the change of tone is the 'chief argument and
        the only one of much force for the existence of Waw Consecutive with
        Perfect,' and adds: 'It is, however, an argument of very little force'
        (1902-4:62).

190-2   The following have made some contribution toward an understanding of
        the inherent problems involved in the tone shift: S. R. Driver (1892:
        §105)(Phonetic approach); G. R. Berry (1903:60-69) who dismisses the
        tone shift as a late development because of the absence of volatili-
        zation of the initial changeable vowel a̱. He suggests that 'the lang-
        uage knew nothing of this change of tone while it was really a living
        language' (p. 68). In this he is supported by M. L. Margolis, <u>JBL</u> 30
        (1911), 42. C. H. Gordon (1938) set out the syllabic structures that
        conditioned the shift. F. R. Blake (1944, 1946) sought a phonemic
        solution to the shift as did G. R. Driver who described the Pf. consec.
        as 'an archaism surviving from the common proto-Semitic speech' (1936:
        90, <u>cf.</u> pp. 89-92). A. S. Hartum (= E. S. Artom) looked for a pho-
        netic solution (1952, Artom, 1963-4). J. F. X. Sheehan wrote a thesis
        on the tone shift but limited it to the Pentateuch (1968). The summary
        of his findings are in <u>Biblica</u> 51 (1970), 545-48. Gordon's article
        dominates this thesis and hence no original contribution was made
        toward the understanding of tone shift. (Gordon was Chairman of the
        Dissertation Committee.) The last contribution to the problem was
        that of J. Blau (1971) who attempts a phonetic solution. He was not
        aware of the work done on the phenomenon since Gordon's article was
        published in 1938.

190-3   <u>Cf.</u> Blake's alternative phonetic principle: 'There is a strong tend-
        ency to shift the accent from a closed penultimate syllable, and a
        contrasting tendency to retain it on a long open penult' (1944:288).
        We are unable to support this 'principle'in the light of our findings,
        see p. 196 last lines. If Blake's 'tendency' is a phonetic rule why
        does it <u>never</u> occur in Narrative Prose style? Blau modifies the sec-
        ond part of Gordon's rule observing that it 'is only a tendency,
        counteracted by several exceptions without any apparent reason' (1971:
        17).

190-4   <u>Cf.</u> G.-K. §491; E. S. Artom (1965:10). Blake described this suggestion
        as a 'pseudo-phonetic principle' (1944:287).

190-5   The consonant following the verb is as follows:

א = 726 (אֶת = 329, אֶל = 43)	ח = 33	גּ = 5
ל = 236	י = 17	ע = 5
עַ = 155 (עַל = 57)	נ = 15	ט = 4
מ = 114	כ = 14	פ = 4
בּ = 86	ס = 14	צ = 3
ו = 68	ר = 11	שׂ = 3
כּ = 61	ג = 8	ת = 3
בְּ = 60	ד = 7	ף = 2
שׁ = 41	ק = 7	שּׂ = 1
ה = 38	ך = 6	

        In 13 cases Sōph Pāsūq intervenes between the verb and the following word and have, accordingly, been left out of these statistics.

194-1   Blake could find only one exception (Jer. 20:9), see his article, 1944: 281 n. 2.

195-1   <u>Cf.</u> Wickes, 1970:107.

196-1   Occasionally there are cases of a conjunctive sign on both the verb and the following word.
GROUP I. Penult tone on verb with accented (conj.) monosyllabic word following:
Jer. 17:27 אֵשׁ וְהִצַּ֤תִּי (That the penult tone is not due to the monosyllabic word see Dt. 24:19 in Group II.)
2 Sam. 9:10 וַעֲבַדְתָּ לֹו

GROUP II. Ultima tone on the verb and conj. tone on monosyllable:
Dt. 24:19 וְשָׁכַחְתָּ עֹמֶר

Ezek. 32:6 וְהִשְׁקֵיתִ֤י אֶרֶץ

Job 5:24 וּפָקַדְתָּ נָוְךָ

GROUP III. Penult tone on verb and conj. tone on following polysyllabic word:
1 Kgs. 18:12 וּבָ֣אתִי לְהַגִּיד

GROUP IV. Ultima tone on verb and conj. tone on following polysyllabic word:
Ezek. 34:10; 37:6; 43:19; 14:19; 37:14; 12:13; 16:60; 4:2;
   16:37; 34:2; 37:6; 39:19; 4:3; 29:12,
Jer. 31:12; 45:5; 49:37; 36:31; 25:9; 24:7, Exod. 8:18;
  25:22; 29:9, Lev. 26:16; 20:5; Dt. 12:20; 17:5; 31:17;
Pss. 89:26, 30, 33; Prov. 23:2; Isa. 66:19; Hos. 2:20;
Am. 9:4; Zch. 12:10; and 2 Chr. 12:7.

196-2   In his 1938 article Gordon understood the principle of <u>nasog 'aḫor</u> to be a purely phonetic phenomenon, <u>i.e.</u> where a verb was followed by an accented monosyllabic word the preceding tone must be <u>two</u> syllables away thus causing penult tone on the verb, hence his criticism of Bergsträsser. There are two points of criticism with his understanding of <u>nasog 'aḫor</u>. Firstly, it is not a purely phonetic phenomenon. It is intimately connected with the logico-syntactical area of Hebrew grammar. Secondly, only when the monosyllabic word following the verb <u>concludes</u> the sense-unit will it cause the verb to take penult tone.
    Even on Gordon's understanding of <u>nasog 'aḫor</u> he is inconsistent in observing its use. In Category I (1938:321) he includes 1 Kgs. 8: 46 but this verb is followed by an accented (disj.) monosyllabic word, <u>i.e.</u>, בָּם; in Category IV 1 Sam. 20:18 is likewise followed by an accented monosyllabic word; also in Category VI he includes Ezek. 32:6 and in Category VII Ezek. 30:12, yet both have an accented monosyllabic word following them. He includes וַיֹּבֵאֲ אֹת in Category IX as a form that does not fulfill the syllabic conditions and hence takes penult tone, yet it is found with ultima tone in Gen. 6:18; Ex. 3:18; Dt. 17:9, 26:3; 1 Sam. 20:19; Jer. 36:6; and Zch. 6:10.

Sheehan based his research work on Gordon's syllabic condition rule, and, unfortunately, on his understanding of nasog 'aḥor which really is surprising. The result was that Sheehan gives a list (App. F List I, pp. 147–152) of 211 verbs that supported Gordon's rule. He failed to notice that in 16 cases an accented monosyllabic word follows the verb. He then gives a list (List VI, p. 156) of 9 verbs said to be affected by nasog 'aḥor. We give just a couple of examples from these two lists:

LIST I : Ultima Tone (Unaffected by nasog 'aḥor)		LIST VI : Penult Tone (Affected by nasog 'aḥor)	
Dt. 23:14	וְהָפַרְתָּ בָּהּ	Lev. 25:35	וְהֶחֱזַקְתָּ בּוֹ
Ex. 34:2	וְנִצַּבְתָּ לִי שָׁם	Dt. 28:36	וְעָבַדְתָּ שָּׁם

A more independent researcher would find these examples puzzling since the same disjunctive sign is on the monosyllabic word following the verb. If nasog 'aḥor were a purely phonetic phenomenon the 16 cases in List I should have received closer attention.

Two other scholars who followed Gordon's faulty understanding of nasog 'aḥor were Blake, who gives 2 Kgs. 5:18 as an example (1944:287), and Blau (1971:16).

197-1   Blau suggests that the different behaviour of verbal forms with qamaṣ in the antepenult might well be due to rhythmical reasons: 'long vowels (both original ones and long by position only) were, it seems, less long than two phonetic units (i.e., e.g. two vowels)' (1971:17).

197-2   There are three apparent exceptions:

Ps. 23:6   וְשַׁבְתִּי בְּבֵית־

Isa. 54:12   וְשַׂמְתִּי כַּדְכֹד

Jer. 20:9   וְנִלְאֵיתִי כַּלְכֵל

There is one apparent exception to Rule 2 but a polysyllabic word follows.

1 Sam. 23:2   וְהִכִּיתָ בַּפְּלִשְׁתִּים

Undoubtedly this has been influenced by analogy since the same clause occurs twice in the sentence. One might explain the 1st pers. by noting that the first two begin with begad kepat letters and O. O. Fletcher has observed that two aspirated consonants cannot come together (Hebraica I (1884-5) p. 146 §4). But we have found exceptions to this observation, e.g., וְצָפוּ בְכָתֵף (with four aspirated consonants in a row) (Isa. 11:14) and יָבָאוּ כָר־ (Jud. 6:5) that the whole phenomenon needs further investigation.

199-1   Cf. Wickes, 1970:108.

200-1   Schroeder seems to have been the first to point out that the 3rd pers. fem. sing. וְהֵבִיאָה took ultima tone (Lev. 15:29)(1810:272). A. S.

Artom has examined the 1st and 2nd pers. sing. of the root בוא but
concluded: 'I must say that I am not in a position to formulate any
hypothesis which would explain why this root should behave differently
from the others' (1965:12). Blake simply states that there are exceptions with בוא but offers no solution (1944:290 n. 35(5)). See the
middle section of f'note 196-2 for Gordon's treatment of the root.

201-1   We have noted only three cases where a conjunctive tone appears on
the verb <u>and</u> the following word, see f'note 196-1 Groups I & III.

202-1   Though it <u>may</u> do so provided the verb takes a disjunctive tone, <u>e.g.</u>,
וְדִבַּרְתָּ בָּם Dt. 6:7. <u>Cf.</u> 1 Kgs. 2:36; 17:9; Ezk. 12:5.

202-2   <u>Cf.</u> also the following pairs: Hag. 1:9 (Past) and Dt. 17:4 (Non-Past);
1 Sam. 3:13 (Past) and Ex. 25:12 (Non-Past); and Lev. 26:41 (Past) and
Zch. 8:18 (Non-Past).

203-1   G.-K. states (§49k) that 'the tone is generally moved forward if the
second syllable has ê in ל"א and ל"ה verbs'. E. S. Artom endorses
this (1965:10). The statement is in fact incorrect. All ל"א Piel
verbs (13x = 13 examples), Niphal (3x) and Hiphil (49x) verbs take ê
in the 1st and 2nd pers. <u>irrespective of the tone</u> position. In the
case of ל"ה verbs the 2nd pers. takes î <u>irrespective of the tone pos-</u>
<u>ition</u> in the Piel (13x) and the Hiphil (16x. There are two exceptions,

וְהִצַּלְתָּ [Ex. 40:4 but <u>cf.</u> Dt. 27:6; Jud. 6:26; and Jer. 38:10] which
may have ê to distinguish it from וְהִדְרִיתָ, and וְהֵבֵאתָ
[נזדה] which may have taken ê to distinguish it from * וְהִדְרִיתָ the
Piel form of another root, הזה 'to dream, rave' [The Piel form is
not extant in the OT.].). In the case of ל"ה verbs the 1st pers.
takes ê <u>irrespective of the tone position</u> in Hiphil(31x); but in the
Piel when the tone is penult the vowel is î (4x) and when the tone is
ultima it is ê (10x; an exception is וְדִרִיתָי [Ezk. 5:10; 6:5; 12:15;

30:26])but this is due to the fact that ר cannot be doubled and hence
the initial <u>i</u> vowel was lengthened to ê in compensation which meant
that if the second vowel was also ê two ê vowels would have come together. The succession of two similar vowels occasioned the dissimil-
ation of one of them, hence the apparent exception (<u>cf.</u> Moscati, 1964:
§9.12). In the Niphal theme we have examples only of penult tone, 1st
pers. (5x), 2nd pers. (1x). They all have the ê vowel. G.-K.'s statement, then, only applies to ל"ה and then only to the Piel theme. It
would seem that the Piel takes the ê vowel <u>because</u> the tone moves forward and not vice versa as G.-K. has stated the rule.

204-1   BH3, BHS, and Snaith's ed., have ultima; the Brit. & Foreign Bib. Soc.
(=BFBS, 1950) and Mandelkern's Heb. Concordance have penult.

204-2   Snaith and BFBS have ultima.

205-1   G.-K. regards all the cases with penult tone as textual corruptions
(§67ee).

207-1   Böttcher rather arbitrarily gives all the forms penult tone on the
assumption that the Massoretes were not always aware of the rules governing the place of the tone, as well as the possibility of scribal
mistakes (1866:§1132 n. 1,3). F. Blake follows Böttcher (1944:289

n. 35(4).

209-1 H. Hurwitz (1831:139) stated that ‎נ"ו‎ and ‎ל"ה‎ could be distinguished by tone position, the former have penult and the latter ultima tone, thus ‎שָׁ֣בוּ‎ from √‎שׁוב‎ signifies, 'they returned', but ‎שָׁבְ֣וּ‎ from √‎שׁבה‎ signifies, 'they captured, took prisoners'.

209-2 BH3 reads ‎וְהָיִ֣ו‎ at Ezek. 44:11, probably a typographical error since BHS reads ‎וְהָיֽוּ‎ .

210-1 As early as 1567 Pierre Martinez noted that ‎וְהִבְדִּ֣ילָה‎ (Ex. 26:33) took ultima tone (see 200-1) and pointed out that ‎וְנָ֣חָה‎ 'and it shall rest' has ultima tone. No thorough investigation into the tone shift of 3rd pers. fem. sing. has been carried out on ‎נ"ו‎ verbs. Bergsträsser has noted two cases where the tone shifts unexpectedly: ‎שָׁ֣תָה‎ (Ps. 90:8) and ‎שַׁ֣תָה‎ (Ps. 73:28), (Heb. Gram., II, p. 146. Cf. Blake, 1944: 287 n. 33).

210-2 Margolis noted: 'The minimal phonetic unit is the stress-group ("Sprechtakt"); its measure is equivalent to the distance between two consecutive strong-stressed syllables. The length of a stress-group is relative to the whole of a connected utterance and varies according to the distribution of forces which itself is <u>conditioned by the tempo of the speaker or the nature of the literary piece</u> as it is recited with more or less solemnity. What in a slow even tempo appears as broken up into a number of groups becomes in a recitation which aims at sense rather than at clear enunciation a compact unit with graded stresses ("Taktgruppe")....In the received system of Hebrew accentuation, there are shorter and longer groups properly graded with reference to one another and to the longest group of which they are component parts....It is well known that the retarded tempo was favoured by Ben Naphtali and the quicker by Ben Asher.' (1911:31-2, emphasis ours.)

ABBREVIATIONS

Abbreviations of Journals

AAL/AfL	Afroasiastic Linguistics
AcOr	Acta Orientalia
AJSL	American Journal of Semitic Languages and Literatures
ALLC	Association for Library and Linguistic Computing
AnOr	Analecta Orientalia
Anthropos	Anthropos. Internationale Zeitschrift für Völker- und Sprachenkunde
AO	See AnOr
ArOr	Archiv Orientální
AS	Assyriological Studies
BA/BASS	Beiträge zur Assyriologie und semitischen Sprachwissenschaft
BASOR	Bulletin of the American Schools of Oriental Research
Bibl	Biblica
Bibl Repos	Biblical Repository (America)
Bib Sac	Bibliotheca Sacra & Theological Review
BiOr	Bibliotheca Orientalis
BJRL	Bulletin of the John Rylands Library, Manchester
BSL/BSLP	Bulletin de la Société de Linguistique de Paris
BSOAS	Bulletin of the School of Oriental & African Studies
BSS	Beiträge zur semitischen Sprachwissenschaft
BT	The Bible Translator
BZ	Biblische Zeitschrift
BZAW	Beihefte zur Zeitschrift für die Alttestamentliche Wissenschaft
CBQ	The Catholic Biblical Quarterly
CdE	Chronique d'Egypte
ExpT	Expository Times
FuF	Forschungen und Fortschritte, Berlin
HCL	Hebrew Computational Linguistics
HistZ	Historische Zeitschrift
HUCA	Hebrew Union College Annual
IOS	Israel Oriental Studies

JA	Journal Asiatique
JANES	Journal of the Ancient Near Eastern Society of Columbia University
JAOS	Journal of the American Oriental Society
JBL	Journal of Biblical Literature
JCS	Journal of Cuneiform
JEOL	Jaarbericht van het Vooraziatisch-Egyptisch Genootschap "Ex Oriente Lux"
JNES	Journal of Near Eastern Studies
JNSL/JNWSL	Journal of Northwest Semitic Languages
JPOS	Journal of the Palestine Oriental Society
JQR	Jewish Quarterly Review
JRAS	Journal of the Royal Asiatic Society
JSL	Journal of Sacred Literature
JSS	Journal of Semitic Studies
JTS/JThS	Journal of Theological Studies
Kush	Journal of the Sudan Antiquities Service. Khartoum
Leš	Lešonénu
MO	Le Monde orientale
Mus	Le Muséon
MUSJ	Mélanges de l'Université Saint Joseph Beyrouth
OLz	Orientalistische Literaturzeitung
Or(OR)	Orientalia
OrGand	Orientalia Gandensia
OrSuec	Orientalia Suecana
OTS	Oud-Testamentische Studiën
PAAJR	Proceedings of the American Academy for Jewish Research
PTR	Princeton Theological Review
RB	Revue Biblique
RÉJ	Revue des Études Juives
RÉS	Revue des Études Sémitiques
RQum	Revue de Qumran
RSO	Rivista degli Studi Orientali
StOr	Studia Orientalia
ThL	Theologische Literaturzeitung
TGUOS	Transactions of the Glasgow University Oriental Society
UF	Ugarit Forschungen

VT/VTS	Vetus Testamentum / Supplement
WO	Die Welt des Orients
WZKM	Wiener Zeitschrift für die Kunde des Morgenlandes
ZA	Zeitschrift für Assyriologie
ZAW	Zeitschrift für die Alttestamentliche Wissenschaft
ZDMG	Zeitschrift der Deutschen Morgenländischen Gesellschaft
ZFP/ZP	Zeitschrift für Phonetik

Other Abbreviations

BDB	F. Brown, S. R. Driver and C. A. Briggs: A Hebrew and English Lexicon of the Old Testament, Oxford, 1907.
BH	Biblical Hebrew
BH3	Biblia Hebraica, ed., R. Kittel (3rd ed.) Stuttgart, 1949.
BHS	Biblia Hebraica Stuttgartensia, eds. K. Elliger & W. Rudolph, Stuttgart, 1967/77.
G.-K.	Gesenius' Hebrew Grammar as Edited and Enlarged by E. Kautzsch, translated by A. E. Cowley, Oxford, 1910.
MT	Massoretic Text
PHVS	Problems of the Hebrew Verbal System, Edinburgh, 1936, by G. R. Driver.

Special Abbreviations

P	Prefix-form, i.e. yiqtol or yqtl
VP	Prefix-form with weak waw (ו) prefixed
WP	Prefix-form with strong waw (וַ / וַ) prefixed
S	Suffix-form, i.e. qatal or qtl
VS	Suffix-form with weak waw (ו) prefixed
CS	Common Semitic
ES	East Semitic
HVS	Hebrew Verbal System
PS	Proto-Semitic
VS	Verbal system
WS	West Semitic

BIBLIOGRAPHY

Andrew, James (1817). <u>Institutes of Grammar, as applicable to the English Language or as an introductory to the Study of other Languages.</u> London.

----- (1823). <u>Hebrew Dictionary and Grammar without Points.</u> London

Arnold, T. K. (1851). <u>The First Hebrew Book.</u> London

Aro, Jussi (1965). 'Parallels to the Akkadian Stative in the West Semitic Language', <u>Studies in honor of Benno Landsberger on his 75th Birthday,</u> eds. H-G. Güterbock, Th. Jacobsen, pp. 407-11. Chicago. (<u>Cf. Assyr. Studies</u> 16 (1965) 407-11)

Artom, E. S. (see also under Hartum, E. S. below) (1950). 'On the Problem of the Accent in the Hebrew Past Converted to the Future', <u>Leš.</u> 17, 88-9 (Hebr.).

----- (1957-8). 'The Accent of the Consecutive Perfect of Verbs tertiae ' and <u>h</u>', <u>Leš.</u> 22, 205-8 (Hebr.).

----- (1965). 'Sull'accento nelle forme verbali ebraiche di perfecto con vav conversive', <u>Annuario di Studi Ebraici</u> (Roma) 1. 1963-64 (1965) 7-14.

Austel, H. J. (1970). <u>Prepositional and Non-Prepositional Complements with Verbs of Motion in Biblical Hebrew.</u> Unpub. Ph.D. Diss., Univ. of Calif., Los Angelos.

Bacher, W. A. (1904). 'Grammar, Hebrew', <u>The Jewish Encyclopedia,</u> N.Y. & London.

Baelper, F. A. (1923). <u>A Survey of Studies upon Hebrew Verb in the Last Twenty-Five Years,</u> Unpub. A.M. Diss., Univ. of Chicago, Chicago.

Baker, David Weston, (1973). <u>The Consecutive Non-Perfective as Pluperfect in the Historical Books of the Hebrew Old Testament (Genesis-Kings).</u> Unpub. Master of Christian Studies Thesis, Regent College, Vancouver, British Columbia.

Ball, C. J. (1877). <u>The Merchant Taylors' Hebrew Grammar.</u> London.

Ballantine, W. G. (1885-6). 'Suggestions towards a more exact nomenclature and definition of the Hebrew Tenses', <u>Hebraica</u> 2, 53-5.

Ballin, A. S. (1881). <u>A Hebrew Grammar, with exercises selected from the Bible.</u> London.

Barker, W. H. (1773). <u>A Plain Grammar of the Hebrew Language.</u> Carmarthen, Scotland.

Barnes, O. L. (1965). <u>A New Approach to the Problem of the Hebrew Tenses and its Solution without Recourse to Waw-Consecutive.</u> Oxford.

Barth, Jacob, (1887). 'Das semitische Perfect im Assyrischen'. <u>ZA</u> 2, 375-86.

Bate, J. (1751). <u>An Hebrew Grammar formed on the usage of the words of the inspired writers being an attempt to make the learning of Hebrew easy.</u> London (Dublin, 1756).

Battle, John Henry, (1969). <u>Syntactic Structures in the Masoretic Hebrew Text of the Psalms.</u> Unpub. Ph.D. Diss., The Univ. of Texas at Austin.

Bauer, Hans, (1910). 'Die Tempora im Semitischen', <u>BA</u> 8/1, 1-53.

—— (1914). 'Semitische Sprachprobleme. Das chronologische Verhältnis von Aorist (Imperfekt) und sogenannten Perfekt in der semitischen Verbalbildung', ZDMG 68, 365–72.

—— & Leander, P. (1922). Historische Grammatik der hebräischen Sprache, Halle (repd. Hildesheim, 1965).

Bayly, Anselm (1773). A Plain and Complete Grammar of the Hebrew Language, London (Facsimile: English Linguistics 186, Menston,1969 of 1772 ed.).

Bayly, Cornelius (1782). An entrance into the sacred language containing the necessary rules of Hebrew Grammar in English...., London.

Beeston, W. (1843). Hieronymian Hebrew; or, a grammar of the sacred language on the system disclosed by the writings of Saint Jerome, London.

Bellamy, John (1818–41). Bible (English), with Commentary. Genesis — Song of Solomon. The Holy Bible newly translated.... London.

Ben David, A. (1972). Parallels in the Bible, Jerusalem. (Heb. Texts)

Ben Yehuda, E. (1952–3). Thesaurus Totius Hebraitatis et Veteris et Recentioris, Jerusalem.

Bennett, W. H. (1885–6). 'Notes on the Use of the Hebrew Tenses', Hebraica 2, 193–208; 3, 22–9.

—— (Jan 1887). 'Notes on a Comparison of the Texts of Psalm XVIII, and 2 Samuel XXII', Hebraica 3, 65–86.

—— (1888/9). 'The Use of the Tenses in Hebrew Narrative', Hebraica 5, 202–4.

Bergsträsser, G. (1918–29). Hebräische Grammatik, repd., Hildesheim, 1962.

—— (1923). 'Mitteilungen zur hebräischen Grammatik. 1. Ist das Hebräische eine Mischsprache?', OLz XXVI, 253–60, 477–81.

Berry, G. R. (1903). 'Waw Consecutive with the Perfect', JBL 22, 60–70.

Bertin, G. (1882). 'Suggestions on the Formation of the Semitic Tenses', JRAS 14, 105–18.

—— (1883). 'Suggestions on the Voice-Formation of the Semitic Verb', JRAS 15, 387–418.

Bevan, A. A. (1927). 'Some Remarks on the Historical Grammar of the Hebrew Language by Bauer and Leander (Halle), 1922', in Old Testament Essays, London, pp. 94–8.

Bickell, G. (See S. I. Curtiss, 1877).

Birkeland, H. (1935). 'Ist das hebräische Imperfectum consecutivum ein Präteritum?', Acta Orient XIII, 1–34.

—— (1950). Laerebok i hebraisk grammatik, Oslo. (Tenses, see pp. 34–5; 107–12).

Blake, F. R. (1903). 'The So-called Intransitive Verbal Forms in Hebrew', JAOS 24, 145–204 (John Hopkins Univ. Ph.D. Thesis).

—— (1942). 'Studies in Semitic Grammar II', JAOS 62, 109–18.

—— (1944). 'The Hebrew Waw Conversive', JBL 63, 271–95.

—— (1946). 'The Form of Verbs after Waw in Hebrew', JBL 65, 51–7.

—— (1951). A Resurvey of Hebrew Tenses, Rome.

Blau, J. (1968). 'Some Difficulties in the Reconstruction of "Proto-Hebrew" and "Proto-Canaan", BZAW 103, 29-43.

————— (1969). 'Some Problems of the Formation of the Old Semitic Languages in the Light of Arabic Dialects', Proceedings of the International Conference on Semitic Studies in Jerusalem, 1965, pp. 38-44.

————— (1971a). 'Studies in Hebrew Verb Formation', HUCA 42, 133-58.

————— (1971b). 'Marginalia Semitica I', IOS 1, 1-35 (espec. Notes 5 & 6).

————— (1976). Grammar of Biblical Hebrew, Weisbaden, W. Germany.

Bobzin, H. (1973). 'Überlegungen zum althebräischen "Tempus"system', WO 7, 141-53.

————— (1974). Die 'Tempora' im Hiobdialog, Marburg/Lahn.

Bornemann, R. E. (1970). Verbal parallelism in Ugaritic and Biblical Poetry, unpub. Ph.D. Diss., The Dropsie University.

Böttcher, F. (1866). Hebräischen Sprache, Leipzig.

Bowman, T. (Part I, 1879; Part II, 1882). A New Easy and Complete Hebrew course: containing a Hebrew Grammar with Exercises in two parts. Edinburgh (Part II reprinted by T & T Clark, 1974).

Boyle, M. L. Jr. (1969). Infix-T forms in Biblical Hebrew, unpub. Ph.D. Diss., Boston University.

Bravmann, M. M. (1951). 'Notes on the Forms of the Imperative in Hebrew and Arabic', JQR n. s. 42, 51-6.

————— (1971). 'The Hebrew Perfect forms: qatᵉlā, qatᵉlū', JAOS 91, 429-30.

Brockelmann, K. (1907-13). Grundriss der vergleichenden Grammatik der semitischen Sprachen, 2 vols., Berlin.

————— (1951). 'Die "Tempora" des Semitischen', ZP 5, 133-54.

Brünnow, R. E. (1893). (Review of:) 'Beiträge zur Assyriologie und vergleichenden semitischen Sprachwissenschaft, herausgegeben von F. Delitzsch und P. Haupt', ZA 8, 121-37.

Buttenweiser, M. (1925). 'The Importance of the Tenses for the Interpretation of the Psalms', Hebrew Union College : Jubilee Volume 1875-1925, Cincinnati, pp. 89-111.

Burney, C. F. (1919). 'A fresh Examination of the current Theory of the Hebrew Tenses', JTS 20, 200-14.

Bush, F. W. (1959-60). 'Evidence from Milḥamah and the Masoretic Text for a Penultimate Accent in Hebrew Verbal Forms', RQum 2, 501-14.

Buxtorf, J. (The Elder) (1651). Thesaurus Grammaticus Linguae Sanctae Hebraicae, Basel.

Bythner [us], V. (1675). לְשׁוֹן לִמּוּדִ֫ים : Lingua eruditorum sive methodica Institutio linguae sanctae; London (Tenses, pp. 61ff.).

Cate, R. L. (1960). An Investigation into the origin of the Hebrew Triliteral Root System: The Theory of Biliteral Roots, unpub. Ph.D Diss., The Southern Baptist Theological Seminary.

Cazelles, H. (1947). 'Note sur l'origine des temps convertis hébreux (d'après quelques textes Ugaritiques)', RB 54, 388-93.

Ceresko, A. R. (1975). 'The A:B::B:A Word Pattern in Hebrew and Northwest Semitic with Special Reference to the Book of Job', UF 7, 73–88.

—— (1976). 'The Chiastic Word Pattern in Hebrew', CBQ 38/3, 303–11.

Cheyne, T. W. (1893). Founders of Old Testament Criticism, London.

Childs, B. S. (1963). 'A Study of the Formula "Until this day"', JBL 82, 279–92.

Chomsky, W. (1952). David Kimchi's Hebrew Grammar (Mikhlol) systematically presented and critically annotated, New York.

Christian, V. (1919–20). 'Akkader und Südaraber als ältere Semitenschichte', Anthropos XIV-XV, 729–39.

—— (1927). 'Das Wesen der semitischen Tempora', ZDMG n.f. 6, 232–58.

Claasen, W. T. (1971). The Hiphil verbal theme in Biblical Hebrew, unpub. Ph.D. Diss., Univ. of Stellenbosch, S. Africa.

—— (1972). 'The Declarative-Estimative Hiph'il', JNWSL II, 5–16.

Cohen, M. S. R. (1924). Le système verbal sémitique et l'expression du temps, Paris.

Comrie, B. (1976). Aspect, Cambridge.

Connellan, T. (1827). Diatessaron...Easy lessons...from the Evangelists, and from the life of Joseph, in...Genesis...to which is added an Hebrew and an Irish grammar.... London.

Corwin, R. (1909). The Verb and the Sentence in Chronicles, Ezra and Nehemiah, Borna (nr. Leipzig).

Cowley, A. E. (1910). Gesenius's Hebrew Grammar, As edited and enlarged by the late E. Kautzsch and revised by A. E. Cowley, Oxford (repd. London, 1966).

Craik, H. (1863). Principia Hebraica; or An Easy introduction to the Hebrew language, exhibiting in twenty-four tables the interpretation of all the Hebrew and Chaldee words...contained in the O.T. Scriptures, London.

Crim, K. R. (1973). 'Hebrew Direct Discourse as a Translation Problem', BT 24/3, 311–16.

Crozier, R. J. (1954). The Semantics of the Hithpael, unpub. S. T. M. thesis, Faith Theo. Seminary, USA.

Curtis, J. J. (1949). An Application of the Syntax of Hebrew Verbs to the Writings of Amos, unpub. Ph.D. Diss., Southern Bapt. Theo. Sem., USA.

Curtiss, S. I. (1877). Outlines of Hebrew Grammar (An annotated translation of G. Bickell's revised Grundriss der hebräischen Grammatik), Leipzig.

Dahood, M. J. & Penar, T. (1970). 'The Grammar of the Psalter', Appendix to The Psalms (Anchor Bible Series), Garden City, N. Y., vol. III, pp. 361–456.

Davidson, A. B. (1894). Hebrew Syntax, Edinburgh.

Davies, B. (1880). Gesenius' Hebrew Grammar, Andover, USA.

Davies, T. W. (1903). Heinrich Ewald: Orientalist and Theologian, 1803–1903, London.

Davis, J. (1656). A Short Introduction to the Hebrew Tongue, London.

Deimal, A. (1934). 'Die sogenannten Tempora im Akkadischen', <u>Orientalia</u>
     III, 196–200.

De Vries, S. J. (1964–6). 'The Syntax of Tenses and Interpretation in the
     Hodayoth', <u>RQum</u> V/3, 375–414.

───── (1965). 'Consecutive Constructions in the 1Q Sectarian Scrolls',
     <u>Doron: Hebraic Studies in Honor of A. I. Katsh,</u> New York, pp. 75–87.

Dietrich, F. E. C. (1846). <u>Abhandlungen zur Hebräischen Grammatik,</u> Leipzig.

Dillmann, A. ((1857). <u>Grammatik der Aethiopischen Sprache,</u> Leipzig (transl.
     by J. A. Crichton, London, 1907).

Dinur, B. Z. (1957–8). 'The Specifying <u>waw</u> in the Bible and its meaning',
     <u>Leš</u> 22, 199–204 (Hebr.).

Donaldson, J. W. (1848). <u>Maskil le-Sopher,</u> London.

Dotan, A. (1976). 'Stress position and vowel shift in Phoenician and Punic;
     Phoenician/Punic – Hebrew linguistic relationship re-examined', <u>IOS</u> 6,
     71–121.

Douglass B. (1885). <u>A Letter to Professors, Scholars and Friends of the
     Holy Tongue criticising "Driver's Hebrew Tenses",</u> Chicago.

Dowling, E. (1797). <u>The Elements and Theory of the Hebrew Language,</u> London.

Driver, G. R. (1936). <u>Problems of the Hebrew Verbal System,</u> Edinburgh.

Driver, S. R. (1874). <u>A Treatise on the Use of the Tenses in Hebrew,</u> Oxford
     (2nd ed. 1881; 3rd ed. 1892).

Duff, A. (1901). <u>A Hebrew Grammar,</u> London.

Duncan, W. W. (1848). <u>A New Hebrew Grammar,</u> London.

Eddleman, H. L. (1943). <u>Waw Consecutive and the Consecution of Tenses as
     reflected by Eight-Century Hebrew,</u> unpub. Ph.D. Diss., Southern Bapt.
     Theo. Seminary, USA.

Eitan, I. (1920). 'Contribution à l'histoire du verbe Hébreu', <u>JPOS</u> 1, 42–7
     (= 'Light on the History of the Hebrew Verb', <u>JQR</u> n.s. 12/1 (1922),
     25–32).

───── (1930). 'Hebrew and Semitic Particles: Comparative Studies in Semitic
     Philology', <u>AJSL</u> 46, 22–51.

<u>Encyclopedia Judaica</u> (1971–2). 'Hebrew Language', vol. 16, pp. 1560–1662;
     'Linguistic Literature', vol. 16, pp. 1351–1402, (Jerusalem).

Engnell, K. I. A. (1960). <u>Grammatik i gammaltestamentlig Hebreiska,</u> Stockholm.

Erman, A. (1900). 'Die Flexion des ägyptischen Verbums', <u>Sitzungsberichte
     der Akademie der Wissenschaften zu Berlin,</u> XIX, 317–353.

Ertelt, B. (1949). <u>Linguistische Untersuchungen zum Verbalsystem des Biblisch-
     Hebräischen,</u> Phil. Diss., Wien.

Ewald, G. H. A. von (1827). <u>Kritische Grammatik der hebräischen Sprache,</u>
     Leipzig (2nd ed. 1835, translated by John Nicholson, London, 1836;
     3rd ed. 1838; 4th ed. 1844.).

───── (1847). (Reply to S. Lee) <u>Churchman's Review</u> 1847, 379–90.

───── (1870). <u>Ausführliches lehrbuch der hebräischen sprache des Alten
     Bundes,</u> Leipzig. (The Syntax of this edition (8th) was translated by

J. Kennedy, Edinburgh, 1879.) 6th ed. 1862-3.

Faus, W. A. (1936). Literary Types in the Writings of the Hebrew Prophets, unpub. Ph.D. Diss., Boston University, USA.

Fenton, T. L. (1963). The Ugaritic Verbal System, unpub. D.Phil. Thesis, Oxford.

―――― (1973). 'The Hebrew "Tenses" in the light of Ugaritic', Proceedings of the Fifth World Congress of Jewish Studies, vol. IV, ed. A. Shinan, Jerusalem, pp. 31-9 (Read to Congress in 1969).

Ferguson, H. (1881-2). 'An Examination of the Use of the Tenses in Conditional Sentences', JBL 1, (1881) 40-94; (1882) 56-58.

Février, J. (1971). 'Le waw conversif en punique', in Hommages à André Dupont-Somer, Paris, pp. 191-4.

Fitzgerald, G. (1813). An Hebrew Grammar for the Use of Students of the University of Dublin, Dublin.

Frankena, R. (1974). 'Some remarks on a new approach to Hebrew', Travels in the World of the Old Testament. Studies presented to Professor M. A. Beek, eds. M. S. H. G. Heerma van Voss, Ph. H. J. Houwink ten Cate, N. A. van Uchelen, Assen, pp. 41-9 (On the common element in Akkad. and Hebrew).

Freytag, G. W. F. (1861). Einleitung in das studium der arabischen sprache, Bonn.

Gelb, I. J. (1952). Morphology of Akkadian. A Comparative and Historical Sketch, Chicago.

Geldart, G. C. (1874). 'On Dr. Hincks's "Permansive Tense" in the Assyrian Verb', Transactions of the International Congress of Orientalists, 1874, ed. R. K. Douglass, London, pp. 25-34.

Gell, P. (1818). Observations on the Idiom of the Hebrew Language, London.

Gesenius, W. F. H. (see A. E. Cowley above)

Ginsberg, H. L. (1930). Studies on the Hebrew Verb, unpub. Ph.D. Diss., London University. (See AJSL 46 (1930), 53-8; 127-38.)

―――― (1970). 'The Northwest Semitic Languages', The World History of the Jewish People, vol. II, ed. B. Mazar, London, pp. 102-24.

―――― (1957). 'The Classification of the N. W. Semitic Languages', Akten des 24 Internat. Orientalisten-Kongresses, München, 1957, Wiesbaden, pp. 256-67.

Givón, T. (1974). 'Verb complements and relative clauses; a diachronic case study in biblical Hebrew', AfL 1/4, 1-22.

Goddard, B. L. (1950). The Origin of the Hebrew Infinitive Absolute in the light of infinitive uses in related languages and its use in the OT, unpub. Ph.D. Diss., Harvard University, USA.

Goetze, A. (1938). 'The Tenses in Ugaritic', JAOS 58, 266-309.

Gordis, R. (1937). The Biblical Text in the Making: A Study of Kethibh-Qere, New York.

Gordon, C. H. (1938). 'The Accentual Shift in the Perfect with Waw Consecutive', JBL 57, 319-26.

―――― (1965). Ugaritic Textbook, Rome.

Green, W. H. (1861). A Grammar of the Hebrew Language, New York (2nd ed. 1866, 3rd ed. 1880).

───── (1890). 'On the Hebrew Tenses', JAOS 14, pp. xxxiv-v.

Greenberg, J. H. (1952). 'The Afro-Asiatic (Hamito-Semitic) Present', JAOS 72, 1-9.

Grimme, H. (1896). Grundzüge der hebräischen Akzent- und Vokallehre, Freiburg (Schweiz).

Gross, W. (1976). Verbalform + Function. Wayyiqtol für die Gegenwart, St. Ottilien, W. Germany.

Gutman, D. (1971). The Morphophonemics of Biblical Hebrew (and a brief comparison with Israeli Hebrew), unpub. Ph.D. Diss., Univ. of Texas at Austin.

Hall, W. R. (1965). A Study of Tense and Aspect in Biblical Hebrew Based on the Translation of Hebrew into Greek, Comparing Genesis in the Kittel-Kahle Biblia Hebraica with Genesis in the Cambridge Septuagint, unpub. Th.D. Diss., Dallas Theological Seminary, USA.

Harper, W. R. (1883). A Hebrew Manual, New York.

Harris, R. L. (1950). Introductory Hebrew Grammar, Grand Rapids, Michigan.

───── (1952). 'Tenses of the Hebrew Verb', The Journal 1, 8-13 (Faith Theo. Sem. Alumni Assoc., USA).

Harris, Z. S. (1939). Development of the Canaanite Dialects, American Oriental Series, vol. 16, New Haven (repd. New York, 1967).

Hartum, A. S. (1952). 'On the Problem of Accent in the Hebrew Past Converted to the Future', World Congress of Jewish Studies, 1952, pp. 81-3 (see also E. S. Artom above).

Haupt, P. (1878). 'Studies on the Comparative Grammar of the Semitic Languages with special Reference to Assyrian: The Oldest Semitic Verb-form', JRAS 10, ccxliv-ccli.

───── (1889). 'Prolegomena to a Comparative Assyrian Grammar', JAOS 13, ccxlix-cclxvii.

Hehn, J. (1920). 'Waw Inversivum', BZAW 34, 83-92.

Herder, J. G. von (1783). Vom Geist der Ebräischen Poesie, transl. from the 3rd ed. of 1822 by J. Marsh, Burlington, 1833 (repd. Naperville, Illinois, 1971).

Herling, C. H. U. (1837). 'Von der Dichotomie in der Tempusformen', in Welcker's: Rheinisches Museum für Philologie, 1837, pp. 522-72.

Hetzron, R. (1969). 'The Evidence for Perfect *yáqtul and Jussive *yaqtúl in Proto-Semitic', JSS 14, 1-21.

Hezel, W. F. (1777). Ausführliche hebräische Sprachlehre, Halle.

Hincks, E. (1832). A Grammar of the Hebrew Language, Dublin.

───── (1855-6). 'On the Assyrian Verb', JSL I, 383-93; II, 141-62; III, 152-71, 392-403.

───── (1866). 'Specimen Chapters of an Assyrian Grammar', JRAS n.s. 2, 480-519.

Hitzig, F. (1870). Die Inschrift des Mesha, Königes von Moab, übersetzt und historisch-kritisch erörtert, Heidelberg.

Hoffmann, G. (1887). Review of Nöldeke's article on Semitic Languages in Literarisches Centralblatt für Deutschland, 1887, No. 18, p. 605, (Leipzig).

Hoftijzer, J. (1974). Verbale vragen. Rede uitgesproken bij de aanvaarding van het ambt van gewoon hoogleraar in het Hebreeuws...aan de Rijksuniversiteit te Leiden, Leiden (Problems of the Verb in Biblical Hebrew).

Huesman, J. E. (1955). The Infinitive Absolute in Biblical Hebrew and Related Dialects, unpub. Ph.D. Diss., John Hopkins University, USA.

—— (1956a). 'Finite Uses of the Infinitive Absolute', Biblica 37, 271-95.

—— (1956b). 'The Infinitive Absolute and the Waw + Perfect Problem', Biblica 37, 410-34.

Hughes, J. A. (1955). The Hebrew Imperfect with Waw Conjunctive and the Perfect with Waw Consecutive and their Interrelationship, Faith Theo. Sem., USA.

—— (1962). Some Problems of the Hebrew Verbal System with particular Reference to the Use of the Tenses, unpub. Ph.D. Diss., Univ. of Glasgow.

—— (1970). 'Another Look at the Hebrew Tenses', JNES 29, 12-24.

Hurwitz, H. (1831). Hebrew Grammar, London.

Hutton, A. R. R. (1898). 'Hebrew Tenses', AJSL 14/2, 57-80.

Jahn, J. (1809). Grammatica linguae Hebraeae, Viennae.

James, J. C. (1918). 'One Tense Semitic', ExpT 29, 376-7.

—— (1920). The Language of Palestine and adjacent Regions, Edinburgh.

Janssens, G. (1957-8). 'De werkwoordelijke "tijden" in het Semietisch, en in het bizonder in het Hebreeuws', JEOL 15, 97-103.

—— (1972). 'Contribution to the Verbal System in Old Egyptian. A new Approach to the Reconstruction of the Hamito-Semitic Verbal System', Or Grand VI, 1-55.

—— (1975). 'The Semitic Verbal System', AAL 2/4, 9-14.

Jarrett, T. (1848). A Hebrew Grammar, London.

Jastrow, M. (1885-9). 'Jewish Grammarians of the Middle Ages', Hebraica 3, (1885/6) 103-06, 171-74; 4, (1887/8) 26-33, 118-122; 5, (1888/9) 115-20.

Johnson, S. (1767). An English and Hebrew Grammar, London.

Joos, M. (1968). The English Verb, Madison, Malwankee and London.

Jotion, P. (1922). 'Examples de waw omis dans le texte Massoretique', Biblica 3, 206-09.

—— (1923). Grammaire de l'Hébreu biblique, Rome (repd. Rome, 1962).

Kalisch, M. M. (1862-3). Hebrew Grammar, London.

Keel, W. A. (1931). Hebrew Syntax in Isaiah and the Problem of Authorship, unpub. Ph.D. Diss., Southern Bapt. Theo. Seminary, USA.

Kelly, F. T. (1920). 'The Imperfect with Simple Waw in Hebrew', JBL 39, 1-23.

Kennedy, J. (1889). Introduction to Biblical Hebrew, London.

Kennett, R. H. (1901). A Short Account of the Hebrew Tenses, Cambridge.

Keyworth, T. (1825). The Analytical Part of Principia Hebraica, London.

Kimchi, D. (1545). ספר מכלול...עם קצת נימוקים שהוסיף ר' אליה אשכנזי. Venice. (J. Rittenberg's edition (Lyck, 1862) of this grammar was translated by W. Chomsky, q.v. above.)

Knudtzon, J. A. (1889). Om det saakaldte PERFECTUM OG IMPERFECTUM i Hebraisk, Denmark.

───── (1891). 'Vom sogenannten Perfekt und Imperfekt im Hebräischen', Actes du 8ᵉ Congrès International des Orientalists tenu en 1889 à Stockholm et à Christiania, Section Sémitique B (1891), Leiden, pp. 73-83.

Koch, A. (1874). Der semitische Infinitiv: Eine sprachwissenschaftliche Untersuchung, Stuttgart.

König, F. E. (1881). Historisch-Kritisches Lehregebäude der hebräischen Sprache, vol. I, Leipzig.

───── (1897). Historisch-comparative Syntax der hebräischen Sprache, vol. II, Leipzig.

───── (1911). 'Neuere Stammbildungstheorien im semitischen Sprachbebiete', ZDMG LXV, 709-28.

Kuryłowicz, J. (1949). 'Le système verbal du sémitique', BSL 45, 47-56.

───── (1959). 'The Accentuation of the Verb in Indo-European and in Hebrew', Word 15, 123-29.

───── (1973). 'Verbal Aspect in Semitic', Orientalia 42, 114-120.

Kustár, P. (1972). Aspekt im Hebräischen, Basel.

Kutscher, E. Y. (1965). 'Contemporary Studies in N. W. Semitics', JSS 10, 21-51.

Lagarde, P. de (1889). Uebersicht über die im aramäischen, arabischen und hebräischen übliche Bildung der Nomina, Göttingen.

Lambert, M. (1890). 'L'accent tonique en Hébreu', RÉJ 20, 73-7.

───── (1892). 'Le déplacement du ton en Hébreu', RÉJ 25, 111-12.

───── (1893). 'Le vau conversif', RÉJ 26, 47-62.

───── (1931-8). Traité de Grammaire Hébraïque, 3 vols., Paris.

Land, J. P. N. (1876). The Principles of Hebrew Grammar, transl. from the Dutch by R. L. Poole, London.

Leander, P. (1928). 'Das Wesen der semitischen Tempora', ZDMG n.f. 7, 142-3.

Lee, A. M. (1896). A Scholar of a Past Generation: A Memoir of Professor Lee, London.

Lee, S. (1820). A Letter to Mr Bellamy on his New Translation of the Bible with some Strictures on a Tract entitled "Remarks, &c.", Oxford.

───── (1827). A Grammar of the Hebrew Language, London. (2nd ed. 1832; 3rd ed. 1841)

───── (1840). A Lexicon, Hebrew, Chaldee and English, London.

───── (1847). An Examination of the Grammatical Principles of Prof. von Ewald as put forth in his Hebrew Grammar, London.

───── (1850). Correspondence, JSL 6, 193-207.

───── (1851). Correspondence, JSL 7, 469-86.

Leech, G. N. (1976). Meaning and the English Verb, London.

Leo, C. (1818). 'An Examination of the Fourteen Verses selected from Scripture, by Mr. J. Bellamy, as a specimen of his emendation of the Bible', Classical Journal 17, 221-40.

—— (1836). Hebrew Grammar, Cambridge.

Leslau, W. (1953). 'The Imperfect in South-East Semitic', JAOS 73, 164-6.

—— (1957). 'The Position of Ethiopic in Semitic: Akkadian and Ethiopic', Akten des XXIV Internationalen Orientalischen-Kongresses, 1957, München, pp. 251-3.

Levita, Elias (1525).ספר הכחור, Basileae.

Levy, H. (1970). Hebrew for All, London, (5th ed. 1976).

Livny, I. J. & Kokhba, M. (1964). A Hebrew Grammar for Schools and Colleges, Jerusalem.

Loretz, O. (1961). 'Perfectum Copulativum in 2 Sam. 7:9-11', CBQ 23, 294-6.

Lowe, W. H. (1887). A Hebrew Grammar, London.

Lowth, R. (1753). De sacra poesi Hebraeorum praelectiones academicae, Oxford.

  (Transl. by G. Gregory, Lectures on the Sacred Poetry of the Hebrews, London, 1787; and by Calvin A. Stowe, Andover, 1829.)

Lowy, S. (1977). The Principles of Samaritan Bible Exegesis, Leiden.

Lund, N. W. (1930). 'The Presence of Chiasmus in the OT', AJSL 46, 104-26.

—— (1933). 'Chiasmus in the Psalms', AJSL 49, 281-312.

Lyons, I. (1735). The Scholars Instructor: An Hebrew Grammar, Cambridge.

Maag, V. (1953). 'Morphologie des hebräischen Narratives', ZAW 65, 86-88.

Marcus, I. D. (1969). 'The Stative and the waw Consecutive', JANES II, 37-40.

—— (1971). Aspects of the Ugaritic Verb in the light of Comparative Semitic Grammar, unpub. Ph.D. Diss., Columbia University.

Margolis, M. L. (1911). 'The Place of the Word Accent in Hebrew', JBL 30, 29-43.

Marks, J. H. & Rodgers, V. M. (1955). A Beginner's Handbook to Biblical Hebrew, Nashville, USA.

Martin, W. (1876). Inquiries concerning the Structure of the Semitic Languages, London.

Martin, W. J. (1957). 'Some Notes on the Imperative in the Semitic Languages', RSO 32, 315-9.

Mason, P. H. & Bernard, H. H. (1853). An Easy Practical Hebrew Grammar, 2 vols., Cambridge. (On the tenses, vol. 2, Letters 51-54.)

Mason, P. H. (1854). 'The Hebrew Tenses', JSL 2nd n.s. April 1854, 111-120.

Mc Alpine, T. (1976). The Perfect with Wâw in Joshua and Judges, unpub. M.A. Thesis, Fuller Theo. Seminary, USA.

Mc Evenue, S. (1971). The Narrative Style of the Priestly Writer, Rome.

Mendenhall, G. E. (1947). The Verb in Early Northwest Semitic Dialects, unpub. Ph.D. Diss., John Hopkins University, Baltimore.

Merx, A. (1867). Grammatica Syriaca, Halis.

Mettinger, T. N. D. (1974). 'The Hebrew Verbal System: A Survey of Recent Research', Annual of the Swedish Theological Institute, IX, 64-84.

Meyer, R. (1953). 'Zur Geschichte des hebräischen Verbums', VT III, 225-35, also FuF XL (1966), 241-3.

––––– (1960). 'Das hebräische Verbalsystem im Lichte der gegenwärtigen Forschung', VTS VII, 309-17.

––––– (1964). 'Aspekt und Tempus im althebräischen Verbalsystem', OLz 59, 117-26.

––––– & Beer, G. (1966-72). Hebräische Grammatik, 4 vols., Berlin.

Michaelis, J. D. (1745). Hebräische Grammatik, Halle.

Michel, D. (1960). Tempora und Satzstellung in den Psalmen, Bonn.

Morag, S. (1974). 'On the Historical Validity of the Vocalization of the Hebrew Bible', JAOS 94, 307-15.

Moran, W. L. (1950). A Syntactical Study of the Dialect of Byblos as Reflected in the Amarna Tablets, unpub. Ph.D. Diss., John Hopkins University.

––––– (1961). 'The Hebrew Language in its Northwest Semitic Background', The Bible and the Ancient Near East, Essays in Honour of W. F. Albright, ed. G. E. Wright, London, pp. 54-72.

Morgenbrod, M. & Serifi, E. (1976). 'Computer-Analysed Aspects of Hebrew Verbs', HCL 10, E1-E17.

Moscati, S. (1969). An Introduction to the Comparative Grammar of the Semitic Languages, Wiesbaden, W. Germany.

Müller, A. (1882). Outlines of Hebrew Syntax, transl. by J. Robertson, Glasgow.

Munk, P. S. (1850). 'Notice sur Abou'l Walid Merwan Ibn-Djan'ah', JA April 1850, 297-337; July 1850, 1-50; Sept. 1850, 201-47; Nov-Dec. 1850, 353-427.

Münster, S. (1544). Opus Grammaticum Consummatum, Basel.

––––– (1524). Institutiones Grammaticae, Basel.

Murphy, J. G. (1850). Correspondence (on the Hebrew Tenses), JSL (Jan.) 5, 194-202.

––––– (1851). Correspondence (Tenses of Hebrew Verbs), JSL (Jan.) 7, 216-23, 469-86.

––––– (1857). The Elements of Hebrew Grammar, London.

Murray, M. A. (1905). Elementary Egyptian Grammar, London.

Murtonen, A. E. (1968). 'The Pre-historical Development of the Hebrew Verbal System', IVth World Congress of Jewish Studies, Papers 2, Jerusalem, pp. 29-33 (= WCJS 4/2).

Nolan, F. (1821). An Introduction to Hebrew Grammar, London.

Nöldeke, Th. (1880). Syrische Grammatik, Leipzig. Transl. by J. A. Crichton, Compendious Syriac Grammar, London, 1904.

───── (1886). 'Semitic Languages', Encyclopaedia Britannica, 9th ed., vol. 21 (1886), Edinburgh, pp. 641-56. (Reprinted: Die Semitischen Sprachen, Leipzig, 1887.)

Nordheimer, I. (1838-41). A Critical Grammar of the Hebrew Language, 2 vols., New York.

Ogden, G. S. (1964). An Examination of the Use of the Verb 'HĀYĀ(H)' (הָיָה), 'Be', in Biblical Hebrew, unpub. Master of Letters Thesis, University of Durham, England.

───── (1971). 'Time, and the Verb היה in O.T. Prose', VT 21/4, 451-69.

Olshausen, J. (1861). Lehrbuch der hebräischen Sprache, 2 vols., Brunswick.

Orlinsky, H. M. (1940-2). 'On the Cohortative and Jussive after an Imperative or Interjection in Biblical Hebrew', JQR n.s. 31, 371-82; 32, 191-205, 273-7.

Palmer, F. R. (1974). The English Verb, London.

Peters, J. P. (1887). 'Miscellaneous Notes (Note 3)', Hebraica III, 111-16.

Philippi, F. W. M. (1892). 'Die semitische Verbal- und Nominalbildung in ihrem Verhältniss zu einander', BASS II, 359-89.

Pick, B. (1884). 'The Study of the Hebrew Language among Jews and Christians', Bib Sac 41, July, pp. 450-77.

Pierce, A. (1947). The Hebrew Tense in the Book of Ruth, unpub. Masters Thesis, Graduate School of Southern Methodist University, USA.

Pococke, E. (The Elder) (1806). Specimen historiae Arabum, Oxford.

Poebel, A. (1916). 'Hans Bauer: Die Tempora im Semitischen, ihre Entstehung und ihre Ausgestaltung in den Einzelsprachen' (Review), OLz 19, 23-8.

───── (1933-4). 'The Tenses of the Intransitive Verb in Sumerian', AJSL 50, 143-70.

───── (1939a). 'The Antepenult Stressing of Old Hebrew and its Influence on the Shaping of the Vowels', AJSL 56, 225-30.

───── (1939b). 'Penult Stressing replacing Ultimate Stressing in Pre-Exilic Hebrew', AJSL 56, 384-7.

───── (1939c). Studies in Akkadian Grammar, Chicago. (Pp. 118-21.)

Polzin, R. M. (1976). Late Biblical Hebrew: Toward an Historical Typology of Biblical Hebrew Prose, Harverd Semitic Monographs.

Pope, M. H. (1953). '"Pleonastic" Waw before Nouns in Ugaritic and Hebrew', JAOS 73, 95-8.

Prätorius, F. (1894). 'Über die hamitischen Sprachen Ostafricas', BA II, 312-341.

Prijs, L. (1964). 'Ein "Waw der Bekräftigung"', BZ 8, 105-9.

Prosser, J. (1838). A Key to the Hebrew Scriptures, London.

Rabin, C. (1943a). 'Saadya Gaon's Hebrew Prose Style', Essays on Saadya, ed. E. Rosenthal, Manchester, pp. 127-38.

───── (1943b). The Evolution of the Syntax of post-biblical Hebrew, unpub. D.Phil. Diss., Oxford.

―――― (1963). 'The Origin of the Subdivisions of Semitic', Hebrew and Semitic Studies presented to G. R. Driver, Oxford, pp. 104-15.

―――― (1968). 'Towards a Descriptive Semantics of Biblical Hebrew', Proceedings of the 26th International Congress of Orientalists, 1964, New Delhi, p. 51.

―――― (1968b). 'The Tense and Mood System of the Hebrew of Sepher Hasidim', IVth World Congress of Jewish Studies, Paper 2 (Jerusalem, 1968), pp.113-6 (Hebr., p. 188 Eng. summary).

―――― (1970). 'Hebrew' (Biblical, Mishnaic, Medieval, and Modern), Current Trends in Linguistics, Vol. 6, ed. T. A. Sebeok, The Hague-Paris, pp. 304-46.

Radday, Y. T. (1974). '"And" in Isaiah', Revue 2, 25-41.

Radday, Y. T. & Shore, H. (1976). 'Waw conjunctivum - A Possible Author-and/ or Type-Specifying Criterion in Biblical Literature', Proceedings of the Sixth World Congress of Jewish Studies, August 1973 (Hebr. with an abstract in English).

―――― (1976). 'The Definite Article: A Type- and/or Author-Specifying Discriminant in the Hebrew Bible', ALLC 4, 23-31.

Rainey, A. F. (1976). 'Enclitic -ma and the Logical Predicate in Old Babylonian', IOS 6, 51-8.

Ramsey, F. P. (1891-2). 'New Names for the Forms of the Hebrew Finite Verbs', Hebraica 8, 101-2.

Raumer, R. von (1863). Gesammelte sprachwissenschaftliche Schriften, Frankfurt.

Reuchlin, J. (= J. Capnio) (1506). Rudimenta Linguae Hebraicae, Pforzheim.

Rich, A. B. (1874). 'The Hebrew Tense', Bib Sac 31 (No. 121), 115-35).

Robertson, D. A. (1972). Linguistic Evidence in Dating Early Hebrew Poetry, SBL Dissertation Series 3.

Robinson, E. (1843). 'Bibliographical Notices of Gesenius & Nordheimer', Bib Sac 1, 361-90.

Robinson, T. H. (1962). Paradigms & Exercises in Syriac Grammar, Oxford.

Rosén, H. B. (1956). 'Aspect and Tense in Biblical Hebrew (The Status of the so-called "conversive waw"), Biram Jubilee Volume (Publ. of the Israel Society of Biblical Research 2), Jerusalem, pp. 205-18 (Hebr.).

―――― (1969). 'The Comparative Assignment of Certain Hebrew Tense Forms', Proceedings of the International Conference of Semitic Studies, Jerusalem 1965, Jerusalem, pp. 212-34.

Rosenthal, F. (1961). A Grammar of Biblical Aramaic, Wiesbaden, W. Germany.

Rössler, O. (1961). 'Eine bisher unerkannte Tempusform im Althebräischen', ZDMG 111, 445-51.

―――― (1962). 'Die präfixkonjugation Qal der Verba Iae Nûn im Althebräischen und das Problem der sogenannten Tempora', ZAW 74, 125-41.

Rowton, M. B. (1962). 'The Use of the Permansive in Classical Babylonian', JNES 21, 233-303.

Rubinstein, A. (1952). 'A Finite Verb continued by an Infinitive Absolute in Biblical Hebrew', VT II, 362-7.

----- (1953). 'Notes on the Use of the Tenses in the Variant Readings of the Isaiah Scroll', VT III, 92-5.

----- (1955). 'Singularities in Consecutive-Tense Construction in the Isaiah Scroll', VT V, 180-8.

----- (1963). 'The Anomalous Perfect with Waw Conjunctive in Biblical Hebrew', Biblica 44, 62-9.

Rundgren, F. (1959). Intensiv und Aspektkorrelation. Studien zur äthiopischen und akkadischen Verbalstammbildung, Uppsala-Wiesbaden.

----- (1960a). 'Der aspekttuelle Charakter des altsemitischen Injunktivs', Or Suec IX, 75-101.

----- (1960b). 'Das altsyrische Verbalsystem. Vom Aspekt zum Tempus', Sprakwetenskapeliga Sällskqpets i Uppsala Forhandlinger 1958-1960, Uppsala, pp. 49-75.

----- (1961). Das althebräische Verbum. Abriss der Aspektlehre, Stockholm.

Ryssel, C. V. (1878). De Elohistae Pentateuchici Sermone, Leipzig.

Sappan, R. (1974). Hajishuf Hatahbiri shel Leshon Hashira Hamiqrait (The Typical Feature of the Syntax of Biblical Poetry in its Classical Period), Jerusalem (Author's Thesis).

Sarauw, C. (1912). 'Das altsemitischen Tempussystem', Festschrift V. Thomsen, Leipzig, pp. 59-69.

Sayce, A. H. (1872). Assyrian Grammar for Comparative Purposes, London.

----- (1875). Principles of Comparative Philology, London.

----- (1878). 'Notes on the Tenses of the Semitic Verb', JRAS n.s. 10, 251-2.

Saydon, P. P. (1954). 'The Inceptive Imperfect in Hebrew and the Verb הָחֵל "to begin"', Biblica 35, 43-50.

----- (1959). 'The Uses of the Tenses in Deutero-Isaiah', Biblica 40, 290-301.

----- (1962). 'The Conative Imperfect in Hebrew', VT XII, 124-6.

Schodde, G. H. (1884-5). 'The Methods in Hebrew Grammar', Hebraica 1, 75-9.

Schramm, G. M. (1957). 'A Reconstruction of Biblical Waw Consecutive', General Linguistics 3/1, 1-8.

Schroeder, N. W. (1766). Institutiones ad fundamenta linguae Hebraicae in usum studiosae juventutis, Groningae. (3rd ed. 1810)

Schultens, A. (1737). Institutiones ad fundamenta linguae hebraeae, Leyden.

Schulz, A. O. (1900). Über das Imperfekt und Perfekt mit וַ(וְ) im Hebräischen, Kirchhain, N.-L.

Scoggin, B. E. (1955). Application of Hebrew Verb States to a Translation of Isaiah 40-55, unpub. Ph.D. Diss., The Southern Bapt. Theo. Sem., USA.

Segert, S. (1965). 'Aspekte des althebräischen Aspektsystems', AO 33, 93-104.

----- (1975). 'Verbal Categories of some Northwest Semitic Languages: A Didactic Approach', AAL 2/5, 1-12.

Sekine, M. (1940-1). 'Das Wesen des althebräischen Verbalausdruck', ZAW n.f. 17, 133-41.

Sharp, G. (1803). Three Tracts on the Syntax and Pronunciation of the Hebrew Tongue, London.

Sharpe, S. (1877). A Short Hebrew Grammar without Points, London.

Sheehan, J. F. X. (1968). Studies in the Perfect with waw in Pentateuchal Prose: A Reexamination of the Accent Shift and Related Problems, unpub. Ph.D. Diss., Brandeis University, USA.

—— (1970). 'Conversive Waw and Accentual Shift', Biblica 51, 545-8.

—— (1971). 'Egypto-Semitic Elucidation of the Waw Conversive', Biblica 52, 39-43.

Sidon, H. (1938). The Order of Words in Hebrew Noun Clauses and Verbal Clauses in Isaiah and its Importance for Exegesis, unpub. Ph.D. Diss., The Southern Bapt. Theo. Seminary, USA.

Siedl, S. H. (1971). Gedanken zum Tempussystem im Hebräischen und Akkadischen, Wiesbaden, W. Germany.

Silverman, M. H. (1973). 'Syntactic Notes on the Waw Consecutive', Orient & Occident: Essays presented to Cyrus H. Gordon.... ed. H. A. Hoffner, Jr., Neukirchen-Vluyn, pp. 167-75.

Simon[is], J. (1753). Introductio grammatico-critica in linguae hebraeae, Halle.

Skoss, S. L. (1955). Saadia Gaon, the Earliest Hebrew Grammarian, Philadelphia. (Reprinted from Proceedings of the American Academy for Jewish Research XXI-XXIII, 1952-4.)

Snell, D. C. (1974). 'Hebrew Verbs', Bi Or 31, 40-2.

Speiser, E. A. (1938). 'The Pitfalls of Polarity', Language 14, 187-202.

Sperber, A. (1939). 'Hebrew based upon Biblical Passages in Parallel Transmission', HUCA 14, 153-249.

—— (1959). A Grammar of Massoretic Hebrew. A General Introduction to the Pre-Massoretic Bible, Copenhagen.

—— (1966). A Historical Grammar of Biblical Hebrew, Leiden.

Stade, B. (1879-). Lehrbuch der hebräischen Grammatik, Leipzig.

Starcky, S. (1938). 'Sur le système verbal de l'hebreu', RÉS 3, 19-31.

Steinthal, H. (1861). Characterisik der hauptsachlichsten Typen des Sprachbaues von F. Misteli: Neubearbeitung des Werkes von H. Steinthal, (Abriss der Sprachwissenschaft II, pp. 414-86) Berlin, 1893.

Stevenson, W. B. (1936-7). 'Illustrations of the Growth of Language taken from the Semitic Languages', TGUOS 8, 6-8.

Storr, G. C. (1779). Observationes ad analogiam et Syntaxin Hebraicam pertinentes, Tubingae.

Strack, H. L. (1883). Hebräische Grammatik, Carlsruhe and Leipsic.

Strong, J. (1885-6). 'Driver on the Hebrew Tense', Hebraica 2, 107-8.

—— (1885-6b). 'Hebrew Syntax', Hebraica 2, 228-33.

Stuart, M. (1831). A Grammar of the Hebrew Language, Andover, USA.

—— (1838). 'The Hebrew Tenses', Biblical Repository 11, 131-74.

Suder, R. W. (1973). The Functional Syntax of the Hebrew Verb Clause in the Sectarian Scrolls from Qumran Cave I, unpub. Ph.D. Diss., Univ. of Wisconsin.

Thacker, T. W. (1954). The Relationship of the Semitic and Egyptian Verbal Systems, Oxford.

Thierry, G. J. (1951). 'Notes on Hebrew Grammar and Etymology', OTS IX, 1-17.

Torczyner, H. (1912). 'Zur semitischen Verbalbildung', ZDMG 66, 87-93.

Tregelles, S. P. (n.d. 1882?). Heads of Hebrew Grammar, London.

Turner, W. (1876). 'The Tenses of the Hebrew Verb', Studies Biblical and Oriental, Edinburgh, pp. 338-407.

Udall, J. (1593). Petrus Martinius' 'The Key of the Holy Tongue' translated by J. Udall.... Leyden (Translated from the Latin Grammar of Pierre Martinez, Paris, 1567.). Facsimile Reprint, Menston, England, 1970.

Waldman, N. M. (1975). 'The Hebrew Tradition', Current Trends in Linguistics, vol. 13, ed. T. A. Sebeok, The Hague, pp. 1285-1330.

Watson, W. G. E. (1972). 'Archaic Elements in the Language of Chronicles', Biblica 53/2, 191-207.

—— (1973). The Language and Poetry of the Book of Isaiah in the Light of Recent Research in Northwest Semitic, unpub. Ph.D. Diss., Aberdeen.

Weidemann, G. F. R. (1849). A Compendious Grammar of the Hebrew Language, with XXVII Tables, Calcutta.

Weir, D. H. (1849). 'Observations on the Tenses of the Hebrew Verb', JSL 4, 308-34.

—— (1850). Correspondence (Prof. Weir's reply to Dr. S. Lee), JSL 6, 484-97.

Wellhausen, J. (1887). Deutsche Litteraturzeitung VII, 968.

Welmers, W. E. (1973). African language structures, Berkeley, California.

Wernberg-Møller, P. (1958). '"Pleonastic" waw in Classical Hebrew', JSS 3, 321-26.

—— (1959). 'Observations on the Hebrew Participle', ZAW 71, 54-67.

—— (1974). 'Aspects of Masoretic Vocalization', Masoretic Studies I, 121-30.

Wheeler, H. M. (1850). Hebrew for Self-instruction, London.

Wickes, W. (1970). Two Treatises on the Accentuation of the Old Testament, New York (First publ. in 1881 (Poetical Books) and 1887 (Prose Books).), Prolegomenon by Aron Dotan.

Wilch, J. R. (1969). 'TIME and EVENT'. An exegetical study of the use of ʿeth in the O.T. in comparison to other temporal expressions in clarification of the concept of time, Leiden.

Williams, R. J. (1971). 'Energic Verbal Forms in Hebrew', Studies on the Ancient Palestinian World, Presented to Prof. F. V. Winnett, ed. J. W. Wevers, Toronto, pp. 75-85.

Wilson, G. H. (1974). A Survey of the Use of the Hebrew Perfect in the Pentateuch, unpub. M.A. Thesis, Fuller Theological Seminary, USA.

Wilson, W. (1850). The Bible Student's Guide, Winchester.

Wright, W. (1859-62). A Grammar of the Arabic Language, London. 2nd. ed. revised and greatly enlarged, 2 vols., 1874-5, London.

----- (1890). Lectures on the Comparative Grammar of the Semitic Languages, Cambridge.

----- (1896-8). A Grammar of the Arabic Language, 3rd ed. revd. by W. Robertson Smith and M. de Goeje, Cambridge (repd. 1962).

Yannay, I. (1970). The Quadriradical Verb in the Hebrew Language, unpub. Ph.D. Diss., University of California, USA.

Yoshikawa, M. (1968). 'The Marû and Ḫamṭu Aspects in the Sumerian Verbal System', Orientalia n.s. 37, 401-16.

Young, G. D. (1953). 'The Origin of the Waw Conversive', JNES 12, 248-52.

Young, R. (1862). Young's Literal Translation of the Bible, Edinburgh. (Revsd. eds. 1887, 1898, and 1900.)

Zimmern, H. (1889-90). 'Das Verhältnis des assyrischen Permansivs zum semitischen Perfekt und zum ägyptischen "Pseudopartizip" untersucht unter Benutzung der El-Amarna Texte', ZA IV, 1-22.

----- (1898). Vergleichende Grammatik der semitischen Sprachen, Berlin.

* * * * * *
* * *
*

INDEX OF BIBLICAL REFERENCES

* Cited for tone position (Appendix 2 & Footnotes)

19^2 The superscript numeral indicates that the text Gen. 17:2 occurs twice on p. 19

Genesis		29:2	71	Leviticus	
1:1	11,22,25,40	30:24	129	2:12	74
1:1-3	41	31:44	69	8:21	215(no 26)
1:1-5	60	31:47	137	9:4	215(no 7)
1:2	19,22	38:5	69	9:22	9
1:3	25,40	38:21	215(no 2)	10:19	11
1:5	18,33,39	*40:15	207	15:11	216(no 96)
1:14	69	41:30-31	93	15:29	232
1:29	19	42:7	47,85	*19:34	195
2:6	69,74	47:15,16	216(no 94)	*20:5	231
2:8	18			22:6	215(no 26)
2:24	69	Exodus		*22:32	204
3:20	215(no 2)	1:1	34	*24:5	193^2,194,195,
3:22	38	3:16	215(no 17)		197, 200,205
6:7	216(no 107)	3:17	18,37	*25:21	194,205
6:18	19,205,231	*3:18	231	*25:35	194,195,232
6:21	201	*3:20	205	*26:16	231
7:11	91	*8:18	231	*26:36	195,203,207
11:3	18	9:7	215(no 12)	*26:41	194,195,204,233
11:27--12:9	116,134	10:14	84	26:44	215(no 8)
12:3	69	14:21	9		
14:14	18,215(no 6)	15:1	8,74	Numbers	
14:16	18	16:20	9	5:13	216(no 111)
15:6	125	*17:6	194	14:2	215(no 22)
15:18	215(no 3)	*21:23	195	14:10	215(nos 7,74)
16:5	215(no 1)	21:37	215(no 4)	15:31	216(no 73)
16:8	47,84,85	22:9	215(nos 5,6)	16:14	70
17:2	19^2	22:13	215(no 12)	18:12	113
17:5	19	23:10	19	21:2	3
17:6	19	*25:12	195,233	*23:3	202
17:7	19	*25:22	231	23:7	47
17:16	19,215(no 1)	*25:29	199	24:17	215(no 9)
17:19	19	*26:29	205	26:63,64	215(no 37)
18:12	19,215(no 2)	26:33	12	*27:13	205
18:18	69	*26:33	195,203,234	*31:28	196
20:6	215(no 3)	*28:17	195,203	35:20	55
20:8	18	*29:5	194		
21:6	86	*29:9	231	Deuteronomy	
22:4	12	*29:43	195,203	1:36	215(no 9)
23:13	215(no 3)	*30:26	195	2:7	215(no 13)
24:27	216(no 67)	33:7	55	*2:28	194,201^2,204
26:4	19	*34:2	196^2,232	*4:39	204
*26:4	205	*40:3	194,195,202	4:41	23
*26:10	194,204	*40:4	233	*6:7	233
27:37	215(nos 3,47)	*40:5	204	*6:18	204
28:20-21	3	*40:7	195,203	*7:25	194,195

Ref		Ref		Ref	
27:7	215(no 57)	*54:12	232	*24:10	194,195,202
28:2	215(no 31)	55:9	124	*25:9	231
29:20	216(no 94)	55:11	216(no 99)	25:14	216(no 110)
31:2	215(no 29)	58:9	73	25:31	215(nos 49,54)
32:10	215(no 28) & 216(no 86)	*59:12	208	*29:14	194
33:5	216(no 95)	59:15	18	29:20	216(no 98)
33:9	215(no 36)	60:7	74	30:17	216(no 61)
33:16	215(no 27)	60:10	216(no 105)	31:3	31
33:23	19,215(no 34)	63:6	19	31:6	216(no 61)
34:2	215(no 49)	64:9	215(no 32)	*31:12	231
34:6	216(no 93)	65:6	216(no 92)	*31:17	208
34:15	215(no 38)	*66:9	194,204	31:25	215(no 45)
34:16	215(no 37)	*66:19	231	31:33	215(no 41)
35:2	215(no 27)	66:19	216(no 101)	33:5	216(no 112)
35:6	216(no 91)			34:15	216(no 109)
*35:10	207	**Jeremiah**		34:18	215(no 40)
36:7	215(no 29)	2:26	215(no 43)	35:15	215(no 41)
37:24	19	2:30	216(no 112)	*36:6	231
37:27	111,215(no 39)	*4:2	204	36:9	216(no 61)
*38:14	206,208	*4:13	206	*36:31	231
38:15	216(no 99)	5:6	215(no 57)	37:16	215(no 54)
39:2	215(no 36)	6:3	215(no 53) & 216(no 62)	38:9	66
39:4	216(no 101)	6:15	215(no 43)	*38:10	194,205,233
40:2	216(no 93)	6:17	19	38:22	216(no 90)
41:5	216(no 101)	*6:17	194,203	38:27	215(no 44) & 216(no 108)
42:9	215(no 23)	6:27	215(no 48)		
42:16	216(no 107)	*7:30	207	38:28	215(no 56)
42:17	216(no 90)	*7:34	204	39:1	215(no 54)
43:14	216(no 98)	*8:9	208	41:9	216(no 95)
43:28	19	8:9	215(nos 39,43)	41:15	216(no 80)
44:26	36	8:12	215(no 43)	*42:17	207
44:28	36	8:16	215(nos 44,55) & 216(no 108)	43:6	215(no 31)
45:1-5	35			*43:12	195
45:13	36	9:18	216(no 108)	44:2	215(no 60)
*45:16	208	10:13	55	*44:12	207
45:16	215(no 52)	*10:18	194,204	44:26	216(no 109)
45:18	215(no 20)	10:21	215(no 42)	*45:5	231
45:24	215(no 20)	*12:3	194	46:5	215(no 24)
46:2	216(no 66)	13:26	215(no 58)	46:21	215(no 24)
47:9	215(no 23)	14:3,4	215(no 52)	46:23	215(no 40)
49:13	215(no 25) & 216(no 106)	*14:4	208	46:24	215(nos 46,59)
49:18	215(no 38)	15:9	215(nos 50,54)	48:1	215(nos 56,59)
50:11	215(no 32)	*17:27	231	48:13	215(no 52)
51:2	19,35	*20:9	194,203,204,231, 232	*48:13	208
51:3	18,215(no 25), 216(no 106)	*20:11	208	48:41	215(no 56) & 216(no 111)
51:11	215(no 24)	20:11	215(nos 42,52)	49:8	215(no 60)
*51:11	208	*21:6	204	49:10	215(no 58)
52:7	215(no 30)	*21:14	195	49:15	215(no 48)
52:9	215(no 25) & 216(no 106)	*22:1	194,195,202	49:21	215(no 55) & 216(no 108)
52:15	216(no 101)	22:26	93	49:23	215(no 50)
54:8	216(no 105)	*23:3	204	*49:27	195
		24:5	216(no 98)	*49:37	231
		*24:7	231	*50:2	208